Fodor's

UTAH

Welcome to Utah

Little did we realize that the emergence of a novel coronavirus in early 2020 would abruptly bring almost all travel to a halt. Although our Fodor's writers around the world have continued working to bring you the best of the destinations they cover, we still anticipate that more than the usual number of businesses will close permanently in the coming months, perhaps with little advance notice. We don't expect things to return to "normal" for some time. As you plan your upcoming travels to Utah, please confirm that places are still open and let us know when we need to make updates by writing to us at this address: editors@fodors.com.

TOP REASONS TO GO

★ **National parks:** Spectacular Zion, Bryce Canyon, Arches, Capitol Reef, and Canyonlands.

★ **Outdoor fun:** Rafting the Colorado River, fishing at Flaming Gorge, and more.

★ **Sundance:** The resort is an artist's dream, the indie film festival a must-do.

★ **Skiing:** Superb snow, varied runs, and swanky resorts like Deer Valley and Snowbird.

★ **Frontier history:** The Pony Express Trail, Wild West towns, and the Golden Spike.

★ **Salt Lake City:** Remarkable Temple Square, plus renowned museums and gorgeous vistas.

Contents

Chapter 1

EXPERIENCE UTAH

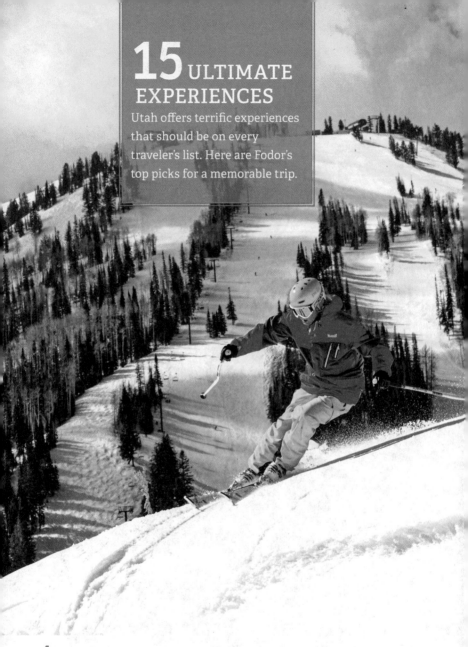

15 ULTIMATE EXPERIENCES

Utah offers terrific experiences that should be on every traveler's list. Here are Fodor's top picks for a memorable trip.

1 Winter sports

The "greatest snow on Earth," plentiful sunshine, and beautiful panoramas make Utah a fabulous winter playground. Deer Valley Resort *(above)* in Park City draws crowds with its groomed ski trails for families as well as experts. *(Ch. 3, 4, 5)*

2 Scenic drives

Mirror Lake Scenic Byway *(above)* through the Uinta Mountains is one of the state's unforgettable drives. Highway 12 is another stunner. *(Ch. 6, 7, 8, 9, 10, 11, 12)*

3 Bryce Canyon National Park

Drive the main park road for breathtaking views into the canyon. For a closer look, accessible hikes take you into the amphitheater to see hoodoos. *(Ch. 9)*

2005 Sundance Film Festival

4 Sundance

A ski resort and year-round artistic retreat, Sundance is best known for the annual independent film festival founded by Robert Redford and based in nearby Park City. *(Ch. 4)*

5 Dinosaur tracking

Utah is a treasure chest of dinosaur remains. See tantalizing footprints at several museums, including the Natural History Museum of Utah *(above)* in Salt Lake City. *(Ch. 3, 6, 10, 13)*

6 Delicate Arch

Recognize this arch? Utah's calling card is this well-known rock formation in Arches National Park. Get up close on a moderate 3-mile hike and marvel at its scale. *(Ch. 11)*

7 Temple Square

The site of the iconic temple in Salt Lake City, 35-acre Temple Square hosts musical performances and other cultural and historic attractions. *(Ch. 3)*

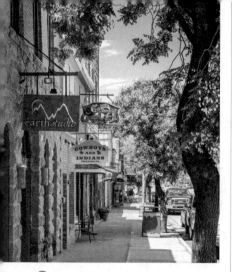

8 Moab

This countercultural frontier town is a hub of artsy activity and a great base for Arches National Park. It's a must for biking, rockclimbing, and rafting as well. *(Ch. 13)*

9 Great Salt Lake

The best place to explore one of the earth's saltiest locales is Antelope Island, home to scores of bison *(above)* and a pit stop for migrating birds. *(Ch. 3)*

10 Water sports

Skiing grabs the headlines but fly fishing, boating, and river rafting, especially on the mighty Colorado River *(above)*, make this a year-round destination. *(Ch. 6, 13)*

11 Salt Lake City

At the foot of the Wasatch Mountains, Utah's capital has a stunning setting, Mormon culture, cosmopolitan dining, and easy access to outdoor activities. *(Ch. 3)*

12 Zion National Park

Angels Landing Trail *(below)*, with its exhilarating overlooks, and the Narrows Trail, set in a river between dramatic 2,000-foot cliffs, make Zion one of America's top parks. *(Ch. 8)*

13 Two-wheeled fun

Mountain-bike trails, such as the world-famous Slickrock Trail near Moab and the White Rim Trail *(above)*, are unparalleled. *(Ch. 6, 12, 13)*

14 Utah Olympic Park

Built for the 2002 Winter Olympic Games, this recreational facility offers fun activities year-round, like tubing, zipline, and more. *(Ch. 4)*

15 Lake Powell

This stunning reservoir and vacation spot provides boat access to Rainbow Bridge National Monument. *(Ch. 13)*

WHAT'S WHERE

1 Salt Lake City. Home of the Church of Jesus Christ of Latter-day Saints, Utah's capital city is surprisingly progressive, and an ideal launch pad for your Utah adventure.

2 Park City and the Southern Wasatch. Miners tunneled throughout the Wasatch Range to build the economy, but modern-day prospectors look skyward to winter snow and summer sunshine to drive it today.

3 Northern Utah. Much of northern Utah is within the boundaries of the Wasatch-Cache National Forest, with breathtaking landscapes, miles of trails, and the turquoise waters of Bear Lake.

4 Dinosaurland and Eastern Utah. Imagine high Western skies and an endless range, and you have a vision of eastern Utah. Mirror Lake, Flaming Gorge, and the Dinosaurland National Monument deliver entirely unique experiences.

5 Capitol Reef National Park. Formed by cataclysmic forces that have pushed and compressed the earth, this otherworldly

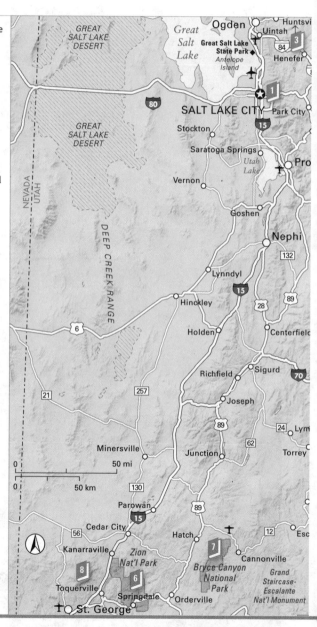

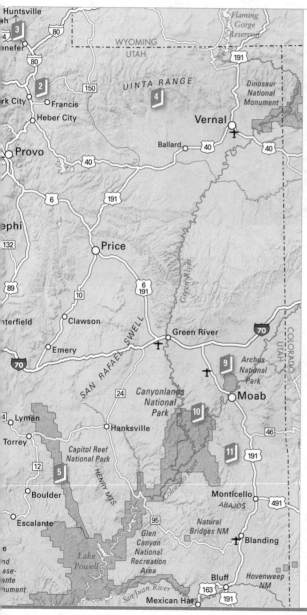

landscape is best known for its 100-mile-long geological feature, the Waterpocket Fold.

6 Zion National Park. Known for its sheer 2,000-foot cliffs and river-carved canyons, Zion deserves to be on every Las Vegas and/or Grand Canyon agenda.

7 Bryce Canyon National Park. The bizarrely shaped, bright red-orange rocks that are this park's signature formation are known as hoodoos.

8 Southwestern Utah. Venture onto trails, view an active dinosaur excavation site, or lose yourself in the mostly road-free, expansive Grand Staircase–Escalante National Monument.

9 Arches National Park. The largest collection of natural sandstone arches in the world are within this park, but the landscapes leave just as lasting an impression.

10 Canyonlands National Park. Canyonlands is best enjoyed on a hike, mountain bike, or raft.

11 Moab and Southeastern Utah. Home to the world-famous Slick Rock mountain bike trail, Moab is a countercultural retreat.

Best Ski Resort Lodges in Utah

MONTAGE, DEER VALLEY

The ultimate getaway at the most alluring ski area in arguably America's best ski town, the Montage Deer Valley opened in 2010 at gorgeous Empire Pass, with its chic-chalet vibe, incomparable service, state-of-the-art 35,000-square-foot spa, and access to the country's most vaunted slopes.

ALTA'S RUSTLER LODGE, ALTA

A strikingly modern mid-rise resort in Little Cottonwood Canyon, Alta's Rustler Lodge contains spacious rooms with balconies overlooking the mountains, while offering quick access to the resort's Transfer Tow and an impressive spa.

STEIN ERIKSEN LODGE, DEER VALLEY

Built in 1982 and impressively upgraded in recent years through millions of dollars of room and amenity upgrades, the venerable Stein Eriksen Lodge was a pioneer in bringing opulence to Utah's ski slopes.

SNOWPINE LODGE, ALTA

Built in 2019 on the site of the Alta's original 1938 hotel and incorporating some of that structure's original beams and stonework, Snowpine Lodge has brought an unprecedented level of luxury and newness to this legendary ski area in Little Cottonwood Canyon. Downy duvets and tasteful throws cover the plush beds in the lodge's dapper rooms, which are outfitted with soft robes and slippers and L'Occitane bath products. There's a gastropub on the property as well as a full-service restaurant with tall windows that afford sweeping views of the slopes, which you can get to from the hotel in a snap via the Grizzly rope tow.

WALDORF ASTORIA, PARK CITY MOUNTAIN

Fans of old-world refinement and glamour rejoiced with the opening of the Waldorf Astoria Park City, with its lobby fit for royalty—guests are greeted by a grand staircase, Baccarat crystal chandelier, and centuries-old marble fireplace. A gondola whisks guests up to Canyons ski village, which merged with neighboring Park City in 2005 to become the nation's largest ski area. Stylish rooms with fireplaces, balconies, and big jetted tubs provide an idyllic retreat from the elements.

SUNDANCE RESORT, SUNDANCE

Forever associated with founder Robert Redford and the prestigious film festival named for it, the lovely 95-room Sundance Resort hotel lies northeast

St. Regis, Deer Valley

of Provo—in the shadows of 11,750-foot Mt. Timpanogos, on the breathtaking Alpine Loop Scenic Highway. The 5,000-acre resort surrounding the hotel enjoys nearly 500 feet of snow annually, making it a favorite hideaway among ardent skiers who are happy without the buzzy scene of Park City (which is a 45-minute drive north).

The convivial Owl Bar and Tree Room offer après-ski hobnobbing and first-rate dining, and the wood-paneled rooms range from cozy standards to roomy high-ceilinged lofts.

THE ST. REGIS, DEER VALLEY

The supremely sumptuous St. Regis, which lies at the base of Deer Valley within a short drive of downtown Park City, offers some of the most inviting accommodations in the state.

MARRIOTT'S MOUNTAINSIDE, PARK CITY MOUNTAIN

A huge perk that comes with staying at Marriott's MountainSide is the opportunity to stay right in the heart of historic downtown Park City, steps from the dozens of bars, restaurants, and shops.

THE CLIFF LODGE, SNOWBIRD

The Cliff Lodge is a mammoth, modern 10-story haven at the base of Little Cottonwood Canyon's Snowbird ski area, offering dozens of activities and amenities, from several bars and restaurants to a huge spa and a rooftop lap pool.

THE INN AT SOLITUDE, SOLITUDE

One of Big Cottonwood Canyon's only ski-in, ski-out lodgings, the upscale if not over-the-top fancy Inn at Solitude stands out for its friendly employees, warmly appointed slope-side room, and utter tranquility. This resort is about resting and relaxing.

The Best Natural Wonders of Utah

FLAMING GORGE, NORTHEASTERN UTAH
Named by explorer John Wesley Powell in 1869 for the brilliant red-rock cliffs, this 91-mile gorge stretches from Wyoming into remote northeastern Utah. A popular reservoir was created via a massive 500-foot-tall dam in 1964.

CAPITOL GORGE, CAPITOL REEF NATIONAL PARK
Best explored from the 8-mile twisting and turning unpaved Scenic Drive that winds through it, this spectacular gorge was traversed by trains of Pioneer wagons in the 1860s. Early travelers carved their names into the canyon walls.

HELL'S BACKBONE, GRAND STAIRCASE-ESCALANTE NATIONAL MONUMENT
The name of both a spectacularly scenic 38-mile gravel road and the rugged tract of dramatic canyons for which it's named, Hell's Backbone is one of the most Instagram-worthy drives or bike rides in the state.

THE NARROWS, ZION NATIONAL PARK
When it comes to amazing scenery, It's difficult to settle on one specific section of this beguiling park, but this 16-mile trail that actually requires wading—and sometimes swimming—through the Virgin River will take your breath away. Sheer orange and tan 2,000-foot walls soar above this improbably steep slot canyon.

DELICATE ARCH, ARCHES NATIONAL PARK
An hour or two before the sun sets, legions of park visitors make the steady 1½-mile uphill hike to view this iconic 52-foot-tall arch—it's depicted in everything from dazzling landscape photos to Utah's license plate—in the most alluring light. Part of the fun is that the hike begins at a 1906 cabin and involves crossing a scenic footbridge over a serene river.

GRAND VIEW POINT, CANYONLANDS NATIONAL PARK
Among the seemingly endless array of overlooks in 527-square-mile Canyonlands National Park, Grand View Point rewards visitors with perhaps the most eye-popping imagery. From this promontory at the end of Island in the Sky scenic drive, you can see for 100 miles up and down the Green and Colorado rivers, toward the rugged rock formations of the park's Needles District, and out toward the jagged peaks of the Henry, Abajo, and La Sal mountain ranges.

The Narrows, Zion National Park

GREAT SALT LAKE, SALT LAKE CITY

Best experienced from the shores of Antelope Island State Park, which you reach via a 7-mile-long causeway north of Salt Lake City, this 1,700-square-mile inland sea is eight times saltier than the ocean—you can float in this buoyant water with the certainty that you will not sink. The island is traversed by hiking and bike trails and is home to a herd of around 600 to 700 bison.

SUNSET PEAK, BIG COTTONWOOD CANYON

Hikeable via the well-marked trails to Catherine Pass from both Brighton ski area in Big Cottonwood Canyon and Alta ski area in Little Cottonwood Canyon, this 10,648-foot summit rewards those who make the strenuous but manageable trek with 360 degree views of Heber Valley, Park City, Mount Timpanogos, and parts of metro Salt Lake City.

BEAR LAKE, NORTH-CENTRAL UTAH

The remarkable azure-blue waters of this 109-square-mile lake on the Utah–Idaho border look like they could be the Mediterranean or even some parts of the Caribbean, and the relative lack of commercialism along the shore results in stunning vistas unspoiled by tourist development. On hot summer days, it's one of the most beautiful places to swim and beachcomb in the state.

BRYCE CANYON, BRYCE CANYON NATIONAL PARK

Although actually a natural amphitheater rather than a canyon, this enormous expanse of fanciful hoodoos and spires seems to stretch as far as the eye can see and is accessible from numerous viewpoints and trails along the 19-mile park road.

What to Eat and Drink in Utah

bees is to pick up a bottle at one of the many excellent farmers' markets around the state, including the Downtown Farmers Market in Salt Lake's Pioneer Park, the Park Silly Sunday Market in Park City, and the Farmers Market on Historic 25th Street in Ogden.

ARTISAN CHEESE
Especially in the north-central region, dairy farming is a big part of Utah's economy, and a natural byproduct of the state's nearly 100,000 dairy cows is cheese. Chefs at many locavore-driven restaurants use local products in their salads, sandwiches, and cheese-boards. Two of particular note, which you can also visit, are Beehive Cheese just outside Ogden, which has earned national acclaim for its espresso- and lavender-rubbed Barely Buzzed cheddar, and the nutty raw-milk Wasatch Mountain Reserve, an alpine cheese produced by Rock Hill Cheese in Richmond (just north of Logan).

SMALL-BATCH SPIRITS
It started with High West, which began producing Rendez-vous Rye afrom a copper pot still in Park City in 2007 and continues to serve it at a world's only ski-in, ski-out distillery and bar. Now Utah has more than a dozen craft distilleries.

STEAKS AND BURGERS
Ranching has deep roots in Utah, and from the tony ski resorts up north to the solitary red rock canyons down south, the state abounds with great places to enjoy a dry-aged, locally raised steak or juicy burger—and that's to say nothing of the many establishments that serve bison, elk, venison, and other wild game meats.

CRAFT BEER
Although Utah has some very strict liquor laws (which have begun to loosen a bit in recent years), the state's craft brewing scene is booming, and it actually dates back many years. Venerable long-time favorites like Squatters Pub in Salt Lake City, Wasatch Brewpub in Park City, and Zion Brewery in Springdale continue to impress, but newcomers keep opening, and there are now more than two dozen craft brewers—as well as a few cideries—around the state.

LOCAL HONEY
Raw honey has been a sweet treat in these parts since the arrival of the region's earliest pioneer homesteaders, and these days you'll find it on ricotta toast in hip breakfast spots, in teas and lattes at cozy coffeehouses, and on plenty of desserts. But the best way to savor the fragrant, distinctive qualities of local

HOUSE-ROASTED COFFEE
Utah's embrace of single-origin, house-roasted coffees has become ever stronger in recent years, and it's now easy to find first-rate indie coffeehouses throughout the state, but Salt Lake City is the undisputed hub of java love. From long-time favorite Salt Lake Roasting to snazzy newer spots like Blue Copper Coffee and Publik Coffee Roasters, the state's largest city is rife with terrific places to sample anything from a refreshing cold brew to a decadent Belgian-chocolate mocha.

Chile Relleno en Nogada

TREE FRUIT

From the moment summer arrives until the cooler nights of autumn, Utahns rejoice at the opportunity to enjoy fresh fruit grown in the state's acres upon acres of peach, apple, cherry, apricot, and pear orchards. Farmers' markets are again a good bet, as are famous farms like the U-pick orchards in the Fruita Historic District in Capitol Reef National Park and Rowley's Red Barn in Washington and Santaquin. Maddox Ranch House restaurant outside Brigham City (aka "Peach" City) is famous for its peach pies, while Bryce Canyon Pines Restaurant serves heavenly apple and cherry pies.

AUTHENTIC MEXICAN FOOD

Immigrants from Mexico have long played a vital role in Utah's workforce, and as the state's percentage of residents who identify as Hispanic has increased from around 8% in 2000 to nearly 20% in 2020, the appetite for and availability of legit Mexican fare has increased. In Salt Lake City, you'll find one of the most celebrated Mexican restaurants in the West, the Red Iguana, which specializes in several varieties of complex mole sauce. Plaza Mexicana in Vernal is beloved for its 22 kinds of burritos, while Miguel's Baja Grill in Moab turns out delicious ceviche and other seafood dishes.

ICE CREAM, FROZEN CUSTARD, AND SHAKES

Another reason to appreciate Utah's impressive tradition of dairy farming: it gives locals and visitors the excuse to sample luscious, locally made ice cream all year-long, and especially during the state's hot and sunny summers. Traditional go-to's include LaBeau's Drive-in up by Bear Lake, which is famous for its raspberry shakes, and Aggie's Ice Cream, on the campus of Utah State University in Logan— regulars swear by the blue-mint flavor. Also keep an eye out for the many fine farm-to-table restaurants that churn out their own small-batch ice cream and sorbet, often with daily-rotating flavors.

FRY SAUCE

Given the devotion with which Utahns seem to worship it, you might think this pink condiment available at virtually every burger-and-fry joint in the state contained some hard-to-procure ingredient. In fact, it's just a blend of ketchup and mayo, developed in the 1940s by the regional fast-food chain Arctic Circle.

What to Read and Watch

A majestic landscape, rich indigenous culture, and famously intertwined Mormon-pioneer history have inspired some of the country's greatest literary minds to write about Utah and its people. And from the very beginning of the film industry, directors have set movies here, sometimes explicitly referencing Utah but in many instances letting the state's red-rock canyons, soaring cliffs, and quaint small towns stand in more vaguely for somewhere out West. Here are some of the most memorable depictions of Utah.

DESERT SOLITAIRE

Ardent environmentalist and provocative essayist Edward Abbey based much of his first—and some say greatest—non-fiction memoir *Desert Solitaire* on the time he spent in the late '50s as a ranger in Moab at Arches National Park. Lyrical, contemplative, and still immensely germane in its critique of America's wildly uneven—to put it charitably—conservation efforts, this 1968 book shines a light on Puebloan culture, the national park service, and southern Utah's singular landscape.

BUTCH CASSIDY AND THE SUNDANCE KID

George Roy Hill's splendid 1969 western, although set mostly in early 1900s western Wyoming, is actually filmed significantly around Zion National Park, St. George's Snow Canyon, and other parts of southwestern Utah where the infamous but allegedly quite charming train robber Butch Cassidy (played by Paul Newman) grew up. His buddy, Harry Longabaugh—better known as the Sundance Kid—actually hailed from back East, but he was depicted by Robert Redford, who would fall in love with the landscape and go on to establish Sundance Resort near Provo as well as the famed Sundance Film Festival. Redford's 1972 classic *Jeremiah Johnson* is filmed entirely in Utah.

UNDER THE BANNER OF HEAVEN

The fourth book from adventurer and best-selling writer Jon Krakauer came out in 2003 and shines a light—and was the source of some controversy—on the renegade fundamentalist outsider communities that exist in Utah and elsewhere in defiance not only of the mainstream LDS Church but government authorities as well. Beyond being a fascinating page-turner, it provides a detailed history of Mormonism.

FOOTLOOSE

Few can forget Kevin Bacon's electrifying performance as a rebellious midwestern teen transplanted to a small western town with a conservative minister (John Lithgow). This rom-com musical from 1984 was shot entirely around Provo and Orem, including the Presbyterian Church in American Fork, Payson High School in Payson, and the Lehi Roller Mills in Lehi.

127 HOURS

Based on Aron Ralston's gripping, autobiographical 2004 *Between a Rock and a Hard Place*, a riveting account of being trapped in, and ultimately forced to amputate his right arm in order to extricate himself from, Bluejohn Canyon—near Canyonlands National Park—this 2010 movie starring James Franco feels all the more intense because it was filmed at the site of the ordeal.

RIDERS OF THE PURPLE SAGE

Penned in 1912 by the great Western novelist Zane Grey, this richly rendered yarn set in a fictional Mormon community in southern Utah, *Riders of the Purple Sage* still ranks among the most popular works of the genre. It's been adapted into a movie no fewer than five times, most recently in 1996 as a made-for-TV vehicle starring Ed Harris and shot partly in Utah.

THELMA AND LOUISE

Although set farther south between Arkansas and Arizona, the most iconic landscape scenes in the 1991 crime drama meets female buddy road movie *Thelma and Louise* were filmed in southern Utah. Most of these shots, including the memorable one in which they drive their 1966 Ford Thunderbird over what's said to be the edge of the Grand Canyon, are in and around Moab and Arches and Canyonlands national parks, which have also appeared prominently in TV's *Westworld* as well as movies like *Indiana Jones and the Last Crusade* and *Once Upon a Time in the West*.

THE SEARCHERS

Among the dozens of celebrated movies filmed in and around Monument Valley, which lies both in Utah and Arizona, John Ford's 1956 western about a troubled Civil War Veteran portrayed by John Wayne captures the region's breathtaking terrain as marvelously as any. Other notable movies in which you may have glimpsed the valley's soaring red rock monoliths include *Forrest Gump, 2001: A Space Odyssey, Easy Rider,* and yet another famed John Ford–John Wayne collaboration, *Stagecoach*.

MORMON COUNTRY

Part of the acclaimed *American Folkways* series of the early 1940s, this early work by the great American novelist Wallace Stegner—who was not Mormon but spent part of his formative years in Salt Lake City—engaged in the migration of Mormon settlers to Utah, where they transformed an unforgiving, parched land into a string of bountiful, dynamic communities.

SLC PUNK!

Director James Merendino based his depiction of Salt Lake City in this 1998 comedy-drama starring Matthew Lillard on his experiences growing up in what was then a far more conservative environment. Irreverent and with a memorable punk rock soundtrack, the film was shot on location at the University of Utah, Memory Grove Park, the Cathedral of the Madeleine, and many other familiar spots around the city.

Utah Outdoor Adventures

Bicycling

Utah's open roads are frequented by Tour de France stars, including locals Levi Leipheimer and David Zabriskie, and since 2010 the Larry H. Miller Tour of Utah has been one of America's premier multiday stage races. Add to that Moab's Slick Rock, Porcupine, and White Rim trails for mountain bikers, and Utah is one of the top destinations for cycling in the United States.

RULES OF THE ROAD

On the road, stay as close as possible to the right side, in single file. If you're nervous about cars, hop on the **Legacy Parkway Trail** near Salt Lake City Airport and ride 15 miles north on a perfectly flat, paved trail that skirts Great Salt Lake. If you're downstate, the rural roads outside St. George, Cedar City, and Moab offer miles of varied topography with relatively little traffic to affect the experience.

BEST RIDES

Antelope Island State Park. It's cheaper to enter Antelope on two wheels, and much more enjoyable, but only strong riders should brave the 7-mile causeway, especially in the heat of summer. Once you reach the island, however, there are miles of rolling and empty trails.

Bonneville Shoreline Trail. Partway up and along the Wasatch Front on the northeast side of Salt Lake City, this hiking and mountain biking trail offers expansive views of the entire Salt Lake Valley, plus points west and south. Its level of difficulty is easy to moderate, with challenging stretches near the University of Utah Hospital.

Flaming Gorge National Recreation Area. Because it mixes high-desert vegetation—blooming sage, rabbit brush, cactus, and wildflowers—and red-rock terrain with a cool climate, Flaming Gorge is an ideal destination for road and trail biking. The 3-mile round-trip Bear Canyon–Bootleg ride begins south of the dam off U.S. 191 at the Firefighters' Memorial Campground and runs west to an overlook of the reservoir.

Klondike Bluffs Trail. This trail offers the less-experienced mountain biker a relatively easy introduction to the sport. The climb to Klondike Bluffs is not difficult, and the reward is a fantastic view into Arches National Park. Access is off U.S. 191, 15 miles north of Moab—not the main park entrance.

Slickrock Trail. America's most famous mountain-biking trail is a 12-mile loop through sagebrush and sand, over slick granite rock and across undulations that can only be described as moonlike. It's well marked, popular, and incredibly challenging. Not recommended for kids under 12.

Wasatch Over Wasatch Trail. Known as the "W.o.W. Trail," this new single-track winds through Pine Canyon and definitely has the coveted wow-factor, with 12 miles of breathtaking views. Be prepared for a lot of climbing and a quick descent at the end. Expansion plans will connect the trail to the Park City–area trail system—almost 400 miles of trail and the first-ever trail system to be designated by the **International Mountain Biking Association** as a "Gold Level Ride Center."

Fishing

Here, blue-ribbon trout streams remain much as they were when Native American tribes, French fur trappers, and a few thousand miners, muleskinners, and sodbusters first placed a muddy footprint along their banks.

WHAT TO BRING

Bring or rent a rod and reel, waders, vest, hat, sunglasses, net, tackle, hemostats, and sunscreen. Always buy a fishing license.

WHEN TO GO

The season is always a concern when fishing. Spring run-offs can cloud the waters. Summer droughts may reduce stream flows. Fall weather can be unpredictable in the west.

BEST FISHING

Flaming Gorge. For some of the finest river fishing, try the Green River below Flaming Gorge Dam, where rainbow and brown trout are plentiful and big. Fed by cold water from the bottom of the lake, this stretch has been identified as one of the best trout fisheries in the world.

Lake Powell. Formed by the construction of Glen Canyon Dam, this popular recreational attraction in southern Utah is home to a wide variety of fish, including bass—striped, smallmouth, and largemouth—as well as bluegill and channel catfish. Ask the locals about night fishing for stripers.

Provo River. One of Utah's world-class fly-fishing rivers, the Provo is divided into three sections, starting in the High Uintas Wilderness about 90 minutes east of Salt Lake City and ending in Utah Lake in Provo. Brown and rainbow trout are the big draw here.

Hiking

Don sturdy boots, pack water, lean on the hardworking park rangers for guidance, and head out for a few hours. Your heart, lungs, and soul will thank you. Trailheads depart from most cities, too, including worthy treks from downtown Salt Lake City, Ogden, Park City, and Moab.

SAFETY

Know your limits, and make sure the terrain you are about to embark on does not exceed your abilities. It's a good idea to check the elevation change on a trail before you set out, and be careful not to get caught on exposed trails at elevation during afternoon storms (rain or snow) any time of year. Dress appropriately, bringing layers to address changing weather conditions, and always carry enough water. Also, make sure someone knows where you're going and when to expect your return. Also be advised that much of rural Utah is a black hole for cellular coverage.

WHEN TO GO

Spring in Utah brings an explosion of wildflowers and color (Alta Ski Area and Mirror Lake are two destinations near Salt Lake City to walk in May or June). Fall brings a turning of cottonwood and cypress leaves that rivals autumn in the Shenandoah mountains. Summer's heat makes many desert locales unbearable, but the shade and breeze of Utah's canyons have offered respite for centuries. The hardiest outdoor types will even gear up in the dead of winter with snowshoes.

BEST HIKES

Angels Landing Trail, Zion National Park. A 5-mile round-trip hike, with 1,500 feet of elevation gain, including a series of steps known as "Walter's Wiggles," this is the one trail in Zion no healthy hiker should miss. If you're afraid of heights, stop short at Scout's Lookout for the breathtaking view and head back down the trail.

Fiery Furnace Walk, Arches National Park. This two- to three-hour walk through narrow sandstone canyons is only offered via ranger-led tour (daily from mid-March to October). The landscape is an unforgettable, physically demanding maze, and the rangers illuminate the geologic history and reassure nervous hikers.

Grandeur Peak. For views of the Salt Lake Valley and Parley's Canyon, start at the trailhead at Church Fork Picnic Area in Mill Creek Canyon. This wide trail follows a stream and tops out at almost 8,300 feet. With quick and easy access from downtown, this 6-mile round-trip hike is a great way to get a bird's-eye view of the capital city.

Hickman Bridge Trail, Capitol Reef National Park. Just 2 miles long, this trail is a perfect introduction to Capitol Reef. You'll walk past a great natural bridge as well as Fremont culture ruins.

Mount Timpanogas. An hour-and-a-half southeast of Salt Lake City, "Timp" is one of the tallest and most striking of the Wasatch Mountains. Access to Timpanogas Cave is via a 3-mile round-trip hike led by park rangers daily in summer. Be aware that outside temperatures can reach triple digits, even at 6,700 feet— but inside the caves it's 45°F year-round.

The Narrows Trail, Zion National Park. Experience the thrill of walking in the Virgin River, peering up at millennia-old rock canyons, hanging gardens, and sandstone grottoes. To see the Narrows you must wade—and occasionally swim— upstream through chilly water and over uneven, slippery rocks, but the views are breathtaking.

Horseback Riding

Horseback-riding options in Utah run the gamut from hour-long rides on a well-worn trail to multiday excursions out into the wilderness. June through August is the peak period for horse-packing trips; before signing up with an outfitter, inquire about the skills they expect.
■ TIP→ **Most horseback-riding outfitters have a weight limit of 250 pounds, and children must be at least seven years old.**

BEST HORSEBACK RIDES

Bryce Canyon National Park. Sign up for a guided tour at Ruby's Horseback Adventures near the park entrance. Let the animals do the work as you descend and emerge hundreds of feet into the Bryce Amphitheatre to see the unrivaled orange-pink spires and hoodoos.

Capitol Reef National Park. Much of this park is accessible only on foot or horseback, which promises an experience of wide-open Western spaces that hark back to the time of cowboys. Indeed, some of the trails may have been used by herdsmen and Native Americans. Sandstone, canyons, mesa, buttes— they're all here. Check at the visitor center for details of horseback-riding outfitters and opportunities for an unforgettable experience.

Zion Ponderosa Ranch Resort. Just east of Zion National Park at the site of a former pioneer logging camp, this multipursuit resort offers plenty of things to do after time spent in the saddle meandering along the multitude of pioneer-era trails. When you're not in the saddle you can drive an ATV, ride a zipline or mountain bike, or learn how to rappel and rock climb on the resort's 40-foot climbing wall. At the end of a long day, relax in a cabin, glamp in a deluxe tent, or hunker down in your own private covered wagon.

Rafting

Dozens of tour companies throughout the West offer relatively tame floats— starting at around $70 for one day. Others cater more to thrill-seeking tourists.

HOW TO CHOOSE A TRIP

Beginners and novices are encouraged to use guides, and many offer luxurious multiday trips in which they do everything, including searing your steak in a beach barbecue, setting up your tent, and rolling out your sleeping bag.

The International Scale of River Difficulty is a widely accepted rating system that ranges from Class I (the easiest) to Class VI (the most difficult—think Niagara Falls). When in doubt, ask your guide about the rating on your route before you book. Ratings can vary greatly throughout the season due to run-off and weather events. Midsummer is ideal for rafting in the West, although many outfitters will stretch the season, particularly on calmer routes.

BEST RIVER RUNS

Cataract Canyon. It begins below Moab and takes three to five days as you wind your way to Lake Powell. Expect a smooth ride for the first day or two, before you dive into the rapids. This multiday adventure offers broad beaches, Native American ruins, deep-color canyon walls, and waves as high as 20 feet.

Colorado River, Moab. The Grand Poobah of river rafting in Utah. There are numerous outfitters in the Moab area with a wide assortment of half, full, and multiday trips on the river. Even though it is the same river, it meanders in parts and rages in others.

Green River. Before it meets up with the Colorado River, the Green River offers plenty of stunning scenery and fast water through canyons such as Desolation and Gray. Desolation Canyon is a favorite family trip, with wildlife sightings, hikes, and beaches. Sign on with an outfitter in the town of Green River.

Weber River. You may see more kayakers than rafters on the Weber, but there are stretches that offer Class II rapids that are commercially run. For a one-day excursion, this is a great side trip from Salt Lake City or Park City.

Westwater Canyon. This short stretch of river can be negotiated in two to three hours, but with notable rapids like Funnel, Sock-it-to-me, and Skull Rapid, it's an action-packed ride.

Skiing and Snowboarding

Utah's "greatest snow on Earth" can be a revelation for skiers and snowboarders familiar only with the slopes of other regions. In Utah the snow builds up quickly, leaving a solid base at each resort that hangs tough all season, only to be layered with thick, fluffy powder that holds an edge, ready to be groomed into rippling corduroy or left in giddy stashes along the sides and through the trees. Off-piste skiing and half-pipe-studded terrain parks are the norm, not the special attractions, here. The added bonus of Utah terrain is that it has something for everyone, often within the same resort.

BEST SLOPES

Alta and Snowbird resorts. These Little Cottonwood Canyon neighbors, within 40 minutes of downtown Salt Lake City, are regularly ranked the top ski resorts in the United States. Seasons with 500 to 600 and more inches of Utah's famous powder are at the root of the accolades. A joint pass lets you ski both mountains on one ticket, but snowboarders are still not allowed at Alta. Snowbird has the longest season in the nation, occasionally staying open through July 4.

Brian Head Resort. The closest Utah ski resort to the Las Vegas airport, Brian Head is worth checking out for the novelty of skiing in southern Utah. The red-orange rocks of Cedar Breaks National Monument form a backdrop to many trails, which tend to focus on beginner and intermediate skiers and snowboarders. Experts can ski off the 11,000-foot summit.

Deer Valley and Park City resorts. The two Park City resorts are known for their great groomed trails, fine dining, and accommodations. Deer Valley is one of three resorts in America that doesn't allow snowboarders, but Park City Mountain Resort, which now encompasses Park City and the resort area formerly known as Canyons, caters to both skiers and riders. The skiing is excellent, but for many it's the whole experience—including the midday feast at Silver Lake Lodge and farm-to-table dining at The Farm—that keeps them coming back.

Snowbasin and Powder Mountain resorts. An hour north of Salt Lake City, Ogden-area residents will tell you the best skiing is at this pair of resorts. Powder Mountain has more skiable terrain than any resort in North America, and Snowbasin was good enough to host the Olympic downhill and slalom during the 2002 Winter Games. These two are often cheaper and less crowded than the Salt Lake City and Park City resorts.

Utah Olympic Park. At the site of the 2002 Olympic bobsled, luge, and ski-jumping events in Park City, you can take recreational ski-jumping lessons or strap in behind a professional driver for a bobsled ride down the actual Olympic course.

A Brief History of Mormonism

From its beginnings in 1830 with just six members, the Church of Jesus Christ of Latter-day Saints has evolved into one of the fastest-growing religions in the world. There are more than 10 million members in more than 185 countries and territories. The faith has drawn increased attention, with the presidential candidacy of Mitt Romney, and a huge increase in tourism since the 2002 Winter Olympics and the 2006–11 HBO show *Big Love*.

IN THE BEGINNING

The church is considered a uniquely American faith, as it was conceived and founded in New York by Joseph Smith, who said God the Father and his son, Jesus Christ, came to him in a vision when he was a young boy. Smith said he also saw a resurrected entity named Moroni, who led him to metal plates that were engraved with the religious history of an ancient American civilization. In 1827 Smith translated this record into the Book of Mormon.

PERSECUTION AND SETTLEMENT IN UTAH

Not long after the creation of the church, religious persecution forced Smith and his followers to flee New York, and they traveled first to Ohio and then to Missouri before settling in Nauvoo, Illinois, in 1839. But even here the fledgling faith was ostracized. Smith was killed by a mob in June 1844 in Carthage, Illinois. To escape the oppression, Brigham Young, who ascended to the church's leadership following Smith's death, led a pilgrimage to Utah, the first group arriving in the Salt Lake Valley on July 24, 1847. Here, under Young's guidance, Mormonism quickly grew and flourished.

In keeping with the church's emphasis on proselytizing, Young laid plans to both colonize Utah and spread the church's word farther afield. This work led to the founding of small towns not only throughout the territory but also from southern Canada to Mexico. Today members of the Church of Jesus Christ of Latter-day Saints continue that work through its young people, many of whom take time out from college or careers to spend two years on a mission at home or abroad.

BELIEFS

Members of the Church of Jesus Christ of Latter-day Saints believe that they are guided by divine revelations received from God by the religion's president, who is viewed as a modern-day prophet in the same sense as other biblical leaders. The Book of Mormon is viewed as divinely inspired scripture, and is used side-by-side with the Holy Bible. Families are highly valued in the faith, and marriages performed in Mormon temples are believed to continue through eternity.

Utah is a conservative state. Utah's civic bodies are overwhelmingly filled by church members who often simultaneously hold leadership positions in their local church units (called wards).

Utah with Kids

Utah is a kid-friendly state.

CITY DIVERSIONS

In and around **Salt Lake City,** start with two very kid-friendly museums in **Gateway Mall.** The **Discovery Gateway** children's museum has a Life Flight helicopter, pinewood derby racing, a story factory, a construction site, and much more—best suited to children under the age of 11. The **Clark Planetarium** opens kids' eyes to the universe and natural phenomena through its interactive exhibits and 3-D and IMAX theaters. The **Leonardo,** an inspirational museum combining science, art, and technology, is on its own a good reason to bring kids to Utah, and the **Natural History Museum of Utah, Red Butte Garden, Tracy Aviary,** and **Hogle Zoo** are also year-round destinations within the city limits—bundle up in the winter and have any one of them virtually to yourself. See bison in a natural setting on **Antelope Island** (if visiting in October, don't miss the annual bison roundup).

In **Ogden,** you can fly like a bird in the wind tunnel, learn to surf, or rock-climb indoors at the state-of-the-art **Salomon Center.** Young children will enjoy the models and playground at the **George S. Eccles Dinosaur Park.** Older kids can catch the Raptors who are, along with Salt Lake's Bees and Orem's Owlz, a fun, inexpensive, entertaining minor-league baseball team.

NATURAL WONDERS

Utah's outdoor attractions provide plenty of outlets for kids' energies. Hikes offer larger-than-life rewards that can even lure kids away from their iPads. Each of Utah's five national parks has special youth-oriented programming and a **Junior Ranger program** that provides them with an interactive booklet of activities and tasks to complete so that they have fun while learning about environmental responsibility.

In **Arches,** hardy kids over the age of 6 can likely make the 3-mile round-trip hike to **Delicate Arch.** Make **Sand Arch** a destination for littler ones—it's right off the road and offers a massive "sandbox" of soft red sand. In **Zion,** kids 10 and up can trek up the Virgin River toward the **Narrows.** At **Bryce** or Zion you can go **horseback riding** to places that might be tough for little legs.

There are **dinosaur excavation** sites near **Vernal, St. George,** and **Price.** Moonlit hikes and telescope tours are nighttime programs offered by park rangers at **Goblin Valley State Park. Moab** has kid-friendly bike trails, and you might find that your BMX-riding teen is more comfortable on the **Slickrock Trail** than you are.

Finally, if you have swimmers, great places to cool off in hot summers include **Lake Powell, Bear Lake,** and glacier-fed rivers and creeks that fill national forest land across the eastern half of the state. And floating in the buoyant waters of the **Great Salt Lake** should be on every kid's bucket list.

Chapter 2

TRAVEL SMART UTAH

Updated by
Shelley Arenas

★ **STATE CAPITAL:**
Salt Lake City

♟ **POPULATION:**
3.2 million

💬 **LANGUAGE:**
English

$ **CURRENCY:**
U.S. Dollar

☎ **AREA CODES:**
385, 485, 801

⚠ **EMERGENCIES:**
911

🚗 **DRIVING:**
On the right

⚡ **ELECTRICITY:**
120–220 v/60 cycles; plugs
have two or three rectangu-
lar prongs

🕐 **TIME:**
Mountain time

🌐 **WEBSITES:**
www.visitutah.com,
www.utah.com,
www.skiutah.com

✈ **AIRPORTS:**
Salt Lake City International
Airport (SLC), St. George
Regional Airport (SGU)

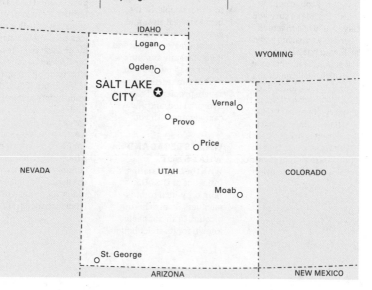

What to Know Before You Go to Utah

Utah is best known for its Mormon roots and the stunning geological features that you can view from scenic drives and amazing national parks. More than 60% of the state's residents are still Mormon, though that drops to less than half in Salt Lake City, and some of the strong Mormon influence over laws and traditions has lessened in recent years.

It's one of the least populated states per square mile, so seclusion is not hard to find, but with that comes the need for preparation before visiting remote areas. Here are some helpful things to know about Utah's climate, staying safe, and more.

ALWAYS WEAR SUNSCREEN

Like the other southwestern states, the sun shines hot and long in Utah. In fact, it's regularly named one of the top 10 sunniest states. Make sure you have and use sunscreen every day. Wearing a wide-brimmed hat helps too. UV exposure increases at high altitudes and Utah's average elevation is 6,100 feet, the third highest in the country. If you're thinking you'll take your chances for a great tan, consider the sobering statistic that the state has the highest rate of skin cancer in the nation.

UNDERSTANDING ALTITUDE SICKNESS

Altitude sickness can be a real downer on vacation. Breathtaking views and outdoor recreation lose appeal fast when you have trouble getting enough oxygen to breathe normally and feel dizzy, nauseous, weak, or get a headache. It happens because the level of oxygen gets lower the higher you go. Most of the ski resorts and many mountain trails are above the 8,000 feet altitude where the sickness begins to affect people. So it's best to take it slow and easy to get used to the mountain air and descend if you feel any symptoms rather than pushing on, as that can cause more severe problems. Stay well hydrated too, and always carry water with you.

WHAT'S LEGAL AND WHAT'S NOT

With the longstanding influence of the LDS religion, which forbids members from drinking alcohol, Utah has been known for its strict liquor laws. One of those laws changed in 2020 when the maximum 4% ABV limit for beer available at grocery stores and beer bars was increased to 5% ABV. You'll still need to go to a liquor store or restaurant for stronger beer, wine, or hard liquor. Don't drink and drive though—Utah has the lowest allowable blood alcohol level in the nation (.05%). Marijuana is not legal in Utah except with a medical card. And (in case you're curious!), while polygamy is considered a crime in all other 49 states, in Utah it was decriminalized in 2020 and is now an infraction similar to a traffic ticket.

GETTING AROUND SAFELY BY CAR

Utah has some amazing scenic drives and you'll cover a lot of miles exploring the state. When driving long stretches, keep an eye on the gas gauge, as gas stations may be few and far between and hours may be limited. Keep your gas tank at least half full; it's a good idea to bring an emergency kit and water. Note that cell service can be spotty so it's wise to bring a map or take screenshots of GPS directions before going off main routes. For winter travel, check road reports and weather forecasts and carry chains if you're not driving a four-wheel drive. Even summer driving can pose challenges, including closed roads due to flash floods from monsoons. Stay alert.

DON'T MISS THE NATIONAL PARKS

Utah is richly blessed with national parks; only California and Alaska have more. Its five parks, all in the southern part of the state, have been nicknamed the "Mighty Five." With canyons, hoodoos, arches and other rock formations, mountains, rivers, wildlife, and exotic flora and fauna, the parks are a delight for outdoor adventurers and photographers. Plan at least a week if you want to see them all and be prepared for crowds, especially at Zion and Bryce Canyon during the summer. If you want to stay in the historic National Park lodges at these two parks, you'll need to book far in advance. At the other parks, there are lodgings in small towns nearby.

UTAH IN THE MOVIES

With its larger-than-life geological majesty and vast expanse of wide-open spaces, Utah has been the setting for many a movie, starting back in 1899 with the first silent Western. It was the backdrop for many other westerns for decades, including nearly a dozen John Wayne movies and *Butch Cassidy and the Sundance Kid* starring Robert Redford and Paul Newman. In more recent years, the docu-drama *127 Hours* (released in 2010) tells the story of a real hiker who was trapped by a boulder against a canyon wall in Canyonlands National Park. The Utah Office of Tourism (⊕ *visitutah.com*) has suggested tours of film locations with an interactive map.

MORMON ORIGINS

In 1847, a group of Church of Jesus Christ of Latter-day Saints members, led by Brigham Young, came west to settle in the Great Salt Lake Valley. Young named the settlement "Deseret," which means honeybee in the Book of Mormon and promoted the idea of bees working cooperatively for the good of the hive. While the name wasn't adopted for the state, the honeybee symbolism remains with its "Beehive State" nickname and the honeybee as the state insect. The early settlers were accompanied by African-American slaves—the first slaves brought to the west. Slavery continued until the end of the Civil War. As the only state with a majority religion, Mormonism plays a big role in its culture and laws. Temple Square in Salt Lake City is a must-see to learn more about the Mormon history in the area.

CAN YOU SWIM IN THE GREAT SALT LAKE?

Locals don't have much interest in swimming in Utah's largest lake; they mention how shallow it is and how smelly from the brine shrimp that live there. Gnats can also be a problem. It's been called "America's Dead Sea" though it lacks the tourist appeal of the real Dead Sea. Still, if you have the time and like to do novel things, it's an interesting experience. The best place to go in is at Antelope Island State Park. You'll wade awhile before reaching the deeper water, where you can float effortlessly, buoyed by the heavy salt. Be careful if you have any cuts or scrapes; the salt will sting. Fortunately, you can shower off all the salt right at the park when you're done.

STAYING SAFE OUTDOORS

There are endless ways to explore the outdoors here—like hiking, biking, climbing, horseback riding, and rafting—but there are definitely risks. The National Park Service recommends outdoor explorers eat well and drink at least a gallon of water a day while in the hot sun, avoid strenuous activities in the middle of the day, and wear sturdy shoes. Always explore with a buddy if you can, and if you get lost, just wait where you are for rescue. When venturing out alone, let someone know where you're going and when you'll be back. Be prepared for sudden weather changes, including flash floods, and stay low if there's lightning.

WHEN TO VISIT

With its legendary powder snow, many people come in winter to enjoy snow sports at the state's 10 world-class ski resorts. The Sundance Film Festival is another reason to visit during the chilly season. Summer is hot and dry but attracts many visitors for the abundant outdoor recreation. There are more programs at national parks during the summer and it's a popular time for families on vacation. If you'd like to avoid crowds and weather extremes, consider the early spring and late fall.

Travel Smart Utah WHAT TO KNOW BEFORE YOU GO TO UTAH

Getting Here and Around

Air

Salt Lake City has a reputation for having one of the nation's easiest airports for travelers—with a low rate of delayed or canceled flights. Plus, it's a western hub for Delta, so your Utah explorations should get off to a timely start. Nonstop flights are available from larger U.S. cities as well as Europe, Mexico, and Canada.

AIRPORTS

The major gateway to Utah is Salt Lake City International Airport. If you're staying in Salt Lake City, you'll appreciate that it's one of the closest airports to downtown of any American city, and security wait times are minimal. The entire airport is being rebuilt in two phases, with the new terminal and parking garage which opened in 2020, and the second phase due to be completed in 2024.

Flights to smaller, regional, or resort-town airports generally connect through Salt Lake. Provo, Cedar City, Logan, Ogden, and Moab all have small airports. A convenient gateway to southern Utah, particularly Zion and Bryce Canyon national parks, is McCarran International Airport in Las Vegas. More and more visitors to southern Utah are using St. George Regional Airport, which has daily flights to Salt Lake City, Phoenix, and Denver. There are limited services, but you can rent cars here and it's less than an hour's drive to Zion National Park once you're on the road.

GROUND TRANSPORTATION

You can get to and from the Salt Lake City Airport by light-rail, taxi, bus, shared ride services, or hotel shuttle. A light-rail line called TRAX connects you in less than 30 minutes (and for just $2.50) to downtown Salt Lake City and the rest of the rapid-transit network. It runs every 15 minutes on weekdays and every 20 minutes on weekends. Taxis, though, are faster (15 minutes); the trip to downtown costs $20–$25. If you're in downtown Salt Lake City, your best bet is to call ahead for a taxi rather than hope to flag one down. Shared-ride shuttle services from the airport are similarly priced to taxis, but can take longer. Lyft and Uber also pick up at the Salt Lake City airport and can cost around half the price of a taxi.

FLIGHTS

Salt Lake City has a large international airport, so you'll be able to fly here from anywhere, though you may have to connect somewhere else first. The airport is a major hub for Delta Airlines. Delta and its affiliates offer almost 250 daily departures to destinations around the country. Southwest ranks second in terms of daily flights, with roughly 30 daily departures. Alaska, American, jetBlue, United, and Frontier also have flights each day.

If you're heading to southern Utah, it may be more convenient to fly into Las Vegas, which has more flights and is often cheaper. Be advised that the 120-mile drive from Las Vegas to St. George passes through extremely remote country, and the Virgin River Canyon near the Arizona/Utah border can make for treacherous driving, especially at night.

Train

Amtrak connects Utah to Chicago and the San Francisco Bay Area daily via the *California Zephyr,* which stops in Salt Lake City, Provo, Helper, and Green River. However, trains are notorious for delays.

Essentials

Dining

Dining in Utah is generally casual. Menus are becoming more varied, but you can nearly always order a hamburger or a steak. There is a growing number of fine restaurants in Salt Lake City and Park City, and good places are cropping up in various other areas. Also look for good dining in Springdale, Moab, and Torrey. Seek out colorful diners along the secondary highways like U.S. 89; they usually serve up meat and potatoes along with the local flavor of each community. Authentic ethnic food is easy to find in Salt Lake City, but generally not available elsewhere. The restaurants we list are the cream of the crop in each price category.

MEALS AND MEALTIMES

Although you can find all types of cuisine in the major cities and resort towns of Utah, be sure to try native dishes like trout, elk, and buffalo (the latter two have less fat than beef and are just as tasty); organic fruits and vegetables are also readily available, especially in finer establishments in Salt Lake City and Park City. Southwestern food is popular, and you'll find several restaurants that specialize in it or show Southwestern influences in menu selections. Asian and Latin American cuisines are both gaining in popularity (and quality) in the Salt Lake area.

Unless otherwise noted, the restaurants listed in this guide are open daily for lunch and dinner. Dinner hours are usually from 6 to 9 pm. Outside of the large cities and resort towns in the high seasons, many restaurants close by 10 and are closed on Sunday.

RESERVATIONS AND DRESS

Reservations are relatively rare outside of the top restaurants in the urban and resort areas. It's a good idea to call ahead if you can. We only mention them specifically when reservations are essential (there's no other way you'll ever get a table) or when they are not accepted. Large parties should always call ahead to check the reservations policy. We mention dress only when men are required to wear a jacket or a jacket and tie—which is almost never in casual Utah. Even at nice resorts dress is usually casual, and in summer you're welcome nearly everywhere in your shorts, T-shirt, and hiking shoes.

WINES, BEER, AND SPIRITS

Despite what you've heard, it's not hard to get a drink in Utah, though you must be 21 to purchase or consume alcohol. The state overhauled liquor laws in 2009 to bring it more in line with the rest of the United States. The state abolished the "private club" system, which required each patron have an annual or short-term membership in order to enter the premises. Many restaurants have licenses, which allow them to serve you wine and beer—and occasionally liquor—with a meal. At restaurants, you will have to order food in addition to alcohol. Some restaurants—generally those that cater to families—opt not to carry a liquor license. If you're set on having a drink with your meal, check before you go. Some restaurants will allow you to bring your own wine, but may charge a corkage fee. Call ahead if you want to take your own wine or other liquor to a restaurant—lots of regulations cover brown bagging.

Utah has a thriving microbrewery scene, with local lagers produced in Salt Lake City, Park City, Moab, Springdale, Vernal, Ogden, and beyond. There are several brewpubs with their own beers on tap—try Latter Day Stout at Desert Edge in Salt Lake City and Polygamy Porter at Wasatch Brew Pubs in Park City and Salt Lake City to get a taste of the local drinking culture. Some brewpubs also have a liquor license that allows the sale of wine and spirits.

Essentials

Most hotel restaurants carry a liquor license, and you'll be able to get your own drinks from the minibar in your room.

Beer with 5% alcohol by volume is available in grocery stores and some convenience stores. For anything else, you'll have to go to a state liquor store. There are 17 liquor stores throughout Salt Lake City and others throughout the state. They are closed on Sunday, Election Day, and holidays.

Note that Utah recently lowered the maximum legal blood alcohol level in drivers from.08% to.05%, giving it the lowest and strictest DUI threshold in the country.

 Lodging

Utah is home to the founders of the Marriott chain of hotels, and its accommodations are plentiful, varied, and reasonably priced throughout the state. Chain motels are everywhere. The ski resorts along the Wasatch Front—especially in Park City—cater to the wealthy jet set, and there are posh resorts such as Deer Valley and the Waldorf Astoria Park City, and pampering at Red Mountain Resort. Salt Lake City has hotels in every price range. National chains like Holiday Inn, Marriott, Hilton, Best Western, Super 8, and Motel 6 are dependable in Utah, and are occasionally the best beds in town. The gateway towns to the national parks usually have a large range of accommodations. Independent motels can also be found all over the state. Look for guest ranches if you're trying to find an authentic Western experience. They often require a one-week stay, and the cost is all-inclusive. During the busy summer season, from Memorial Day to Labor Day, it's a good idea to book your lodging in advance. Most motels and resorts have off-season rates. Take advantage of these, because hiking is best in the south in cool weather, and the mountains are beautiful even without snow.

■ TIP → **Assume that hotels do not include any meals in their room rates, unless we specify otherwise.**

APARTMENT AND HOUSE RENTALS

Increasingly, condos and private homes are available for rent, with more and more options on websites such as Airbnb, Homeaway, and Vrbo. Rentals range from one-night to month-long stays. Enjoy slope-side accommodations with all the amenities of home such as multiple bathrooms and full kitchens at most ski resorts. Condo and home rentals are also available outside Zion, Bryce, Arches, and Canyonlands national parks.

HOTELS

Most Salt Lake City hotels cater to business travelers with such facilities as restaurants, cocktail lounges, Wi-Fi, swimming pools, exercise equipment, and meeting rooms. Most other Utah towns and cities have less expensive hotels that are clean and comfortable but have fewer facilities.

Many properties have special weekend rates, sometimes up to 50% off regular prices. However, these deals are usually not extended during peak months (summer near the national parks and winter in the ski resorts), when hotels are normally full. Salt Lake City hotels are generally full only during major conventions.

All hotels listed have private bath unless otherwise noted.

RESORTS

Ski towns throughout Utah such as Park City, Sundance, and Brian Head are home to resorts in all price ranges (but primarily high-end); any activities lacking in any individual property are usually available in the town itself—in summer as well as winter. Off the slopes, there are both wonderful rustic and luxurious resorts in the southern part of the state: Red Mountain Resort in St. George, Zion Ponderosa Ranch Resort near Zion, Sorrel River Ranch near Arches, and Amangiri near Lake Powell and Four Corners.

⊕ Health

Salt Lake City and Logan are surrounded by mountains, which can trap pollution and create some of the worst air quality in the nation, particularly in winter. Red Alert action days happen several times a year (often for more than a week at a time) when strenuous activity, particularly by young and elderly people, is discouraged. Visit the Utah Department of Environmental Quality website to find out about air quality if you have asthma, allergies, or other breathing sensitivities.

COVID-19

A new novel coronavirus brought all travel to a virtual standstill in the first half of 2020. Although the illness is mild in most people, some experience severe and even life-threatening complications. Once travel started up again, albeit slowly and cautiously, travelers were asked to be particularly careful about hygiene and to avoid any unnecessary travel, especially if they are sick.

Older adults, especially those over 65, have a greater chance of having severe complications from COVID-19. The same is true for people with weaker immune systems or those living with some types of medical conditions, including diabetes, asthma, heart disease, cancer, HIV/AIDS, kidney disease, and liver disease. Starting two weeks before a trip, anyone planning to travel should be on the lookout for

some of the following symptoms: cough, fever, chills, trouble breathing, muscle pain, sore throat, new loss of smell or taste. If you experience any of these symptoms, you should not travel at all.

And to protect yourself during travel, do your best to avoid contact with people showing symptoms. Wash your hands often with soap and water. Limit your time in public places, and, when you are out and about, wear a cloth face mask that covers your nose and mouth. Indeed, a mask may be required in some places, such as on an airplane or in a confined space like a theater, where you share the space with a lot of people.

You may wish to bring extra supplies, such as disinfecting wipes, hand sanitizer (12-ounce bottles were allowed in carry-on luggage at this writing), and a first-aid kit with a thermometer.

Given how abruptly travel was curtailed in March 2020, it is wise to consider protecting yourself by purchasing a travel insurance policy that will reimburse you for any costs related to COVID-19 related cancellations. Not all travel insurance policies protect against pandemic-related cancellations, so always read the fine print.

ⓢ Money

Hotel prices in Salt Lake City run the gamut, but on average the prices are a bit lower than in most major cities. You can pay $100–$350 a night for a room in a major business hotel, though some "value" hotel rooms go for $50–$75, and budget motels are also readily available. Weekend packages at city hotels can cut prices in half (but may not be available in peak winter or summer seasons). As a rule, costs outside cities are lower, except in the deluxe resorts, where costs can be at least double those anywhere

Essentials

else in the state. Look for senior and kids' discounts at many attractions.

Prices throughout this guide are given for adults. Substantially reduced fees are almost always available for children, students, and senior citizens.

CREDIT CARDS

Some small-town restaurants may not accept credit cards, but otherwise plastic is readily accepted at dining, lodging, shopping, and other facilities throughout the state. Minimum purchase amounts may apply.

Throughout this guide, we only mention credit cards when they are not accepted.

🖰 Packing

Informality reigns here; jeans, sport shirts, and T-shirts fit in almost every-where. The few restaurants and perform-ing-arts events where dressier outfits are required, usually in resorts and larger cities, are the exception.

If you plan to spend much time out-doors, and certainly if you go in winter, choose clothing appropriate for cold and wet weather. Cotton clothing, including denim—although fine on warm, dry days—can be uncomfortable and even dangerous when it gets wet and when the weather's cold. A better choice is clothing made of wool or any of a number of new synthetics that provide warmth without bulk and maintain their insulating properties even when wet.

In summer you'll want shorts during the day. But because early morning and night can be cold, and high passes windy, pack a sweater and a light jacket, and perhaps also a wool cap and gloves. Try layering—a T-shirt under another shirt under a jacket—and peel off layers as you go. For walks and hikes, you'll need

sturdy footwear. To take you into the wilds, boots should have thick soles and plenty of ankle support; if your shoes are new and you plan to spend much time on the trail, break them in at home. Bring a day pack for short hikes, along with a canteen or water bottle, and don't forget rain gear, a hat, sunscreen, and insect repellent.

In winter, prepare for subfreezing temperatures with good boots, warm socks and liners, thermal underwear, a well-insulated jacket, and a warm hat and mittens. Dress in layers so you can add or remove clothes as the temperatures fluctuate.

If you attend dances and other events at Native American reservations, dress conservatively—skirts or long pants—or you may be asked to leave.

When traveling to mountain areas, remember that sunglasses and a sun hat are essential at high altitudes, even in winter; the thinner atmosphere requires sunscreen with a greater SPF than you might need at lower elevations. Bring moisturizer even if you don't normally use it. Utah's dry climate can be hard on your skin.

➕ Safety

It's always best to tell someone—the hotel desk clerk, the ski-rental person—where you're going. Cell phones don't always work in the backcountry, and even a general idea of where you are can help rescuers find you quickly. Know your limits.

Many trails are at high altitudes, where oxygen is thinner. They're also frequently desolate. Hikers and bikers should carry a flashlight, a compass, waterproof matches, a first-aid kit, a knife, and a light plastic tarp for shelter. Backcountry skiers should add a repair kit, a blanket, an avalanche beacon, and a lightweight shovel to their lists. Always bring extra food and a canteen of water. Never drink from streams or lakes, unless you boil the water first or purify it with tablets. Giardia, an intestinal parasite, may be present.

Always check the condition of roads and trails, and get the latest weather reports before setting out. In summer take precautions against heat stroke or exhaustion by resting frequently in shaded areas; in winter take precautions against hypothermia by layering clothing.

You may feel dizzy and weak and find yourself breathing heavily—signs that the thin mountain air isn't giving you your accustomed dose of oxygen. Take it easy and rest often for a few days until you're acclimatized. Throughout your stay, drink plenty of water and watch your alcohol consumption, as dehydration is a common occurrence at high altitudes. If you experience severe headaches and nausea, see a doctor. It is easy to go too high too fast. The remedy for altitude-related discomfort is to go down quickly into heavier air.

Flash floods can strike at any time and any place with little or no warning. The danger in mountainous terrain intensifies when distant rains are channeled into gullies and ravines, turning a quiet stream-side campsite or wash into a rampaging torrent in seconds; similarly, desert terrain can become dangerous when heavy rains fall on land that is unable to absorb the water and thus floods quickly. Check weather reports before heading into the backcountry, and be prepared to head for higher ground if the weather turns severe.

One of the most wonderful features of Utah is its abundant wildlife. To avoid an unpleasant situation while hiking, make plenty of noise and keep dogs on a leash and small children between adults. While camping, be sure to store all food, utensils, and clothing with food odors far away from your tent, preferably high in a tree or in a bear box. If you do come across a bear or big cat, do not run. For bears or moose, back away while talking calmly; for mountain lions, make yourself look as big as possible. In either case, be prepared to fend off the animal with loud noises, rocks, sticks, and so on. And, as the saying goes, do not feed the bears—or any wild animals, whether they're dangerous or not.

When in any park, give all animals their space. If you want to take a photograph, use a long lens and keep your distance. This is particularly important for winter visitors. Approaching an animal can cause stress and affect its ability to survive the sometimes-brutal climate. In all cases, remember that the animals have the right-of-way; this is their home, and you are the visitor.

Tours

BICYCLING

Utah offers a wide range of topography and scenery to satisfy cyclists of all styles. Moab has been heralded for years as a mecca for mountain bikers, but fat-tire lovers pedal all corners and all elevations of the state; bike shops in St. George, Salt Lake City, Park City, and Ogden can also help you find an itinerary. Excellent multiday (and multisport) tours crisscross the desert including the incomparable White Rim Trail in Canyonlands National Park. Hard-core road cyclists, including pros in training, challenge themselves by climbing the

Essentials

grueling canyons to the east of Salt Lake City. But there are plenty of roads for the less gonzo rider to explore, and biking is an excellent way for a family to bond while getting some exercise.

■ TIP→ **Most airlines accommodate bikes as luggage for an extra fee, provided they're dismantled and boxed.**

Bicycle Adventures

BICYCLE TOURS | Several multiday tours in southern Utah including an epic seven-day national parks ride that starts at St. George and zooms through Zion, Capitol Reef, Glen Canyon, Lake Powell, Natural Bridges, and more. ☎ 800/443–6060 ⊕ www.bicycleadventures.com ✉ From $2,798.

Escape Adventures

BICYCLE TOURS | More than 20 itineraries for road cyclists and mountain bikers alike range from three to seven days, departing from Moab and St. George. Beginners can enjoy road rides of less than 30 miles per day, single-track daredevils can conquer slickrock trails, and independent travelers will love the "do-it-yourself" itineraries. Half-day and full day tours are also available from Moab. ☎ 800/596–2953 ⊕ www. escapeadventures.com ✉ From $75 for half-day, from $695 for three-day tour.

Rim Tours

BICYCLE TOURS | Half-, full-, or multiday camping- and hotel-based tours in southern Utah include Slickrock, Navajo Rocks, Magnificent 7, White Rim, and Moab Brand Trails. ☎ 435/259–5223, 800/626–7335 ⊕ www.rimtours.com ✉ From $105 for a half-day tour.

Western Spirit

BICYCLE TOURS | **FAMILY** | This outfitter offers nine fully supported mountain biking itineraries (such as Bryce to Zion national parks) that range from family-oriented to expert-only, and from three to six days. The common denominator is challenging wilderness conditions that are best undertaken with an expert guide, unless you're a seasoned back-road or off-road biker. There are also a couple of five-day road bike tours and a six-day tour that rides on both gravel and paved roads. ☎ 435/259–8732 ⊕ www. westernspirit.com ✉ From $945.

FISHING

Close to Salt Lake City, the Provo and Logan rivers are world-class trout-fishing rivers that attract anglers from around the globe. In some parts of the Provo, it is said that there are upward of 3,000 trout per square mile.

Fish Heads Fly Shop

GUIDED TOURS | Fish the trout-filled streams of the Provo River and surrounding waters under the guidance of these experienced anglers. Half- and full-day guided trips are available. ☎ 435/657–2010 ⊕ www.fishheadsflyshop.com ✉ From $275 for half-day.

GOLF

From a dozen public courses in the Salt Lake Valley, to world-class courses in Park City, to the sunny southern Utah courses set against red-rock backdrops, Utah offers a proliferation of golf courses, many of which are highlighted on the Utah tourism website (⊕ utah.com/golf-courses). You will find variety in terrain, scenery, and level of difficulty.

HORSEBACK RIDING

You can still throw on some jeans and boots and head out on a multiday horseback trek. Several Utah operators will match you with your steed, give you as much or as little instruction as you need, and get you out on the trail. Excursions range from day trips to week-long adventures. Find guides and rides on the Utah tourism website (⊕ utah.com/horseback-riding).

RAFTING

For an instant respite from summer heat that ranges from toasty to torrid, book a one-to-five-day river-rafting adventure. Itineraries exist for families with adventurers as young as three years old and range from leisurely multiday floats to days that culminate in unforgettable rapids. Utah's river guides have been at it for decades, and will gladly share river-bottom views of red rock cliffs, petroglyphs, and wildlife. The Utah tourism website (⊕ *www.utah.com/river-rafting*) is a useful resource.

SKIING

If ever an outdoor activity was synonymous with Utah tourism, skiing is it. The bulk of the state's resorts, known for the fluffy powder that falls on average 500 inches a year, are within a one-hour drive from the Salt Lake City Airport. Ski the same runs that Olympians traversed in 2002: the downhill and slaloms were held at Snowbasin near Ogden, while aerials, slalom, and snowboarding took place at Park City or Deer Valley. Finally, challenge yourself on the Nordic competition trails at Heber Valley's Soldier Hollow Olympic venue. The season traditionally begins Thanksgiving week at many resorts and runs through July 4 at some resorts. Plan to ski in late November, March, or April to avoid the biggest crowds. Prices spike and accommodations fill around major holidays like President's Day. Every ski resort and many private travel agents can assist you with your ski planning. Ski Utah is the state's official and very useful website for ski information; it should be your starting point for any ski activity in the state.

SkiUtah

SPECIAL-INTEREST | Whether you have 2 days or 10, Ski Utah can help you make the most of your time on the snow. The Interconnect Tour gives advanced to expert skiers the chance to ski back-country terrain in and around as many as six resorts in one day. ☎ *800/754–8824* ⊕ *www.skiutah.com* ✉ *From $430 for Interconnect tour.*

Taxes

State sales tax is 4.85% in Utah. Most areas have additional local sales and lodging taxes, which can be quite significant. For example, in Salt Lake City the combined sales tax is 7.25%; the highest rates are in Alta (8.75%) and Park City (9.05%). Utah sales tax is reduced for some items, such as groceries.

Time

Utah is in the mountain time zone. In summer Utah observes Daylight Savings Time.

Tipping

It is customary to tip at least 15% at restaurants; 18%–20% in resort towns is increasingly the norm. For coat checks and bellhops, $1 per coat or bag is the minimum. Taxi drivers expect 15% to 20%, depending on where you are. In resort towns, ski technicians, sandwich makers, baristas, and the like also appreciate tips. For ski instructors, a 10%–15% tip is standard.

Essentials

Tipping Guidelines for Utah

Bartender	$1 to $5 per round of drinks, depending on the number of drinks
Bellhop	$1 to $5 per bag, depending on the level of the hotel
Hotel Concierge	$5 or more, if he or she performs a service for you
Hotel Doorman	$1–$2 if he or she helps you get a cab
Hotel Housekeeper	$2–$5 a day (tip daily since staff may vary)
Hotel Room-Service Waiter	15–20% unless gratuity has been added
Skycap at Airport	$1 to $2 per bag checked
Taxi Driver	15%–20%, but round up the fare to the next dollar amount
Tour Guide	10% of the cost of the tour
Valet Parking Attendant	$1–$2, but only when you get your car
Waiter	15%–20%, with 20% being the norm at high-end restaurants; nothing additional if gratuity is added to the bill

🧭 Trip Insurance

Comprehensive trip insurance is valuable if you're booking a very expensive or complicated trip (particularly to an isolated region) or if you're booking far in advance. Comprehensive policies typically cover trip cancellation and interruption, letting you cancel or cut your trip short because of illness, or, in some cases, acts of terrorism in your destination. Such policies might also cover evacuation and medical care. Some also cover you for trip delays because of bad weather or mechanical problems as well as for lost or delayed luggage. Some policies offer an add-on "Cancel for any Reason (CFAR)" option that covers 50%–75% of nonrefundable and prepaid deposits; these can be used for reasons not covered in standard policies (such as pandemics, vacation scheduling conflicts, personal issues, etc.), but must be purchased within two to three weeks of the initial trip deposit.

Another type of coverage to consider is financial default—that is, when your trip is disrupted because a tour operator or airline goes out of business. Generally you must buy this when you book your trip or shortly thereafter, and it's available to you only if your operator isn't on a list of excluded companies.

Always read the fine print of your policy to make sure that you're covered for the risks that most concern you. Compare several policies to be sure you're getting the best price and range of coverage available.

🧭 Visitor Information

Utah Office of Tourism has an excellent website, and its office (across the street from the state capitol) is open weekdays.

On the Calendar

January

Sundance Film Festival. Presented by Robert Redford's Sundance Institute, the annual festival is on par with international festivals like Cannes and Toronto and attracts serious film buffs, locals, and plenty of celebrities. It takes place over 11 days at the end of January, primarily in Park City, but also in Salt Lake City and at Redford's Sundance Resort. The festival features both independent filmmakers and major studios, and the best go home with the coveted Sundance Awards. ⊕ *www.sundance.org.*

June

Utah Arts Festival. Salt Lake City's Library Square fills with art booths, performers, interactive art, kids activities, tasty food, and plenty of people (around 70,000 over four days) for Utah's largest outdoor festival. The award-winning celebration of the arts highlights primarily regional artists and is a wonderful opportunity to bring home locally made art to remember your visit to Utah. The festival happens the last weekend of June from Thursday through Sunday. ⊠ *Library Square, 200 East 400 South, Salt Lake City* ⊕ *www.uaf.org.*

Bryce Canyon Astronomy Festival. Held in late June at Bryce Canyon National Park, the four-day festival has plenty of activities for the whole family, including model rocket building and launching, solar scope viewings, stories and talks on astronomy by park rangers and scientists, and of course stargazing. ⊠ *Bryce Canyon National Park* ⊕ *www.nps.gov/ brca.*

July

Pioneer Day. On this state holiday every July 24, community celebrations mark the arrival on July 24, 1847, of Brigham Young and the first Mormons that settled the area. Statewide, you will find fireworks, historical reenactments, rodeos, parades, and fairs. Though meant to be inclusive of all pioneer history from the era, not just the Mormons, the holiday has inspired a smaller alternative celebration called "Pie & Beer Day" for the non-LDS folks and a Native American Powwow at Liberty Park in Salt Lake City.

September

Moab Music Festival. This two-week festival in early September highlights chamber, jazz, and global traditional music played in stunning outdoor settings around Moab. The unique venues include a grotto that is accessed by jet boat and surrounded by red rock, secluded canyons that you hike to, and two multiday luxury adventure experiences that add on rafting, swimming, floating, and hiking, and a plane ride back to the start. A few venues are indoors in Moab and there's a free concert in the city park too. ⊠ *Moab* ⊕ *www.moabmusicfest.org.*

Great Itineraries

Utah's Five Glorious National Parks, 7 Days

DAYS 1 AND 2: ZION NATIONAL PARK
(3 hours from McCarran Airport in Las Vegas)

Start early from Las Vegas, and within three hours you'll be across the most barren stretches of desert and marveling at the bends in the Virgin River gorge. Just past St. George, Utah, on I–15, take the Route 9 exit to **Zion National Park.** Spend your afternoon in the park—if you're visiting in February through November, the National Park Service bus system does the driving for you on Zion Canyon Scenic Drive (in fact, when the bus is running, cars are not allowed on the drive).

For a nice introductory walk, try the short and easy **Weeping Rock Trail.** Follow it along the **Emerald Pools Trail** in Zion Canyon itself, where you might come across wild turkeys and ravens. Before leaving the park, ask the rangers to decide which of Zion's two iconic hikes is right for you the next day—the 1,488-foot elevation gain to **Angel's Landing** or river wading along the improbably steep canyon called the **Narrows.** Overnight at **Zion Lodge** inside the park (book well in advance or call for last-minute cancellations), but venture into the bustling gateway town of **Springdale** for dinner and a peak into an art gallery or boutique. Try **Bit & Spur** for tasty Southwestern food.

Start at dawn the next day to beat the crowds and heat if you're ascending Angel's Landing (allow three to four hours).

DAY 3: BRYCE CANYON NATIONAL PARK
(2 hours from Zion)

It's a long 85 miles from Zion to Bryce via Route 9 (the scenic Zion–Mount Carmel Highway), particularly as traffic must be escorted through a 1.1-mile-long tunnel. Canyon Overlook is a great stopping point, providing views of massive rock formations such as East and West Temples. When you emerge, you are in slickrock country, where huge petrified sandstone dunes have been etched by ancient waters. Stay on Route 9 for 23 miles and then turn north onto U.S. 89 and follow the signs to the entrance of **Bryce Canyon National Park.**

Start at **Sunrise Point.** Check out **Bristlecone Loop Trail** and the **Navajo Loop Trail,** both of which you can easily fit into a day trip and will get you into the heart of the park. Listen for peregrine falcons deep in the side canyons, and keep an eye out for a species of prairie dog that only lives in these parts. If you can't stay in the park (camping or **The Lodge at Bryce Canyon** are your options), overnight at **Ruby's Inn,** near the junction of Routes 12 and 63, or the full-featured **Bryce Canyon Grand Hotel** across the street; both are on the park's free shuttle route.

DAY 4: CAPITOL REEF NATIONAL PARK
(2½ hours from Bryce Canyon)

If you can, get up early to see sunrise paint Bryce's hoodoos, then head out on the spectacular Utah Scenic Byway–Route 12. Route 12 winds over and through **Grand Staircase–Escalante National Monument.** Boulder's **Hell's Backbone Grill,** for example, may be the best remote restaurant you'll find in the West, and you don't want to bypass **Fruita's** petroglyphs and bountiful orchards in the late summer and fall.

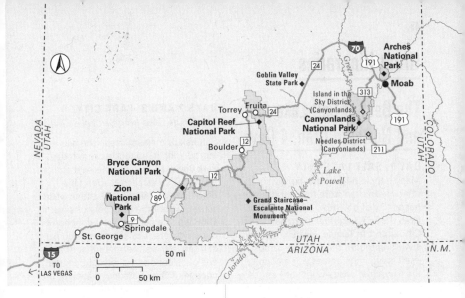

At the intersection of Routes 12 and 24, turn east onto Route 24 toward **Capitol Reef National Park.** The crowds are smaller here than at other national parks in the state, and the scenery is stunning. Assuming it's still daylight when you arrive, hike the 1-mile **Hickman Bridge Trail,** stop in at the visitor center, open until 4:30 (later in the spring through fall), and view pioneer and Native American exhibits, talk with rangers about geography or geology, or watch a film. Nearby **Torrey** is your best bet for lodging and you can get a tasty pizza to enjoy with a microbrew and gorgeous red rock views from the **Rim Rock Patio.**

DAYS 5–7: MOAB, ARCHES, AND CANYONLANDS NATIONAL PARKS
(2½ hours from Capitol Reef to Canyonlands)

Explore Capitol Reef more the next morning. An easy way to do this is to drive the 10-mile **Capitol Reef Scenic Drive,** which starts at the park Visitor Center. When you leave, travel east and north for 75 miles on Route 24. If you want a break after about an hour, stop at the small **Goblin Valley State Park.** Continue on Route 24 to I–70 and turn east toward Colorado.

Take Exit 182 south onto U.S. 191, proceeding about 19 miles to Island in the Sky Road. Make sure you have water, food, and gas, as **Canyonlands National Park** offers no services, with the exception of water at The Needles visitor center year-round and the Island in the Sky visitor center seasonally. Be sure to follow the drive out to **Grand View Point** to look down on the convergence of the Colorado and Green rivers. Along the way, **Mesa Arch** is a half-mile walk and offers a sneak preview of what to expect at Arches. More ambitious individuals should hike the mysterious crater at **Upheaval Dome,** which is a steep 1-mile round-trip hike. Whether you plan to explore Canyonlands further the next day or move onto **Arches National Park,** backtrack to U.S. 191 and turn right for the final 12-mile drive into **Moab,** a good basecamp for both parks.

Build your Arches itinerary around hikes to **Delicate Arch** (best seen at sunrise to avoid the crowds) and **Landscape Arch.** The guided hike in the **Fiery Furnace.**

You can raft the Colorado River from Moab or bike the **Slickrock Trail.** Or, explore **Needles District** of Canyonlands (about 90 minutes south), viewing petroglyphs on Route 279 (Potash Road), and driving along the Colorado River north of town to **Fisher Towers.**

Great Itineraries

The Best of Salt Lake City and Northern Utah, 4 Days

DAY 1: SALT LAKE CITY

Many people begin their explorations of northern Utah from the comfortable hospitality of downtown **Salt Lake City.** Grab the TRAX light rail from Salt Lake City Airport to **Temple Square** and begin a walking tour of the city. The temple itself is off-limits unless you belong to the Church of Jesus Christ of Latter-day Saints, but its grounds and the rest of the complex make for interesting wandering. Immediately south is **City Creek Center,** the city's first upscale shopping district. The **Discovery Gateway** children's museum and **Clark Planetarium** are best bets here, as well as the **Olympic Legacy Plaza.** Complete your walk by crossing Pioneer Park, heading east through Gallivan Plaza (you may catch live music midday or evenings) as far as **Salt Lake City Main Library**—a modern architectural gem that includes a soaring roof that you can ascend for one of the best views of the city. **Salt Lake Roasting Co.,** in the library promenade, is a good place for a drink or snack. There's ample downtown lodging to choose from. Pamper yourself at the **Grand America Hotel** or bring your pooch to the pet-friendly **Kimpton Hotel Monaco.** Dining and drinking options are varied. Sample the microbrews from **Squatters Pub Brewery,** then fill up on America's best Mexican food at **Red Iguana** or check out **The Copper Onion** for Continental cuisine.

DAYS 2 AND 3: PARK CITY
(40-minute drive from Salt Lake City)

Salt Lake's majesty lies in the hills surrounding it, so tackle them today. **Park City** is 25 miles to the east along I–80 and you can easily spend the entire day wandering its historic Main Street, where the discovery of silver in 1868 led to a boom era of prospectors, mine workers, and schemers. You can still see in the storefronts that dozens of saloons and a red-light district once flourished here in defiance of the Mormon Church. The **Park City Museum** is the perfect place to discover the town's colorful history, and the **Park Silly Sunday Market** (June to September) portrays its modern-day fun side. For lunch or dinner, **Wasatch Brew Pub** is at the top of Main Street, and **Handle** and **High West Distillery** are just off Main on Heber Avenue and Park Avenue, respectively. You can't go wrong with any of them for a meal. If it's winter, hit the slopes; if it's summer hit the trails, where you might just encounter a moose. Either season, stop at **Utah Olympic Park** where you will often glimpse America's next gold-medal hopefuls training in any of a half-dozen disciplines including ski jumping, bobsled, or luge. If you have time and love roller coaster thrills, ride the bobsled course from top to bottom with a trained driver. Indulge in the spa, lounge, or restaurant at Deer Valley's **Stein Ericksen Lodge,** or opt for the equally refined (but no less expensive) **Waldorf Astoria Park City.** The **Newpark Resort** is a more affordable option near the outlet mall.

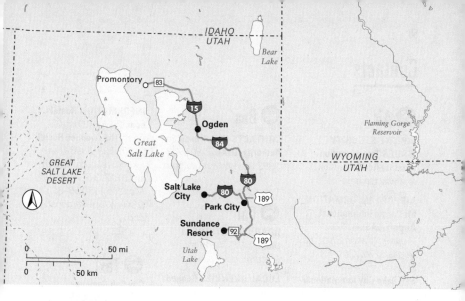

DAY 4: SUNDANCE RESORT OR OGDEN

(45-minute drive from Park City to Sundance; or 1 hour 10 minute drive to Ogden)

You can easily spend several more days in Park City, but its environs are beckoning. There's fly-fishing and rafting on the Provo River, balloon rides, and hot springs. Robert Redford's **Sundance Resort** is a year-round destination for artists, film-makers, and musicians—not just tourists and skiers. It's about 45 minutes south of Park City through the gorgeous Provo River canyon. Dine at the **Foundry Grill** or **Tree Room** and keep your eyes open for Mr. Redford. Railroad buffs may prefer to make the hour drive north to **Ogden,** where **Union Station** has welcomed trains on the transcontinental route since it opened in 1924. Historic 25th Street has a multitude of restaurants. From there, head west to **Promontory,** Utah, to see where the golden spike was hammered in to connect East and West in 1869.

Contacts

Air

AIRLINE SECURITY ISSUES Transportation Security Administration. ⊕ *www.tsa.gov.*

AIRPORT INFORMATION McCarran International Airport (LAS). ✉ *5757 Wayne Newton Blvd., Las Vegas* ☎ *702/261–5211* ⊕ *www.mccarran.com.* **Salt Lake City International Airport (SLC).** ✉ *776 N. Terminal Dr., Salt Lake City* ☎ *801/575–2400* ⊕ *www. slcairport.com.* **St. George Regional Airport (SGU).** ✉ *4550 S. Airport Pkwy., St. George* ☎ *435/627–4080* ⊕ *www.flysgu.com.*

AIRLINE CONTACTS Alaska Airlines. ☎ *800/252–7522* ⊕ *www.alaskaair. com.* **American Airlines.** ☎ *800/433–7300* ⊕ *www. aa.com.* **Delta Airlines.** ☎ *800/221–1212 for U.S. reservations, 800/241–4141 for international reservations* ⊕ *www. delta.com.* **Frontier.** ☎ *801/401–9000* ⊕ *www. flyfrontier.com.* **jetBlue.** ☎ *800/538–2583* ⊕ *www. jetblue.com.* **Southwest Airlines.** ☎ *800/435–9792* ⊕ *www.southwest.com.* **United Airlines.** ☎ *800/864–8331 U.S. and Canada reservations* ⊕ *www. united.com.*

Bus

CONTACTS Utah Transit Authority (UTA). ☎ *801/743–3882* ⊕ *www.rideuta.com.*

🚗 Car

ROAD CONDITIONS In Utah. ☎ *511* ⊕ *commuterlink.utah.gov.*

LOCAL AGENCIES Rugged Rental. ☎ *801/977–9111* ⊕ *www.ruggedrental.com.*

MAJOR RENTAL AGENCIES Advantage. ☎ *800/777–5500* ⊕ *www. advantage.com.* **Alamo.** ☎ *844/354–6962* ⊕ *www.alamo.com.* **Avis.** ☎ *800/633–3469* ⊕ *www.avis.com.* **Budget.** ☎ *800/218–7992* ⊕ *www. budget.com.* **Hertz.** ☎ *800/654–3131* ⊕ *www. hertz.com.* **National Car Rental.** ☎ *844/382–6875* ⊕ *www.nationalcar.com.*

➕ Health

INFORMATION Utah Department of Environmental Quality. ⊕ *www.airquality. utah.gov.*

🛏 Lodging

RENTAL INFORMATION Airbnb. ⊕ *www.airbnb. com.* **Vrbo.** ⊕ *www.vrbo. com.*

INFORMATION Hostels. com. ⊕ *www.hostels. com* . **The Avenues Hostel.** ☎ *801/539–8888* ⊕ *salt-lakehostel.com.* **Lazy Lizard.** ✉ *1213 S. Hwy. 191, Moab* ☎ *435/259–6057* ⊕ *www.lazylizardhostel. com.*

Taxi

City Cab Company. ☎ *801/363–5550* ⊕ *www. citycabut.com.* **Ute Cab Company.** ☎ *801/359–7788* ⊕ *utecabco.com.* **Yellow Cab.** ☎ *801/521–2100* ⊕ *yellowcabutah.com.*

🚆 Train

TRAIN INFORMATION Amtrak. ☎ *800/872–7245* ⊕ *www.amtrak.com.* **Heber Valley Historic Railroad.** ✉ *450 S. 600 W, Heber* ☎ *435/654–5601* ⊕ *www.hebervalleyrr.org.*

📍 Visitor Information

CONTACTS Utah Office of Tourism. ✉ *Council Hall, Capitol Hill, 300 N. State St., Salt Lake City* ☎ *801/538–1900, 800/200–1160* ⊕ *www. visitutah.com.*

Chapter 3

SALT LAKE CITY

3

Updated by
Andrew Collins

⊙ Sights
★★★★★

🍴 Restaurants
★★★★★

🛏 Hotels
★★★☆☆

🛍 Shopping
★★★☆☆

🍸 Nightlife
★★★★☆

WELCOME TO SALT LAKE CITY

TOP REASONS TO GO

★ **A downtown renaissance:** Venture into Salt Lake's vibrant downtown, with its respected theater scene, farm-to-table restaurants, craft breweries and coffeehouses, and the impressive City Creek Center retail plaza.

★ **Wander the Wasatch Front:** Lace up your hiking boots and enjoy the dramatic canyons on the city's east side.

★ **Catch the indie spirit:** This region, which has historically embraced chain franchises, has in recent years blossomed with hip independently owned businesses.

★ **Shore adventures:** Explore the city's namesake, the Great Salt Lake, by car, on foot, or by bicycle. If you're here in the summer, try floating off the beaches at Antelope Island—the water is so salty it's impossible to sink.

★ **Pow-pow-powder:** Experience the "greatest snow on earth" within an hour's drive of the airport at one of nine renowned ski resorts.

1 Temple Square. The hub of the Church of Jesus Christ of Latter-day Saints is home to both the Salt Lake Temple and Tabernacle.

2 Downtown and Central City. Salt Lake City's core is downtown, a quadrant containing most of the city's top hotels, and a slew of theaters, restaurants, and bars.

3 Capitol Hill and the Avenues. Surrounding the capitol on all sides are residential areas known for historic houses.

4 East Side and Sugar House. This scenic area of the city hugs up against the dramatic Wasatch Range.

5 Great Salt Lake and West Side. Great Salt Lake, the remnants of the ancient Bonneville Lake that covered much of the northern half of Utah.

6 Midvalley and South Valley. The Midvalley and South Valley suburbs contain mostly bedroom communities.

7 Big Cottonwood Canyon. This famed canyon is home to Solitude and Brighton ski areas.

8 Little Cottonwood Canyon. This smaller canyon to the south is arguably even more prestigious among skiers.

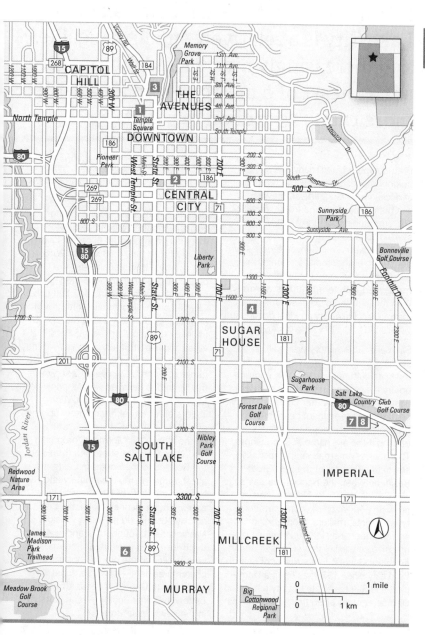

Nestled at the foot of the rugged Wasatch Mountains and extending to the south shore of the Great Salt Lake, Salt Lake City is a relatively small, navigable, and increasingly diverse and vibrant city at the heart of a metropolitan area with more than 1.25 million residents.

Both downtown and many outlying neighborhoods have become hot beds of acclaimed dining, artisan brewing and coffee-roasting, and trendy retail. The surrounding Salt Lake Valley offers striking landscapes and accessible outdoor adventures. Canyon breezes turn hot summer afternoons into enjoyable evenings, and snowy winter days are moderated with temperatures warmer than those at most ski destinations, making Salt Lake City an ideal destination year-round.

Salt Lake City's history was built on the shoulders of its Mormon founders, but today its culture draws equally contemporary events and influences, such as hosting the 2002 Winter Olympics, and becoming a preeminent destination for technological or innovative pursuits, earning it the nickname "Silicon Slopes." The city has emerged as the economic and cultural center of the vast Great Basin, between the Rocky Mountains and California's Sierra Nevada. And its growing population of young outdoorsy types, artists, makers, foodies, and entrepreneurs has infused it with a progressive sensibility that surprises many first-time visitors. Every mayor of Salt Lake City since 1976 has been a Democrat, and Salt Lake City County has voted Democrat more often than not in the last few presidential elections. Furthermore, the city has a sizable and visible LGBTQ community.

Despite recent demographic changes, including the percentage of Mormon-identifying residents of Salt Lake County falling below 50% as of 2018 (it's far lower than that in Salt Lake City proper), since Brigham Young led his first party of pioneers here in 1847, Salt Lake City has been synonymous with the Mormon Church, formally called the Church of Jesus Christ of Latter-day Saints. The valley appealed to Young because, at the time, it was under the control of Mexico rather than the U.S. government, which the Mormons believed was responsible for much of their persecution. Within days of his arrival, Young drew up plans for Salt Lake City, which was to be the hub of the Mormons' promised land, a vast empire stretching from the Rockies to the Southern California coast. Although the area that eventually became the state of Utah was smaller than Young planned, Salt Lake City quickly outstripped his original vision. Missionaries throughout Scandinavia and the British Isles converted thousands, who flocked to the city to live near their church president—a living prophet, according to Church of Jesus Christ of Latter-day Saints doctrine—and worship in the newly built temple.

In the 1860s, income from railroads and mines created a class of industrialists who built mansions near downtown and whose businesses brought thousands of workers—mainly from Europe and few of whom were Mormon—to Utah Territory. By the time Utah became a state in 1896, Salt Lake was a thriving city. Although the majority of the city was members of the Church of Jesus Christ of Latter-day Saints, it claimed a healthy mix of Protestant, Catholic, and Jewish citizens. The Church of Jesus Christ of Latter-day Saints's presence is still evident, as both its headquarters and the Tabernacle, home to the world-famous Tabernacle Choir at Temple Square, call Temple Square home.

Today the city is an important center for business, medicine, education, and technology, and it's a major worldwide hub of Delta Airlines. A growing commitment to the arts from both the public and private sector has led to a booming cultural scene, and sports fans appreciate the presence of two major-league franchises—basketball's Utah Jazz and soccer's Real Salt Lake.

Although the former mining town and now ritzy getaway of Park City—just a 40-minute drive up the hill—receives the lion's share of Utah's skiing acclaim, Salt Lake County is home to four world-class resorts: Alta, Brighton, Snowbird, and Solitude. And the foothills just north and east of the city teem with amazingly scenic hiking and mountain-biking trails and myriad opportunities for wildlife viewing, as does Antelope Island, at the eastern end of Great Salt Lake.

MAJOR REGIONS

Salt Lake City proper lies at the northern center of the greater Salt Lake Valley, at the confluence of two huge freeways that cross the country, east–west I-80 (which connects the city with nearby Park City) and north–south I-15, which runs north to the suburbs of Ogden and south into Utah County and Provo.

Apart from Great Salt Lake and Antelope State Park, which are 15 miles west and 40 miles north of the city respectively, most of the side trips you're likely to make from town are to the south and east. Immediately south, in the Midvalley and South Valley regions, you'll find the sometimes sprawling (especially as you head farther west from the Wasatch Range) suburbs of Millcreek, West Valley City, Murray, Sandy, Draper, and others. Heading due east of these suburbs, Big Cottonwood Canyon and Little Cottonwood Canyon are home to the county's four renowned ski areas.

Planning

When to Go

Spring and fall are the best times to visit, as cooler afternoons give way to idyllic breezy evenings. Summertime high temperatures average more than 90° (June–August), with a few days above 100° each month. Winters bring snow, but abundant sunshine melts it quickly in the valley. If your plans include trips to Park City or the Cottonwood Canyons, follow weather forecasts closely, because a fluffy 6-inch snowfall in the city will often be accompanied by 3 to 5 feet "up the hill." Extreme heat or cold without any wind often brings about "inversions" of polluted air that sometimes linger for longer than a week and prompt red alert warnings against activity in the valley, especially for people who suffer from respiratory issues. Locals often escape to the mountains on these days to get some fresh air above the clouds. Most years, ski season kicks off by mid-November and ends in early April. (During a heavy snow year, Snowbird Ski Resort will stay open on weekends as late as July 4.) Expect larger crowds at the airport and higher rates at hotels and resorts near the ski slopes on winter weekends, particularly around holidays such as Christmas, Martin Luther King Jr. Day, and Presidents' Day, as well as during the Sundance Film Festival, based in nearby Park City but with some screenings in Salt Lake. Most of the rest of the year, city accommodations are cheaper than in other big cities across the country, but occasional large conventions sometimes drive up prices. Utahns reserve much of their patriotism for July 24, rather than July 4, as it's a recognized statewide holiday known as Pioneer Day, celebrated with a parade, a marathon, and fireworks; expect road and business closures.

Getting Here and Around

AIR

For a relatively small city, Salt Lake is served by large airport, which is one of the major hubs of Delta Airlines, which offers direct flights to most major U.S. cities and a number of international ones. Additionally, most other U.S. airlines and a couple of international ones (AeroMexico, KLM) fly to Salt Lake.

AIR INFORMATION Salt Lake City International Airport. ☒ *776 N. Terminal Dr.* ☎ *801/575–2400, 800/595–2442* ⊕ *www. slcairport.com.*

GROUND TRANSPORTATION

Salt Lake City International Airport is just 7 miles northwest of downtown via I–80, or you can take North Temple, which leads to the city center. A taxi or ride-share, such as Uber or Lyft, from the airport to town costs about $21. The Utah Transit Authority (UTA) operates TRAX light-rail to and from the airport in less than 30 minutes for $2.50 each way.

TAXI CONTACTS City Cab Company. ☎ *801/363–5550* ⊕ *www.citycabut.com.* **Yellow Cab.** ☎ *801/521–2100* ⊕ *www. yellowcabutah.com.*

BUS AND RAIL

Salt Lake has a very workable public transportation system, although it's used more by locals than visitors. One feature that even tourists rely heavily on is the Free Fare Zone for travel by bus within a roughly 36-square-block area downtown and on Capitol Hill. The TRAX light-rail system moves passengers quickly around the city and to the suburbs south of Salt Lake. There are 50 stations, originating from Salt Lake Central Station, where you can connect to FrontRunner (inter-county light rail), Amtrak, and buses. The Blue Line runs north–south from downtown to the suburb of Draper, serving the downtown landmarks and Rio Tinto Stadium (home of Real Salt Lake soccer) in Sandy. The Red line extends eastward to the University of Utah and southwest to the suburb of South Jordan. The Green line originates at the airport and loops into downtown before heading west to the suburb of West Valley. More than 20 stations have free park-and-ride lots. One-way tickets cost $2.50 and can be purchased from platform vending machines, online, or using the UTA mobile app called Transit.

BUS AND RAIL INFORMATION Utah Transit Authority (UTA). ☎ *801/743–3882* ⊕ *www.rideuta.com.*

CAR

Although traffic has increased a bit as Salt Lake continues to grow, it's still comparatively less daunting than in most U.S. cities. On the whole, it's an easy city to explore by car. Free or inexpensive parking is easy to find in most neighborhoods, and even downtown garages charge a fraction of what you'll pay in many large cities. Finding your way around Salt Lake City is easy as the city is laid out on an orthogonal grid, but keep in mind that city blocks are longer than in many other cities.

Tours

City Sights (AKA Salt Lake City Tours)
BUS TOURS | A four-hour, 20-mile bus tour of the city includes dozens of major sights and many interesting lesser-known places you wouldn't necessarily find on your own, with a 30-minute organ recital at the Tabernacle and a stop for lunch in Brigham Young's Lion House. A 4½-hour tour also includes a Tabernacle Choir at Temple Square concert or rehearsal. A few other tours cover sights outside the city. ☎ 801/531–1001 ⊕ www.saltlakecity-tours.org ✉ From $49.

Mountain West Birding
SPECIAL-INTEREST | Run by incredibly knowledgeable birder Tim Avery, this tour company located just outside Salt Lake City can show you all of the best places to see the nearly 500 year-round and migratory birds that frequent this part of the world, including flammulated owls, gray partridges, Himalayan snowcocks, cassis crossbills, and more. Half-, full-, and multiday tours are available. ⊕ www.mwbirdco.com ✉ From $150.

★ Preservation Utah
WALKING TOURS | Tours led by knowledgeable guides from nonprofit Preservation Utah include a walking tour of the Marmalade Historic District, the Kearns Mansion, McCune Mansion, and the City and County Building. It's a good idea to book several days in advance. You can also explore on your own using the organization's app, "Utah Heritage Walks." ✉ Memory Grove Park, 375 N. Canyon Rd., Capitol Hill ☎ 801/533–0858 ⊕ www.preservationutah.org ✉ From $10.

Restaurants

Restaurant reviews have been shortened. For full information, visit Fodors.com.

What it Costs			
$	$$	$$$	$$$$
RESTAURANTS			
under $16	$16–$22	$23–$30	over $30

Hotels

Hotel reviews have been shortened. For full information, visit Fodors.com.

What it Costs			
$	$$	$$$	$$$$
HOTELS			
under $125	$125–$175	$176–$225	over $225

Visitor Information

CONTACTS Salt Lake Convention and Visitors Bureau. ✉ 90 S. West Temple, Downtown ☎ 801/534–4900, 800/541–4955 ⊕ www.visitsaltlake.com. **Utah Office of Tourism.** ✉ 300 N. State St., Capitol Hill ☎ 800/200–1160, 801/538–1900 ⊕ www.visitutah.com.

Temple Square

When Mormon pioneer and leader Brigham Young first entered the Salt Lake Valley, he chose this spot at the mouth of City Creek Canyon for the headquarters of the Church of Jesus Christ of Latter-day Saints, a role it maintains to this day. The buildings in Temple Square

The iconic Salt Lake Temple in Temple Square took 40 years to build.

vary in age, from the Tabernacle constructed in the 1860s to the Conference Center constructed in 2000. Perhaps the most striking aspect of the Square is the attention to landscaping, which turns the heart of downtown Salt Lake City into a year-round oasis. The Church takes particular pride in its Christmas decorations, which make a nighttime downtown stroll, or horse-and-buggy ride, a must on December calendars.

The Salt Lake Temple and parts of Temple Square are currently undergoing a four-year renovation and restoration. The Temple and grounds immediately surrounding it will be under construction until 2024.

Sights

Beehive House
HOUSE | Brigham Young's home was constructed in 1854 and is topped with a replica of a beehive, symbolizing industry. Inside are many original furnishings; a tour of the interior will give you a fascinating glimpse of upper-class 19th-century life. ✉ *67 E. South Temple, Temple Square* ☎ *801/240–2681* ⊕ *history.churchofjesuschrist.org* ⊘ *Closed Sun.*

Church of Jesus Christ of Latter-day Saints Conference Center
CONVENTION CENTER | Completed in 2000, this massive center features a 21,000-seat auditorium with a 7,708-pipe organ and a 900-seat theater. Equally impressive are the rooftop gardens landscaped with native plants and streams to mirror the surrounding mountains. Visitors can find flexible tour times that last roughly 45 minutes, but all guests must be accompanied by a guide. The Center is home to the biannual General Conference and regular concerts by the Tabernacle Choir at Temple Square. ✉ *60 W. North Temple, Temple Square* ☎ *801/240–0075* ⊕ *www.templesquare.com/explore.*

Family History Library
LIBRARY | **FAMILY** | This four-story library houses the world's largest collection of genealogical data, including books, maps, and census information. Mormons

and non-Mormons alike come here to research their family history. ✉ *35 N. West Temple, Temple Square* ☎ *801/240–6996* ⊕ *www.familysearch.org/locations.*

Joseph Smith Memorial Building

HISTORIC SITE | Previously the Hotel Utah, this stately 1911 building is now owned and operated by the Church of Jesus Christ of Latter-day Saints. Inside you can learn how to do genealogical research online at the FamilySearch Center (no charge; volunteers will assist you) or watch an hour-long film about the Church's teaching of how Jesus Christ appeared in the western hemisphere after his resurrection. The center has two restaurants and an elegantly restored lobby. Upstairs is the 1920 census and 70,000 volumes of personal histories of the faithful. ✉ *15 E. South Temple, Temple Square* ☎ *801/531–1000* ⊕ *www.templesquare.com/explore* ☾ *Closed Sun.*

Museum of Church History and Art

MUSEUM | Here you can view a variety of artifacts and works of art relating to the history and doctrine of the Mormon faith, including personal belongings of church leaders Joseph Smith and Brigham Young. There are also samples of Mormon coins and scrip used as standard currency in Utah during the 1800s, and beautiful examples of quilting, embroidery, and other handicrafts. Upstairs galleries exhibit religious and secular works by Mormon artists from all over the world. ✉ *45 N. West Temple, Temple Square* ☎ *801/240–3310* ⊕ *history.churchofjesuschrist.org* ☾ *Closed Sun.*

★ Salt Lake Temple

FOUNTAIN | Although the interior is closed as of this writing for renovation through 2024, this centerpiece and spiritual capital of the Church of Jesus Christ of Latter-day Saints is a sacred pilgrimage destination for members of the faith. Brigham Young chose this spot for a temple as soon as he arrived in the Salt Lake Valley in 1847, but work on

the building didn't begin for another six years. Built of blocks of granite hauled by oxen and train from Little Cottonwood Canyon, the Temple took 40 years to the day to complete. Its walls are 16 feet thick at the base. Enjoy the serene fountains and pristine landscaping that decorates the Temple area. ✉ *50 N. West Temple, Temple Square* ☎ *801/240–2640* ⊕ *www.churchofjesuschristtemples.org/salt-lake-temple.*

The Tabernacle

RELIGIOUS SITE | The Salt Lake City Tabernacle, also known as the Tabernacle, is home to the famous Tabernacle Choir and its impressive organ with 11,623 pipes. Visitors can hear organ recitals Monday through Saturday at noon and 2 pm, and Sunday at 2 pm. You're also welcome Thursday from 7:30 pm to 9:30 pm to listen to the choir rehearse Sunday hymns, as well as from 9:30 am to 10 am as the choir performs for the world's longest-running continuous network broadcast, *Music and the Spoken Word.* ✉ *50 N. West Temple, Temple Square* ☎ *801/240–2534* ⊕ *www.templesquare.com.*

Temple Square Visitors' Center

INFO CENTER | The history of the Mormon Church and the Mormon pioneers' trek to Utah is outlined in a visitor center on the north side of Temple Square (50 W. North Temple). Diligent missionaries stand by to offer tours and answer questions. ✉ *Temple Sq.* ☎ *801/240–2534* ⊕ *www.templesquare.com.*

🎭 Performing Arts

MUSIC

★ Tabernacle Choir at Temple Square

MUSIC | Nearly 400 volunteers make up this famous choir, which performs sacred music, with some secular (classical and patriotic) works. Visitors can hear organ recitals Monday through Saturday at noon and 2 pm, and Sunday at 2 pm. You're also welcome Thursday from 7:30

pm to 9:30 pm to listen to the choir rehearse Sunday hymns, as well as from 9:30 am to 10 am as the choir performs for the world's longest-running continuous network broadcast, *Music and the Spoken Word.* ✉ *50 N. West Temple, Temple Square* ☎ *801/240–4150* ⊕ *www. thetabernaclechoir.org.*

Downtown and Central City

Although businesses and homes stretch in all directions, downtown's core is a compact, several-block area that contains most of the city's most prominent hotels, plus a good number of high-profile restaurants, historic buildings, theaters, and bars. Although it sounds like it might just be another name for downtown, Central City is a larger quadrant that extends east and south from downtown, as far as 1300 East and 1300 South. This area contains a mix of residential and commercial pockets and some charming shopping and eating districts, such as Trolley Square and 9th and 9th, and also gracious Liberty Park. Extending south from Downtown along the Main Street and State Street corridor, you'll find some more recently emerging hives of dining as well as craft breweries and distilleries, including the Granary/Ballpark area.

 Sights

Clark Planetarium
OBSERVATORY | FAMILY | With an array of free hands-on exhibits and state-of-the-art 3-D and IMAX theaters, Clark Planetarium is an appealing, affordable family attraction. Traipse across a moonscape and learn about Utah's contributions to spaceflight, but save a few minutes for the Planet Fun store. ✉ *110 S. 400 W, Downtown* ☎ *385/468–7827* ⊕ *www. clarkplanetarium.org* 🎟 *Exhibits free; movies $9.*

Discovery Gateway Children's Museum
MUSEUM | FAMILY | The region's premier children's museum, geared toward kids ages 2 to 10, has three floors of lively hands-on experiences. Kids can participate in a television newscast, tell stories through pictures or radio, climb into a Life Flight helicopter, or revel in a kid-size town with grocery store, vehicles, a house, and a construction site. ✉ *444 W. 100 S, Downtown* ☎ *801/456–5437* ⊕ *www.discoverygateway.org* 🎟 *$12.50.*

Gallivan Center
PLAZA | FAMILY | Sometimes dubbed Salt Lake City's "living room," the John W. Gallivan Center anchors downtown and offers an amphitheater, ice rink, and various art projects, and it hosts numerous events, including popular Food Truck Thursdays and several annual summer festivals. ✉ *239 S. Main St., Downtown* ☎ *801/535–6110* ⊕ *www.thegallivancenter.com.*

Land Cruiser Heritage Museum
MUSEUM | Nearly 100 models of Toyota Land Cruisers, some dating back to the early '50s, fill this quirky museum that has something of a cult following among fans of old autos and four-wheel vehicle enthusiasts. In a rugged state like Utah, these rugged SUVs have quite a fan base, but folks come from all over the world, admiring the extensive collection of memorabilia, scale models, artwork, and a very cool 10-by-13-foot 3-D map of the state of Utah. ✉ *470 W. 600 S* ☎ *505/615–5470* ⊕ *www.landcruiserhm. com* 🎟 *$10* 🕐 *Closed Sun.–Tues.*

The Leonardo
MUSEUM | FAMILY | Salt Lake's only museum devoted to the convergence of science, art, and technology hosts large-scale national touring exhibits as well as hands-on permanent exhibits dedicated to inspiring the imaginations of children. In this former library building, you'll be greeted by a main-floor lab space where revolving artists-in-residence offer a variety of free programs where kids

can sculpt with clay, draw, design, or write. Head upstairs to the workshop, where volunteers help you build with repurposed household objects and deconstruct electronics. ✉ *209 E. 500 S, Downtown* ☎ *801/531–9800* 🌐 *www.theleonardo.org* 🎟 *$13; more for special exhibits.*

Salt Lake City and County Building

GOVERNMENT BUILDING | The castle-like seat of city government was the city's tallest building from its 1894 opening to 1973. On Washington Square, at the spot where the original Mormon settlers circled their wagons on their first night in the Salt Lake Valley, this building served as the state capitol for 19 years. Hundreds of trees, including species from around the world, and many winding paths and seating areas make the grounds a calm downtown oasis. In summer the grounds host major Salt Lake arts and music festivals. Free tours are given on Monday during the summer and by request outside the summer months through the Preservation Utah. ✉ *451 S. State St., Downtown* ☎ *801/535–7704* 🌐 *www.slc.gov* 🕒 *Closed weekends.*

★ Salt Lake City Public Library

BUILDING | **FAMILY** | Designed by Moshe Safdie and built in 2003, this spectacular contemporary structure has become the city's cultural center and one of the country's most architecturally noteworthy libraries. Inspired by the Roman Coliseum, it features a six-story walkable wall that serves as both sculpture and function, allowing for great views and a path up the building. From the rooftop garden you get a 360-degree view of the valley and mountains. The on-site branch of Salt Lake Roasting Co. coffeehouse, the Hemingway Cafe, a handful of shops, a writing center, and a public radio station provide ways to spend the entire day here. Kids can fall in love with reading in the Crystal Cave and Treehouse Room in the huge children's section. There are several other libraries in the system, including the Tudor-style Sprague Library that opened in 1928 in the city's popular Sugar House neighborhood. ✉ *210 E. 400 S, Downtown* ☎ *801/524–8200* 🌐 *www.slcpl.org.*

🍴 Restaurants

Bambara

$$$$ | **MODERN AMERICAN** | Set in an ornate former bank lobby adjacent to swanky Hotel Monaco, the building itself is as much of a draw as the food. The kitchen crafts big plates of seasonally sourced modern American fare, including seared elk loin, whole-roasted branzino, steak-frites, and other hearty dishes with bold sauces. **Known for:** stylish, see-and-be-seen dining room; three eggs Benedict options at brunch; creative cocktails. [$] *Average main: $36* ✉ *202 S. Main St., Downtown* ☎ *801/363–5454* 🌐 *www.bambara-slc.com.*

The Bayou

$ | **CAJUN** | You'll find more than 200 microbrews, both bottled and on tap, at this lively, often crowded Louisiana-inflected bar and restaurant. The menu offers plenty of Cajun specialties such as crawfish étouffée and blackened catfish sandwiches, along with more regionally American grub like fried chicken and pizza. **Known for:** savory alligator cheesecake; gumbolaya (jambalaya smothered with crawfish gumbo); great live music many nights. [$] *Average main: $14* ✉ *645 S. State St., Downtown* ☎ *801/961–8400* 🌐 *www.utahbayou.com* 🕒 *No lunch on weekends.*

Café Trio Downtown

$$ | **MODERN ITALIAN** | In this comfortable, modern dining room with clean lines and great location near Trolley Square and 9th and 9th, you might whet your appetite with a selection of cheeses or flatbread, but save room for balsamic-drizzled stone-fired pizzas, hearty baked pastas, and roasted half chicken, all of which vie for attention at this chatter-filled Italian

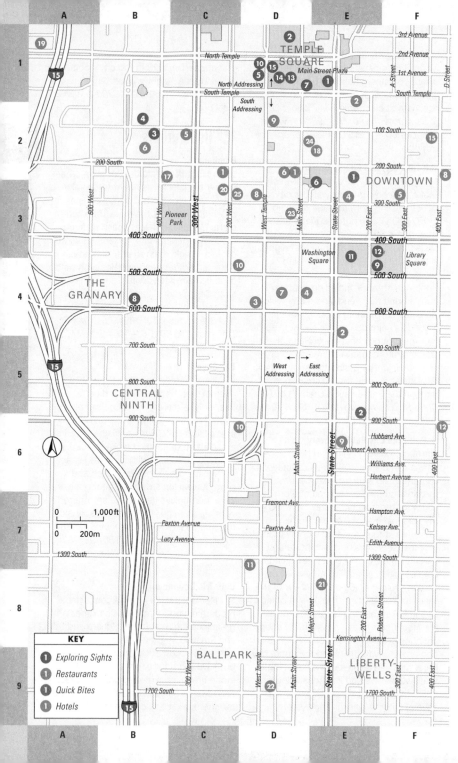

Temple Square, Downtown, and Central City

Sights ▼

1 Beehive House............ **E1**
2 Church of Jesus Christ of Latter-day Saints Conference Center **D1**
3 Clark Planetarium........ **B2**
4 Discovery Gateway Children's Museum..... **B2**
5 Family History Library.................... **D1**
6 Gallivan Center........... **E3**
7 Joseph Smith Memorial Building...... **D1**
8 Land Cruiser Heritage Museum **B4**
9 The Leonardo **E4**
10 Museum of Church History and Art.......... **D1**
11 Salt Lake City and County Building......... **E3**
12 Salt Lake City Public Library **E3**
13 Salt Lake Temple........ **D1**
14 The Tabernacle **D1**
15 Temple Square Visitor's Center.......... **D1**

Restaurants ▼

1 Bambara................ **D2**
2 The Bayou **E4**
3 Café Trio Downtown...... **I5**
4 The Copper Onion **E3**
5 Current Fish & Oyster ... **F3**
6 HallPass **B2**
7 Hires Big H **H3**
8 HSL...................... **F2**
9 La-Cai Noodle House.... **E6**
10 Laziz Kitchen **D6**
11 Lucky 13 Bar and Grill............. **D7**
12 Manoli's.................. **F6**
13 Mazza **I6**
14 Oasis Cafe **G2**
15 Oquirrh................... **F2**
16 Pago...................... **I6**
17 Pallet.................... **B2**
18 Pretty Bird Chicken...... **E2**
19 Red Iguana **A1**
20 Settebello Pizzeria Napoletana.............. **C3**
21 Seasons Plant Based Bistro...................... **E8**
22 Sweet Lake Biscuits & Limeade..... **D9**
23 Takashi.................. **D3**
24 Tin Angel................ **D2**
25 Zest Kitchen & Bar **C3**

Quick Bites ▼

1 Campos Coffee SLC **E2**
2 Normal Ice Cream....... **E6**
3 Salt Lake Roasting Company...... **H3**
4 Tulie Bakery **I5**

Hotels ▼

1 AC Hotel by Marriott Salt Lake City Downtown................ **C2**
2 Carlton Hotel **E1**
3 DoubleTree Suites by Hilton Salt Lake City Downtown.............. **D4**
4 The Grand America Hotel...................... **D4**
5 Hyatt House Salt Lake City– Downtown............... **C2**
6 Kimpton Hotel Monaco Salt Lake City............ **D2**
7 Little America Hotel **D4**
8 Peery Hotel, Tapestry Collection by Hilton..... **D3**
9 Salt Lake Marriott Downtown at City Creek............... **D2**
10 Sheraton Salt Lake City Hotel...... **C4**

The Salt Lake City Public Library was inspired by the Roman Coliseum.

eatery. You'll want to linger for the crème brûlée, flavored martinis, and espresso. **Known for:** pizzas and pastas with creative toppings; poached eggs with polenta at brunch; knowledgeable, friendly service. $ *Average main: $21* ✉ *680 S. 900 E, Downtown* ☎ *801/533–8746* ⊕ *www. triodining.com.*

★ The Copper Onion

$$ | **MODERN AMERICAN** | Celebrated chef-owner Chef Ryan Lowder brings joy with the basics—artful salads, house-made pastas, and charcuterie—and then dazzles with mouthwatering locally sourced dishes, from Cast Iron Mary's Chicken to rainbow trout with charred lemon and Greek yogurt. Stop in at this chic modern downtown bistro before or after a film, gallery tour, or live theater on Salt Lake's Broadway. **Known for:** cavatelli pasta with rich pork ragu; selection of Amari and after-dinner drinks; Valrhona chocolate pudding with sea salt and olive oil. $ *Average main: $22* ✉ *111 E. Broadway, Downtown* ☎ *801/355–3282*

⊕ *www.thecopperonion.com* ⊙ *Closed Mon. and Tues.*

Current Fish & Oyster

$$$ | **SEAFOOD** | Being in a city with a major international hub airport has its advantages, including access to daily shipments of incredibly fresh fish, which are the stars on the menu of this post-in-dustrial space with a soaring arched ceiling and exposed rafters and air ducts. Expect seafood sourced from east and west—consider Japanese kumamoto oysters on the half shell, Gulf shrimp and grits, and Prince Edward Island mussels with house-smoked pork belly. **Known for:** ceviche with citrus, jicama, and melon; Irish coffee with sweet cream; stellar international wine list. $ *Average main: $28* ✉ *279 E. 300 S* ☎ *801/326–3474* ⊕ *www.currentfishandoyster.com* ⊙ *No lunch weekends.*

HallPass

$ | **INTERNATIONAL** | Set in downtown's Gateway Center shopping mall and offering eight distinct dining stations and seating at gorgeous carved-wood tables, the city's first food hall opened in early 2020 and has quickly become a trendy spot to eat and people-watch. The options are varied and consistently good and include Nashville hot chicken, Belgian-style waffles and crepes, slow-cooked ramen, prodigious lobster rolls, and Japanese-Mexican-fusion izakaya fare. **Known for:** large outdoor dining area; nice variety of healthy and decadent international options; terrific craft beer bar. $ *Average main: $12* ⊠ *153 S. Rio Grande St.* ☎ *801/415–9886* ⊕ *www. hallpassslc.com.*

Hires Big H

$ | **BURGER** | **FAMILY** | A family tradition in Salt Lake since 1959, this old-school burger and shakes joint with curbside car service elevates traditional diner favorites by using fresh, local products prepared in-house. Inside the renovated dining room, root-beer floats are a staple, as are "H" burgers such as the New York H, Canadian H, and Mountain H, all of which pair fresh patties, tasty buns, and the owner's proprietary fry sauce (a Utah staple) with a variety of condiments. **Known for:** retro-style car-side service; frosted root beer mugs; fry sauce. $ *Average main: $8* ⊠ *425 S. 700 E, Downtown* ☎ *801/364–4582* ⊕ *www.hiresbigh.com* ⊗ *Closed Sun.*

★ HSL

$$$$ | **MODERN AMERICAN** | On the east edge of downtown and within a short, pretty stroll of the Avenues and Capitol Hill, this outpost of the original, nationally acclaimed Handle restaurant in Park City turns heads with its stunning plated, locavore-driven cuisine and a fetching interior with marble-top tables, a wood-beam ceiling, and a gleaming, tiled open kitchen. What's served on any given night varies according to what's in season, but you might encounter truffled agnolotti pasta filled with Swiss chard, corn, and goat's whey cream, or slow-cooked pork shank with carrot-frisee salad, whipped ranch dressing, and apple butter. **Known for:** artful, Instagram-worthy food; exquisitely curated spirits, wine, and beer list; roasted-miso chess pie with lemongrass ice cream. $ *Average main: $33* ⊠ *418 E. 200 S* ☎ *801/539–9999* ⊕ *www.hslrestaurant.com.*

La-Cai Noodle House

$ | **VIETNAMESE** | Named for a historic restaurant district in Ho Chi Minh City, this low-frills eatery set amid auto-parts shops south of downtown re-creates the cuisine of southern Vietnam. The menu ranges from traditional basics like beef-brisket pho and stir-fried crispy egg noodles to more creative fare, such as walnut shrimp in a creamy white sauce, salt-baked calamari, and a massive hot pot that's perfect for groups of two to four. **Known for:** pho and noodle soups; huge portions; hot and iced Vietnamese coffee. $ *Average main: $12* ⊠ *961 S. State St., Downtown* ☎ *801/322–3590* ⊕ *www.lacainoodlehouse.com* ⊗ *Closed Sun.*

★ Laziz Kitchen

$$$ | **MIDDLE EASTERN** | Run by a friendly husband-and-husband team who began with a hummus stand at the farmers' market, Laziz has grown into an outstanding full-service Lebanese restaurant in the burgeoning Central Ninth neighborhood, with a cheerfully hip plant-filled dining room and street-side terrace. The most delicious strategy here is to make a feast of a selection of small plates: spiced labneh, eggplant baba ghanoush, grilled haloumi cheese, kibbeh, fried cauliflower with garlic-cilantro pesto, red-wine-braised lamb shank, and maybe a kafta burger or two. **Known for:** shared dips and mezze appetizer platters; blueberry, lavender, and other kefir sodas; chocolate halva cake. $ *Average main: $24* ⊠ *912 Jefferson St. W.* ☎ *801/441–1228* ⊕ *www.lazizkitchen.com* ⊗ *Closed Sun.*

Lucky 13 Bar and Grill

$ | **AMERICAN** | There may be no better place in the valley to order a monstrous burger (with intriguing toppings like hickory-smoked pastrami and peanut butter, plus house-baked buns) and wash it down with a local beer or a shot of whiskey. This rollicking tavern is across from Smith's Ballpark baseball stadium, home to the Salt Lake Bees, the Triple A team for the Los Angeles Angels. **Known for:** creatively topped burgers; ice cream sandwiches; locally produced whiskies. [$] *Average main: $12* ✉ *135 W. 1300 S, Downtown* ☎ *801/487–4418* 🌐 *www.lucky13slc.com.*

Manoli's

$$ | **GREEK** | Venture into this sleek, angular neighborhood bistro to savor some of the tastiest contemporary Greek food in Utah, best enjoyed with a selection from the nicely curated wine list (which lists some excellent Hellenic offerings). The menu is broken down into tapas-style vegetable, meat, and seafood plates, such as piquillo peppers with smoked feta and olive oil, charred octopus with bean salad and sherry vinaigrette, and pork-beef meatballs with a soul-warming cinnamon-tomato sauce. **Known for:** seasoned side dishes; ouzo and resin-y skinos mastiha Greek liqueurs; Greek doughnuts with spiced-honey syrup. [$] *Average main: $20* ✉ *402 E. 900 S* ☎ *801/532–3760* 🌐 *www.manolison9th.com* 🕓 *Closed Mon. No lunch weekdays.*

Oasis Cafe

$$ | **ECLECTIC** | From early morning to well into the evening, a selection of fine teas and espresso drinks, big breakfasts, and healthful entrées draw regulars to this café and its serene patio courtyard, and also to adjacent New Age bookstore and gift shop, the Golden Braid. The menu leans toward vegetarian and seafood selections, such as multigrain waffles and eggs Benedict Florentine in the morning and sesame-blackened ahi with sticky rice and peanut stir-fry with udon noodles later in the day. **Known for:** short stroll to the Avenues and City Creek Park; diverse, New Age vibe; seasonal house-made sorbets. [$] *Average main: $20* ✉ *151 S. 500 E, Downtown* ☎ *801/322–0404* 🌐 *www.oasiscafeslc.com.*

★ Oquirrh

$$$ | **MODERN AMERICAN** | An unprepossessing neighborhood restaurant near the leafy Avenues district, Oquirrh (rhymes with "poker") is named for the snowcapped mountain range west of downtown and focuses on seasonal fare with locally sourced ingredients. Boldly flavored dishes like spaghetti with butter-poached lobster and curried lamb shank with garam masala–roasted vegetables are presented artfully on handmade stoneware in an intimate, art-filled dining room. **Known for:** beef tartare with fermented vegetables; excellent French- and West Coast–centric wine selection; Sunday brunch. [$] *Average main: $28* ✉ *368 E. 100 S* ☎ *801/359–0426* 🌐 *www.oquirrhslc.com* 🕓 *Closed Mon.–Wed. No lunch weekends.*

Pago

$$$ | **MODERN AMERICAN** | More than living up to its promise of farm-to-table freshness, this welcoming, microscopic, chef-driven neighborhood bistro capitalizes on local artisan farmers, with big and small plates anchored around simple ingredients like radishes, beets, or mountain stream trout. There's plenty to satisfy big appetites, too, such as bavette steak with duck fat potatoes, and fettuccine with braised hen, sofrito, pistachio, chile, and lemon. **Known for:** cute, art-fille dining in 9th and 9th neighborhood; excellent service; Pago eggs Benedict (with prosciutto and arugula). [$] *Average main: $26* ✉ *878 S. 900 E, East Side* ☎ *801/532–0777* 🌐 *www.pagoslc.com.*

Pallet

$$$$ | **MODERN AMERICAN** | In a charming vintage warehouse space with exposed brick walls, dim lighting, and antique framed paintings, this buzzy mod

American bistro within walking distance of downtown hotels is ideal for a cozy date night or a chatter-filled feast with friends. The deft cooking crew turns out creative versions on classic American dishes—think pork ribs with rice porridge, kimchi, and tapioca crisp, or grilled venison with barley, cabbage, horseradish foam, and a port reduction. **Known for:** fantastic cheese and charcuterie boards; expertly crafted (tho expensive) cocktails; ginger cake with parsnip anglaise sauce. *[$] Average main: $31 ✉ 237 S. 400 W ☎ 801/935–4431 🌐 www.eatpallet.com 🕑 Closed Sun. No lunch.*

Pretty Bird Chicken

$ | **AMERICAN** | As its name hints, this usually packed downtown fast-casual eatery with counter service and a small seating area specializes in poultry, and the menu couldn't be simpler. Pick your spice level (from medium to the excruciatingly fiery "hot behind"), choose either quarter bird or a boneless-chicken sandwich, and add some sides if you'd like (crinkle-cut fries, cider slaw, pickles). **Known for:** in midst of downtown shopping and theater scene; astoundingly spicy fried chicken (as requested); day-glo purple cider slaw. *[$] Average main: $12 ✉ 146 S. Regent St. 🌐 www.prettybirdchicken.com.*

★ Red Iguana

$$ | **MEXICAN** | Visitors are sometimes taken aback to find stunningly authentic, richly flavorful house-made moles, chile verde, carnitas, and other self-described "killer Mexican" dishes in Salt Lake City, and especially in a modest old building on the other side of I–15 from downtown. But the lines out the door attest to the longstanding adoration of the Red Iguana, which in addition to doling out great food also serves first-rate premium margaritas, good Mexican beers, and delicious and free salsa and chips. **Known for:** chilaquiles for breakfast; richly complex turkey and mole dishes; fried ice cream with shredde coconut and cinnamon-sugar. *[$] Average main: $16 ✉ 736 W. North Temple, Downtown ☎ 801/322–1489 🌐 www.rediguana.com.*

Seasons Plant Based Bistro

$$ | **VEGETARIAN** | Close to Smith's Ballpark and Liberty Park, you'll find this simple but homey go-to for creative, beautifully presented vegan cuisine, much of it with Italian and French preparations. Dishes like papardelle Stroganoff noodles with smoked Portobello mushrooms and a marsala-dill sauce, and house-made ravioli with butternut squash and brown-butter consumme are both hearty and robustly flavored. **Known for:** tasty veggie versions of Philly cheesesteaks, Cuban sandwiches, and burgers; fine selection of wine and craft beer; cheesecakes with daily-rotating flavors. *[$] Average main: $22 ✉ 1370 State St. ☎ 385/267–1922 🌐 www.seasonsslc.com 🕑 Closed Sun.–Mon.*

Settebello Pizzeria Napoletana

$ | **PIZZA** | Two ambitious restaurateurs set out to re-create authentic, ultra-thin-crust pizza from Naples using an oven, flour, cheese, and other ingredients shipped from the Old Country. The still wildly popular result of this undertaking is Settebello Pizzeria, which continues to draw raves for its blistered-crust pies with simple, top-quality toppings like crusted tomatoes, artichokes, pancetta, and a few nontraditional options, like jalapeño marmalade and slow-cooked brisket. **Known for:** fig-and-prosciutto pie; burrata crostini; Nutella-topped dessert pizzas. *[$] Average main: $15 ✉ 260 S. 200 W, Downtown ☎ 801/322–3556 🌐 www.settebello.net 🕑 Closed Sun.*

Sweet Lake Biscuits & Limeade

$ | **SOUTHERN** | This super-casual café with a smattering of sidewalk tables serves up heavenly biscuits in an assortment of ways, from blueberry-biscuit pudding French toast to fried chicken biscuit sandwiches with spicy pickles and mustard. Head to the refreshment stand at one end of the dining room to order a refreshing raspberry, habanero, or mint limeade. **Known for:** limemades with rotating seasonal flavors; biscuit-dough breakfast pizzas; strawberry "tall cake" with fresh cream. [$] *Average main: $12* ✉ *54 W. 1700 S* ☎ *801/953–1978* 🌐 *www.sweetlakefresh.com* 🕐 *No dinner.*

★ Takashi

$$$ | **JAPANESE** | You'll often see chef-owner Takashi Gibo behind the sushi bar at this hip and lively Japanese restaurant across from the Gallivan Center. Takashi is known for sublime, melt-in-your mouth sushi as well as a slew of izakaya-style treats, like miso-grilled eggplant, baked marinated sablefish, and shiitake lamb shank in Japanese yellow curry. **Known for:** barbecue pork ribs; riceless sushi rolls wrapped in cucumber; superb wine and saki selection. [$] *Average main: $26* ✉ *18 W. Market St., Downtown* ☎ *801/519–9595* 🌐 *www.takashisushi.com* 🕐 *Closed Sun. No lunch Sat.*

Tin Angel

$$$ | **MODERN EUROPEAN** | This bustling, art-filled restaurant inside the snazzy Eccles Theater draws plenty of folks for meals before or even during shows (there's a quick-bites intermission menu). Food here tends toward regional American and Southern European, with plenty of modern twists, such as a stew of chunky wild boar agrodolce over creamy polenta, and a satisfying Moroccan-style duck confit salad with chickpeas, harissa, and feta. **Known for:** pre-theater people-watching; hard-cider-braised short ribs; flourless chocolate-hazelnut torte. [$] *Average main: $25* ✉ *131 S. Main St.* ☎ *801/328–4155* 🌐 *www.thetinangel.com* 🕐 *Closed Sun. No lunch Sat.*

Zest Kitchen & Bar

$ | **VEGETARIAN** | The charms of festive bar and grill near downtown theaters and Pioneer Park include quirky decor (including a chandelier *and* a disco ball), a super-friendly staff, and focus on organic spirits and wines, and healthy farm-to-fork-inspired plant-based cuisine. Drop in a thyme-infused grapefruit-vodka cocktail (with CBD on request) and cashew-quinoa-stuffed poblano pepper before a show, or a smoothie, jackfruit pizza, or miso ramen bowl to break up an afternoon of exploring. **Known for:** luscious smoothies; creative vegetarian fare; extensive selection of teas and healthy elixirs. [$] *Average main: $15* ✉ *275 S. 200 W* ☎ *801/433–0589* 🌐 *www.zestslc.com* 🕐 *Closed Mon.*

Coffee and Quick Bites

★ Campos Coffee SLC

$ | **CAFÉ** | This airy, plant-filled, hipster-approved coffeehouse and daytime eatery tucked down a side street near the Gallivan Center is where you should go when you're seeking an alternative to the lame or overpriced breakfast at your downtown hotel. The morning menu here is terrific, featuring ginger oatmeal with coconut creme, Idaho trout eggs Benedict, and exceptional coffees and Smith-brand teas. **Known for:** smoked-salmon toast with caper cream cheese; exceptional single-origin coffees; build your own mimosas. [$] *Average main: $11* ✉ *228 S. Edison St., Downtown* ☎ *801/953–1512* 🌐 *us.camposcoffee.com* 🕐 *No dinner.*

★ Normal Ice Cream

$ | **CAFÉ** | Begun by a pastry chef from trendy HSL restaurant, this off-beat artisan ice cream shop turns out exceptional all-natural soft-serve ice cream in a riot of interesting flavors (horchata, brown butter, banana, apple cider sorbet, olive oil), along with "composed" cones with interesting toppings mixed in—like house-made cake bits, gingersnap cookies, and honeycomb. If you're looking for sweet picnic treats, pick up a pint or a slice of ice cream cake. **Known for:** vegan sorbets in cool flavors (pomegranate, blood orange, etc.); Oregon's renowned Coava coffee; ice cream sandwiches. [$] *Average main: $6* ✉ *169 E. 900 S* ☎ *385/299–5418* 🌐 *www.normal.club.*

Salt Lake Roasting Company

$ | **CAFÉ** | Since 1981 the Roasting Company has sourced, bought, imported, roasted, and sold dozens of varieties of coffees. Great pastries, desserts, light breakfast and lunch fare, free Wi-Fi, and friendly, knowledgeable staff make this a Salt Lake institution. **Known for:** lots of space to spread out and work, read, or socialize; great range of herbal teas; opens at 6:30 am. $ *Average main: $5* ⊠ *820 E. 400 S, Downtown* ☎ *801/363–7572* ⊕ *www.roasting.com* ⊗ *Closed Sun.*

Tulie Bakery

$ | **BAKERY** | This cozy neighborhood bakeshop between Trolley Square and 9th and 9th turns out absolutely ethereal cookies (the salted caramel bars are legendary), tarts, cakes, and sandwiches on soft and crusty savory breads. The sopressata and provolone, and prosciutto-fig-gorgonzola sandwiches are among the favorites, and there's a full roster of espresso drinks and fine teas. **Known for:** fine Japanese green teas; breakfast toast with apricot honey and garlic chevre; olive oil–orange cake with brown-butter buttercream. $ *Average main: $8* ⊠ *863 E. 700 S* ☎ *801/883–9741* ⊕ *www.tuliebakery.com* ⊗ *No dinner.*

Hotels

★ AC Hotel by Marriot Salt Lake City Downtown

$$ | **HOTEL** | Across from the convention center and Vivint Arena, this dapper midsize property—part of Marriott's hip AC boutique brand—stands out for its smartly designed rooms, each with plush duvets and linens, 55-inch flat-screen TVs, and bathrooms with rainfall showers, as well as a 24-hour gym and a spacious lobby with high ceilings and comfy chairs you can actually enjoy sitting in. **Pros:** many restaurants and bars within walking distance; airy, stylish rooms; nice restaurant and bar on-site. **Cons:** busy downtown location; gym overlooks parking lot; fills up during conventions. $ *Rooms from: $169* ⊠ *225 W. 200 S, Downtown* ☎ *385/722–9600* ⊕ *www.marriott.com* ⇄ *164 rooms* ⦿ *No meals.*

Carlton Hotel

$ | **HOTEL** | An absolute steal on the quieter eastern side of downtown and Temple Square, this atmospheric 1920s hotel with a gorgeous brick exterior has remained resolutely old-fashioned, offering few frills but plenty of value, especially in the spacious suites. **Pros:** excellent downtown location; friendly service; made-to-order breakfast is quite good. **Cons:** some rooms are small; partly hemmed in by high-rises and a parking garage; no gym. $ *Rooms from: $89* ⊠ *140 E. South Temple, Downtown* ☎ *801/355–3418* ⊕ *www.carltonsaltlakecity.com* ⇄ *25 rooms* ⦿ *Free breakfast.*

Doubletree Suites by Hilton Salt Lake City Downtown

$$ | **HOTEL** | The sunlit atrium with its soaring ceiling gives this entire well-maintained, nine-story hotel a light, airy feeling, and its roomy suites are furnished with two TVs and sofa sleepers—perfect for families. **Pros:** indoor pool and 24-hour fitness room; decent on-site restaurant and bar; two blocks from TRAX light rail. **Cons:** at one of downtown's duller intersections; breakfast costs extra; rooms fill up when conventions come to town. $ *Rooms from: $155* ⊠ *110 W. 600 S, Downtown* ☎ *801/359–7800* ⊕ *www.hilton.com* ⇄ *241 suites* ⦿ *No meals.*

★ The Grand America Hotel

$$$$ | **HOTEL** | Built to impress dignitaries and celebs attending the 2002 Winter Olympics, this 24-story luxury tower is by far Salt Lake City's most opulent hotel, a huge complex with similarly huge rooms (averaging 700 square feet), most of them with balconies and sweeping views. **Pros:** big, sumptuous rooms; excellent pool and plush full-service spa; attentive, personable staff. **Cons:** expensive for SLC; immense hotel that can feel a little overwhelming; quality of restaurants is

uneven. $ *Rooms from: $305* ✉ *555 S. Main St., Downtown* ☎ *801/258–6000, 800/304–8696* ⊕ *www.grandamerica.com* ⤳ *775 rooms* ⦿ *No meals.*

Hyatt House Salt Lake City–Downtown

$$ | HOTEL | Depending on your needs, this mid-rise Hyatt across from the Vivint Arena and the convention center works either as a reasonably priced option with simple but contemporary standard rooms or as an ideal choice for longer stays if you book one of the suites with well-designed kitchens and ample sitting areas. **Pros:** super convenient to attractions and dining; nice pool and hot tub; suites have stylish, fully outfitted kitchens. **Cons:** neighborhood can get very crowded during games and events; breakfast is pretty ordinary; lower floors can receive a bit of road noise. $ *Rooms from: $139* ✉ *140 S. 300 W* ☎ *801/359–4020* ⊕ *www.hyatt.com* ⤳ *159 rooms* ⦿ *Free breakfast.*

★ Kimpton Hotel Monaco Salt Lake City

$$$ | HOTEL | This swank hotel resides in an ornate 14-story former bank tower (built in 1924), distinguished by a sophisticated, eclectic, and upbeat interior design and rooms offering extra touches like big-fringed ottomans, oversize framed mirrors, and lots of pillows. **Pros:** sparkling design, inside and out; exceptional restaurant; short walk to many fun bars and eateries. **Cons:** parking is $26 nightly; in a busy downtown location; some rooms have street noise. $ *Rooms from: $180* ✉ *15 W. 200 S, Downtown* ☎ *801/595–0000, 800/805–1801* ⊕ *www.monaco-saltlakecity.com* ⤳ *223 rooms* ⦿ *No meals.*

Little America Hotel

$ | HOTEL | FAMILY | This enormous but reliably comfortable hotel stands in the shadow of its world-renowned and much more expensive sister property, but Little America has even more rooms and its own loyal following. **Pros:** large indoor-outdoor pool; trees make the courtyard an oasis; central downtown location. **Cons:** restaurants and bar are rather ordinary; huge property that can feel a little impersonal; sometimes packed with conventioneers. $ *Rooms from: $119* ✉ *500 S. Main St., Downtown* ☎ *800/281–7899, 801/596–5700* ⊕ *www.saltlake.littleamerica.com* ⤳ *850 rooms* ⦿ *No meals.*

Peery Hotel, Tapestry Collection by Hilton

$$$ | HOTEL | Since becoming part of Hilton's indie-spirited Tapestry collection, this elegant 1910 classic hotel with a distinctive mulberry exterior has undergone a complete top-to-bottom renovation, with a substantial increase in room rates to go with it. **Pros:** well-maintained and charmingly historic; two full-service restaurants on-site; steps from several good bars and eateries. **Cons:** receives noise from traffic and nearby bars; $12 self parking; quirky heating and a/c system. $ *Rooms from: $185* ✉ *110 W. Broadway, Downtown* ☎ *801/521–4300* ⊕ *www.peeryhotel.com* ⤳ *73 rooms* ⦿ *No meals.*

Salt Lake Marriott Downtown at City Creek

$$ | HOTEL | The more centrally located of Marriott's two large downtown convention hotels, this gleaming, 16-story hotel lies between the City Creek shopping mall and the Salt Lake Convention Center. **Pros:** steps from many restaurants and shops; upper floors have mountain views; on-site restaurant, lounge, and Starbucks. **Cons:** not a lot of character; breakfast is expensive; often booked up with conventions. $ *Rooms from: $155* ✉ *75 S. West Temple, Downtown* ☎ *801/531–0800* ⊕ *www.marriott.com* ⤳ *510 rooms* ⦿ *No meals.*

Sheraton Salt Lake City Hotel

$ | HOTEL | This reliable, reasonably priced full-service hotel that delivers exactly what you expect from a Sheraton has comfortably outfitted rooms, many with balconies offering views of downtown and the Wasatch Range. **Pros:** upper-floor balcony rooms have great views; rates are often lower than comparable downtown properties; nice outdoor pool and hot tub. **Cons:** a bit of a walk from downtown bar-dining district; on busy stretch of 500 South; bland design. $ *Rooms from: $115* ✉ *150 W. 500 S, Downtown* ☎ *801/401–2000* ⊕ *www. sheratonsaltlakecityhotel.com* ⇆ *362 rooms* ⦿ *No meals.*

Nightlife

BARS AND LOUNGES

★ Beehive Distilling
BARS/PUBS | At the forefront of South Salt Lake's burgeoning spirits and craft brewing scene, this acclaimed small-batch gin and vodka producer has a stylish, post-industrial bar where you can sample expertly crafted cocktails and nibble on tasty apps and sandwiches. Serious enthusiasts might want to book one of Beehive's occasional behind-the-scenes tours. ✉ *2245 S. West Temple* ☎ *801/326–3913* ⊕ *www.beehivedistilling.com.*

★ Bodega + The Rest
BARS/PUBS | There's more than meets the eye to this modest-looking downtown bar with pinball machines and cheap drinks. A locked door leads to "the Rest," a basement speakeasy decorated with quirky framed portraits, mounted animals, and odd bric-a-brac. Here you'll discover well-curated menus of creative cocktails and well-prepared modern American food. Reservations are advised for the speakeasy. ✉ *331 S. Main St.* ☎ *801/532–4042* ⊕ *www.bodegaslc.com.*

BTG Wine Bar
WINE BARS—NIGHTLIFE | Close to downtown hotels and attractions, this classy, expansive lounge offers plenty of comfy seating and one of the most impressive lists of wines—by the glass and the bottle—in town. Flights are a good way to try a few different sips, and there's a nice menu of tapas and rich desserts (consider the dark-chocolate cake), too. ✉ *404 S. West Temple* ☎ *801/359–2814* ⊕ *www.btgwinebar.com.*

The Red Door
BARS/PUBS | Martinis are a specialty at this cosmopolitan bar with an attractive patio, but you'll find plenty of other intriguing elixirs. ✉ *57 W. 200 S, Downtown* ☎ *801/363–6030* ⊕ *www.thereddoorslc.com.*

Tavernacle Social Club
MUSIC CLUBS | Dueling pianos (Wednesday through Saturday) and karaoke (Sunday to Tuesday) make for a festive atmosphere in this bar just east of downtown. The musicians only play requests, and if you don't like the current song, you can pay $1 to change it. ✉ *201 E. 300 S, Downtown* ☎ *801/519–8900* ⊕ *www. tavernacle.com.*

Water Witch
BARS/PUBS | An intimate, minimalist space on the west edge of downtown, the Water Witch is an exemplar of the city's farm-to-cocktail scene. Creative drinks using fresh herbs and extracts and artisan spirits in served with a flourish in colorful vessels. ✉ *163 W. 900 S* ☎ *801/462–0967* ⊕ *www.waterwitchbar. com.*

BREWPUBS AND MICROBREWERIES

Beer Hive Pub
BREWPUBS/BEER GARDENS | Set in an atmospheric vintage brick downtown building with a lively patio out front, this hive of hops enthusiasts stocks perhaps the most exhaustive selection of craft beer in the city, with about two-dozen IPAs alone. ✉ *128 S. Main St.* ☎ *801/364–4268.*

Desert Edge Brewery
BREWPUBS/BEER GARDENS | A fixture in Salt Lake City since the early 1970s, this Trolley Square microbrewery offers tasty pub fare, loft seating, a sheltered patio, and good music, plus a good selection of house beers. ✉ *273 Trolley Square* ☎ *801/521–8917* ⊕ *www.desertedgebrewery.com.*

★ Fisher Brewing Company

BREWPUBS/BEER GARDENS | Local food trucks dispense tasty eats at this lively craft brewery and beer garden with a dog-friendly patio. The saison and cream ale are among the standout offerings. ✉ *320 W. 800 S* ☎ *801/487–2337* ⊕ *www.fisherbeer.com.*

Kiitos Brewing

BREWPUBS/BEER GARDENS | This festive purveyor of first-rate craft beer is as known for its smooth Coconut Stout and tangy Blackberry Sour as for its impressive selection of vintage pinball and arcade games. ✉ *608 W. 700 S* ☎ *801/215–9165* ⊕ *www.kiitosbrewing.com.*

Squatters Pub Brewery

BREWPUBS/BEER GARDENS | Arguably Utah's most famous microbrewery, Squatters' flagship downtown pub is lined with well-deserved awards from the Great American Beer Festival and World Beer Cup. The pub has friendly staff and an easygoing, casual vibe, although it can get crowded on weekends and when there are conventions in town. ✉ *147 W. Broadway, Downtown* ☎ *801/363–2739* ⊕ *www.squatters.com.*

LGBTQ+

Bottoms Up

BARS/PUBS | On the west side of downtown in the city's lively LGBTQ+ quadrant, Bottoms Up stands out for its sprawling roof deck and for presenting some of the best drag shows in SLC. ✉ *579 W. 200 S* ☎ *385/528–3734.*

The Sun Trapp

BARS/PUBS | This spacious dance club and lounge with a popular patio has long been a favorite hangout of Salt Lake's LGBTQ+ community. ✉ *102 S. 600 W* ☎ *385/235–6786* ⊕ *www.thesuntrapp.com.*

 Performing Arts

MAJOR PERFORMANCE VENUES

★ Abravanel Hall

ARTS CENTERS | Home of the Utah Symphony and other distinguished events like the Wasatch Speaker Series featuring names such as Dr. Sanjay Gupta and Jane Goodall. ✉ *123 W. South Temple, Downtown* ☎ *801/468–1010* ⊕ *www.saltlakecountyarts.org.*

Capitol Theatre

ARTS CENTERS | This grand 1913 theater built originally for vaudeville has been masterfully restored and features Ballet West and the Utah Opera in addition to hosting Broadway touring companies. ✉ *50 W. 200 S, Downtown* ☎ *801/468–1010* ⊕ *www.saltlakecountyarts.org.*

★ Eccles Theater

THEATER | Notable for its five-story glass-wall lobby and starry-sky ceiling, this striking 2,500-seat venue with a smaller black box theater helped spur a revitalization of Regent Street, the narrow lane just east of it. The Eccles hosts major Broadway touring shows as well as big-name concerts. ✉ *131 S. Main St.* ☎ *385/468–1010* ⊕ *www.saltlakecountyarts.org.*

Rose Wagner Performing Arts Center

ARTS CENTERS | Comprising the Black Box Theatre, the Jeanné Wagner Theatre, and the Studio Theatre, the Center is home to the Ririe-Woodbury Dance Company and the Repertory Dance Theatre, and provides performance space for many of the city's smaller theater companies, including Plan-B and Pygmalion Productions. ✉ *138 Broadway, Downtown* ☎ *801/355–2787* ⊕ *www.saltlakecountyarts.org.*

FILM
Brewvies Cinema Pub
FILM | Enjoy craft beer and tasty pub fare while you watch the new releases and indie films at this intimate downtown cinema. ⊠ *677 S. 200 W, Downtown* ☎ *801/322–3891* ⊕ *www.brewvies.com.*

Broadway Centre Theatre
FILM | The Salt Lake Film Society shows newly released, independent, and foreign films at this hugely popular downtown venue. ⊠ *111 E. Broadway, Downtown* ☎ *801/321–0310* ⊕ *www.saltlakefilmsociety.org.*

★ Tower Theatre
FILM | Head to Central City's hip 9th and 9th district to catch first-run and classic indie and foreign films at this historic art deco theater that's also a Sundance Film Festival venue. ⊠ *876 E. 900 S, East Side* ☎ *801/321–0310* ⊕ *www.saltlakefilmsociety.org.*

MUSIC
★ Utah Symphony
MUSIC | The premier orchestra in the state, the Utah Symphony performs in the acoustically acclaimed Abravanel Hall and calls the Deer Valley Music Festival its summer home. ⊠ *Downtown* ☎ *801/533–6683* ⊕ *www.usuo.org.*

OPERA
Utah Opera
OPERA | Since 1978, this company has performed new and classical works at Capitol Theatre and throughout the state. ⊠ *Downtown* ☎ *801/533–6683* ⊕ *www.usuo.org.*

THEATER
★ Plan-B Theatre
THEATER | The resident company of the Rose Wagner Performing Arts Center stages modest productions built on fine original scripts and timely social and cultural themes. ⊠ *Downtown* ☎ *801/297–4200* ⊕ *www.planbtheatre.org.*

⬤ Shopping

ANTIQUES
Capital City Antique Mall
ANTIQUES/COLLECTIBLES | This expansive, multi-dealer emporium specializes in antiques of all periods, plus jewelry and vintage clothing. You're sure to encounter some great finds. ⊠ *959 S. West Temple, Downtown* ☎ *801/521–7207.*

ART GALLERIES
★ Phillips Gallery
ART GALLERIES | The highly respected, longest-running gallery in Utah features three floors of local and regional artists' work, including mixed media, paintings, and sculptures. Check out the sculptures on the rooftop garden. ⊠ *444 E. 200 S, Downtown* ☎ *801/364–8284* ⊕ *www.phillips-gallery.com.*

BOOKS
★ Weller Book Works
BOOKS/STATIONERY | The name of this store has been synonymous with independent book sales in Salt Lake City since 1929. Catherine and Tony Weller are the third generation to operate this bookstore, which relocated to the historic former train yard in 2012. Bibliophiles will love the space and the helpful and knowledgeable staff. ⊠ *607 Trolley Sq., East Side* ☎ *801/328–2586* ⊕ *www.wellerbookworks.com.*

CLOTHING
Hip & Humble
CLOTHING | Look to this dapper little 9th and 9th lifestyle shop for casually stylish women's attire, from cheerful floral midi dresses to handmade silver jewelry, platform sandals, and cotton totes. There's also a big selection of housewares and gifts, including handpainted planters, charcuterie boards, and detox soaking-tub teas. ⊠ *1043 E. 900 S* ☎ *801/467–3130* ⊕ *www.hipandhumble.com.*

★ IconoClad

CLOTHING | In this beloved consign-
ment and vintage shop, bargain-priced
treasures abound, from previously worn
to brand-new gear and clothing, plus
fun gifts, LGBTQ Pride items, and much
more. Keep an eye out for the friendly
feline staffers working the aisles. ✉ *414
E. 300 S* ☎ *801/833–2272* ⊕ *www.
iconoclad.com.*

The Stockist

CLOTHING | This cosmopolitan fashion
boutique carries women's and men's
attire and lifestyle products from Aesop,
Citizens of Humanity, Gitman Vintage,
Neuw Denim, Richer Poorer, and dozens
of other brands, both internationally
renowned and emerging. ✉ *875 E. 900
S* ☎ *801/532–3458* ⊕ *www.thestockist-
shop.com.*

FOOD

★ Caputo's Market & Deli

FOOD/CANDY | A must for stocking up on
snacks and picnic goods before hiking,
skiing, or just hanging out across the
street in Pioneer Park, Caputo's boasts
a fantastic butcher shop, bean-to-bar
chocolates, fine cheeses and charcuterie, Italian baked goods, and a deli that
produces some of the tastiest to-go
sandwiches in town. ✉ *314 W. 300 S,
Downtown* ☎ *801/531–8669* ⊕ *www.
caputos.com.*

★ Fillings & Emulsions

FOOD/CANDY | Employing a team of world-
class pastry chefs, including acclaimed
owner and Food Network competitor
Adalberto Diaz, this sumptuous little
cake shop produces artful and delicious
sweet treats and offers one-day classes,
too, on all sorts of topics—from French
macarons to creamy custards. Stop by
and treat yourself to a guava tart, a slice
of raspberry chocolate cheesecake, or
a savory ham-and-cheese croissant.
✉ *1475 S. Main St.* ☎ *385/229–4228*
⊕ *www.fillingsandemulsions.com.*

Goodly Cookies

FOOD/CANDY | It's all about the cookie at
this delightful little shop whose best sell-
ers include the cobbler-inspired Peachy
Keen, the gooey Choc PB Love, and the
ethereal White Chocolate Raspberry
Delight. But wait, there's more: the store
partners with locally renowned Howdy
Homemade to produce decadent cookie–
ice cream sandwiches. ✉ *432 S. 900 E*
☎ *801/784–4848* ⊕ *www.goodlycookies.
com.*

Liberty Heights Fresh

FOOD/CANDY | This gourmet grocery near
Liberty Park and 9th and 9th is a go-to
for high-quality foods as well as delicious
prepared items, such as rosemary
ham–Brie–balsamic sandwiches and
roasted-veggie lasagna with house-made
pasta. ✉ *1290 S. 1100 E* ☎ *801/583–7374*
⊕ *www.libertyheightsfresh.com.*

GIFTS
Cahoots

BOOKS/STATIONERY | Arguably SLC's most
irreverent little retailer, Cahoots is where
you go when seeking the perfect smart-
ass greeting card, campy T-shirt, LGBTQ
Pride tchotchke, or NSFW gag gift. ✉ *878
E. 900 S* ☎ *801/538–0606.*

HOUSEHOLD GOODS
Salt & Honey Market

HOUSEHOLD ITEMS/FURNITURE | A well-
stocked maker market that very much
captures the hipster spirit of the surrounding 9th and 9th neighborhood, Salt
& Honey carries large and small items for
every room of the house, from arty bowls
and vases to fine jewelry and some
locally made apparel, too. ✉ *926 E. 900 S*
☎ *385/368–6088* ⊕ *www.saltandhoney-
market.com.*

OUTDOOR AND GREEN MARKETS
★ Downtown Farmers Market

OUTDOOR/FLEA/GREEN MARKETS | Farm-
ers and artisan food producers proffer
fresh fruit and veggies, flowers, and
other goodies to the popular downtown
farmers' market at **Pioneer Park** each

Saturday from June through late October. Local bakeries and restaurants also sell tasty treats ranging from fresh salsa to cinnamon rolls, and there is live music, too. At the same location, there's also a Tuesday afternoon market in August and September, a smaller winter market takes place on Saturdays from November through April. Additional farmers' markets take place around the city, generally in summer, in Liberty Park, Sugar House, Murray, South Jordan, and several other locales around the city. ⊠ *300 W. 300 S* ☎ *801/328–5070* ⊕ *www.slcfarmers-market.org.*

PLAZAS AND MALLS

City Creek Center

STORE/MALL | The centerpiece of a $1 billion downtown redevelopment across from Temple Square, this attractive outdoor mall has brought upscale shopping to the city with stores like Apple, Anthropologie, Louis Vuitton, Lululemon, Nordstrom, and Tiffany. Note that most stores are closed on Sunday. ⊠ *50 S. Main St., Downtown* ☎ *801/521–2012* ⊕ *www.shopcitycreekcenter.com.*

Trolley Square

SHOPPING CENTERS/MALLS | The wares in this converted historic railyard near Central City, not far from trendy 9th and 9th, run the gamut from estate jewelry and designer clothes to bath products and fine groceries. Stores include chains and indie boutiques, such as Pottery Barn, Weller Books, Tabula Rasa, and an assortment of restaurants, as well as Whole Foods. ⊠ *600 S. 700 E, Downtown* ☎ *801/521–9877* ⊕ *www.trolleysquare. com.*

SPORTSWEAR AND OUTDOOR GEAR

Canyon Sports

SPORTING GOODS | This big and well-stocked downtown retailer geared toward skiing, snowboarding, and other winter-sports gear and apparel—both for sale and for rent—also stocks plenty of warm-weather items, including paddle boards, mountain bikes, tents, and more. You can also buy lift tickets. ⊠ *517 S. 200 W* ☎ *801/322–4220* ⊕ *www.canyonsports.com.*

★ Cotopaxi

SPORTING GOODS | The boldly colored backpacks, fleeces, running wear, and ski jackets hint at Cotopaxi's mission and aesthetic. Named for a massive Andean stratovolcano in Ecuador, the B Corporation shop sources its goods from Latin America and pays its makers a fair, sustainable wage while also giving back through charitable action. ⊠ *74 S. Main St.* ☎ *385/528–0855* ⊕ *www.cotopaxi. com.*

Utah Ski & Golf

SKIING/SNOWBOARDING | Discounted lift tickets, advance equipment, and clothing rental reservations are available at Utah Ski & Golf's downtown and Cottonwood Canyon locations and in Park City, with free shuttle service from downtown hotels to their stores. ⊠ *134 W. 600 S, Downtown* ☎ *385/202–2448* ⊕ *www. utahskigolf.com.*

 Activities

BASEBALL

Salt Lake Bees

BASEBALL/SOFTBALL | The AAA affiliate of the Los Angeles Angels plays at attractive Smith's Ballpark, its backdrop of the Wasatch Mountains making a fantastic place to enjoy a game. The season runs April through August. ⊠ *77 W. 1300 S, Downtown* ☎ *801/325–2337* ⊕ *www. slbees.com.*

BASKETBALL

Utah Jazz

BASKETBALL | Salt Lake's NBA team plays at the Vivint Smart Home Arena. Basketball buffs should check out the statues of Hall of Famers John Stockton and Karl Malone outside. ⊠ *301 W. South Temple, Downtown* ☎ *801/325–2500* ⊕ *www.nba. com/jazz.*

3

Salt Lake City DOWNTOWN AND CENTRAL CITY

BICYCLING
Bingham Cyclery
BICYCLING | With four locations around metro Salt Lake, including one downtown Salt Lake City across from Pioneer Park, this friendly shop sells and rents bikes or will tune up the one you already have. Other branches are in Ogden, Sunset, and Sandy. ✉ *336 Broadway, Downtown* ☎ *888/611–2453* ⊕ *www.binghamcyclery. com.*

★ Contender Bicycles
BICYCLING | In trendy 9th and 9th, the store that vows to "make every bike a dream bike" is a must-visit for cyclists, offering a full slate of sales and services, including rentals. You might catch Tour de France veterans Levi Leipheimer or Dave Zabriskie stopping by to chat or ride with this shop's competitive team. ✉ *989 E. 900 S, Downtown* ☎ *801/364–0344* ⊕ *www.contenderbicycles.com* ⊙ *Closed Sun.*

Capitol Hill and the Avenues

These picturesque, historic neighborhoods overlook the city from the foothills north of downtown. Two days after entering the future Salt Lake City, Brigham Young brought his fellow religious leaders to the summit of the most prominent hill here, which he named Ensign Peak, to plan out their new home. New arrivals built sod homes into the hillside of what is now the Avenues. Two-room log cabins and adobe houses dotted the area. Meanwhile, on the western slope of the hill, fruit and nut trees were planted. Some still remain, as does a neighborhood known as Marmalade, with streets named Apricot, Quince, and Almond.

With the coming of the railroad came Victorian homes. The city's rich and prominent families built mansions along South Temple. As the city has grown over the years, wealthy citizens have continued to live close to the city but farther up the hill where the views of the valley are better. Since the early 1970s the lower Avenues has seen an influx of residents interested in restoring the older homes, adding diversity and energy to this evolving community.

The state capitol, for which Capitol Hill is named, was completed in 1915. State offices flank the capitol on three sides. City Creek Canyon forms its eastern boundary. The Avenues denotes the larger neighborhood along the foothills, north of South Temple, extending from Capitol Hill east to the University of Utah.

 Sights

Cathedral of the Madeleine
BUILDING | Although the Salt Lake Temple just to the west is Salt Lake's most prominent religious landmark, this 1909 cathedral stands high above the city's north side and is a stunning house of worship in its own right. The exterior sports gargoyles, and its Gothic interior showcases bright frescoes, intricate wood carvings, and a 4,066-pipe organ. The highly regarded Madeleine children's choir gives concerts regularly (especially during the Christmas season). ✉ *331 E. South Temple, The Avenues* ☎ *801/328–8941* ⊕ *www.utcotm.org.*

Governor's Mansion
HISTORIC SITE | Built by silver-mining tycoon Thomas Kearns in 1902, this limestone structure—reminiscent of a French château with all its turrets and balconies—is now the official residence of Utah's governor. In its early days the mansion was visited by President Theodore Roosevelt and other dignitaries from around the world. The mansion was faithfully restored after Christmas lights caused a fire in 1993 that destroyed much of the interior. Free hour-long tours are given by Preservation Utah from June through August and December on

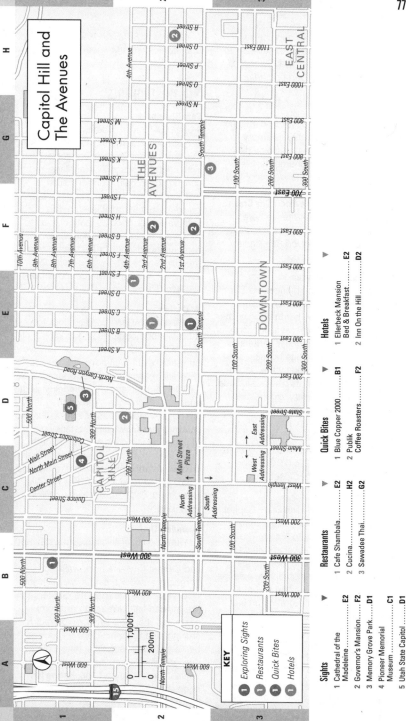

Capitol Hill and The Avenues

KEY

- ① Exploring Sights
- ① Restaurants
- ① Quick Bites
- ① Hotels

Sights ▶

1 Cathedral of the
   Madeleine..................**E2**
2 Governor's Mansion.....**F2**
3 Memory Grove Park.....**D1**
4 Pioneer Memorial
   Museum......................**C1**
5 Utah State Capitol......**D1**

Restaurants ▶

1 Cafe Shambala.............**E2**
2 Cucina..........................**H2**
3 Sawadee Thai...............**G2**

Quick Bites ▶

1 Blue Copper 2000........**B1**
2 Publik
   Coffee Roasters...........**F2**

Hotels ▶

1 Ellerbeck Mansion
   Bed & Breakfast...........**E2**
2 Inn On the Hill..............**D2**

77

3

Salt Lake City CAPITOL HILL AND THE AVENUES

Thursday afternoons, by appointment only (call at least 24 hours in advance). ✉ *603 E. South Temple, The Avenues* ☎ *801/533–0858* 🌐 *governor.utah.gov/mansion.*

Memory Grove Park

NATIONAL/STATE PARK | Severely damaged by a freak tornado in 1999, Memory Grove was carefully restored as a city park with veterans' monuments, beautiful landscaping, and the waters of City Creek. You can hike, jog, or bike on the paved road or dirt trails along **City Creek Canyon.** More trails commence here, including the 100-mile Bonneville Shoreline Trail. ✉ *300 N. Canyon Rd., Capitol Hill* 🌐 *www.slc.gov/parks.*

Pioneer Memorial Museum

MUSEUM | Covering the pioneer era from the departure of the Mormons from Nauvoo, Illinois, to the hammering of the Golden Spike, this massive collection traces the history of pioneer settlers in 38 rooms—plus a carriage house—on four floors. Administered by the Daughters of Utah Pioneers, its displays include clothing, furniture, tools, wagons, and carriages. Be careful with kids—this museum is as cluttered as a westbound covered wagon loaded with all of a family's possessions. ✉ *300 N. Main St., Capitol Hill* ☎ *801/532–6479* 🌐 *www.dupinternational.org* 🕒 *Closed Sun.*

★ **Utah State Capitol**

GOVERNMENT BUILDING | The State Capitol, built in 1912, hosts Utah's legislature annually from January to March. The exterior steps offer marvelous views of the Salt Lake Valley. In the rotunda beneath the 165-foot-high dome, a series of murals, commissioned as part of a Works Progress Administration project during the Depression, depicts the state's history. Don't miss the gold-leafed State Reception Room, the original state supreme court, and the Senate gallery. Free guided tours are offered weekdays 9–4 (until 1 pm on Friday), on the hour, except for holidays. ✉ *350 N. State St., Capitol Hill* ☎ *801/538–1800* 🌐 *www.utahstatecapitol.utah.gov* 🕒 *Closed weekends.*

🍴 Restaurants

Cafe Shambala

$ | TIBETAN | Savory Tibetan food at bargain prices is the big attraction at this small, clean restaurant decorated with brightly colored Tibetan flags. You can indulge in hearty entrées such as spicy potatoes, chicken curry, and beef *phingsha,* a traditional Tibetan dish with vermicelli noodles, potatoes, dried mushrooms, and spices. **Known for:** bargain-priced lunch buffet; herbal teas; friendly service. [$] *Average main: $9* ✉ *382 4th Ave., The Avenues* ☎ *801/364–8558* 🕒 *Closed Sun.*

★ **Cucina**

$$ | MODERN ITALIAN | Foodies flock to this neighborhood café and food market for creative salads and colorful, creative entrées like ahi tuna poke with guajillo chile and mango, or lobster gnocchi in a saffron beurre blanc with dandelion pesto and candied oranges. Also on the menu are house-made soups and generous deli sandwiches. **Known for:** outstanding list of wines by the glass and bottle; hefty deli sandwiches to go; panna cotta with creative rotating preparations. [$] *Average main: $22* ✉ *1026 E. 2nd Ave., The Avenues* ☎ *801/322–3055* 🌐 *www.cucinawinebar.com.*

Sawadee Thai

$ | THAI | Consider this popular restaurant on the border between the Avenues and Central City—its brick walls and gorgeous artwork create a warm, inviting vibe—for authentic Thai fare. Starters like minced-fish cakes with red-curry paste and Thai beef salad are perfect for sharing, and the main dishes—such as barbecue sweet-soy pork, pineapple-fried rice, and duck in red curry sauce—arrive in generous portions. **Known for:** eggplant, garlic, and Thai basil stir fries;

fragrant Thai iced tea; jackfruit with Thai sweet sticky rice. $ *Average main: $14* ✉ *754 E. S Temple St., The Avenues* ☎ *801/328–8424* ⊕ *www.sawadee1.com* ⊗ *Closed Sun.*

☕ Coffee and Quick Bites

Blue Copper 2000

$ | **CAFÉ** | This newer location of the already well-established Blue Copper coffeehouse opened in an atmospheric old building a few blocks west of the capitol is a perfect place to relax on the patio with an Earl Grey latte or flat white, maybe while enjoying a slice of raspberry shortbread. It's also a great stop for grabbing cold brew or kombucha to take with you on a hike in nearby City Creek Canyon. **Known for:** carefully sourced coffees; matcha lattes; rich pastries and fluffy muffins. $ *Average main: $5* ✉ *401 N. 300 W* ☎ *801/225–2092* ⊕ *www. bluecopperslc.com.*

★ Publik Coffee Roasters

$ | **CAFÉ** | This terrific, uber-cool artisan-coffee purveyor has several locations around town, with this simple, streamlined shop in the Avenues arguably the most inviting, in part because of its handsome wooden tables and for its location along a block of lovely historic homes. Publik sources its fair-trade beans from high-quality farms throughout Latin America and Africa, and always offers an interesting array of seasonal espresso drinks, like the wintertime favorite Sweet Melissa, a honey syrup–infused latte with lemon balm, sage, and sweet mint. **Known for:** artisan toasts; inviting, hip aesthetic; white mochas. $ *Average main: $6* ✉ *502 3rd Ave.* ☎ *385/229–4836* ⊕ *www.publikcoffee.com.*

Hotels

Ellerbeck Mansion Bed & Breakfast

$$ | **B&B/INN** | A stay in this lovely brick Victorian mansion, with its tree-lined streets and gentle pace, will give you a real appreciation of why city residents flock to live in the historic Avenues district. **Pros:** free parking; gorgeously appointed guest and common rooms; pleasant walk to Temple Square and City Creek Canyon. **Cons:** sometimes books up for weddings; service can be a bit impersonal for a B&B; not a good fit for children. $ *Rooms from: $152* ✉ *140 N. B St., Capitol Hill* ☎ *801/903–3916* ⊕ *www.ellerbeckbedandbreakfast.com* ⊅ *6 rooms* ⏸ *Free breakfast.*

★ Inn on the Hill

$$$ | **B&B/INN** | Owned and restored by former *Salt Lake Tribune* publisher Philip McCarthey, this spectacular turn-of-the-20th-century Renaissance Revival mansion makes a striking impression with its red-rock exterior and princely setting on the lower slopes of tony Capitol Hill. **Pros:** short walk from Temple Square and the state capitol; jetted tubs and radiant-heat bathroom floors in every room; exceptionally friendly and helpful staff. **Cons:** lots of steps and no elevator; no kids except in the carriage house; books up fast many weekends. $ *Rooms from: $180* ✉ *225 N. State St., Capitol Hill* ☎ *801/328–1466* ⊕ *www.inn-on-the-hill. com* ⊅ *13 rooms* ⏸ *Free breakfast.*

Nightlife

BARS AND LOUNGES
Garage on Beck

BARS/PUBS | Set inside a transformed former auto garage a short drive north of Capitol Hill, this rollicking tavern with a big patio hosts live rock, blues, and the like. The kitchen turns out tasty comfort food—think chicken or vegan wings with habanero-molasses "sludge" or burgers topped with candied jalapeños and crispy bacon. There's a popular Sunday brunch, too. ✉ *1199 Beck St.* ☎ *801/521–3904* ⊕ *www.garageonbeck.com.*

★ Mountain West Cider
BREWPUBS/BEER GARDENS | One of the state's only craft cider producers, Mountain West uses local ingredients—prickly pear puree, and a wide variety of apples—to create its crisp and refreshing concoctions. In the cheerful tap room and sunny garden, where live bands often perform, you can sample the ciders along with local beers and spirits. ✉ *425 N. 400 W* ☎ *801/935–4147* ⊕ *www. mountainwestcider.com.*

 ## Performing Arts

Salt Lake Acting Company
THEATER | Recognized for its development of new regionally and locally written plays, this year-round company presents thought-provoking plays while promoting arts education for Utahns in kindergarten up through the university level. ✉ *168 W. 500 N, Capitol Hill* ☎ *801/363–7522* ⊕ *www.saltlakeactingcompany.org.*

 ## Shopping

ART GALLERIES
Alice Gallery at Glendinning
ART GALLERIES | This gallery housed inside the gracious and historic Glendinning Mansion, which is also home to the Utah Arts Council, features rotating exhibits that focus on contemporary Utah artists. ✉ *617 E. South Temple, Downtown* ☎ *801/245–7272* ⊕ *artsandmuseums. utah.gov/alice-gallery.*

FOOD
Hatch Family Chocolates
FOOD/CANDY | For a sweet treat, stop by this friendly candy- and ice-cream shop. Jerry Hatch uses his mother's secret recipe for creamy caramel, and each piece of chocolate is hand-dipped and sold by weight. They also serve espresso, Italian soda, ice cream, and decadent hot chocolate. ✉ *376 8th Ave.* ☎ *801/532–4912* ⊕ *www.hatchfamilychocolates.com.*

 ## Activities

RECREATIONAL AREAS
★ City Creek Canyon
BICYCLING | A favorite of bikers as well as walkers and joggers, City Creek Canyon and its lush 5.6-mile trail—just east of the capitol—rewards visitors with dramatic views of the city and mountains. Part of the hike is along a pristine alpine stream. Cyclists can ride the trail on odd-number days from Memorial Day through Labor Day, and every day between Labor Day and Memorial Day, when the road is closed to vehicles. ✉ *N. Canyon Rd. at Bonneville Rd., Capitol Hill* ☎ *801/972–7800* ⊕ *www.slc.gov/parks.*

Ensign Peak Park
PARK—SPORTS-OUTDOORS | Close to City Creek Canyon and the Capitol building, this peaceful wildlife-rich habitat can be reached via a short, moderately steep trail of just under a mile, which leads to a 5,400-foot-elevation summit. Well-marked and maintained, the trail ascends from a residential neighborhood, and there's usually plenty of free parking on the street. ✉ *1002 N. Ensign Vista Dr., Capitol Hill* ☎ *801/972–7800* ⊕ *www.slc. gov/parks.*

East Side and Sugar House

Home to the city's lofty University/Foothill district, the East Side is both a lively urban neighborhood and a scenic slice of nature, with its many trails twisting and turning into the Wasatch Range. Occupying what was once the eastern shoreline of ancient Lake Bonneville, the University of Utah is the state's largest higher-education institution and the oldest university west of the Mississippi.

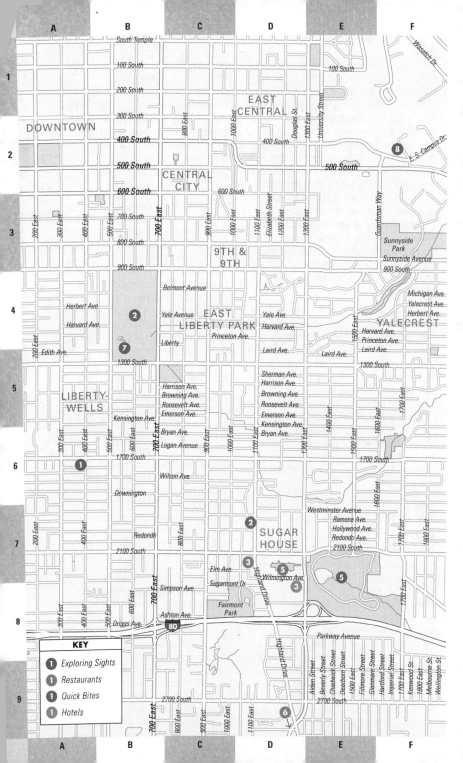

It's the cultural hub of University/Foothill, home to museums, the football stadium that was the site of the opening and closing ceremonies during the 2002 Winter Olympics, a 15,000-seat indoor arena, numerous prominent medical facilities and Research Park, which houses scores of private companies and portions of 30 academic departments in a cooperative enterprise in which research and technology partner to produce marketable products. Near campus, the scenic Red Butte Garden and Arboretum is a great place to learn about plants that thrive in dry climates such as Utah's, and the gleaming copper-colored Natural History Museum of Utah is one of the city's must-see attractions.

A bit south, you'll find the charming Sugar House neighborhood. Utah pioneers tried to produce sugar out of beets at a mill here, and although sugar never made it to their tables, it is a sweet place to find eclectic shops and hip restaurants. The beautiful **Sprague Library** (⊠ 2131 S. 1100 E), in a historic Tudor-style building, is worth a visit. Pick up picnic food and head for tiny Hidden Hollow Park, or cross 1300 East to the expansive Sugar House Park, which hosts the city's most spectacular fireworks and arts festival every July 4.

Sights

Hogle Zoo
ZOO | FAMILY | This 42-acre zoo, nestled at the base of Emigration Canyon, has been a delightful half-day destination for families since 1931. In the African Savanna you can spy zebras, giraffes, and ostriches; Asian Highlands showcases big cats in natural surroundings; Rocky Shores includes underwater viewing of polar bears, sea lions, seals, and otters; and Elephant Encounter has elephants and white rhinos in a simulated African plain. In between you'll find many exhibits with species native to the West, including wolves and bison. A children's

zoo, interactive exhibits, and special presentations make visits informative all ages. Just for fun is the Lighthouse Point Splash Zone, with a tube slide, the Zoo Train, and a carousel. ⊠ 2600 E. Sunnyside Ave., East Side ☎ 801/584–1700 ⊕ www.hoglezoo.org ⊠ $19 summer, $17 winter.

★ Liberty Park
NATIONAL/STATE PARK | Salt Lake's oldest park contains a wealth of intriguing amenities, including the Tracy Aviary, the Chase Home Museum, several playgrounds, a large pond, a swimming pool, and a tennis complex on its eight square city blocks. Weekly farmers' markets on Friday nights and the city's biggest Pioneer Day celebration (July 24) mark a busy summer schedule annually. Make a wish and toss a coin into Seven Canyons Fountain, a symbol of the seven major canyons of the Wasatch Front. ⊠ 600 E. 900 S, East Side ☎ 801/521–0962 ⊕ www.slc.gov/parks.

★ Natural History Museum of Utah
MUSEUM | FAMILY | Stop and admire the sleek copper and granite form of this contemporary museum on the University of Utah campus before stepping inside to learn about the formation of the region's incredible landscape of parks, mountain ranges, lakes, and basins. Immerse yourself in prehistoric Utah, home to prolific research on dinosaurs and some of the most famous fossil recoveries in history. ⊠ 301 Wakara Way, University of Utah ☎ 801/581–6927 ⊕ www.nhmu.utah.edu ⊠ $15.

★ Red Butte Garden and Arboretum
GARDEN | With more than 100 acres of gardens and undeveloped acres, this tranquil, mesmerizing nature space provides many enjoyable hours of strolling. Of special interest are the Perennial, Fragrance, and Medicinal gardens, the Daylily Collection, the Water Pavilion, and the Children's Garden. Lectures on everything from bugs to gardening in arid climates, workshops, and concerts are

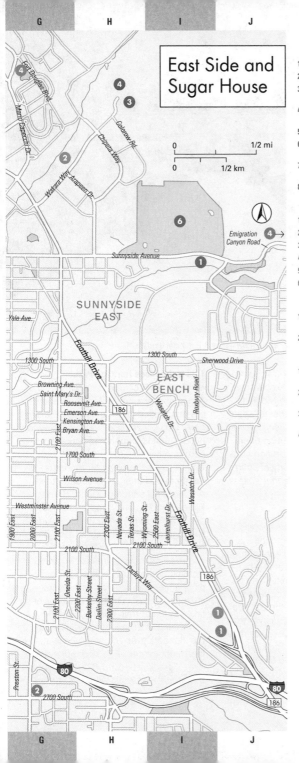

East Side and Sugar House

0 — 1/2 mi
0 — 1/2 km

Emigration
Canyon Road

See emus, parrots, and bald eagles at the Tracy Aviary & Botanical Garden.

presented regularly. The popular Summer Concert Series attracts well-known musicians from the B-52s to Modest Mouse. The pristine amphitheater seats approximately 3,000 people on its expansive lawn. The Botanic Gift Shop offers books, soaps, sculptures, and fine gifts. ✉ *300 Wakara Way, University of Utah* ☎ *801/585–0556* ⊕ *www.redbuttegarden. org* ✆ *$14.*

Sugar House Park

CITY PARK | FAMILY | Rolling grassy hills, athletic fields, multiple playgrounds, a creek, and a pond provide plenty of room to fly a kite or have a picnic at this big and popular neighborhood city park. Take in stunning mountain views or head to the hill on the south end of the park—a go-to destination for sledding in winter. Odd fact: the park once housed a federal prison famous for incarcerating Utah's polygamists. ✉ *1330 E. 2100 S, East Side* ⊕ *www.sugarhousepark.org.*

This Is the Place Heritage Park

MUSEUM VILLAGE | FAMILY | Brigham Young and his band of Mormon followers descended into the Salt Lake Valley here. On July 24, 1847 (now a statewide holiday that is bigger than July 4 in many communities), he famously declared that this was the place for the Latter-day Saints to end their cross-country trek. A 60-foot-tall statue of Young, Heber Kimball, and Wilbur Woodruff stands prominently in the park, which includes Heritage Village, a re-created 19th-century community and visitor center. In summer, volunteers dressed in period clothing demonstrate what Mormon pioneer life was like. You can watch artisans at work in historic buildings and take wagon or train rides around the compound. A 20-minute movie depicts the pioneers' trek across America at the visitor center. ✉ *2601 E. Sunnyside Ave., East Side* ☎ *801/582–1847* ⊕ *www. thisistheplace.org* ✆ *Village: $14 (Sun. $8). Monument: free.*

Tracy Aviary & Botanical Garden
ZOO | **FAMILY** | Easily walkable for even the smallest kids, this family-friendly facility in gracious Liberty Park features more than 100 species of birds found on the Western Hemispheric Flyway, a migratory pattern that includes Great Salt Lake. You will see emus, bald eagles, flamingos, parrots, several types of waterfowl, and maybe even a wandering peacock. There are bird shows and educational activities daily. ✉ *589 E. 1300 S, East Side* ☎ *801/596–8500* 🌐 *www.tracyaviary.org* 🎟 *$12.*

Utah Museum of Fine Arts
MUSEUM | Spanning 74,000 square feet and offering more than 20 galleries, this well-regarded art museum on University of Utah campus contains a vast permanent collection of Egyptian, Greek, and Roman relics, Italian Renaissance and other European paintings, and Chinese ceramics and scrolls. Special exhibits are mounted regularly, and a café and a sculpture court offer further diversions. ✉ *410 Campus Center Dr., University of Utah* ☎ *801/581–7332* 🌐 *www.umfa.utah.edu* 🎟 *$16* 🕒 *Closed Mon.*

🍴 Restaurants

Bombay House
$ | **INDIAN** | You'll be enveloped in electrifying aromas the minute you step into this dark, intimate space that ranks among the best Indian restaurants in the state. You'll find all the standards, including soft garlic naan, chicken-coconut korma, piquant lamb vindaloo, fragrant tandoori dishes, and lots of vegetarian options. **Known for:** attentive service; several excellent shrimp and halibut curries; rosewater lassi. [$] *Average main: $15* ✉ *2731 E. Parleys Way, University of Utah* ☎ *801/581–0222* 🌐 *www.bombayhouse.com* 🕒 *Closed Sun. No lunch.*

★ Feldman's Deli
$ | **DELI** | A bustling space with high ceilings, brick walls, and live music some evenings. this contemporary take on a traditional Jewish deli is in a cheerful neighborhood on the south edge of Sugar House. It's a must for classic dishes—in enormous portions—of Reuben sandwiches, blintzes with fruit compote, matzo ball soup, everything bagels with smoked sockeye salmon and a schmear. **Known for:** plenty of distinctive local beers; authentic boiled bagels baked fresh daily; rugelach pastries. [$] *Average main: $14* ✉ *2005 E. 2700 S* ☎ *801/906–0369* 🌐 *www.feldmansdeli.com* 🕒 *Closed Sun. and Mon.*

Mazza
$$ | **MIDDLE EASTERN** | A warmly inviting and reasonably priced option in the buzzy 9th and 9th district, Mazza presents a long menu of well-prepared, traditional Middle Eastern favorites, like falafel, Aleppan walnut-pomegranate dip, cheese and za'atar flatbread, lamb kebabs, and oven-baked chicken and potatoes *mutabbak* (served with sweet onions and a tangy tamarind sauce over basmati rice). The desserts—including honey-drenched baklava—are noteworthy. **Known for:** wide variety of meat and veggie skewers; casually sophisticated dining room; apricot-cream turnovers for dessert. [$] *Average main: $21* ✉ *912 E. 900 S, East Side* ☎ *801/521–4572* 🌐 *www.mazzacafe.com* 🕒 *Closed Sun.*

Ramen Legend
$ | **RAMEN** | Fantastic murals adorn the walls of this trendy Sugar House ramen parlor and izakaya that also specializes in creamy milk boba teas and smoothies. From the ramen menu, you can't go wrong with aromatic black sesame broth with pork slices and boiled eggs, while fans of Japanese bar fare might want to consider the cold tofu with ground pork, shrimp tempura, and soft-shell crab buns. **Known for:** several

86

varieties of richly satisfying ramen; spicy tuna poke bowls; noisy, bustling dining room. $ *Average main: $14* ✉ *2118 Highland Dr.* ☎ *801/758–8950* ⊕ *www. ramenlegend.com.*

★ Ruth's Diner

$ | **AMERICAN** | **FAMILY** | Families love the gussied-up old railcar that serves as Ruth's dining room and the best creek-side patio in the city—you just have to navigate your way up gorgeous Emigration Canyon to find it. Breakfast (served until 4 pm) has been the diner's trademark since 1930, and it starts with 3-inch-high biscuits followed by massive omelets like the King of Hearts (artichokes, garlic, mushrooms, and two cheeses). **Known for:** scenic canyon setting; live music on the patio in summer; long wait times on weekend mornings. $ *Average main: $14* ✉ *4160 Emigration Canyon Rd., East Side* ☎ *801/582–5807* ⊕ *www.ruthsdiner.com.*

SOMI Vietnamese Bistro

$$ | **VIETNAMESE** | The expertly prepared, contemporary Vietnamese food is but one reason for this buzzy, contemporary bistro's success—there's also a good wine list and a range of distinctive cocktails. The kitchen specializes in modern and traditional fare, along with some nods to countries that border Vietnam—try the piquant lemongrass beef noodle soup, before graduating to steamed whole branzino fish with a ginger-scallion sauce, and tender sliced Peking-style pork chops with sweet-and-sour sauce. **Known for:** slow-simmered beef-meatball pho; traditional Peking duck; fried bananas with toasted sesame and organic vanilla ice cream. $ *Average main: $22* ✉ *1215 E. Wilmington Ave.* ☎ *385/322–1158* ⊕ *www.somislc.com.*

★ Table X

$$$ | **MODERN AMERICAN** | Serving artfully crafted modern American fare in a sceney cathedral-ceilinged restaurant and tall black leather booths, a pair of SLC's most esteemed chefs have created the most alluring dining destination in the Sugar House area. The menu changes frequently and is based on what's in season, but recent offerings have included locally raised lamb shank accompanied by smoked and pickled alliums and saffron lamb jus, and a vegetable "steak" topped with coconut-leek curry, spiced ghee, and garden chili oil. **Known for:** fresh produce grown in the on-site garden; outstanding service; daily-changing selection of house-made ice creams and sorbets. $ *Average main: $25* ✉ *1457 E. 3350 S* ☎ *385/528–3712* ⊕ *www. tablexrestaurant.com* ⊗ *Closed Sun. and Mon. No lunch.*

🍩 Coffee and Quick Bites

Alchemy Coffee

$ | **CAFÉ** | In the Liberty Wells district a little west of Sugar House, this eclectically furnished café with cozy armchairs, rotating art exhibits, and high ceiling rafters is an inviting place to while away a morning or afternoon. Veggie quiche with house-made aioli, thick-cut sourdough avocado toast, and well-crafted espresso drinks provide sustenance, and there's always good music playing. **Known for:** diverse crowd; sweet chocolate chai lattes; almond and chocolate croissants. $ *Average main: $9* ✉ *390 E. 1700 S* ☎ *801/322–0735* ⊕ *www.alchemycoffee. com.*

Tea Zaanti

$ | **CAFÉ** | In a city known for healthy living and spiritualism, this Sugar House purveyor of exceptional loose-leaf teas and light snacks has a devoted following. Pick your tea from the lengthy menu—the blueberry matcha is a standout—and enjoy it hot, as a latte, or iced. **Known for:** tomato soup with grilled cheese; iced peach tea; decadent drinking chocolates. $ *Average main: $6* ✉ *1944 1100 E* ☎ *801/906–8132* ⊕ *www.teazaanti.com* ⊗ *Closed Mon.*

Hotels

Home2 Suites Salt Lake City–East

$ | **HOTEL** | **FAMILY** | This modern and cheerful member of Hilton's extended-stay Home2 Suites brand offers smartly designed suites with sitting areas, sofa beds, fully equipped kitchens, and a wonderful location for being close to East Side hiking and attractions—it's also one of the closest hotels in town to Park City, as it's just off I–80. **Pros:** very pet-friendly; kitchens and extra beds are great for families; convenient to Sugar House and University of Utah. **Cons:** rear-facing rooms overlook a Walmart; not much within walking distance; 15-minute drive from downtown. [$] *Rooms from: $119* ✉ *2350 S. Foothill Dr., University of Utah* ☎ *801/384–5785* 🌐 *www.hilton.com* 🛏 *105 rooms* 🍴 *Free breakfast.*

Salt Lake City Marriott University Park

$$ | **HOTEL** | Away from the downtown bustle and steps from hiking and biking trails as well as University of Utah attractions, this airy and inviting hotel is popular with business travelers but is actually a great choice if you'd rather be closer to nature and a little away from the bustle of downtown. **Pros:** near Natural History Museum and Red Butte Garden; sweeping Wasatch Mountain views; good on-site restaurant and bar, plus Starbucks. **Cons:** not many businesses within walking distance; expensive breakfast; 10- to 15-minute drive from downtown. [$] *Rooms from: $132* ✉ *480 Wakara Way, University of Utah* ☎ *801/581–1000* 🌐 *www.marriott.com* 🛏 *218 rooms* 🍴 *No meals.*

★ **SpringHill Suites Salt Lake City Sugar House**

$$$ | **HOTEL** | The first hotel in the city's colorful Sugar House neighborhood is a sleek all-suites lodging with large entertainment-work areas, a comfy lobby with a convenience market, and an east side location near I–80 that's handy for hiking and skiing. **Pros:** spacious, contemporary rooms with big sitting areas; across from a pretty park in a lively neighborhood; indoor pool with lots of natural light. **Cons:** pricey for Salt Lake; walls are a little thin; 10- to 15-minute drive from downtown. [$] *Rooms from: $199* ✉ *2206 S. 1330 E* ☎ *385/297–8300* 🌐 *www.marriott.com* 🛏 *125 rooms* 🍴 *Free breakfast.*

University Guest House

$$ | **HOTEL** | Located on campus and operated by the University of Utah, this reasonably priced 210-room hotel is favored by those doing business with the school or its hospital, but the general public is welcome, and those wanting to be near hikes in the East Side foothills as well as the Avenues appreciate this property's convenience and value. **Pros:** safe, quiet location on University of Utah campus; near Red Butte Gardena and other East Side attractions; free parking and shuttle around campus and points nearby. **Cons:** 10- to 15-minute drive from downtown; some rooms are a little dark; books up well ahead during school events and conferences. [$] *Rooms from: $155* ✉ *110 Fort Douglas Blvd., University of Utah* ☎ *801/587–1000, 877/412–8159* 🌐 *www.universityguesthouse.com* 🛏 *210* 🍴 *Free breakfast.*

Nightlife

BARS AND LOUNGES

★ **Osteria Amore**

BARS/PUBS | Although it's a full-service restaurant serving very good Italian fare, Osteria Amore is also one of the best spots near the University of Utah and the Avenues for a glass of wine—the selection is impressive, and the setting warm and inviting. On warm nights, sip and eat on the sidewalk patio. ✉ *224 1300 E* ☎ *385/270–5606* 🌐 *www.osteriaamore.com.*

Riverbank Bar

BARS/PUBS | A high-ceilinged, contemporary tavern between Sugar House and Millcreek is a fun spot after skiing in Big Cottonwood Canyon or exploring the city's south side and adjacent suburbs. The talented mixologists turn out both classic and contemporary cocktails, and the kitchen serves some of the best bar food in the area. ✉ *1306 Woodland Ave.* ☎ *801/484–1718* ⊕ *www.riverbankbar. com.*

The Ruin

BARS/PUBS | This darkly lighted, stylish lounge in Sugar House stands out for its well-crafted cocktails, like the Thistle & Wool, with Sheep Ditch Scotch, cardamaro, benedictine, black walnut bitters, and orange zest. There's a nice selection of tapas-style bites, too. ✉ *1215 Wilmington Ave.* ☎ *801/869–3730* ⊕ *www.ruinslc. com.*

BREWPUBS AND MICROBREWERIES

⭐ **Hopkins Brewing**

BREWPUBS/BEER GARDENS | Grab a table in this handsome, brick-walled tap room and try some of the finest and most distinctive craft ales in the city, such as crisp Sauvin Blanc Brut produced with hops and Chardonnay grapes, and a roasty Black Sesame Stout. The kitchen is known for its Thai-style and chipotle-honey wings. ✉ *1048 E. 2100 S* ☎ *385/528–3275* ⊕ *www.hopkinsbrewingcompany.com.*

Performing Arts

Pioneer Theatre Company

THEATER | This professional company, in residence at the University of Utah, stages classic and contemporary musicals and plays to consistently positive critical acclaim. ✉ *300 S. 1400 E, University of Utah* ☎ *801/581–6961* ⊕ *www.pioneertheatre.org.*

Shopping

BOOKS

The King's English Bookshop

BOOKS/STATIONERY | **FAMILY** | With works by local authors, a wide selection of children's books, a dozen reading groups, and a community writing series, this converted cottage is a great place to browse and a terrific literary resource. ✉ *1511 S. 1500 E, East Side* ☎ *801/484–9100* ⊕ *www.kingsenglish.com.*

SPORTSWEAR AND OUTDOOR GEAR

Sports Den

SKIING/SNOWBOARDING | A four-season store, Sports Den can handle any ski, snowboard, and snowshoeing need—as well as bicycles, golf, swimming, and summer gear. ✉ *1350 Foothill Dr., East Side* ☎ *801/582–5611* ⊕ *www.sportsden.com.*

Activities

HIKING

⭐ **Big Beacon–Living Room Trail**

HIKING/WALKING | One of the most popular treks on the East Side, this Big Beacon Trail leaves from Georges Hollow, near the Natural History Museum of Utah, and twists and turns for nearly 5 miles through wildflower meadows and sunny canyons to Mount Wire. Along the way, a popular (sometimes a bit too much so on weekends) side trail to Living Room cuts off to the side, providing some of the best views in the city. ✉ *383 Colorow Rd.*

Great Salt Lake and West Side

A visit to northern Utah isn't complete without a trip to the Great Salt Lake. The best way to experience this 1,700-square-mile body of water (it's a little smaller than the state of Delaware) is a half-day excursion to Antelope Island. There's no place in the country like this state park, home to millions of waterfowl and hundreds of bison and antelope, and surrounded by some of the saltiest water on earth. Drive the 7-mile narrow causeway that links the shoreline, then explore the historic ranch house and miles of hiking trails, and try a buffalo burger at the small café.

◉ Sights

★ Antelope Island State Park

ISLAND | In the 19th century, settlers grazed sheep and horses on Antelope Island, ferrying them back and forth from the mainland across the waters of the Great Salt Lake. Today, the park is the most developed and scenic spot in which to experience the lake. Hiking and biking trails crisscross the island, and the lack of cover—cottonwood trees provide some of the only shade—gives the place a wide-open feeling and makes for some blistering hot days. You can go saltwater bathing at several beach areas. Since the salinity level of the lake is always greater than that of the ocean, the water is extremely buoyant (and briny smelling). Hot showers at the marina remove the chill and the salt afterward.

The island has historic sites, as well as desert wildlife and birds in their natural habitat. The most popular inhabitants are the members of a herd of more than 700 bison descended from 12 brought here in 1893. Each October at the **Buffalo Round-up** more than 250 volunteers on horseback round up the free-roaming animals and herd them to the island's north end to be counted. The island's **Fielding-Garr House,** built in 1848 and now owned by the state, was the oldest continuously inhabited home in Utah until the last resident moved out in 1981. The house displays assorted ranching artifacts, and guided horseback riding is available from the stables next to the house. Be sure to check out the modern visitor center, and sample a bison burger at the stand that overlooks the lake to the north. If you're

lucky, you'll hear coyotes howling in the distance. Access to the island is via a 7½-mile causeway, which is reached from I–15 about a half-hour drive north of Salt Lake City. ✉ 4528 W. 1700 S, Syracuse ☎ 801/773–2941 ⊕ stateparks.utah. gov ⌨ $15 per vehicle, $3 per pedestrian.

Great Salt Lake State Park

BEACH—SIGHT | The Great Salt Lake is eight times saltier than the ocean and second only to the Dead Sea in salinity. What makes it so briny? There's no outlet to the ocean, so salts and other minerals carried by rivers and streams become concentrated in this enormous evaporation pond. Ready access to this wonder is possible at this state park on the lake's south shore, 16 miles west of Salt Lake City. A pavilion, souvenir shop, and dance floor honor the park's glory days when ballroom dancing and the lake brought thousands of visitors to its shores.

The state park used to manage the beaches north of the pavilion, but the lake is too shallow here for floating (Antelope Island is better for that). What you can do here is walk down the boat ramp to Great Salt Lake State Marina and stick your legs in the water to experience the unique sensation of floating on water that won't let you sink. Your feet will bob to the surface, and you'll see tiny orange brine shrimp floating with you. You can also rent boats and stand-up paddleboards here, and shower off at the marina. ✉ 13312 W. 1075 S, Magna ☎ 801/828–0787 ⊕ www.stateparks. utah.gov ⌨ $5 per vehicle.

⑪ Restaurants

Island Buffalo Grill

$ | **BURGER** | It may feel a little odd eating buffalo burgers on a bison sanctuary, but if you're an ardent carnivore, you're in for a treat (the less expensive beef burgers are pretty tasty, too). There are no frills here, except for an unparalleled view. **Known for:** juicy buffalo burgers; spectacular views; snow cones. $ *Average main: $10* ✉ *4528 W. 1700 S, Syracuse* ☎ *801/897–3452* ⏲ *No dinner. Closed Nov.–Feb.*

Nomad Eatery

$ | **MODERN AMERICAN** | Located in something of a food desert amid the chain hotels southwest of Salt Lake International Airport, there's one terrific gastropub with a rustic-chic vibe, serving elevated comfort fare and creative cocktails. A nice option before or after a flight or on your way to or from Great Salt Lake State Park, Nomad doles out such eclectic dishes as Korean barbecue pulled-pork sandwiches and thin-crust pizzas topped with broccoli rabe, garlic cream, and taleggio cheese. **Known for:** friendly, easy-going staff; ginger-pear-bourbon cocktails; choco-tacos with cinnamon ice cream. $ *Average main: $11* ✉ *2110 W. North Temple* ☎ *801/938–9629* 🌐 *www.nomad-eatery.com* ⏲ *Closed Sun.*

Roosters Brewing Company

$ | **AMERICAN** | An outpost of the original Roosters that's farther north in Ogden, this Layton brewpub is a great spot to relax with a beer and some pub grub after or before visiting Antelope Island. The array of stouts, IPAs, and pale ales are accompanied by individual-size pizzas, full-meal salads, burgers, and pastas. **Known for:** homemade root beer; spicy shrimp tacos; green-chile farm burgers. $ *Average main: $14* ✉ *748 W. Heritage Park Blvd., Layton* ☎ *801/774–9330* 🌐 *www.roostersbrewingco.com.*

Hotels

Tru by Hilton Salt Lake City Airport

$ | **HOTEL** | Among the dozen or so chain properties close to the airport, this boldly designed member of Hilton's budget-boutique Tru brand stands out for its smartly appointed rooms with 55-inch TVs, laminate-wood floors, and clean aesthetic. **Pros:** sleek design; free parking and airport shuttle; convenient I–80 and Great Salt Lake State Park. **Cons:** bland office park setting; not too many frills; 15-minute drive from downtown. $ *Rooms from: $109* ✉ *206 N. Jimmy Doolittle Rd., Airport* ☎ *801/783–3170* 🌐 *www.hilton.com* 🛏 *90 rooms* 🍴 *Free breakfast.*

Activities

HIKING

Antelope Island State Park offers plenty of space for the avid hiker to explore, but keep a few things in mind. All trails are also shared by mountain bikers and horseback riders—not to mention the occasional bison. Trees are few and far between on the island, making for high exposure to the elements, so bring (and drink) plenty of water and dress appropriately. In the spring, biting insects make bug repellent a must-have. Pick up a trail map at the visitor center.

Once you're prepared, hiking Antelope Island can be a very enjoyable experience. Trails are fairly level except for a few places, where the hot summer sun makes the climb even more strenuous. Mountain ranges, including the Wasatch Front to the east and the Stansbury Mountains directly to the west, provide beautiful background in every direction, though haze sometimes obscures the view. Aromatic sage plants offer shelter for a variety of wildlife, so don't be startled if your next step flushes a chukar partridge, horned lark, or jackrabbit. A bobcat is a rarely seen island resident that will likely keep its distance.

MOUNTAIN AND ROAD BIKING

Bountiful Bicycle Center

BICYCLING | With two locations north of Salt Lake City, one just Kaysville on the way to Antelope Island, this reputable shop is a great place to pick up rentals to cycle around the state park. ✉ *151 Main St., Layton* ☎ *801/444–2453* 🌐 *www.bountifulbicycle.com.*

Midvalley and South Valley

The swatch of suburban communities south of Salt Lake are divided into the Midvalley and South Valley regions, with more of the notable attractions, eateries, and businesses of interest to visitors in the former, chiefly in the towns of Murray, Millcreek, Holladay, and Cottonwood Heights. In addition to being home to some interesting museums and parks, these areas also have some hotels and dining and nightlife options that are popular with winter skiers and summer hikers and bikers making their way to and from the Cottonwood canyons.

 ## Sights

Kindig It Design

MUSEUM | Having earned a cult following as the star of Motortrend TV's long-running show *Bitchin' Rides,* Dave Kindig's custom auto design and restoration shop in near Millcreek produces stunning, high-profile cars, sometimes for famous clients. Fans of the show and others who simply love cars that have been customized to look like works of art enjoy checking out the showroom gallery, where you might see an immaculately detailed '57 Corvette or '67 Pontiac GTO. Tours are given on some Fridays—these cost $5 and last about 45 minutes (check the website for the schedule). ⊠ *164 E. Hill Ave., Millcreek* ☎ *801/262–3098* ⊕ *www. kindigit.com* ☉ *Closed weekends.*

★ Millcreek Canyon

NATIONAL/STATE PARK | Running parallel to and just north of Big Cottonwood Canyon, this lush mountain canyon east of Millcreek and the Salt Lake County Parks office and the U.S. Forest Service is a wonderful destination for hiking, picnicking, mountain and road-biking, and scenic drives. Certain trails are open to bikes only on odd- or even-numbered days, and dogs are welcome but can only be off-leash on odd-number days. There are about two-dozen well-maintained trails within the Millcreek Canyon system, ranging from quick scrambles to challenging 11-mile round-trip adventures, but even the short jaunts usually entail an elevation gain of at least 1,000 feet. Although accessible on foot year-round, the canyon closes to vehicles from November through around mid-June, depending on snowfall. ⊠ *3800 Millcreek Canyon Rd.* ☎ *801/733–2660* ⊕ *www. slco.org/parks* ⊠ *$5 per vehicle.*

Wheeler Historic Farm

FARM/RANCH | FAMILY | Now a 75-acre park and living history museum with numerous historic structures and a country store selling snacks, toys, and farm-related gifts, this verdant oasis and still-working farm on Little Cottonwood Creek in suburban Murray was settled in 1898 and is one of the only pioneer-era farmsteads left in the metro area. Activities here include cow-milking, observing the farm animals, tours of the impressive Victorian homestead (which is packed with farming implements and artifacts), and wagon rides and easy hikes on an extensive trail network. A farmers' market is held here on summer Sundays. There's no charge to walk around the property, but tours and various activities have small fees. ⊠ *6351 S. 900 E* ☎ *385/468–1755* ⊕ *www.slco. org/wheeler-farm* ☉ *Closed Sun.*

Restaurants

Angry Korean

$$ | KOREAN | With an irreverent name and somewhat remote suburban location in the District retail-dining center in South Jordan, this contemporary post-industrial space pulls in ardent fans of Korean food from points far and near. Once you've tucked into a plate of kalbi flame-grilled short ribs, beef bulgogi, or fusion-style garlic-ginger tacos with Asian slaw or a Korean fried shrimp po'boy slathered in house sweet-and-sour sauce, you'll

understand what all the fuss is about. **Known for:** spicy house-made kimchi; crab and pork belly steamed buns; refreshing Italian sodas in a variety of flavors. $ *Average main: $16* ⊠ *11587 District Main Dr., South Jordan* ☎ *801/307–8300* ⊘ *Closed Sun.*

Franck's

$$$$ | MODERN AMERICAN | Celebrated for its art-filled dining room and lushly tree-shaded terrace, this romantic spot occupies a converted house near the mouth of Big Cottonwood Canyon. The kitchen specializes in modern French and American fare, such as preserved-heirloom-tomato pie with cilantro aioli and toasted-parmesan sabayon, and Franck's signature meat loaf with whipped potatoes and a blueberry-lavender sauce. **Known for:** family-style platters that serve two to six people; well-chosen old-world wine list; carrot cake with cream cheese frosting and a marbled chocolate shell. $ *Average main: $31* ⊠ *6263 S. Holladay Blvd.* ☎ *801/274–6264* ⊕ *www. francksfood.com* ⊘ *Closed Sun. and Mon. No lunch.*

Layla Grill and Mezze

$$ | MEDITERRANEAN | Venture a few miles south from downtown to Holladay to enjoy savory Mediterranean dishes—with an emphasis on hearty Moroccan and Middle Eastern grills—in a crisp, contemporary dining space. Tangy spices enliven old-world favorites such as shawarma and moussaka, and not-so-common dishes like muhamarra (think hummus but with walnuts) may tempt you away from your comfort zone. **Known for:** combination mezze platters; Lebanese-influenced cocktails; Turkish coffee ice cream. $ *Average main: $19* ⊠ *4751 S. Holladay Blvd., Holladay* ☎ *801/272–9111* ⊕ *www.laylagrill.com.*

★ Log Haven

$$$$ | MODERN AMERICAN | This elegant 1920s mountain retreat brings inventive takes on American wild game–focused cuisine by incorporating Asian ingredients with a Rocky Mountain style—consider grilled bison steak with sweet potato orzo, duck breast with butternut squash puree and pomegranate syrup, and sake-marinated market fish with wood-ear mushrooms and shrimp dumplings. With its romantic setting in a beautifully renovated log home amid the pine trees, waterfalls, and wildflowers of Millcreek Canyon, this is definitely a restaurant to remember. **Known for:** breathtaking mountain views; inventive East meets West cuisine; chocolate flourless cake with raspberry sauce. $ *Average main: $35* ⊠ *6451 E. Millcreek Canyon Rd., Millcreek* ☎ *801/272–8255* ⊕ *www. log-haven.com* ⊘ *No lunch.*

Lone Star Taqueria

$ | MEXICAN | You can't miss this tiny lime green joint, marked by an old sticker-covered car off Fort Union Boulevard and often packed with skiers from the nearby Cottonwood canyons. The kitchen serves tasty, inexpensive Mexican food—including house special fish tacos, handmade tamales, burritos, and plenty of chilled Mexican beer. **Known for:** shrimp tacos with cilanto-jalapeño aioli; mammoth burritos; Mexican beers on tap. $ *Average main: $8* ⊠ *2265 E. Fort Union Blvd., Cottonwood* ☎ *801/944–2300* ⊕ *www. lstaq.com* ⊘ *Closed Sun.*

★ Provisions

$$ | MODERN AMERICAN | Renowned for its delicious weekend brunches and a bright and colorful dining room with a lively open kitchen, this modern American bistro with a focus on organic ingredients also turns out flavorful dinner fare. Brunch favorites include slow-roasted pork shoulder with poached eggs and wood-roasted blueberry pancakes, while homemade pappardelle with braised rabbit and smoked bacon stars among the dinner options. **Known for:** shareable, creative small plates; extensive list of artisan spirits; white chocolate–salted yuzu cheesecake. $ *Average main: $21* ⊠ *3364 S. 2300 E* ☎ *801/410–4046* ⊕ *www.slcprovisions. com* ⊘ *No lunch weekdays.*

Hotels

Castle Creek Inn

$$ | **B&B/INN** | Designed like a grand castle, complete with ornate medieval-inspired theme suites (all with jetted tubs and fireplaces), this striking B&B with pretty gardens is popular for celebrating romantic special occasions and being fairly close to skiing in Big and Little Cottonwood canyons. **Pros:** convenient to ski areas; distinctive architecture; extensive breakfast included. **Cons:** small in-room TVs; not suitable for kids; 20 minutes from downtown SLC. [$] *Rooms from: $159* ✉ *7391 Creek Rd., Cottonwood Heights* ☎ *801/567–9437* 🌐 *www.castlecreekbb.com* 🛏 *10 rooms* 🍴 *Free breakfast.*

Embassy Suites West Valley

$ | **HOTEL** | The West Valley offers some of the best values in metro Salt Lake City, and this modern property with two-room suites that sleep four to six guests offers terrific rates with plenty of perks, from evening receptions on weeknights to free parking and a large indoor pool and fitness center. **Pros:** spacious suites are great for families and groups; convenient to I–215; free breakfast and evening appetizers and drinks. **Cons:** no pets; on a busy road; 15- to 20-minute drive from downtown SLC. [$] *Rooms from: $109* ✉ *3524 S. Market St., West Valley City* ☎ *801/963–4760* 🌐 *www.hilton.com* 🛏 *162 rooms* 🍴 *Free breakfast.*

★ **Hyatt Place Salt Lake City–Cottonwood**

$$$ | **HOTEL** | This mid- to upscale pet-welcoming Hyatt mid-rise near the mouth of Big Cottonwood Canyon is a perfect roost for skiers and hikers but also a comfortable base for the metro area, with its access to I–215. **Pros:** outdoor pool and hot tub; nice views of Wasatch Range; convenient to I–215 and ski areas. **Cons:** pleasant but nondescript interior design; not many restaurants within walking distance; 20-minute drive from downtown SLC. [$] *Rooms from: $179* ✉ *3090 E. 6200 S* ☎ *801/890–1280* 🌐 *www.hyatt.com* 🛏 *124 rooms* 🍴 *Free breakfast.*

Residence Inn Murray

$$$ | **HOTEL** | With a central suburbs location near I–15, this bright, light-filled all-suites property is handy for families and groups and within striking distance of downtown, the ski areas, and Utah County to the south. **Pros:** good soundproofing; full kitchens in every room; convenient base location for entire SLC region. **Cons:** breakfast area can be a zoo on ski-season weekends; humdrum suburban setting; 15- to 20-minute drive to downtown SLC. [$] *Rooms from: $189* ✉ *171 E. 5300 S* ☎ *801/262–4200* 🌐 *www.marriott.com* 🛏 *136 rooms* 🍴 *Free breakfast.*

Nightlife

BARS AND LOUNGES

★ **Porcupine Pub and Grille**

BARS/PUBS | Above a ski- and board-rental shop at the mouth of Big and Little Cottonwood canyons, this lively pub offers a huge menu of hearty dishes, cocktails, and craft beers. Inside the large A-frame chalet-like building you'll find bright polished wood floors and trim, and a friendly vibe. There's a second popular location on Salt Lake City's East Side, near the University of Utah. ✉ *3698 E. Fort Union Blvd., Cottonwood Heights* ☎ *801/942–5555* 🌐 *www.porcupinepub.com.*

Prohibition

BARS/PUBS | Close to Fashion Place Mall, this speakeasy-style cocktail bar feels far more urbane than its suburban location, with its exposed-brick walls, leather booths, and offbeat artwork. Burlesque shows are part of the fun. ✉ *151 E. 6100 S, Murray* ☎ *801/281–4852* 🌐 *www.prohibitionutah.com.*

 Performing Arts

Off Broadway Theatre

THEATER | Musicals and plays, with a focus on sketch comedy, parody, and improv, are the bill of fare from this company that moved from downtown Salt Lake to Midvale Performing Arts Center in 2020. ⊠ *695 W. Center St., Midvale* ☎ *801/355-4628* ⊕ *www.theobt.org.*

USANA Amphitheater

CONCERTS | This 20,000-seat open-air venue in West Valley City brings in top pop, country, and rock acts throughout the warmer months. ⊠ *5150 Upper Ridge Rd., West Valley City* ☎ *801/417-5343* ⊕ *www.saltlakeamphitheater.com.*

 Shopping

SPORTSWEAR AND OUTDOOR GEAR

Backcountry.com

SPORTING GOODS | One of the country's top outdoor-equipment retailers, Backcountry has a small showroom and massive (200,000-square-foot) back room where you can shop or pick up products you've ordered online. Skiers, boarders, campers, and climbers all favor this place. ⊠ *2607 S. 3200 W, West Valley City* ☎ *800/409-4502* ⊕ *www.backcountry.com.*

L9 Sports

LOCAL SPORTS | The Millcreek branch of Utah's acclaimed ski and bike shop is convenient for adventures in the mountains east of town, including Alta, Snowbird, Brighton, and Solitude ski areas. ⊠ *2927 E. 3300 S, Millcreek* ☎ *801/466-9880* ⊕ *www.levelninesports.com.*

 Activities

GOLF

★ **Stonebridge Golf Club**

GOLF | One of the state's top public courses is just a five-minute drive from the airport and just 20 minutes from downtown. The links-style course, designed by Gene Bates

and Johnny Miller, offers 27 holes amid beautiful scenery. Water hazards come in the form of lakes and streams, and there are plenty of bunkers, but fairways are wide and generally quite forgiving. ⊠ *4415 Links Dr., West Valley City* ☎ *801/957-9000* ⊕ *www.golfstonebridgeutah.com* 🖃 *$46* ⚡ *18 holes, 7200 yards, par 36.*

ICE SKATING

★ **Utah Olympic Oval**

ICE SKATING | The stunning venue was built for the 2002 Winter Olympics and is the home of the U.S. speed skating team. Watch the world's best skaters in major competitions every winter. It's open to the public year-round for myriad activities, including skating, curling, and running on the 442-meter indoor track. ⊠ *5662 Cougar La., Kearns* ☎ *801/968-6825* ⊕ *www.utaholympiclegacy.org/oval.*

SOCCER

Real Salt Lake

SOCCER | Since 2005, Real Salt Lake has competed in Major League Soccer. The gleaming Rio Tinto Stadium also hosts concerts and other events. ⊠ *9256 S. State St., Sandy* ☎ *801/727-2700* ⊕ *www.rsl.com.*

Big Cottonwood Canyon

31 miles from Downtown Salt Lake City.

The history of mining and skiing in Utah often go hand in hand, and that's certainly true of Big Cottonwood Canyon, with its adjacent ski resorts of **Brighton** and **Solitude.** In the mid-1800s, 2,500 miners lived at the top of this canyon in a rowdy tent city. The old mining roads make great hiking, mountain-biking, and backcountry ski trails. Rock climbers congregate in the lower canyon for excellent sport and traditional climbing. Opened in 1936, Brighton is the second-oldest ski resort in Utah, and one of the oldest in North America. Just down the canyon, Solitude has undergone several incarnations since it opened in 1957, and has invested heavily in overnight accommodations and new base facilities in recent years. Among local ski areas, Big Cottonwood is quieter than Park City or neighboring Little Cottonwood Canyon, home of Alta and Snowbird resorts.

GETTING HERE AND AROUND

From downtown Salt Lake City it's a 40-minute drive to Big Cottonwood via I–80 and I–215, then Highway 190 E. Most downtown hotels offer free shuttles to the ski resorts, and Utah Transit Authority runs bus shuttles for $4.50 each way.

🍴 Restaurants

★ Yurt at Solitude

$$$$ | **MODERN AMERICAN** | One of the most memorable and dramatic restaurant experiences in the state, dining in this secluded yurt begins with a guided ¼-mile snowshoe trek beneath a canopy of nighttime stars, and the dinner price—$140 per person—includes rentals, guides, corkage fee, and a grand four-course meal. The seasonally driven menu changes regularly, and the Yurt's chef describes the meal as he prepares it before your eyes in the cozy exhibition kitchen. **Known for:** unique snowshoeing tour to dinner; rich steaks and seafoods; festive yet intimate dining space. [$] *Average main: $140* ✉ *12000 Big Cottonwood Canyon Rd., Building 15, Solitude* ☎ *801/536–5765* 🌐 *www.solitudemountain.com* ⏲ *Closed Mon., Tues., and in summer. No lunch.*

🛏 Hotels

★ The Inn at Solitude

$$$$ | **RESORT** | Enjoy ski-in ski-out convenience and VIP treatment at this well-appointed hotel with comfortable and spacious rooms and a slew of creature comforts, including an atmospheric bar, a lovely spa with a range of treatments, and an outdoor heated pool and hot tub. **Pros:** steps from lifts and ski village dining; outdoor heated pool and full-service spa; dazzling mountain views. **Cons:** social butterflies may find it a bit quiet; breakfast not included; no pets. [$] *Rooms from: $309* ✉ *12000 Big Cottonwood Canyon Rd., Solitude* ☎ *800/748–4754, 801/536–5500* 🌐 *www.solitudemountain.com* ⏲ *Closed May–mid-June and mid-Oct.–Nov.* 🛏 *46 rooms* 🍴 *No meals.*

Silver Fork Lodge

$$ | **B&B/INN** | Log furniture and wood paneling give the rooms in the cozy and rustic 1940s ski lodge just down the road from Solitude and Brighton a warm and inviting feel; the views are unbeatable and the food in the excellent restaurant is a major attraction year-round (you can dine on the patio in summer). **Pros:** popular on-site restaurant; full breakfast included; free shuttle to ski lifts. **Cons:** not ski-in, ski-out; no in-room phones or TVs; three-night minimum during ski season. [$] *Rooms from: $175* ✉ *11332 Big Cottonwood Canyon Rd.* ☎ *801/533–9977* 🌐 *www.silverforklodge.com* 🛏 *6 rooms, 1 suite* 🍴 *Free breakfast.*

🍸 Nightlife

Molly Green's

BARS/PUBS | Ski bums and snowboarders come together to tip back a few at this retro-fun 1950s watering hole in the A-frame at the base of Brighton Ski Resort. ✉ *8302 S. Brighton Loop Rd., Brighton* ☎ *801/532–4731* 🌐 *brightonresort.com/molly-greens* ⏲ *Call for hrs, May–Nov.*

🏃 Activities

BICYCLING

Solitude Mountain Resort

BICYCLING | Mountain bikers will love Solitude for its single-track trails that span 20 miles within Big Cottonwood Canyon as well as routes that connect neighboring canyons. Solitude Mountain Resort offers lift-served mountain biking with rentals available at Solitude Village on weekends from mid-to-late June to early October, weather permitting. ✉ *12000 Big*

Cottonwood Canyon Rd. ☎ 801/534–1400 ⊕ www.solitudemountain.com.

HIKING

★ Brighton Lakes Trail

HIKING/WALKING | The upper section of Big Cottonwood Canyon is a glacier-carved valley with many side drainages that lead to picturesque alpine lakes. In the Brighton area, you can access beautiful mountain lakes (Dog, Mary, Martha, and Catherine), about a 4½-mile round-trip jaunt. The elevation at Brighton's parking lot is 8,700 feet and the lakes are at 9,400 to 10,000 feet, so take it easy, rest often, drink plenty of water, and keep an eye on the weather no matter the season. This beautiful hike along the Brighton Lakes Trail eventually ascends to Catherine Pass. From here you can choose to descend into Little Cottonwood's Albion Basin near Alta (but remember, you'll need a car for the 45-minute ride back to Brighton), or return back along the Brighton Lakes Trail. ⊠ Mary Lake La. at S. Brighton Loop Rd., Brighton.

Lake Blanche Trail

HIKING/WALKING | This moderately challenging 7-mile round-trip trek leads to three stunning, glacially carved lakes, the largest of which is Lake Blanche—there's a beautiful waterfall, too. With an elevation gain of nearly 3,000 feet, this one will give you a pretty serious workout, but the scenery is amazing. The trailhead is just a 10-minute drive from Cottonwood Heights, less than midway before you get to Brighton. ⊠ Big Cottonwood Canyon Rd. ⊹ about 4½ miles from jct. with Hwy. 210.

SKIING

CROSS-COUNTRY

Solitude Nordic Center

SKIING/SNOWBOARDING | Accessible from Solitude and Brighton villages, the Solitude Nordic Center has 12 miles of groomed cross-country trails, 6 miles of snowshoe trails, and a small shop offering rentals, lessons, food, and guided tours. For $20 you can use the trails all day; for $75 you can get a private lesson,

rental, and all-day trail pass. ⊠ 12000 Big Cottonwood Canyon Rd. ☎ 801/534–1400 ⊕ www.solitudemountain.com.

DOWNHILL

Brighton Ski Resort

SKIING/SNOWBOARDING | The smallest of the Cottonwood resorts just outside Salt Lake City, Brighton is nonetheless a favorite among serious snowboarders, parents (who flock to the resort's ski school), and some extreme skiers and riders. There are no megaresort amenities here, just a nice mix of terrain for all abilities, and a basic lodge, ski shop, and ski school. The snow is as powdery and deep as nearby Alta and Snowbird, and advanced (and prepared) skiers can access extensive backcountry areas. There's something for everyone here at a fraction of the cost of the bigger resorts. ⊠ 8302 S. Brighton Loop Rd., Brighton ☎ 801/532–4731 ⊕ www.brightonresort. com ⊠ Lift tickets $104 ☞ 1,875-ft vertical drop; 1,050 skiable acres; 21% beginner, 40% intermediate, 39% advanced/expert; 4 high-speed quad chairs, 1 triple chair.

Solitude Mountain Resort

SKIING/SNOWBOARDING | Since 1957, Solitude has offered Big Cottonwood Canyon's most intense ski experience. It's now anchored by a European-style village with lodges, condominiums, an upscale hotel, and some good restaurants. Downhill skiing and snowboarding are still the main attractions, with steep, pristine terrain in Honeycomb Canyon attracting the experts, and a mix of intermediate cruising runs and beginner slopes beckoning the less accomplished. You can enjoy relaxing after a hard day on the slopes at the comfortable Solitude Mountain Spa. ⊠ 12000 Big Cottonwood Canyon Rd., Solitude ☎ 801/534–1400, 800/748–4754, 801/536–5777 snow report ⊕ www.solitudemountain.com ⊠ Lift tickets $125 ☞ 2,047-ft vertical drop; 1,200 skiable acres; 10% beginner, 40% intermediate, 50% advanced; 4 high-speed quad chairs, 2 quad chairs, 1 triple chair, 1 double chairs.

Alta, Utah, is a dramatic place to enjoy the slopes, or to take in the sights during the off-season.

Little Cottonwood Canyon

25 miles from Brighton and Solitude; 20 miles from Salt Lake City.

Skiers have been singing the praises of Little Cottonwood Canyon since 1938, when the Alta Lifts Company pieced together a ski lift using parts from an old mine tram to become the **Alta Ski Resort,** the second such area in North America. With its 550 inches per year of dry, light snow and unparalleled terrain, this canyon is legendary among diehard snow enthusiasts. A mile down the canyon from Alta, **Snowbird Ski and Summer Resort,** which opened in 1971, shares the same mythical snow and terrain quality—the two areas are connected via the Mineral Basin area. You can purchase an Alta Snowbird One Pass that allows you on the lifts at both areas, making this a huge skiing complex.

But skiing isn't all there is to do here. Dazzling mountain-biking and hiking trails access the higher reaches of the Wasatch-Cache National Forest, and the trails over Catherine Pass will put you at the head of Big Cottonwood Canyon at the Brighton Ski Area. Formed by the tireless path of an ancient glacier, Little Cottonwood Canyon cuts a swath through these pristine woodlands. Canyon walls are composed mostly of striated granite, and traditional climbing routes of varied difficulty abound. At Snowbird's base area, modern structures house accommodations, restaurants, and bars. The largest of these buildings, the Cliff Lodge, is an entire ski village under one roof. The resort mounts a variety of entertainment throughout the year, including pop and jazz concerts, and Oktoberfest in fall.

GETTING HERE AND AROUND

To get here, take I–80 East to I–215 South, then hop off the highway at Exit 6 and venture into Little Cottonwood Canyon, following signs for Alta and Snowbird. The canyon's dramatic topography invites very occasional avalanches that block the road, the only entrance and egress.

ESSENTIALS

VISITOR INFORMATION Alta Chamber & Visitors Bureau. ☎ *435/633–1394* 🌐 *www.discoveralta.com.*

🍴 Restaurants

★ Shallow Shaft

$$$$ | **MODERN AMERICAN** | For finely prepared steaks and game dishes—from braised beef ribs with mushroom butter to sea scallops with crispy pork belly—Alta's only sit-down restaurant not in a hotel is the place to go. The small interior is cozy, with a sandy color scheme and walls adorned with 19th-century mining tools found on the mountain. **Known for:** big windows overlooking the mountains; phenomenal wine selection; house-made, daily rotating ice creams. [$] *Average main: $41* ✉ *10199 E. Hwy. 210, Alta* ☎ *801/742–2177* 🌐 *www.shallowshaft.com* 🕓 *No lunch. Closed Apr.–Nov.*

Steak Pit

$$$$ | **STEAKHOUSE** | Views and food take precedence over interior design at Snowbird's oldest restaurant, with a menu full of well-prepared steak and seafood entrees, including opulent Wagyu New York strip steaks and 16-ounce lobster tails. The dining room is warm and unpretentious, with some wood paneling and an expanse of glass. **Known for:** exceptional steaks with rich sauces; a number of high-ticket bottles on the extensive wine list; signature mud pie dessert. [$] *Average main: $44* ✉ *Snowbird Plaza Center, Level 1, Snowbird* ☎ *801/933–2222* 🌐 *www.snowbird.com* 🕓 *No lunch.*

Swen's

$$$$ | **MODERN AMERICAN** | With its sleek, contemporary vibe, warm lighting and wood accents, open kitchen, and floor-to-ceiling windows overlooking the fantastic ski terrain, this upscale restaurant in the ritzy Snowpine Lodge is Alta's trendiest dining destination. The kitchen takes a farm-to-table approach to its hearty but creative mountain fare, with standout dishes like a warm truffled goat cheese dip with chives and house-made potato chips, and a succulent peppercorn-crusted rib-eye steak with mashed potatoes and merlot-braised mushrooms. **Known for:** breathaking mountain views; thin-crust pizzas; impressive wine list. [$] *Average main: $32* ✉ *10420 E. Hwy. 210, Alta* ☎ *801/742–2000* 🌐 *www.snowpine.com.*

🛏 Hotels

Alta Lodge

$$$$ | **B&B/INN** | Many families have been booking the same week each year for several generations at this low-key 1939 lodge that's home to the famed Sitzmark Club bar as well as saunas and hot pools to help you work out the kinks after a day on the slopes. **Pros:** steps from lift to Alta's steep slopes; magnificent Wasatch Mountain views; breakfast and dinner included during ski season. **Cons:** not many amenities for the price; no TVs in guest rooms; 4-night minimum stay in high ski season. [$] *Rooms from: $410* ✉ *10230 E. Hwy. 210, Alta* ☎ *801/742–3500, 800/707–2582* 🌐 *www.altalodge.com* 🕓 *Closed mid-Apr.–May and early Oct.–mid-Nov.* 🛏 *53 rooms* 🍴 *All-inclusive.*

Alta's Rustler Lodge

$$$$ | **HOTEL** | Alta's sleekest lodge is a contemporary, full-service hotel with warmly decorated guestrooms and seating areas. **Pros:** plush full-service spa; adjacent to Alta's ski lifts; superb, unpretentious service. **Cons:** avalanches are rare, but you could get snowed in; pricey, especially for a family; 5-night minimum stay during ski season. [$] *Rooms from: $525* ✉ *10380 E. Hwy. 210, Alta* ☎ *801/742–4200* 🌐 *www.rustlerlodge.com* 🕓 *Closed late Apr.–mid-Nov.* 🛏 *89 rooms* 🍴 *All-inclusive.*

Cliff Lodge

$$$$ | **RESORT** | The stark concrete walls of this 10-story structure, designed to complement the surrounding granite cliffs, enclose a self-contained ski-in, ski-out village with restaurants, bars, shops, and a high-end, two-story spa. **Pros:** central Snowbird ski village location; nice rooftop spa; several eateries and bars on-site. **Cons:** stark, monolithic design isn't to every taste; furnishings are a bit dated; huge property that can feel impersonal. [$] *Rooms from: $510* ✉ *9320 Cliff Lodge Dr., Snowbird* ☎ *801/933–2222, 888/205–7322* 🌐 *www.thecliffl odgeandspasnowbird.com* 🛏 *511 rooms* 🍴 *No meals.*

★ **Snowpine Lodge**

$$$$ | **RESORT** | The level of luxury, and the lofty prices to go with it, that's commonplace in Park City finally arrived in Alta in 2019 with the opening of this ultra-posh slopeside retreat built using timber and stone from the original lodge on the site, and featuring a glamorous full-service spa with a heated outdoor pool, a swanky restaurant and hip gastropub, and stylishly kitted rooms and suites, many with mountain-view balconies. **Pros:** just steps from ski lifts; excellent on-site restaurants; gorgeous full-service spa. **Cons:** multi-night minimum stay during busy times; some might find it a bit glitzy for laid-back Alta; steep rates. [$] *Rooms from: $485* ✉ *10420 E. Hwy. 210, Alta* ☎ *801/742–2000* 🌐 *www.snowpine.com* 🛏 *63 rooms* 🍴 *No meals.*

Nightlife

★ **Gulch Pub**

BARS/PUBS | The handsome gastropub in Alta's swanky new Snowpine Lodge has big windows and an inviting terrace overlooking the slopes and plush leather seats and rustic stone columns. Upscale but easy-going, it's a terrific spot for a glass of wine or local IPA, and light dining on tasty bar fare, such as kale Caesar salads, pickle-brined fried chicken, and New Haven–style white clam pizza. ✉ *10420 E. Hwy. 210, Alta* ☎ *801/742–2000* 🌐 *www.snowpine.com.*

Tram Club

BARS/PUBS | Windows looking into the gears of the Snowbird tram give the Tram Club its name. Swank leather couches, live music, pool tables, big screens, and video games draw a lively crowd. ✉ *Hwy. 210, Snowbird* ☎ *801/933–2222* 🌐 *www.snowbird.com.*

Activities

HIKING

★ **Sunset Peak**

HIKING/WALKING | The trailhead for the 4-mile out-and-back hike to Sunset Peak starts high in Little Cottonwood Canyon, above Alta Ski Resort, in Albion Basin. This is a popular area for finding wildflowers in July and August. After an initial steep incline, the trail wanders through flat meadows before it climbs again to Catherine Pass at 10,240 feet. From here intermediate hikes continue along the ridge in both directions. Continue up the trail to the summit of Sunset Peak for breathtaking views of the Heber Valley, Park City, Mount Timpanogos, Big and Little Cottonwood Canyons, and even a part of the Salt Lake Valley. You can alter your route by starting in Little Cottonwood Canyon and ending your hike in neighboring Big Cottonwood Canyon, by following the Catherine Pass as it descends along the Brighton Lakes Trail to Brighton Ski Resort (from which it's a nearly an hour's drive back to Alta). ✉ *Cecret Lake/Catherine Pass Trailhead, Albion Basin Rd., Alta.*

White Pine Trailhead

HIKING/WALKING | **FAMILY** | White Pine Trailhead, ¾ mile below Snowbird on the south side of the road, runs alongside gurgling Little Cottonwood Creek and accesses some excellent easy hikes to overlooks with great opportunities for spotting wildlife. If you want to keep going on more intermediate trails, continue up the trail to the lakes in White Pine Canyon, Red Pine

Canyon, and Maybird Gulch. All of these hikes share a common path for the first mile. ✉ *Hwy. 210, Snowbird.*

SKIING

★ Alta Ski Area

SKIING/SNOWBOARDING | Alta Ski Area has perhaps the best snow anywhere in the world—an average of nearly 550 inches a year, and terrain to match it. Alta is one of the few resorts left in the country that doesn't allow snowboarding. Sprawling across two large basins, Albion and Wildcat, Alta has a good mixture of expert and intermediate terrain, but relatively few beginner runs. Much of the best skiing (for advanced or expert skiers) requires either finding obscure traverses or doing some hiking. It takes some time to get to know this mountain so if you can find a local to show you around you'll be ahead of the game. Albion Basin's lower slopes have a terrific expanse of novice and lower-intermediate terrain. Rolling meadows, wide trails, and light dry snow create one of the best places in the country for less-skilled skiers to learn to ski powder. Two-hour lessons start at $80. In addition to downhill skiing, Alta also has 3 km of groomed track for skating and classic skiing (on a separate ticket), plus a good selection of rental equipment. ✉ *10230 Hwy. 210, Alta* ☎ *801/359–1078, 801/572–3939 snow report* ⊕ *www.alta.com* 🎟 *Lift tickets $125* ☞ *2,020-ft vertical drop; 2,200 skiable acres; 15% novice, 30% intermediate, 55% advanced; 3 high-speed quads, 1 triple chairs, 2 double chairs, 5 surface tows.*

★ Snowbird Resort

SKIING/SNOWBOARDING | For many skiers, this is as close to heaven as you can get. Soar aboard Snowbird's signature 125-passenger tram straight from the base to the resort's highest point, 11,000 feet above sea level, and then descend into a playground of powder-filled chutes, bowls, and meadows—a leg-burning top-to-bottom run of more than 3,000 vertical feet if you choose. The terrain here is weighted more toward experts—35% of Snowbird is rated black diamond—and if

there is a drawback to this resort, it's a lack of beginner terrain. The open bowls, such as Little Cloud and Regulator Johnson, are challenging; the Upper Cirque and the Gad Chutes are hair-raising. On deep-powder days—not uncommon at the Bird—these chutes are exhilarating for skiers who like that sense of a cushioned free fall with every turn. With a nod to intermediate skiers, Snowbird opened North America's first skier tunnel in 2006. Skiers and boarders now ride a 600-foot magic carpet through the Peruvian Tunnel, reducing the trek to Mineral Basin. If you're looking for intermediate cruising runs, there's the long, meandering Chip's Run. After a day of powder turns, you can lounge on the 3,000-square-foot deck of Creekside Lodge at the base of Gad Valley. Beginner's lessons start at $120 and include lift ticket, tuition, and rentals. ✉ *Hwy. 210, Snowbird* ☎ *801/933–2222, 801/933–2100 snow report* ⊕ *www. snowbird.com* 🎟 *Lift tickets $130* ☞ *3,240-ft vertical drop; 2,500 skiable acres; 27% novice, 38% intermediate, 35% advanced; 125-passenger tram, 4 quad lifts, 6 double chairs, 1 gondola, and a skier tunnel with surface lift.*

SKI TOURS

Ski Utah Interconnect Adventure Tour

SKIING/SNOWBOARDING | Strong intermediate and advanced skiers can hook up with the Ski Utah Interconnect Adventure Tour for a guided alpine ski tour that takes you to as many as six resorts (including Brighton, Solitude, Alta, and Snowbird) in a single day, all connected by backcountry ski routes with unparalleled views of the Wasatch Mountains. Guides test your ski ability before departure. The tour includes guide service, lift tickets, lunch, and transportation back to the point of origin. You'll even walk away with a finisher's pin. The Deer Valley Departure Tour operates Sunday, Monday, Tuesday, Wednesday, and Friday; the Snowbird Departure Tour operates Thursday and Saturday. Reservations are required. ☎ *801/534–1907* ⊕ *www. skiutah.com* 🎟 *From $430.*

Chapter 4

PARK CITY AND THE SOUTHERN WASATCH

Updated by
Jenie Skoy

◉ Sights	🍴 Restaurants	🛏 Hotels	👜 Shopping	🍸 Nightlife
★★★★★	★★★★★	★★★★★	★★★★★	★★★★☆

WELCOME TO PARK CITY AND THE SOUTHERN WASATCH

TOP REASONS TO GO

★ **Outdoor fun:** Regardless of the season, Park City is the epicenter of mountain adventure.

★ **Two top-tier resorts:** No place in North America has two world-class and distinct resorts so close to one another, not to mention as expansive, dynamic, luxurious, and unique as Deer Valley and Park City Mountain Resort.

★ **Olympic spirit:** This town seems to contain more Olympians per capita than any town in the country, if not the world.

★ **Old Town Park City:** First laid out by silver miners in the late 1800s, Park City's historic Main Street is especially lively during big events like the Sundance Film Festival and Kimball Arts Festival.

★ **Sundance Resort:** At the base of Mount Timpanogos, Robert Redford's intimate resort pays homage to art and nature.

1 Park City and the Wasatch Back. With a high desert climate, you'll smell both sagebrush and pine in this alpine outback. There are rivers, streams, and lakes to fish from and thousands of trails to hike and mountain bike.

2 Heber Valley. This valley is what Salt Lake Valley probably looked like 50 years ago. It's still fairly pristine and with an agricultural and small town vibe. A winding river runs through the verdant valley on the west side and horses still clop down the side streets. People come here for the golfing, fishing, and recreational opportunities near Kamas and in the Uinta mountains. Close by is Midway, a Swiss-like village built on the west side where you can find pampered stays at European-like resorts and a dairy farm where you can get ice cream.

3 Sundance Resort. Robert Redford bought and preserved this swath of paradise under the snowy head of Mount Timpanogos and shares it with the public. The Provo River is also a famous blue-ribbon fly-fishing destination.

4 Provo. A youthful college town that's equally devoted to their raucous Freedom Festival in July and their fall football season at Brigham Young University (BYU). Be sure to wear blue on game days. The town is home to a gorgeous art museum on the campus of BYU as well as many orchard stands that run along the eastern edge near Provo Canyon. Provo Canyon is a great place to go tubing or have a picnic while you watch Bridal Veil Falls cascade down the cliffs.

5 American Fork. At the foot of the Wasatch Range, American Fork (named after the river) is a base from which you can access the Timpanogos Cave National Monument and the Alpine Loop Scenic byway.

6 Lehi. A quaint pioneer town on the west side of the valley, Lehi has an operational historic roller mill (*Footloose* was filmed here) and Porter's Place, a restaurant named after one of Lehi's first residents, a famous pistol-packing bodyguard named Porter Rockwell. Thanksgiving Point is here, too, with its extensive flower gardens, farmers' and artisan markets, and restaurants. In the fall, it's a great place to enjoy a local harvest festival with pumpkins, doughnuts, and hot apple cider.

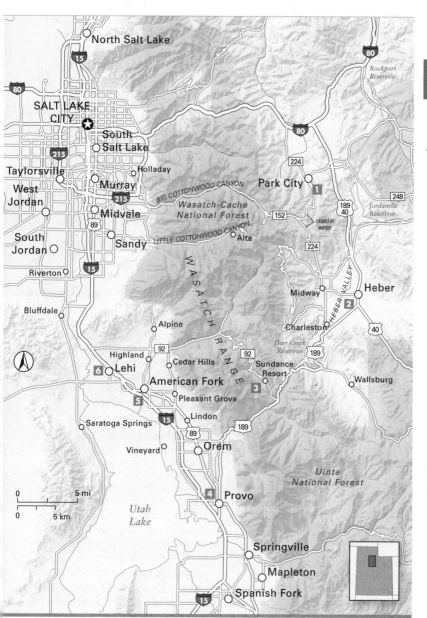

North Salt Lake

15

80

Rockport
Reservoir

80

SALT LAKE
CITY

215

South
Salt Lake

Holladay

224

Park City　1

189
40

248

Jordanelle
Reservoir

Taylorsville

Murray

215

BIG COTTONWOOD CANYON

Wasatch-Cache
National Forest

152

closed in
winter

West
Jordan

Midvale

89

LITTLE COTTONWOOD CANYON　Alta

224

South
Jordan

Sandy

Riverton

15

W
A
S
A
T
C
H

Midway

HEBER VALLEY

Heber
2

Bluffdale

Alpine

R
A
N
G
E

Charleston

40

189

Deer Creek
Reservoir

Highland

92

Cedar Hills

92

Sundance
Resort

Lehi
6

American Fork
3

Wallsburg

5

Pleasant Grove

Saratoga Springs

15

Lindon

89

189

Vineyard

Orem

Uinta
National Forest

0　　5 mi

0　　5 km

Utah
Lake

4　Provo

Springville

Mapleton

15

Spanish Fork

The Wasatch Range shares the same desert climate as the Great Basin, which it rims, but these craggy peaks rise to more than 11,000 feet, and stall storms moving in from the Pacific causing massive precipitations. The 160-mile stretch of verdure is home to 2 million people, or three-fourths of all Utahns. Although its landscape is crisscrossed by freeways and dappled by towns large and small, the Wasatch still beckons adventurers with its alpine forests and windswept canyons.

Where three geologically distinct regions—the Rocky Mountains, the Colorado Plateau, and the Basin and Range provinces—converge, the Wasatch Range combines characteristics of each. You'll find broad glacial canyons with towering granite walls, stream-cut gorges through purple, tan, and green shale, and red-rock bluffs and valleys.

Most people associate Park City with its legendary skiing in winter, but this is truly a year-round destination. Bright-blue lakes afford fantastic boating and water sports, and some of the West's best trout streams flow from the high country. Add miles of hiking and biking trails and you have a vacation that's hard to beat.

You can also find cultural activities and entertainment at every turn. The Sundance Film Festival, hosted by Sundance Institute (which was founded

by actor-director Robert Redford), attracts movie stars and independent filmmakers from all over. Major recording artists of all types play indoor and outdoor venues, and nightlife abounds in the city and resorts, with an increasing number of nightclubs and music venues.

MAJOR REGIONS

Park City and the Wasatch Back. This is the hospitality heart of the mountains, and you'll be spending a good deal of your time in Park City whatever your budget. There's everything from fine dining on Main Street to athlete training and shows at Utah Olympic Park to nonstop year-round activity at the resorts. Mountain valleys north and south of Park City are home to stunning wildlife.

South of Salt Lake City. It's worth venturing south to the glorious Sundance Resort for a slice of rural Utah. Even farther south, Provo, home to Brigham Young University, counters Park City's "Sin City" reputation with an overwhelming Mormon temperance.

Planning

When to Go

Winter is long in the mountains (ski resorts buzz from November to mid-April) but much more manageable in the valleys. The snow stops falling in April or May, and a month later the temperatures are in the 80s. In spring and fall, rates drop and crowds lessen. Late spring is also a good time for fishing, rafting on rivers swollen with snowmelt, birding, and wildlife viewing. In summer, water-sports enthusiasts of all stripes flock to the region's reservoirs, alpine lakes, rivers, and streams. The Wasatch Mountains draw those seeking respite from the heat of the valley from June through Labor Day. Fall's colors rival those of New England; a tradition here is to drive along the Alpine Loop east of Provo or up Pine Canyon out of the Heber Valley.

Planning Your Time

At your home base in Park City you can ski, snowboard, hike, mountain bike, or simply take in the scenery at local resorts. Head east to Heber City or Midway for golfing at Wasatch State Park, swimming in the Homestead Crater, horseback riding, or fly-fishing on the meandering Provo River. Plan at least a half-day trip to Sundance Resort and a hike on the foothills of Mt. Timpanogos. For a glimpse of Utah's Mormon culture, spend a day in the college town of Provo, catch a Brigham Young University football game, and follow with a scoop of ice cream at the BYU Creamery. Warm-weather drives on the Alpine Loop or Mirror Lake scenic byways offer alpine

breezes, views of golden aspens, and snow-peaked mountains.

Getting Here and Around

AIR
Commercial air traffic flies in and out of Salt Lake International Airport, which is less than an hour from all destinations in the Wasatch and 7 miles northwest of downtown Salt Lake City. The airport is served by Alaska, American, Delta, Southwest, jetBlue, Frontier, United, Air Canada, and KLM. Provo Airport has commercial flights from Los Angeles, Oakland, San Diego, and Mesa, Arizona, on Allegiant Airlines. Heber's airport is open to private planes only.

CONTACTS Salt Lake City International Airport. ✉ *776 N. Terminal Dr., Salt Lake City* ☎ *801/575–2400* ⊕ *www.slcairport.com.*

CAR
Highway travel around the region is quick and easy. The major routes in the area include the transcontinental I–80, which connects Salt Lake City and Park City; and U.S. 40/189, which connects southwest Wyoming, Utah, and northwest Colorado via Park City, Heber City, and Provo. Along larger highways, roadside stops with restrooms, fast-food restaurants, and sundries stores are well spaced. Scenic routes and lookout points are clearly marked, enabling you to slow down and pull over to take in the views. Off the main highways, roads range from well-paved multilane blacktop routes to barely graveled backcountry trails. Watch out for wildlife on the roads just about anywhere in Utah.

ROAD CONDITIONS Utah Highway Patrol; Wasatch, Summit and Rich Counties. ✉ *10420 No. Jordanelle Blvd., Heber* ☎ *435/655–3445* ⊕ *highwaypatrol.utah. gov.* **Utah Road Condition Information.** ☎ *511 Salt Lake City area, 866/511–8824 within Utah* ⊕ *www.udot.utah.gov.*

SHUTTLE

Shuttles are the best way to travel between the airport and Park City, and fares start at $39 per person one way. A free, efficient Park City transit system operates a reliable network of bus routes, connecting Old Town, the local ski resorts, Kimball Junction, and most neighborhoods.

SHUTTLE CONTACTS Canyon Transportation. ☎ 801/255–1841 ⊕ www.canyontransport.com. **Park City Direct Shuttle.** ☎ 866/655–3010 toll-free, 435/655–3010 ⊕ www.parkcitydirectshuttle.com.

Restaurants

American cuisine dominates the Wasatch dining scene, with great steaks, barbecue, and traditional Western fare. There's also an abundance of good seafood, which the busier eateries fly in daily from the west coast. Restaurants range from Swiss to Japanese, French, and Mexican. Hours vary seasonally, so it's a good idea to call ahead. Reservations are essential during winter holiday weekends and the Sundance Film Festival. Park City restaurants offer great deals, such as two-for-one entrées from spring to fall, so check the local newspaper for coupons or ask your concierge which eateries are offering discounts. *Restaurant reviews have been shortened. For full information, visit Fodors.com.*

Hotels

Chain hotels and motels dot I–15 all along the Wasatch Front and nearly always have availability. Every small town on the back side of the range has at least one good bed-and-breakfast, and most towns have both independent and chain motels. Condominiums dominate Park City lodging, but you also find high-end hotels, luxurious lodges, and well-run bed-and-breakfast inns. All this luxury means prices here tend to be higher than in other areas in the state during the winter. Prices drop significantly in the warmer months, when package deals or special rates are offered. Lodging in Provo tends to be most expensive during the week. Make reservations well in advance for busy ski holidays like Christmas, Presidents' Day, and Martin Luther King Jr. Day, and during January's Sundance Film Festival. As the mountain country is often on the cool side, lodgings at higher elevations generally don't have air-conditioning. *Hotel reviews have been shortened. For full information, visit Fodors.com.*

What it Costs			
$	$$	$$$	$$$$
RESTAURANTS			
under $16	$16–$22	$23–$30	over $30
HOTELS			
under $125	$125–$175	$176–$225	over $225

Campgrounds

There are a number of wonderful campgrounds across the Wasatch–Cache National Forest. Between Big and Little Cottonwood canyons there are four higher-elevation sites. In the vicinity of Provo, American Fork, Provo Canyon, and the Hobble Creek drainage, there are dozens of possibilities. Additional campgrounds are at the region's state parks and national monuments.

Sites range from rustic (pit toilets and cold running water) to posh (hot showers, swimming pools, paved trailer pads, full hookups). Fees vary from $6 to $20 a night for tents and up to $50 for RVs, but are usually waived once the water is turned off for the winter. Site reservations are accepted at most campgrounds, but are usually limited to seven days (early birds reserve up to a year in advance). Campers who prefer a more remote setting may camp in the vast National Forest Service and Bureau of Land Management backcountry. You might need a permit, which is available from park visitor centers and ranger stations.

Visitor Information

CONTACTS Park City Convention and Visitors Bureau. ✉ *1850 Sidewinder Dr., #320, Park City* ☎ *800/453–1360* ⊕ *www.visitparkcity.com.* **Ski Utah.** ✉ *2749 E. Parleys Way, Suite 310, Salt Lake City* ☎ *801/534–1779, 800/754–8824* ⊕ *www.skiutah.com.* **Utah Valley Convention and Visitors Bureau.** ✉ *220 W. Center St., Suite 100, Provo* ☎ *801/851–2100, 800/222–8824* ⊕ *www.utahvalley.com.*

Park City and the Wasatch Back

The best-known areas of the Wasatch Mountains lie east of Salt Lake City. Up and over Parley's Canyon via I–80 you'll find the sophisticated mountain town of Park City, with its world-class ski resorts and myriad summer attractions.

After silver was discovered in Park City in 1868, it quickly became a rip-roaring mining town with more than two-dozen saloons and a thriving red-light district. In the process, it earned the nickname "Sin City." A fire destroyed many of the town's buildings in 1898; this, combined with declining mining fortunes in the early 1900s, caused most of the residents to pack up and leave. It wasn't until 1946 that its current livelihood began to take shape in the form of the small Snow Park ski hill, which opened where Deer Valley Resort now sits.

Park City once again profited from the generosity of the mountains as skiing became popular. In 1963 Treasure

Mountain Resort began operations with its skier's subway—an underground train and hoist system that ferried skiers to the mountain's summit via old mining tunnels. Facilities were upgraded over time, and Treasure Mountain became the Park City Mountain Resort. Although it has a mind-numbing collection of condominiums, at Park City's heart is a historic downtown that rings with the authenticity of a real town with real roots.

GETTING HERE AND AROUND
If you're arriving via Salt Lake City, a rental car or shuttle bus will get you to Park City in about 35 minutes. Park City has a free transit system running between neighborhoods and to the ski resorts. It operates from roughly 6 am to midnight in summer and winter. The schedule is more limited in fall and spring, so be sure to check schedules at the Transit Center on Swede Alley or on the buses.

Old Town is walkable, but the rest of greater Park City is best explored by bicycle in the spring, summer, and fall. More than 400 miles of bike trails help Park City earn accolades as one of the top cycling communities in the world, including the designation of Gold Level Ride Center by International Mountain Biking Association. Automobile traffic is relatively minimal and limited to slowdowns during morning and evening commutes and the post-ski exodus from the resorts. There are several local taxi businesses.

ESSENTIALS
VISITOR INFORMATION Park City Visitor Information Center. ✉ *1794 Olympic Pkwy., Kimball Junction* ☎ *435/649–6100* ⊕ *www.visitparkcity.com* ✉ *Park City Museum, 528 Main St., Park City* ☎ *435/649–7457.*

FESTIVALS
Robert Redford's Sundance Film Festival comes to Park City every January, but the city hosts a number of other festivals

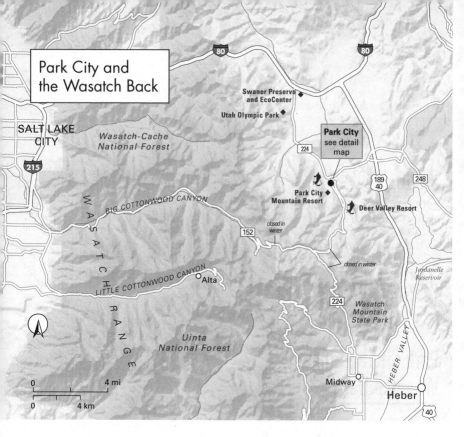

Park City and
the Wasatch Back

SALT LAKE CITY

Wasatch-Cache
National Forest

Swaner Preserve
and EcoCenter

Utah Olympic Park

Park City
see detail
map

Park City
Mountain Resort

Deer Valley Resort

BIG COTTONWOOD CANYON

WASATCH RANGE

LITTLE COTTONWOOD CANYON

Alta

closed in winter

closed in winter

Joydanelle Reservoir

Uinta
National Forest

Wasatch
Mountain
State Park

HEBER VALLEY

Midway

Heber

0   4 mi
0   4 km

and events that might sway your decision about when to visit.

Canyons Village Summer Concert Series
CONCERTS | FAMILY | Rock, reggae, funk, and country bands draw fans of all ages to Park City Mountain Resort's village stage at Canyons Village in July and August. Food vendors and family activities surround the Resort Village, and picnics are welcome. ⊠ 4000 Canyons Resort Dr., Park City ☎ 435/649–8111 ⊕ www.parkcitymountain.com.

★ **Deer Valley Snow Park Amphitheater**
CONCERTS | Everything from Utah Symphony performances to country music features on stage. Big name stars like Willie Nelson, Bonnie Raitt, Chris Isaak, and Judy Collins have graced the outdoor amphitheater, which sits on the resort's beginner ski area. ■TIP→ Go on Wednesday evenings for free concerts with local

and regional bands and pack a picnic.
⊠ Park City ☎ 435/649–1000 ⊕ www.deervalley.com.

Independence Day Celebration
FESTIVALS | FAMILY | A traditional freedom celebration, complete with a pancake breakfast, parade down Main Street, and all-day activities in City Park, is a sure sign summer has arrived. The day culminates in fireworks that illuminate the sky over Old Town. ⊠ Park City ☎ 435/649–6100 ⊕ www.visitparkcity.com.

Miner's Day
FESTIVALS | FAMILY | The end of the summer season is heralded with an old-fashioned parade down Main Street and the Rotary Club's "Running of the Balls"— with golf balls in place of Pamplona-style bulls—followed by miners' competitions of mucking and drilling at Library Park. This Labor Day tradition is a Park City

favorite. ✉ *Park City* ☎ *435/649–6100* ⊕ *www.visitparkcity.com.*

Park City Food & Wine Classic

FESTIVALS | Held in early July, this festival allows diners and wine-enthusiasts to sample from wineries, distilleries, and breweries from all over the world and to taste delicious fare from the region's best restaurants. Educational seminars are offered and the festival culminates in a grand tasting at Montage Deer Valley. ■**TIP**➔ **It's increasingly popular, and many events now sell out in advance, so plan ahead.** ✉ *Park City* ☎ *877/328–2783.*

★ Park City Kimball Arts Festival

ARTS FESTIVALS | Celebrating visual and culinary art, this three-day festival, held the first weekend in August, is the biggest summer event in town. More than 200 artists from all over North America exhibit and offer their work to 40,000 festival attendees. Culinary vendors and beer and wine gardens offer plenty of refreshment to art lovers, and live music is around every corner. ✉ *Main St., Park City* ☎ *435/649–8882* ⊕ *www.parkcity-kimballartsfestival.org.*

Savor the Summit

FESTIVALS | When more than 25 of Park City's restaurants—both gourmet and casual dining—take over Main Street on the Saturday nearest the Summer Solstice in June, it's a spectacle of food, drink, and music unrivaled in the country. Restaurateurs line the length of Main Street with a mile-long "Grande Table," creating the largest dinner party you'll witness in Utah. Pick one restaurant (many sell out) and be treated to a special menu, often with a theme related to Park City's colorful history. Visit the website for participating restaurants and reservation information. ✉ *Main St., Park City* ☎ *435/640–7921* ⊕ *www.parkcityrestaurants.com/savor-the-summit.*

★ Sundance Film Festival

FESTIVALS | For 10 days each January, movie stars, film executives, and independent film lovers gather in a mountain setting for the Sundance Film Festival, hosted by Robert Redford's Sundance Institute. It's a chance to view the screenings of new, risk-taking documentaries, features, and other creative film projects from around the globe. Moviegoers can also participate in Q&A conversations with filmmakers, producers, and creatives after screenings. Participants can add their names to a waiting list even if shows are sold out. The festival is held at many venues in Park City, Sundance, Ogden, and in downtown Salt Lake City, and there are music and culinary events as well.

■**TIP**➔ **Book your hotel months in advance. Skip the rental car and use the free shuttle. Park City's legendary ski slopes empty out while the filmgoers attend the screenings, so build in a day of crowd-free skiing.** ✉ *Park City* ☎ *435/658–3456* ⊕ *www.sundance.org/festival.*

 ## Sights

Park City and the surrounding area hosted the lion's share of skiing and sliding events during the 2002 Winter Olympic Games, and the excited spirit of the Games is still evident around town. Visitors often enjoy activities at the Utah Olympic Park or simply taking candid photos at various memorable sports venues.

The city also serves as an excellent base camp for summer activities. Hiking trails are plentiful. A scenic drive over Guardsman Pass is now mostly paved and passable for most vehicles, providing incredible mountain vistas. There are top-rated golf courses, hot-air ballooning is popular, and mountain bikers find the ski slopes and old mining roads truly exceptional pedaling. With so much to offer both summer and winter visitors, dozens of hotels of all levels have sprung up to complement the three resorts, each with its own scene.

Both Park City ski resorts consistently earn high skier-snowboarder rankings. Whereas Park City Mountain Resort is known for its central location, superb family amenities, and gnarly parks and pipes for snowboarders and free skiers, Deer Valley is in a peaceful spot at the edge of town and is renowned for its creature comforts—and its prohibition on snowboarding. A city-run free shuttle-bus system serves the resorts.

Kimball Art Center

MUSEUM | A thriving nonprofit community art center, this venue hosts national and regional exhibitions, sells art supplies, provides educational opportunities including seminars and art classes for all ages, and hosts special events. ⊠ 1401 Kearns Blvd., Park City ☎ 435/649–8882 ⊕ www. kimballartcenter.org ✉ Free.

Park City Farmers Market

MARKET | Held rain or shine each Wednesday from June through October, the Farmers Market is always a good spot to pick up locally sourced bread, fruits and vegetables, flowers, and more. ⊠ Canyons Village, 4000 Canyons Resort Dr., Park City ☎ 435/671–1455 ⊕ parkcityfarmersmarket.com.

Park City Mountain Resort

AMUSEMENT PARK/WATER PARK | FAMILY | In the warmer months, the resort transforms itself into a mountain amusement park, with attractions such as the Alpine Slide, ziplines, Alpine Coaster, and a climbing wall. Visitors take a chairlift up the mountain to the Alpine Slide, then hop aboard special sleds that carry them down 3,000 feet of winding concrete and fiberglass track at speeds controlled by each rider. Two ziplines offer a high-flying adrenaline rush as riders strap into a harness suspended from a cable. The gravity-propelled Alpine Coaster (which operates year-round) zooms through aspen-lined twists and turns at speeds up to 35 mph. There's also a climbing wall, miniature golf course, trampolines, an adventure zone for younger children,

and some of the West's best lift-served mountain biking and hiking. ⊠ 1345 Lowell Ave., Park City ☎ 435/649–8111, 800/222–7275 ⊕ www.parkcitymountain. com.

Park City Museum

JAIL | A must-see for history buffs, this museum is housed in the former library, city hall, and the Bell Tower on Main Street. With a two-story scale model of the 19th-century Ontario Mine, a 20th-century gondola hanging overhead, and the old jail below, this is an authentic tribute to Park City's mining and skiing past. Climb aboard a re-created Union Pacific train car, hold on to a quivering and noisy jack drill for a feel of the mining experience, and, if you dare, step inside a jail cell. Tours of historic Main Street also depart from here. ⊠ 528 Main St., Park City ☎ 435/649–7457 ⊕ www.parkcityhistory.org ✉ $12.

Park Silly Sunday Market

MARKET | A funky and constantly changing assortment of artisans, entertainers, and culinary vendors transform Old Town into a street festival complete with beer garden and Bloody Mary bar on Sunday, June through September. The Silly Market strives to be a no-waste event with everything recycled or composted. Look for the free bike valet to park your ride while you walk through the crowds. ⊠ Lower Main St., Park City ☎ 435/714–4036 ⊕ www.parksillysundaymarket. com.

Swaner Preserve and EcoCenter

NATURE PRESERVE | Home to more than 100 migratory and native birds (most notably sandhill cranes) and small critters (like the spotted frog), as well as foxes, deer, elk, moose, and coyotes, this 1,200-acre preserve is both a bird-watchers' paradise and an example of land restoration in action. Naturalist-led walks, snowshoe tours in winter, and other events are hosted here throughout the year. The EcoCenter is filled with interactive exhibits, such as a climbing wall

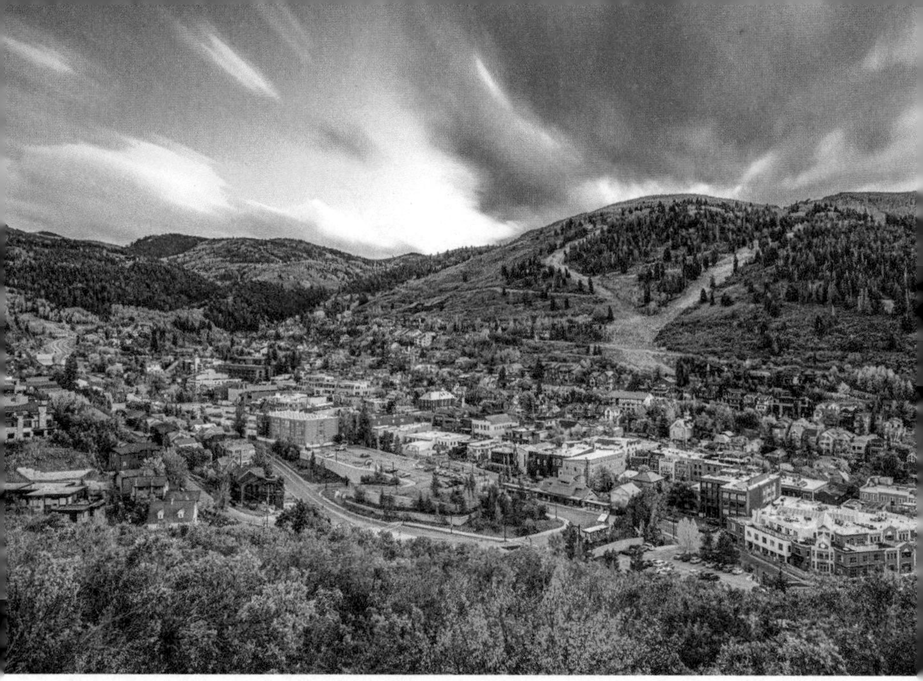

Park City has been known since its mining heyday as Utah's "Sin City."

with microphones emitting the sounds of the wetlands as climbers move through habitats. The facility serves as an exhibit in itself, given its eco-friendly construction, incorporating everything from recycled denim insulation to solar panels. More than 10 miles of hiking and biking trails and 15 wetland ponds give visitors a great place to unwind and get away from the urban life. ✉ *1258 Center Dr., Newpark* ☎ *435/649–1767* 🌐 *www.swanerecocenter.org* 🎟 *Free (donation appreciated)* 🕒 *Closed Mon. and Tues.*

★ Utah Olympic Park

MUSEUM | **FAMILY** | An exciting legacy of the 2002 Winter Olympics, this is a mecca of bobsled, skeleton, luge, and ski jumping. As it is one of the only places in America where you can try these sports, you might have to wait your turn behind U.S. Olympians and aspirants who train here year-round. In summer or winter, screaming down the track in a bobsled at nearly 80 mph with a professional driver is a ride you will never forget. In summer, check out the freestyle ski jumpers doing flips and spins into a splash pool and Nordic jumpers soaring to soft landings on a synthetic outrun. Ride the ziplines or Alpine Slide, or explore the adventure course. There's also an interactive ski museum and an exhibit on the Olympics; guided tours are offered year-round, or you can take a self-guided tour. ✉ *3419 Olympic Pkwy., Park City* ☎ *435/658–4200* 🌐 *www.utaholympiclegacy.com* 🎟 *Museum and self-guided tours free, guided tours $13.*

🍴 Restaurants

Adolph's Restaurant

$$$ | **SWISS** | The Swiss Alps meet Park City at this beloved stomping ground of longtime locals and athletes from around the globe. Chef Adolph Imboden's food is European, with strong ties to his Alpine roots. **Known for:** Swiss fondue; escargots; rack of lamb; European-inspired ambience. [$] *Average main: $30* ✉ *1500 Kearns Blvd., Park City* ☎ *435/649–7177* 🌐 *www.adolphsrestaurant.com.*

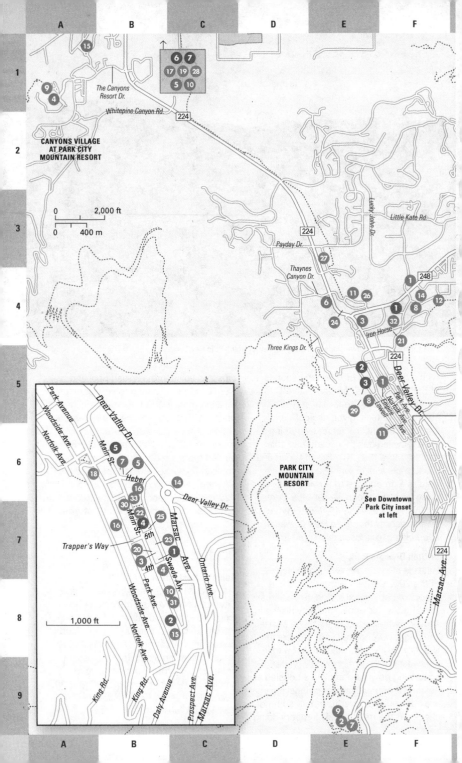

Park City

Sights ▼

1 Kimball Art Center **F4**
2 Park City
   Farmers Market.......... **E5**
3 Park City
   Mountain Resort......... **E5**
4 Park City Museum **B7**
5 Park Silly
   Sunday Market.......... **B6**
6 Swaner Preserve and
   EcoCenter **C1**
7 Utah Olympic Park....... **C1**

Restaurants ▼

1 Adolph's Restaurant..... **F4**
2 Apex...................... **E9**
3 Café Terigo **B7**
4 Chimayo.................. **B7**
5 Coal & Lumber **B6**
6 Deer Valley
   Grocery Cafe **H6**
7 Deer Valley's
   Empire Lodge
   Fireside Dining **E9**
8 El Chubasco **F4**
9 The Farm................. **A1**
10 Firewood................. **C8**
11 Five5eeds................. **E4**
12 Freshies Lobster Co..... **F4**
13 Glitretind Restaurant ... **G9**
14 Good Karma **F4**
15 Grappa **C8**
16 Handle **B6**
17 Hearth & Hill............. **C1**
18 High West Distillery **A6**
19 Maxwell's
   East Coast Eatery........ **C1**
20 Purple Sage **B7**
21 Ritual Cafe &
   Chocolate Factory....... **F4**
22 Riverhorse on Main **B7**
23 Shabu **B7**
24 Squatters Roadhouse
   Grill & Pub **E4**
25 Tupelo **B7**
26 Twisted Fern............. **E4**
27 Versante
   Hearth + Bar............. **E3**
28 Vessel Kitchen **C1**
29 The Viking Yurt **E5**
30 Wahso **B7**
31 Wasatch Brew Pub...... **C8**
32 Windy Ridge Café........ **F4**
33 Yuki Yama Sushi......... **B6**

Quick Bites ▼

1 Java Cow
   Cafe & Bakery............ **C7**
2 Riverhorse Provisions... **C8**

Hotels ▼

1 Chateau Après **F5**
2 The Chateaux
   Deer Valley **G8**
3 DoubleTree by
   Hilton Park City–
   The Yarrow **E4**
4 Grand Summit
   Resort Hotel **A1**
5 Holiday Inn
   Express & Suites......... **C1**
6 Hotel Park City,
   Autograph Collection.... **E4**
7 Main & SKY.............. **B6**
8 Marriott MountainSide
   Resort **E5**
9 Montage Deer Valley.... **E9**
10 Newpark Resort,
   A Destination Hotel...... **C1**
11 Old Town
   Guest House.............. **F6**
12 The St. Regis
   Deer Valley **H7**
13 Stein Eriksen Lodge **G9**
14 Torchlight Inn............. **C6**
15 Waldorf Astoria
   Park City **A1**
16 Washington
   School House **B7**

KEY

1 *Exploring Sights*
1 *Restaurants*
1 *Quick Bites*
1 *Hotels*

Apex

$$$$ | STEAKHOUSE | Suitably named as this restaurant is the highest year-round restaurant in Park City, Apex is also at the top of its class for dining and service. The restaurant is within Montage Deer Valley, and at dinner transforms into a mountain steak house. **Known for:** steak; superior service. $ *Average main: $50* ⊠ *9100 Marsac Ave., Park City* ☎ *435/604–1402* ⊕ *www.montagedeervalley.com.*

Café Terigo

$$$ | ITALIAN | This Main Street staple has delighted guests for more than 25 years with a modern Italian menu in an airy café with the best patio in town. The restaurant serves well-prepared pasta and seafood dishes using only fresh ingredients for lunch and dinner. **Known for:** traditional bolognese; hearty salads; alfresco dining. $ *Average main: $30* ⊠ *424 Main St., Park City* ☎ *435/645–9555* ⊕ *www.cafeterigo.com* ⊙ *Call for seasonal hrs.*

★ Chimayo

$$$$ | SOUTHWESTERN | Chef Arturo Flores will delight you with tantalizing dishes such as duck breast enchiladas, tortilla soup (his grandmother's recipe), a giant ahi tuna taco, or his melt-off-the-bone spareribs in this upscale Southwestern restaurant. Order a house-made margarita (try the serrano margarita for an extra kick) and enjoy the cozy and intimate feel of this popular restaurant. **Known for:** upscale southwestern fare; margaritas; friendly staff. $ *Average main: $40* ⊠ *368 Main St., Park City* ☎ *435/649–6222* ⊕ *www.chimayorestaurant.com* ⊙ *Call for seasonal hrs.*

★ Deer Valley's Empire Lodge Fireside Dining

$$$$ | EUROPEAN | After a day of playing in the snow, Empire Lodge's Fireside Dining is the perfect way to warm up by dining in a timber-framed lodge around several stone fireplaces. You'll feel like a medieval lord as you go from fireplace to fireplace to be served hearty fare like veal stew, elk, or a slice of perfectly roasted lamb cooked over a spit. **Known for:** dining around the fire; decadent dining options; lengthy meals. $ *Average main: $90* ⊠ *9200 Marsac Ave. #306, Park City.*

Deer Valley Grocery Cafe

$ | AMERICAN | FAMILY | An extension of the ski resort's famous culinary offerings, this gourmet grocery/café serves breakfast, lunch, and early dinner and features menu items ranging from the famous Deer Valley turkey chili, to shrimp tacos, to a chicken tandoori wrap, and everything in between. The expansive outdoor deck provides waterfront al fresco dining (the only place in Park City) and views of the ski resort. **Known for:** waterfront dining; high-quality ingredients; fast-casual atmosphere. $ *Average main: $10* ⊠ *1375 Deer Valley Dr., Park City* ☎ *435/615–2400* ⊕ *www.deervalley.com.*

★ El Chubasco

$ | MEXICAN | For quick and hearty traditional Mexican food, this popular place is perfect. Favorites are *camarones a la diabla* (spicy shrimp), chiles rellenos, and fish tacos. **Known for:** extensive salsa bar; fast-casual dining. $ *Average main: $10* ⊠ *1890 Bonanza Dr., Park City* ☎ *435/645–9114* ⊕ *www.elchubascomexicangrill.com.*

★ The Farm

$$$ | MODERN AMERICAN | The team at The Farm relentlessly seeks new, fresh, and unique ingredients to infuse into memorable meals in the restaurant's open kitchen. Seasonal menus always spotlight items from regional sustainable farmers, including root vegetables, truffles, berries, and meat. **Known for:** charcuterie board; fresh ingredients; cozy atmosphere. $ *Average main: $30* ⊠ *Canyons Village, 4000 Canyons Resort Dr., Park City* ☎ *435/615–8080* ⊕ *www.canyonsresort.com* ⊙ *Call for seasonal hrs.*

★ Firewood

$$$$ | **AMERICAN** | At this warm establishment, dishes are cooked over an open flame, and antique leather chairs look out onto the open kitchen. Self-described as "heirloom American," the seasonal, locally sourced menu changes frequently. **Known for:** open-fire cooking; locally sourced menu; downstairs bar. [$] *Average main: $36* ✉ *306 Main St., Main Street* ☎ *435/252–9900* 🌐 *firewoodonmain.com* 🕒 *Call for seasonal closures.*

★ Five5eeds

$ | **CONTEMPORARY** | This breakfast and lunch hotspot offers up nourishing dishes that look and taste like works of art. The restaurant manages to pull in flavors from all over the globe while using Utah-sourced ingredients with an Aussie twist, a nod to the owners' roots. **Known for:** iced coffee with ice cream; breakfast served all day. [$] *Average main: $14* ✉ *1600 Snow Park Dr., #EF, Park City* ☎ *435/901–8242* 🕒 *No dinner.*

★ Freshies Lobster Co

$$ | **SEAFOOD** | It may seem a bit out of place, but Freshie's Lobster Co started as a food truck by East Coast natives, and became so popular in the mountains of Utah that a brick-and-mortar location opened in 2016. Lobsters are flown in fresh daily, and the lobster roll is now nationally recognized as the "World's Best Lobster Roll" after taking home the win at a competition in Portland, Maine, in 2017. **Known for:** lobster rolls; casual atmosphere. [$] *Average main: $20* ✉ *1897 Prospector Ave., Prospector* ☎ *435/631–9861* 🌐 *www.freshieslobsterco.com.*

Glitretind Restaurant

$$$$ | **MODERN AMERICAN** | Beloved Chef Zane Holmquist is the culinary king behind the restaurants within the Stein Eriksen collection. Holmquist's inventive and soulful dishes are as much of a staple here as the wood trim, crisp white linens, crystal glasses, and fresh-cut flowers. **Known for:** private wine seminars and tastings; excellent wine pairings; Sunday brunch. [$] *Average main: $40* ✉ *7700 Stein Way, Deer Valley* ☎ *435/645–6455* 🌐 *www.steinlodge.com/dining.*

Good Karma

$$ | **INDIAN** | This Indo-Persian restaurant is a nice break from the New American found all over town, and you'll immediately feel at home in the intimate, comfortable dining room where chef-owner Houman Gohary personally greets guests. Open for breakfast, lunch, and dinner, locals love the house-made lamb curry and the tandoori shrimp vindaloo. **Known for:** house-made curries; vegetarian and gluten-free friendly; welcoming and friendly atmosphere. [$] *Average main: $20* ✉ *1782 Prospector Ave., Prospector* ☎ *435/313–6986.*

Grappa

$$$$ | **ITALIAN** | This restaurant specializes in regional Italian cuisine. Heavy floor tiles, rustic bricks, and exposed timbers lend a warm, rustic farmhouse feel. **Known for:** ambience; osso bucco; wine list. [$] *Average main: $40* ✉ *151 Main St., Main Street* ☎ *435/645–0636* 🌐 *www.grapparestaurant.com* 🕒 *No lunch.*

Handle

$$$ | **AMERICAN** | Handle was voted Best Restaurant in Park City in 2017 thanks to chef Briar Handly's inventive American dishes. Small plates make it easy to try everything, and you'll want to with dishes like buffalo cauliflower, smoked trout sausage, and the chef's famous fried chicken. **Known for:** chef's fried chicken; creative cocktails; $10 burger Wednesday (during off-season). [$] *Average main: $30* ✉ *136 Heber Ave., Old Town* ☎ *435/602–1155* 🌐 *www.handleparkcity.com* 🕒 *Call for seasonal closures.*

★ Hearth & Hill

$$$$ | **AMERICAN** | Started in 2017 by Brooks Kirchheimer who returned to his Park City hometown, Hearth and Hill—though not in the sexiest neighborhood—has quickly become a hangout for locals

in search of comfort food and community. Built with floor-to-ceiling windows inside a modernized industrial space, the restaurant has plenty of elbow room, and the natural lighting and white-tiled open kitchen give the place a distinctive communal vibe. **Known for:** dog-friendly patio; chef-driven menu; inventive cuisine. [$] *Average main: $35* ✉ *1153 Center Drive, Newpark Retail Center, Park City* ✣ *Between Jupiter Bowl and Best Buy* ☎ *435/200–8840* 🌐 *hearth-hill.com.*

★ High West Distillery

$$ | **AMERICAN** | Touted as the only ski-in, ski-out distillery in the world, High West Saloon sits at the base of the Park City Mountain's Town Lift, serving an eclectically Western, locally focused menu that changes seasonally, and delicious handcrafted cocktails using the distillery's own whiskey and vodka. The family-friendly restaurant and bar, housed in a historical home and livery, is a favorite among locals and visitors alike. **Known for:** whiskey; handcrafted cocktails; lively atmosphere. [$] *Average main: $21* ✉ *703 Park Ave., Old Town* ☎ *435/649–8300* 🌐 *www.highwest.com.*

Maxwell's East Coast Eatery

$$ | **PIZZA** | **FAMILY** | Located between the Swaner Preserve and a swath of shops, this casual eatery is popular with locals and welcomes the late-night crowd. Nearly 2 feet in diameter, the Fat Kid "pie" will remind you of Brooklyn or the Bronx—grab a slice of the "Goodfella" veggie pizza or the "Italian Stallion" meat-lovers version. **Known for:** east coast-style pizza; sports bar; family-friendly. [$] *Average main: $21* ✉ *1456 Newpark Blvd., Newpark* ☎ *435/647–0304* 🌐 *www.maxwellsparkcity.com.*

Purple Sage

$$$ | **AMERICAN** | Plenty of purple-hue touches—velvet upholstered booths, hand-painted scrims, and Western murals—brighten the 1898 brick building that was once the local telegraph office. "Fancy cowboy" cuisine includes such dishes as grilled veal meat loaf with poblano peppers and pine nuts or the lime-grilled black tiger shrimp. In summer, eat on the back deck under the charming bistro lights. **Known for:** Western fare; meat loaf; intimate dining. [$] *Average main: $30* ✉ *434 Main St., Main Street* ☎ *435/655–9505* 🌐 *www.purplesageparkcity.com* 🕓 *Call for seasonal hrs.*

★ Ritual Cafe & Chocolate Factory

$ | **AMERICAN** | **FAMILY** | Experience a rush of senses when you visit this fixture in Park City's culinary scene opened in 2015 by Robbie Stour and Anna Davies. Smell just-baked brownies with toasted Peruvian cocoa nibs and watch through an observation window as cocoa beans go into the factory's roll mill as a thick gritty paste then come out smooth and flaky. **Known for:** sustainability; observation window; sipping chocolate. [$] *Average main: $15* ✉ *1105 Iron Horse, Park City* ☎ *435/200–8475* 🌐 *www.ritualchocolate.com.*

★ Riverhorse on Main

$$$$ | **AMERICAN** | With two warehouse loft rooms, exposed wood beams, sleek furnishings, and original art,this award-winning restaurant feels like a big-city supper club where chef-owner Seth Adams pairs imaginative fresh food with a world-class wine list in this elegant—but ski-town relaxed—atmosphere. The menu changes seasonally, but look out for the braised buffalo short rib, pan-roasted tomahawk pork, or signature macadamia-nut-crusted Alaskan halibut. **Known for:** Alaskan halibut; vegan and gluten-free friendly; Sunday brunch. [$] *Average main: $42* ✉ *540 Main St., Park City* ☎ *435/649–3536* 🌐 *www.riverhorseparkcity.com* 🕓 *No lunch Mon.–Sat.*

Shabu

$$$$ | **ASIAN** | The wagyu hot rock, volcano sushi roll (tuna, wasabi, pineapple, jalapeño, and cilantro) and shabu shabu, a Japanese hot pot, are all favorites at this trendy eatery. Go for a Ginger Snap

sake martini (saketini) in the red-hued dining room. **Known for:** excellent sushi; wagyu hot rock; trendy spot. $ *Average main: $33* ✉ *442 Main St., Main Street* ☎ *435/645–7253* ⊕ *www.shabuparkcity. com* ⊗ *Call for seasonal hrs.*

Squatters Roadhouse Grill & Pub

$ | **AMERICAN** | **FAMILY** | If you are looking for a place to grab a burger and delicious craft beer while your kids enjoy house-made mac-and-cheese, Squatters is the spot. With a sleek and bustling brewpub vibe, it's a great place for both an evening out and a stop by after a spin on your mountain bike to enjoy truffle fries and share a pint of Pale Ale. **Known for:** local favorite; one of the largest craft breweries in Utah; open all day. $ *Average main: $14* ✉ *1900 Park Ave., Park City* ☎ *435/649–9868* ⊕ *www.squatters.com.*

Tupelo

$$$$ | **AMERICAN** | Southern comfort dishes with a sophisticated twist are lovingly crafted at this ambitious restaurant started by veteran Park City Chef Matt Harris, formerly at J&G Grill and the St. Regis Bar. An ambience of soft lighting, exposed brick, warm wood, and soft, modern furnishings will help you feel right at home. **Known for:** southern comfort food; chicken and waffles; Sunday brunch. $ *Average main: $50* ✉ *508 Main St., Park City* ☎ *435 /615–7700* ⊕ *tupeloparkcity.com.*

Twisted Fern

$$ | **MODERN AMERICAN** | The brainchild of chef/owner Adam Ross, this hot spot serves comfort food such as pork chops, cheesy short-rib sandwiches, and Utah trout hash. Dedicated to locally sourced and seasonal fare, Twisted Fern offers lunch, après-ski, and dinner daily. **Known for:** welcoming atmosphere; friendly staff; local food. $ *Average main: $21* ✉ *1300 Snow Creek Dr., Suite RS, Park City* ☎ *435/731–8238* ⊕ *www.twisted-fern.com.*

Versante Hearth + Bar

$$ | **AMERICAN** | Located in the newly remodeled Park City Peaks Hotel, Versante opened in January of 2017 and quickly became a favorite among locals. The welcoming, casual atmosphere paired with menu favorites such as flatbread pizzas, hearty pastas, and specialty cocktails is hard to beat. **Known for:** flatbread pizzas; welcoming atmosphere. $ *Average main: $18* ✉ *2346 Park Ave., Park City* ☎ *435/649–5000* ⊗ *No lunch.*

Vessel Kitchen

$ | **FAST FOOD** | In a part of town where fast-food reigns, Vessel Kitchen has a sustainable and healthy menu without sacrificing the fast-casual environment and reasonable prices. Here, you'll find hearty grain bowls, proteins such as braised beef and pork confit, and seasonal vegetables for sides. **Known for:** healthy dining; hearty grain bowls; fast-casual dining. $ *Average main: $12* ✉ *1784 Uinta Way, #1E, Kimball Junction* ☎ *435/200–8864* ⊕ *www.vesselkitchen. com.*

The Viking Yurt

$$$$ | **EUROPEAN** | Don your Scandinavian sweater for a brisk sleigh ride (pulled by a snow-cat rather than reindeer) through wintery pines up to this Nordic hut, built in a mountainous enclave in Park City Mountain Resort. After a hot cup of glogg, tuck into a European-style feast, featuring six hearty courses which might feature braised short ribs, lobster soup, and a traditional cheese course. **Known for:** unique dining experience; traditional Nordic cuisine. $ *Average main: $140* ✉ *1345 Lowell Ave., Old Town* ☎ *435/615–9878* ⊕ *www.thevikingyurt. com* ⊗ *Closed Apr.–Nov.*

Wahso

$$$$ | **ASIAN** | This restaurant instantly transports you to Shanghai in the 1930s, with art deco decor and Asian artifacts from around the world. Start your evening with a sake martini shaken table-side, then ask your server about starters

that span the continent, from steamed Chinese buns to *tom kha gai*, a delicious chicken-and-lemongrass soup from Thailand. **Known for:** warm atmosphere; steamed Chinese buns; attentive service. [$] *Average main: $41* ✉ *577 Main St., Main Street* ☎ *435/615–0300* 🌐 *www.wahso.com* 🕓 *Call for seasonal hrs.*

Wasatch Brew Pub

$$ | **AMERICAN** | **FAMILY** | It's hard to believe it's been more than 30 years since Wasatch became Park City's first brewery in the post-Prohibition era. At the top of Main Street, this pub stays on top of its game with celebrated beers and down-to-earth yet elevated pub food. **Known for:** local craft beer; outdoor dining in summer; elevated pub food. [$] *Average main: $18* ✉ *250 Main St., Park City* ☎ *435/645–0900* 🌐 *www.wasatchbeers.com.*

Windy Ridge Café

$$ | **AMERICAN** | **FAMILY** | Don't overlook Windy Ridge because of its industrial park neighborhood, the dining room is warm and inviting and the baked goods are delicious. Lighter appetites might fancy the homemade chicken noodle soup and a Southwest salad, or if you've spent the day skiing or biking, tackle the meat loaf or a rack of smoked ribs. **Known for:** comfort food; warm atmosphere; Taco Tuesdays. [$] *Average main: $20* ✉ *1250 Iron Horse Dr., Prospector* ☎ *435/647–0880* 🌐 *www.windyridgecafe.com.*

Yuki Yama Sushi

$$ | **SUSHI** | The name means "snow mountain" in Japanese, and the menu has a whirling blend of sushi, sashimi, and maki, as well as hot entrées, including noodle dishes. Observe sushi-making theatrics at the bar while they prepare the 84060 roll in homage to the local zip code, or retreat to the sunken seating of the tatami room. **Known for:** fresh sushi; sake; lively atmosphere. [$] *Average main: $18* ✉ *586 Main St., Main Street* ☎ *435/649–6293* 🌐 *www.yukiyamasushi.com* 🕓 *Check for seasonal closures.*

Coffee and Quick Bites

Java Cow Cafe & Bakery

$ | **DELI** | **FAMILY** | Java Cow has long been a staple on Main Street. Stop in for a panini, a caffeine pick-me-up, or delicious ice cream to satisfy your sweet tooth. **Known for:** excellent coffee; house-made ice cream; quick breakfast or lunch spot. [$] *Average main: $10* ✉ *402 Main St., Main Street.*

Riverhorse Provisions

$ | **CAFÉ** | A casual sister to Riverhorse on Main (with the same award-winning chef behind it), Riverhorse Provisions is a café, specialty market, and deli all in one. Come here for one of the few breakfasts served on Main Street, or stop in on your way to an outdoor concert and pick up a signature picnic basket filled with fried chicken, cornbread and peach cobbler, or a chilled lobster salad. **Known for:** signature picnic baskets; gourmet market; café-style fare. [$] *Average main: $12* ✉ *221 Main St., Main Street* ☎ *435/649–0799* 🌐 *www.riverhorseprovisions.com.*

Hotels

Chateau Après

$$ | **B&B/INN** | In one of the most expensive ski towns around, this reasonably priced classic skiers' lodge is a throwback to bygone ski days. **Pros:** comfortable rooms; close to the slopes; longtime local owners. **Cons:** basic accommodations. [$] *Rooms from: $145* ✉ *1299 Norfolk Ave., Park City* ☎ *435/649–9372, 800/357–3556* 🌐 *www.chateauapres.com* 🛏 *32 rooms* 🍴 *Free breakfast.*

The Chateaux Deer Valley

$$$$ | **HOTEL** | **FAMILY** | Just steps away from the Deer Valley lifts at Silver Lake Village, this modern interpretation of a luxury European château incorporates designer furnishings, heated towel racks, full kitchens in suites, gas fireplaces, and numerous windows with spectacular mountain views. **Pros:** luxury digs without

stuffy atmosphere; great Italian dining at Cena; rooms can accommodate any family size. **Cons:** too far from Old Town to walk; evenings are quiet. *[$] Rooms from: $448 ✉ 7815 Royal St. E, Park City ☎ 435/658–9500, 877/288–2978 🌐 www.the-chateaux.com 🛏 160 rooms 🍴 No meals.*

Doubletree by Hilton Park City - The Yarrow
$$$$ | **HOTEL** | Guests love its central location with easy access to Park City's ski resorts and to historic Main Street with its many upscale and casual restaurants, shopping options, and even a cinema close by. **Pros:** clean, basic rooms; rates suit cost-conscious tourists; easy access to all Park City has to offer. **Cons:** location has no charm; traffic during peak season; confusing layout. *[$] Rooms from: $239 ✉ 1800 Park Ave., Park City ☎ 435/649–7000, 800/927–7694 🌐 www.doubletree3.hilton.com 🛏 173 rooms, 8 suites 🍴 No meals.*

Grand Summit Resort Hotel
$$$$ | **RESORT** | **FAMILY** | Located in the heart of Canyons Village, the hotel is just steps from a heated chairlift and golf course, making lodgings here ideal year-round. **Pros:** luxury accommodations; countless activities; on-site spa. **Cons:** very large, can sometimes feel cavernous; expensive daily resort fee; no nightlife on property. *[$] Rooms from: $368 ✉ 4000 Canyons Resort Dr., Park City ☎ 435/615–8040 front desk, 888/226–9667 reservations 🌐 www.parkcitymountain.com 🛏 375 units 🍴 No meals.*

Holiday Inn Express & Suites
$ | **HOTEL** | Just off the main Park City exit near I–80, this chain hotel has a mountain-lodge feel. **Pros:** affordable; walking distance to shops and restaurants; continental breakfast included. **Cons:** you'll need a car or to take free public bus to get to the resorts; close to interstate; rooms are small. *[$] Rooms from: $122 ✉ 1501 W. Ute Blvd., Park City ☎ 435/658–1600, 877/662–6241 🌐 www.holidayinn.com 🛏 73 rooms 🍴 Free breakfast.*

Hotel Park City, Autograph Collection
$$$$ | **HOTEL** | On the Park City golf course, this all-suites hotel is built in the tradition of the grand old stone-and-timber lodges of the West. **Pros:** close to town and the ski hills; grand lodge-style rooms with views; on 18-hole golf course. **Cons:** rooms are expensive; must drive to restaurants and resorts; long outdoor walk to some of the rooms. *[$] Rooms from: $569 ✉ 2001 Park Ave., Park City ☎ 435/200–2000 🌐 www.hotelparkcity.com 🛏 100 suites 🍴 No meals.*

Main & SKY
$$$$ | **HOTEL** | Smack in the middle of Old Town, this contemporary hotel blends chic modern design with a mountain feel. **Pros:** prime location; large, luxurious rooms; great views. **Cons:** location on Main Street means no escaping the action; large suites mean expensive rates; pricey valet parking. *[$] Rooms from: $650 ✉ 201 Heber Ave., Park City ☎ 435/658–2500 🌐 www.skyparkcity.com 🛏 33 suites 🍴 No meals.*

Marriott MountainSide Resort
$$$$ | **HOTEL** | Watch skiers go by from the heated outdoor pool at this hotel near the lifts in arguably the most ideal location at Park City Base Area, offering traditional rooms and one- and two-bedroom suites. **Pros:** ski-in, ski-out convenience; heated outdoor pool and hot tubs; helpful, pleasant staff. **Cons:** busy and somewhat congested area; rooms are plain; no great dining nearby. *[$] Rooms from: $400 ✉ 1305 Lowell Ave., Park City ☎ 435/940–2000, 800/845–5279 🌐 www.marriott.com 🛏 365 rooms 🍴 No meals.*

★ **Montage Deer Valley**
$$$$ | **RESORT** | Montage is nestled into Empire Pass at 9,000 feet above the sea like a jewel atop Park City's alpine crown. **Pros:** exquisite location with beautiful views; top-level dining; ample amenities and activities on-site. **Cons:** remote

location; car or shuttle required to get to Main Street; can feel cavernous at times. $ *Rooms from: $805 ⊠ 9100 Marsac Ave., Park City ☎ 435/604–1300 ⊕ www.montagedeervalley.com ⇌ 88 rooms, 66 suites ⦿ No meals.*

Newpark Resort, A Destination Hotel

$$$ | HOTEL | At Newpark you'll find a busy shopping and dining scene on one side, and a gorgeous nature preserve on the other. **Pros:** comfortable suites; affordable rates; within walking distance of shops and restaurants. **Cons:** a drive to ski resorts and Main Street; location is in congested area; not all rooms have views. $ *Rooms from: $180 ⊠ 1476 Newpark Blvd., Newpark ☎ 435/649–3600, 877/649–3600 ⊕ www.newparkresort.com ⇌ 126 rooms, 24 townhomes ⦿ No meals.*

★ Old Town Guest House

$$ | B&B/INN | Listed on the National Register of Historic Places, this four-room inn, steps from the slopes and trails, is warm and cozy with its country style and lodgepole-pine furniture. **Pros:** walking distance to Park City Base Area and Main Street; hearty mountain breakfast and afternoon snacks included; year-round hot tub. **Cons:** rooms are small; only one suite can accommodate more than two people; strict cancellation policy. $ *Rooms from: $169 ⊠ 1011 Empire Ave., Park City ☎ 435/649–2642, 800/290–6423 ⊕ www.oldtownguesthouse.com ⇌ 4 rooms ⦿ Free breakfast.*

★ The St. Regis Deer Valley

$$$$ | RESORT | A 90-second ride up the funicular will take you to one of the most luxurious hotels at any alpine resort. **Pros:** glitz, glam, and butlers; ski-in, ski-out convenience; award-winning dining on property. **Cons:** additional restaurants are a drive away; layout is confusing, easy to get lost inside; après is popular with locals, get there early. $ *Rooms from: $946 ⊠ 2300 Deer Valley Dr. E, Park City ☎ 435/940–5700, 866/932–7059 ⊕ www.marriott.com ⇌ 115 rooms, 66 suites ⦿ No meals.*

★ Stein Eriksen Lodge

$$$$ | RESORT | As enchanting as it gets for a slope-side retreat, this lodge is as perfectly groomed, timelessly gracious, and uniquely charming as its namesake founder, the winner of an Olympic Gold Medal in 1952. **Pros:** award-winning dining on property; service is impeccable and exemplary; only five-star-rated spa in Utah. **Cons:** isolated location means a drive to Main Street and Park City; rooms require a walk outside, which can be cold in the winter; the high-altitude location (8,000-plus feet) can be difficult for some. $ *Rooms from: $900 ⊠ 7700 Stein Way, Park City ☎ 435/649–3700, 800/453–1302 ⊕ www.steinlodge.com ⇌ 180 rooms ⦿ No meals.*

Torchlight Inn

$$$$ | B&B/INN | This bed-and-breakfast inn offers a nice mix of contemporary and traditional style and incredible views from its rooftop deck and hot tub. **Pros:** rooms are spacious; delicious and personal breakfast; one block from Main Street and a short drive to the slopes. **Cons:** location is near a loud congested traffic circle; no a/c; limited parking. $ *Rooms from: $361 ⊠ 255 Deer Valley Dr., Park City ☎ 435/612–0345 ⊕ www.torchlight-inn.com ⇌ 6 rooms ⦿ Free breakfast.*

★ Waldorf Astoria Park City

$$$$ | RESORT | A sweeping staircase, Baccarat crystal chandelier, and 300-year-old marble fireplace lend grandeur to the first Waldorf Astoria hotel in an alpine location. **Pros:** celebrated restaurant; steps from the gondola; decadent spa. **Cons:** very little within walking distance; gondola nearby is very slow; only one dining option on-site. $ *Rooms from: $740 ⊠ 2100 Frostwood Dr., Park City ☎ 435/647–5500, 866/279–0843 ⊕ www.waldorfastoriaparkcity.com ⇌ 215 rooms ⦿ No meals.*

★ Washington School House

$$$$ | B&B/INN | Since 2011, this spectacular boutique hotel has been the hottest "must-stay" destination in Old Town Park

City, providing beautifully designed and well-appointed rooms within a National Historic Registry landmark. **Pros:** central location; stellar service (they'll even pack and unpack for you); chefs provide delicious (included) breakfast and après-ski. **Cons:** not family-friendly; rooms fill up quickly, so book far in advance. $ *Rooms from: $875 ⊠ 543 Park Ave., Box 536, Park City ☎ 435/649–3800, 800/824–1672 ⊕ www.washingtonschoolhouse. com ⇌ 12 rooms ¡O¡ Free breakfast.*

CONDOS

Deer Valley Resort Lodging

The reservationists at Deer Valley Resort Lodging are knowledgeable and the service is efficient at this high-end property-management company. They can book distinctive hotel rooms, condominiums, or private homes throughout Deer Valley and Park City. Complimentary shuttle service to/from resorts and around town in Cadillac Escalades is a perk. ⊠ *Park City ☎ 435/645–6428, 800/558–3337 ⊕ www. deervalley.com.*

Resorts West

Resorts West manages roughly 150 properties around town, ranging from two-bedroom condos to eight-bedroom ski homes. More than 90% of their properties are on the slopes or a short walk to the lifts. Your concierge will take care of everything from grocery delivery and private chefs to ski rental delivery, and each reservation includes daily housekeeping and shuttle service around town. ⊠ *1795 Sidewinder Dr., Suite 100, Park City ☎ 435/655–7006 ⊕ www.resortswest.com.*

Nightlife

In a state where nearly every town was founded by Mormons who eschewed alcohol and anything associated with it, Park City has always been an exception. Founded by miners with healthy appetites for whiskey and gambling, Park City has been known since its mining heyday as Utah's "Sin City." The miners are gone, but their legacy lives on in this town that has far more bars per capita than any other place in Utah.

Boneyard Saloon and Kitchen

BARS/PUBS | This hot spot is in a somewhat unlikely place—in fact, you might think you're lost as you pull into the industrial-looking area in Prospector. But its off-Main location means it's popular with the locals, and ample parking is a huge plus. TVs lining the wall and a special weekend breakfast menu have made Boneyard the new go-to for Sunday football, and the rooftop deck has stunning views of the mountains. A sister restaurant of No Name on Main Street, Boneyard features beers on tap and an extensive bottle list. Head next door to Wine Dive (same ownership) to find 16 wines on tap and artisan pizza. ⊠ *1251 Kearns Blvd., Prospector ☎ 435/649–0911 ⊕ www.boneyardsaloon.com.*

★ No Name Saloon

BARS/PUBS | A Park City favorite anchoring Main Street's nightlife, this is a classic wood-backed bar with lots of memorabilia, a shuffleboard table, and a regular local clientele. The upstairs outdoor deck is great for enjoying cool summer nights, but heaters in the winter make this deck comfortable year-round. The eclectic decor looks like everything was purchased at a flea market in the best way possible. If you are looking for some late-night grub, No Name has the best buffalo burgers in town. ⊠ *447 Main St., Park City ☎ 435/649–6667 ⊕ www. nonamesaloon.net.*

Old Town Cellars

WINE BARS—NIGHTLIFE | The first of its kind in the area, this private label winery opened on Main Street in 2016. Stop in to learn about the urban wine-making process, buy a bottle of their house wine, or enjoy an après-ski tasting in their Bar and Lounge where local beers and spirits are also available. Local meats and chocolate, available on their fare menu, pair perfectly with the experience. ⊠ *408*

Main St., Main Street ☎ *435/649–3759* ⊕ *www.otcwines.com.*

The Spur Bar and Grill

MUSIC CLUBS | If you are looking for live music, look no further than The Spur, which hosts bands seven nights a week. A renovation in 2016 more than doubled the size of The Spur, adding two additional bar areas and a Main Street entrance. The front room provides a lively bar atmosphere; head upstairs if you want to hear your conversation. The back room is where you'll find the live music and the dancing. A full kitchen means breakfast, lunch, and dinner are served until 10 pm. ⊠ *352 Main St., Park City* ☎ *435/615–1618* ⊕ *www.thespurbarandgrill.com.*

Troll Hallen Lounge

BARS/PUBS | If quiet conversation and a good single-malt scotch or Swiss raclette in front of a fire is your idea of nightlife, this is the place for you. ⊠ *Stein Eriksen Lodge, 7700 Stein Way, Park City* ☎ *435/645–6455.*

 Performing Arts

MUSIC

★ Mountain Town Music

MUSIC | FAMILY | This nonprofit organization books dozens of local, regional, and national musical acts in the Park City area, using many different venues around town including the ski resorts and Main Street. No matter what show you go to, you're likely to see every age group represented and enjoying the music. Most performances are free. ⊠ *Park City* ☎ *435/901–7664* ⊕ *www.mountaintownmusic.org.*

THEATER AND DANCE

Eccles Center for Performing Arts

ARTS CENTERS | Dance, theater, wide-ranging concerts, family shows, and other performances are on the bill in a state-of-the-art auditorium that also holds the biggest premieres during the Sundance Film Festival. ⊠ *1750 Kearns Blvd., Park*

City ☎ *435/655–3114 box office* ⊕ *www.parkcityinstitute.org.*

Egyptian Theatre

THEATER | This historical building has been a Park City theater since its mining days in the 1880s. In 1922 the Egyptian Theatre was constructed on the site of the original Dewey Theatre that collapsed under record-breaking snow. Patrons enjoy an eclectic array of local and regional music, theater, and comedy in the 266-seat space. ⊠ *328 Main St., Park City* ☎ *435/649–9371* ⊕ *www.egyptianheatrecompany.org.*

 Shopping

Within the colorful structures that line Park City's Main Street are a number of clothing boutiques, sporting-goods stores, and gift shops. In recent years, brand name stores like Lululemon, Patagonia, and Gorsuch have opened their doors along Historic Main Street, but alongside these recognizable names are locally owned boutiques and shops that help preserve the Park City charm.

ART GALLERIES

Park City Gallery Stroll

ART GALLERIES | Main Street is packed with great art galleries, and the best way to see them all is the Park City Gallery Stroll, a free event hosted by the Park City Gallery Association on the last Friday of the month 6–9 pm, sun or snow. ⊠ *Park City* ⊕ *www.parkcitygalleryassociation.com.*

BOOKS AND TOYS

Dolly's Bookstore

BOOKS/STATIONERY | FAMILY | For many returning visitors, the first stop in town is Dolly's Bookstore to check on the two cats: Dolly and Pippi Longstocking. Oh, and to browse a great selection of regional books as well as national best-sellers. Dolly's also has a uniquely complete selection of children's books and toys. While you are at it, swing through neighboring Rocky Mountain

Chocolate Factory to satisfy your sweet tooth. ⊠ *510 Main St., Park City* ☎ *435/649–8062.*

J. W. Allen & Sons Toys & Candy

TOYS | FAMILY | Jam-packed with classic toys and modern fun, J. W. Allen & Sons rescues parents who forgot to pack toys for their kids on family vacation. Scary dinosaurs, giant stuffed bears, dolls, sleds, scooters, and kites are as irresistible as the candy. ⊠ *1675 W. Redstone Center, No. 105, Park City* ☎ *435/575–8697.*

CLOTHING
Indigo Highway

CLOTHING | This eclectic boutique, located in Newpark Town Center, is worth a visit. Here you'll find clothing, gifts, scented candles, Park City keepsakes, and more, all with a modern nomad twist. They sell handmade bags from all over the world (with notes about the women who made them) next to Park City embroidered caps. There's even a full section of small batch, artisanal apothecary items (think body oils, detoxifying bath salts, and more). ⊠ *1241 Center Dr. #L170, Newpark* ☎ *435/214–7244* ⊕ *www.indigohighway.com.*

Mary Jane's

CLOTHING | This independently owned boutique has an eclectic selection of trendy clothing and designer jeans, lingerie, statement jewelry, shoes, and handbags. ⊠ *613 Main St., Park City* ☎ *435/645–7463* ⊕ *www.maryjaneshoes.com.*

Olive and Tweed

CLOTHING | This artist-driven boutique sells local handmade jewelry, women's clothing accessories, home decor, baby items, and local art. ⊠ *608 Main St., Park City* ☎ *435/649–9392* ⊕ *www.oliveandtweed.com.*

FOOD AND CANDY
Rocky Mountain Chocolate Factory

FOOD/CANDY | You'll find a quick fix for your sweet tooth here, and you can watch them make fudge, dozens of different carameled apples, and other scrumptious treats. There's another location at 1385 Lowell Avenue. ⊠ *510 Main St., Park City* ☎ *435/649–0997, 435/649–2235.*

 Activities

BICYCLING

In 2012, Park City was the first community ever designated a Gold Level Ride Center by the International Mountain Bicycling Association, thanks in large part to the relentless work of the Mountain Trails Foundation, which oversees and maintains more than 400 miles of area trails. The accolade is based upon bike shops, trail access, variety, and more. Pick up a map at any local bike shop or get details from the Mountain Trails Foundation (☎ *435/649–6839* ⊕ *www.mountaintrails.org*). You can join local road or mountain bikers most nights in the summer for free group rides sponsored by Park City bike shops.

Cole Sport

BICYCLING | Road bikers of all abilities can ride with a pack one evening a week from June to mid-September from this shop. You can rent mountain and road bikes here, too; be ready to ride at 6 pm. ⊠ *1615 Park Ave., Park City* ☎ *435/649–4806* ⊕ *www.colesport.com* ☞ *Call in advance for weekly schedule.*

Deer Valley Resort

BICYCLING | Mountain bikers from across the world flock to Deer Valley's single track trails for mountain biking each summer, and it's easy to see why with the variety of terrain and bike offerings available. Nearly 70 miles of trails can be accessed from three chairlifts, spanning all levels of ability, including down-hill flow trails. Bike clinics and lessons, both group and private, are offered through the Deer Valley Mountain Bike School, and rentals are available at the base areas. Trails are open June through September. ✉ *2250 Deer Valley Dr. S, Park City* ☎ *435/649–1000* ⊕ *www.deervalley. com.*

Jans Mountain Outfitters

BICYCLING | When the snow melts, Jans has everything you need to hit the road on two wheels. Whether you're into mountain bikes, road bikes, or cruisers, stop by to rent or demo something new, or to tune your own wheels. ✉ *1600 Park Ave., Park City* ☎ *435/649–4949* ⊕ *www. jans.com.*

Park City Mountain Resort

BICYCLING | Utah's largest ski resort transforms into a summer adventure land for cyclists, with a lift-served bike park at Canyons Village and miles of cross-country and downhill trails across the whole resort. Park City Base Area provides a number of trails accessible directly from the base, or haul your bike up the lift for some downhill riding. Canyons Village is the home of Park City Bike Park, with a dozen downhill flow and jump trails, many of which are accessible to all skill levels. Lessons are available with certified instructors for those who are new to the sport, and cyclists can find bike rentals at both base areas. ✉ *Park City Base Area, 1345 Lowell Ave., Park City* ☎ *435/649–8111* ⊕ *www.parkcitymountain.com.*

Silver Star Ski & Sport

BICYCLING | Look for Tallulah, the English bulldog at Silver Star Ski & Sport. While the dog watches the shop, friendly staff help find the best bike or piece of outdoor equipment to suit your needs. In addition to the retail area of the store offering top-of-the-line gear and clothing, Silver Star offers cruiser, road, and mountain bike rentals. ✉ *1825 Three Kings Dr. #85, Park City* ☎ *435/645–7827* ⊕ *www. silverstarskiandsport.com.*

White Pine Touring

BICYCLING | Every Thursday in summer, mountain bikers of all levels gather at 6 pm for a free guided mountain-bike ride. On the last Thursday of June, July, and August, the White Pine guides prepare a barbecue, too. There's also a women-only ride on Tuesday. For both rides, meet at the shop at 6 pm—earlier if you need to rent a bike. Guided road-biking, mountain-biking, climbing, and hiking tours are also available throughout the summer. In the winter, experience their Fat Bike Tours to ride snow-covered singletrack on a bike. ✉ *1790 Bonanza Dr., Park City* ☎ *435/649–8710* ⊕ *www.whitepinetouring.com.*

FLY-FISHING

The mountain-fed waters of the Provo and Weber rivers and several smaller streams near Park City are prime trout habitat.

Jans Mountain Outfitters

FISHING | During the summer, the entire upstairs of this store is dedicated solely to fly-fishing, and knowledgeable staff will help you find the best equipment and gear for your time on the river. Specializing in trout fishing, guides lead fly-fishing excursions year-round in nearby rivers, rent equipment, and provide insight and advice to the local area. Jans also has exclusive access to private waters in the surrounding areas. Guides also give free casting lessons at the Deer Valley ponds on Monday at 5 pm from Memorial Day to Labor Day. ✉ *1600 Park Ave., Park City* ☎ *435/649–4949* ⊕ *www.jans.com.*

Park City Fly Shop and Guide Service

FISHING | See Chris Kunkel, the owner of this shop, for good advice, guide service, and a modest selection of fly-fishing necessities. ✉ *2065 Sidewinder Dr., Park City* ☎ *435/640–2864* ⊕ *www.pcflyshopguideservice.com.*

Trout Bum 2

FISHING | This full-service fly shop can outfit you with everything you need, then guide you to where the fish are. This shop has the largest selection of flies in town, and is the only guide service in all of Park City to have access to the renowned Green River below Flaming Gorge Reservoir. Check the website for fishing reports of the area rivers and streams. ✉ *4343 N. Hwy. 224, Suite 101, Park City* ☎ *435/658–1166, 877/878–2862* ⊕ *www.troutbum2.com.*

GOLF

Within 20 minutes of Park City are 12 golf courses. An equal amount of private and public courses provide a variety of terrain, views, and holes to play.

Canyons Golf

GOLF | The newest course in Park City (opened for play in 2015), this 97-acre course uses the mountainous terrain at the base of the ski resort for a challenging game. Six holes interact with ski runs, with more than 550 feet of elevation change throughout the course. With seven par-3s, the course is not for the faint of heart, but the views alone make it worth checking out no matter your level. ✉ *4000 Canyons Resort Dr., Canyons Resort* ☎ *435/615–4728* ⊕ *www.parkcitymountain.com/golf* 🖃 *$95; rates drop to $70 during off-peak times* ⅄ *18 holes, 6256 yards, par 70.*

Park City Golf Club

GOLF | On this gorgeous and challenging 6,800-yard, par-72 public course, you'll love the views of ski runs, rising peaks, historic Main Street, and an occasional moose. Popular among locals, it's considered one of the best public courses in the area. Everything you need is in the pro shop, in the Hotel Park City right along the course. ✉ *1541 Thaynes Canyon Dr., Park City* ☎ *435/615–5800* ⊕ *www.parkcity.org/departments/park-city-golf-club* 🖃 *$26 for 9 holes, $33 with cart; $52 for 18 holes, $67 with cart* ⅄ *18 holes, 6800 yards, par 72.*

Promontory Club

GOLF | The only private club in the area to make selected tee times available to the general public, Promontory Club welcomes nonmembers on its challenging and sometimes windy Pete Dye–designed course. The club is renowned for extraordinary views and exemplary service. Six sets of tees on this course make for what some call the most level playing field on any course in Utah. ✉ *8758 Promontory Ranch Rd., Park City* ☎ *435/333–4000* ⊕ *www.promontoryclub.com* 🖃 *$250 for nonmembers; check with hotel concierge for better price* ⅄ *18 holes, 7700 yards, par 72.*

HIKING

The Wasatch Mountains surrounding Park City offer more than 400 miles of hiking trails, ranging from easy, meandering meadow strolls to strenuous climbs up wind-blown peaks. Getting away from civilization and into the aspens is easy, and lucky hikers might spy foxes, coyotes, moose, elk, deer, and red-tailed hawks. Many of the trails take off from the resort areas, but some of the trailheads are right near Main Street. For beginners, or for those acclimating to the elevation, the Rail Trail is a good place to start. Another alternative is to take the McLeod Creek Trail from behind The Market all the way to the Redstone Center. The Round Valley and Lost Prospector trails are still mellow but slightly more challenging. To really get the blood pumping, head up Spiro or do a lengthy stretch of Mid-Mountain.

For interactive trail maps, up-to-date information about trail conditions and events, and answers to your trail questions, contact the nonprofit Mountain Trails Foundation (⊕ *www.mountaintrails.org*) whose mission is to promote, preserve, advocate for, and maintain Park City's local trail system. Maps detailing trail locations are available at most local gear shops.

Few places in the world can show off such distinct geologic features in an area as small as the 50 to 70 miles along the Wasatch Front.

HORSEBACK RIDING

Blue Sky Adventures

HORSEBACK RIDING | Located just outside of Park City in Wanship, this Vaquero-style equestrian center sits on 3,500 acres of land available for exploring. Using the vaquero method of finding harmony and togetherness between horse and rider, each ride is private and includes a unique gourmet culinary experience. ⊠ Blue Sky Ranch, 27659 Old Lincoln Hwy. ☎ 435/252–0662 ⊕ www. blueskyutah.com.

Red Pine Adventures

HORSEBACK RIDING | This outfitter leads trail rides through thousands of acres of private land. ⊠ 2050 W. White Pine Canyon Rd., Park City ☎ 435/649–9445 ⊕ www. redpinetours.com ⊠ From $75.

Rocky Mountain Recreation

HORSEBACK RIDING | Saddle up for a taste and feel of the Old West with guided mountain trail rides, from one hour to all-day or overnight excursions, departing from several locations in the Park City area, complete with fantastic scenery and good cowboy grub. ⊠ Stillman Ranch, Oakley ☎ 435/645–7256 ⊕ www. rockymtnrec.com ⊠ From $66.

Wind In Your Hair Riding

HORSEBACK RIDING | Only experienced riders who are looking for a get-up-and-go kind of mountain riding adventure are allowed on these trail rides, so there will be no inexperienced riders to slow you down, and the Paso Fino horses are noted for their smooth ride. Plan to tip the trail leader. Lessons are available for beginners. ⊠ Cherry Canyon Ranch, 46 E. Cherry Canyon Dr., Wanship ☎ 435/336–4795, 435/901–4644 ⊕ www.windinyour-hair.com ⊠ From $150.

HOT-AIR BALLOONING

Park City Balloon Adventures

BALLOONING | Hour-long scenic sunrise flights are offered daily, weather permitting. Fliers meet at Starbucks in Kimball Junction and are shuttled to the take-off site, which varies from day to day. A champagne or nonalcoholic toast is offered on touchdown. Reservations are required. ✉ *Park City* ☎ *435/645–8787, 800/396–8787* 🔗 *$225 per person.*

ICE-SKATING

Park City Ice Arena

ICE SKATING | The Olympic-size rink here provides plenty of space for testing out that triple-toe loop or slap shot. The hill outside the building is popular sledding terrain. ✉ *600 Gillmor Way, Park City* ☎ *435/615–5700* ⊕ *www.parkcityice.org* 🔗 *$11.*

RAFTING

Park City Rafting

WHITE-WATER RAFTING | Two-hour, mostly class II rafting adventures are offered, as well as full-day trips that end with a class III splash. Given the Weber's mostly benign water, there are plenty of breaks between plunges to look for moose, deer, beavers, badgers, and feathered friends along the shore. ✉ *1245 Taggart La., Morgan* ☎ *435/655–3800, 866/467–2384* ⊕ *www.parkcityrafting. com* 🔗 *From $49.*

Utah Outdoor Adventures

WHITE-WATER RAFTING | This company specializes in half-day and full-day excursions, all of which are private groups. Tours take place on the Weber River on class II and class III rapids. Perfect for all age groups. ✉ *3310 Mountain La., Park City* ☎ *801/703–3357* ⊕ *www.utahoutdooradventures.com* 🔗 *$60.*

ROCK CLIMBING

White Pine Touring

CLIMBING/MOUNTAINEERING | If you're looking for some hang time on the local rocks but don't know the area, White Pine Touring offers guided climbing tours, equipment rental, and private and group lessons. Reservations are required. ✉ *1790 Bonanza Dr., Park City* ☎ *435/649–8710* ⊕ *www.whitepinetouring.com* 🔗 *From $325.*

SKIING AND SNOWBOARDING

★ Deer Valley Resort

SKIING/SNOWBOARDING | FAMILY | Just to the south of downtown Park City, this resort set new standards in the ski industry by providing such amenities as ski valets and slope-side dining of the highest caliber. For such pampering, the resort has drawn rave reviews from virtually every ski and travel magazine, consistently rated #1 Ski Resort in America by *SKI* magazine. The careful layout of runs and the impeccable grooming makes this an intermediate skier's heaven. With the Empire Canyon and Lady Morgan areas, the resort also offers bona fide expert terrain. For many, part of the ski experience includes a two- to three-hour midday interlude of feasting at one of the many world-class dining locations on the mountain and catching major rays on the snow-covered meadow in front of Silver Lake Lodge. The ski experience fits right in with the resort's overall image. With lessons for kids from preschool through teens, Deer Valley's acclaimed children's ski school is sure to please both children and parents. Note: this is one of the only ski resorts in the United States that prohibits snowboards. ✉ *2250 Deer Valley Dr., Park City* ☎ *435/649–1000, 800/424–3337 reservations* ⊕ *www.deervalley.com* 🔗 *Lift ticket $135* ⛷ *3,000-ft vertical drop; 2,026 skiable acres; 27% beginner, 41% intermediate, 32% advanced; 101 total runs.*

★ Park City Mountain Resort

SKIING/SNOWBOARDING | FAMILY | Although this has been one of North America's most popular ski and snowboard destinations for quite some time, in 2015 Vail Resorts joined neighboring Canyons Resort to Park City Mountain, creating the largest ski resort in the United States. With more than 330 trails, 17 mountain peaks, 7,300 skiable acres, and 41 lifts, it is almost impossible to ski the entire resort in one day. The trails provide a great mix of beginner, intermediate, and advanced terrain, with Jupiter Peak providing the highest elevation and steepest terrain in town. Three distinct base areas provide a great starting point for the ski day—Park City Base Area has a variety of dining and retail options, along with a stellar après-ski scene. Park City is the only resort with lift access to Historic Main Street with Town Lift, allowing for guests staying near or on Main Street direct access to the slopes. Canyons Village, located on the other side of the mountain, gives ski-in/ski-out access to many of the base areas hotels and lodging properties. The resort is widely acclaimed for being a free-skiing and snowboarding mecca with official Olympic qualifying events each year; you're likely to see Olympic athletes training and playing on the slopes. ⊠ *1345 Lowell Ave., Park City* ☎ *435/649–8111* ⊕ *www.parkcitymountain.com* 🎟 *Lift ticket prices change daily; check online for daily rate* ⚲ *3,200-ft vertical drop; 7,300 skiable acres; 8% beginner, 42% intermediate, 50% advanced; 41 lifts; 2 halfpipes (including 1 super pipe) and 8 terrain parks.*

Wasatch Powderbird Guides

SKIING/SNOWBOARDING | If you don't mind paying for it, the best way to find untracked Utah powder is with Wasatch Powderbird Guides. A helicopter drops you on the top of the mountain, and a guide leads you back down. Itineraries are always weather dependent. Call to inquire about departures from Snowbird (Little Cottonwood Canyon) or Park City Mountain Resort (Canyons Village). ⊠ *3000 Canyons Resort Dr., Park City* ☎ *801/742–2800* ⊕ *www.powderbird.com* 🎟 *From $1260.*

White Pine Nordic Center

SKIING/SNOWBOARDING | Just outside Old Town, White Pine Nordic Center offers around 20 km (12 miles) of set track, in 3-km (2-mile), 5-km (3-mile), and 10-km (6-mile) loops, plus cross-country ski instruction, equipment rentals, and a well-stocked cross-country ski shop. The fee to use the track is $18, or $10 after 3 pm. Reservations are required for their guided backcountry ski and snowshoe tours in the surrounding mountains. ⊠ *On Park City Golf Course, 1541 Thaynes Canyon Dr., Park City* ☎ *435/649–6249* ⊕ *www.whitepinetouring.com.*

SKI RENTALS AND EQUIPMENT

Many shops in Park City rent equipment for skiing and other sports. From old-fashioned rental shops that also offer discount lift tickets to luxurious ski-delivery services that will fit you in your room, you have dozens of choices. Prices tend to be slightly lower if you rent in Salt Lake City. ■ TIP→ **If you happen to be visiting during holidays, reserve skiing and snowboarding gear in advance.**

Breeze Winter Sports Rentals

SKIING/SNOWBOARDING | You can reserve your equipment online in advance with this company (often for less than day-of rentals), which has two locations in Park City. You'll find them near Canyons Village and at Park City Base Area. They're owned by Vail Resorts, and you can expect good quality and service at a value price. ⊠ *4343 N. Hwy. 224, Park City* ☎ *435/655–7066, 888/427–3393* ⊕ *www.skirentals.com.*

Cole Sport

SKIING/SNOWBOARDING | With four locations from Main Street to Deer Valley, Cole Sport carries all of your winter ski, snowboard, and snowshoe rental needs. Come back in summer for bikes, standup paddleboards, hiking gear, and more. No matter the season, Cole Sport offers expert fitting and advice with a broad range of equipment. ⊠ *1615 Park Ave., Park City* ☎ *435/649–4806, 800/345–2938* ⊕ *www.colesport.com.*

Jans Mountain Outfitters

SKIING/SNOWBOARDING | For almost 40 years, this has been the locals' choice for gear rentals, with ski and snowboard equipment packages and clothing in winter, and bikes and fly-fishing gear in summer. With the most knowledgeable staff around, they'll assist you with any outdoor adventure. There are multiple locations, including the flagship Park Avenue store, Deer Valley, and Park City Mountain Resort. ⊠ *1600 Park Ave., Park City* ☎ *435/649–4949* ⊕ *www.jans.com.*

Park City Sport

SKIING/SNOWBOARDING | At the base of Park City Mountain Resort, this is a convenient place to rent ski and snowboard equipment, goggles, and clothing. You can drop off your personal gear at the end of a ski day, and they'll have it tuned and ready for you the next morning with free overnight storage for customers. A second location on Main Street is across from Town Lift. ⊠ *1335 Lowell Ave., #104, Park City* ☎ *435/645–7777, 800/523–3922* ⊕ *www.parkcitysport.com.*

Silver Star Ski & Sport

SKIING/SNOWBOARDING | This company rents, tunes, and repairs ski equipment, snowshoes, bike gear, and stand-up paddleboards. It doesn't get much more convenient for winter rentals/gear adjustments, as the shop is located at the base of the Silver Star lift at Park City Mountain Resort. ⊠ *1825 Three Kings Dr., #85, Park City* ☎ *435/645–7827* ⊕ *www. silverstarskiandsport.com.*

Ski Butlers

SKIING/SNOWBOARDING | The most prominent of a number of companies offering ski and snowboard delivery, Ski Butlers carries top-of-the-line Rossignol equipment. Their experts will fit you in your hotel room or condo and meet you at any of the resorts should something go wrong. You'll pay a little more, but you'll avoid the hassle of rentals when the snow is falling on your first morning in the mountains. ⊠ *Park City* ☎ *877/754–7754* ⊕ *www.skibutlers.com.*

Utah Ski & Golf

SKIING/SNOWBOARDING | Downhill equipment, snowshoes, clothing, and golf-club rental are available here, at Park City Base Area and Town Lift, as well as in downtown Salt Lake City. ⊠ *698 Park Ave., Park City* ☎ *435/649–3020* ⊕ *www. utahskigolf.com.*

SKI TOURS

Ski Utah Interconnect Tour

SKIING/SNOWBOARDING | Strong intermediate and advanced skiers can hook up with the Ski Utah Interconnect Tour for a guided alpine ski tour that takes you to as many as six resorts, including Deer Valley and Park City, in a single day, all connected by backcountry ski routes with unparalleled views of the Wasatch Mountains. Guides test your ski ability before departure. The tour includes guide service, lift tickets, lunch, and transportation back to the point of origin. You'll even walk away with a finisher's pin. Reservations are required. ⊠ *Park City* ☎ *801/534–1907* ⊕ *www.skiutah.com* 🖃 *$395.*

★ White Pine Touring

SKIING/SNOWBOARDING | Specializing in telemark, cross-country, and alpine touring gear and guided tours, White Pine Touring also has top of the line clothing, as well as mountain bikes, fat bikes, snowshoes, and climbing shoes. ⊠ *1790 Bonanza Dr., Park City* ☎ *435/649–8710* ⊕ *www.whitepinetouring.com.*

SNOWMOBILING

Red Pine Adventures

SNOW SPORTS | For a winter speed thrill of the machine-powered variety, hop on a snowmobile and follow your guide along private groomed trails adjacent to Park City Mountain Resort. Pick up is in Park City. ⊠ *2050 W. White Pine Canyon Rd., Park City* ☎ *435/649–9445* ⊕ *www. redpinetours.com* 🖃 *From $199 single rider, $239 double.*

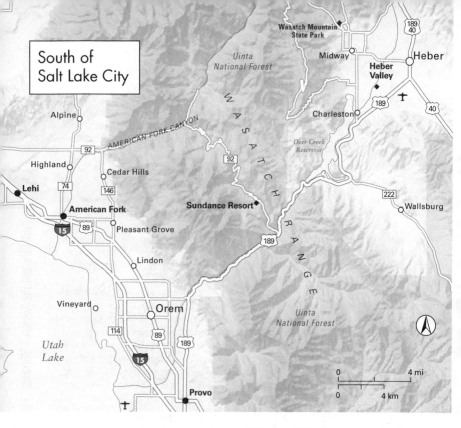

South of
Salt Lake City

Wasatch Mountain
State Park

Uinta
National Forest

Midway   Heber

Heber
Valley

189
40

Charleston

Alpine

AMERICAN FORK CANYON

92

Deer Creek
Reservoir

189

40

Highland

Cedar Hills

92

W
A
S
A
T
C
H

222

Wallsburg

Lehi

74

146

American Fork

Sundance Resort

15

89

Pleasant Grove

189

R
A
N
G
E

Lindon

Vineyard

Orem

Uinta
National Forest

114

89

189

Utah
Lake

15

Provo

0   4 mi

0   4 km

Thousand Peaks Snowmobile Adventures
SNOW SPORTS | Backcountry snowmobile
tours are on one of Utah's largest private
mountain ranches, just outside of Park
City. Clothing is available to rent. ✉ Office, 698 Park Ave., Park City ☎ 888/304–
7669 ⊕ www.powderutah.com 🖾 From
$169 single rider, $218 double.

SNOW TUBING
Woodward Park City
SNOW SPORTS | **FAMILY** | Lift-served snow
tubing (with 7 lanes) and minisnowmo-
bile rentals bring families here. ✉ 3863
W. Kilby Rd., Park City ☎ 435/658–2648
⊕ www.woodwardparkcity.com/tick-
ets-passes/tubing 🖾 From $40.

Heber Valley

*20 miles south of Park City; 22 miles
northeast of Sundance.*

Bounded by the Wasatch Mountains on
the west and the rolling foothills of the
Uinta Mountains on the east, the Heber
Valley, including the towns of Heber,
Midway, and Charleston, is well-supplied
with snow in winter for cross-country
skiing, snowmobiling, and other snow
sports. Summers are mostly cool and
green. Events throughout the year enter-
tain locals and visitors alike.

GETTING HERE AND AROUND
From Park City, head east on Highway 40
to enter the Heber Valley. The highway
turns into Main Street, which leads
straight through Heber City. Turn right on
100 South to reach the Swiss-influenced

town of Midway. If you're coming from Sundance, take Highway 92 south then Highway 189 east.

ESSENTIALS

VISITOR INFORMATION Heber Valley County Chamber of Commerce. ✉ *475 N. Main St.* ☎ *435/654–3666* ⊕ *www.gohebervalley.com.*

FESTIVALS

Heber City Concerts in the Park
CONCERTS | From June through August, enjoy the free and family-friendly Heber City Concerts in the Park. A farmers' market fills City Park with fresh produce and rock, reggae, or folk tunes every Thursday evening from 6:30 to 9. ✉ *City Park, S. 6th W, Heber* ☎ *435/654–3666* ⊕ *www. gohebervalley.com.*

Soldier Hollow Classic International Sheepdog Championship
FESTIVALS | Held over Labor Day weekend, this is a four-day event that draws approximately 20,000 spectators for an extraordinary display of canine skill. There are also bagpipers, culinary treats, and entertainment for wee ones. ✉ *2002 Soldier Hollow La., Midway* ☎ *435/654–2002* ⊕ *www.soldierhollowclassic.com* 🎟 *$17.*

Swiss Days
FESTIVALS | Each Labor Day Weekend, Midway's Swiss Days honor the town's original Swiss settlers with a parade, entertainment, and contests. More than 300 gallons of sauerkraut are consumed during the two-day event that takes place in the Town Square. ✉ *Midway* ✛ *Main St. and 100 North* ☎ *801/234–0673* ⊕ *www.midwayswissdays.com.*

Wasatch County Fair
FESTIVALS | A 60-car demolition derby is the popular kickoff for the weeklong Wasatch County Fair in late July/early August; a rodeo caps the action. Events are based at the Wasatch County Fairground in Southfield Park. ✉ *895 W. 100 S, Heber* ☎ *435/657–3240* ⊕ *www. wasatchcountyfair.com.*

 # Sights

The Heber Creeper: Heber Valley Historic Railroad
TOUR—SIGHT | FAMILY | This steam train takes passengers on a nostalgic trip along a line that first ran in 1899 past the Deer Creek Reservoir and through beautiful Provo Canyon. It continues past Bridal Falls, a veil-like waterfall near snow-capped Mt. Timpanogos. Each car has been restored, and two of the engines are fully operational, steam-powered locomotives. The railroad offers special events including cheese-tasting rides, the local favorite North Pole Christmas Train, Raft 'n Rails (pairing rafting with a train excursion), Reins 'n Trains (with horseback riding), and Wilderness. Lunch is available for an extra cost. ∎TIP➔ **There's no climate control in the rail cars, so dress for the weather.** ✉ *450 S. 600 W, Heber* ☎ *435/654–5601* ⊕ *www.hebervalleyrr.org* 🎟 *Provo Canyon $30; Deer Creek $20; call for special event and activity trip prices.*

Mirror Lake Highway
SCENIC DRIVE | East of Park City, this scenic byway winds through aspens and ponderosa pines, skirts alpine lakes and waterfalls, and reaches 11,943-foot Bald Mountain. The ride is good, but getting out of the car is better. A spectacular hike is the 5-mile, five-lake Lofty Lake Loop, which starts at the Pass Lake Trailhead at mile 32. It's also a great place to snowshoe in the winter. Keep an eye out for moose, wildflowers, and changeable weather. Reward yourself with jerky from Samak Smoke House, an usual dry goods store, or a berry shake at Uinta Drive-In, near the Uinta-Wasatch-Cache National Forest's Kamas entrance. ✉ *Kamas* ☎ *435/783–4338* ⊕ *www.fs.fed.us/r4/ uwc* 🎟 *$6 per car for 3-day pass* ☉ *Road closed in winter, depending on snowfall.*

Soldier Hollow
NATIONAL/STATE PARK | On the southern end of the park, this activity center was one site for the 2002 Winter Olympics

To the west of Heber Valley are the Wasatch Mountains; to the east are the Uinta Mountains.

and still hosts the national championship Nordic ski events and other events, including powwows and sheepdog championships. It's open to the public year-round for hiking, horseback riding, cross-country skiing, tubing, snowshoeing, biathlon, and other events. A beautiful lodge has food concessions, equipment rentals, and a souvenir shop. ✉ *2002 Soldier Hollow La., Midway* ☎ *435/654–2002* 🌐 *www.soldierhollow.com.*

Wasatch Mountain State Park

NATIONAL/STATE PARK | **FAMILY** | This 22,000-acre preserve is 3 miles from Heber City and provides for a number of activities, ranging from serene hikes along winding mountain trails to golfing at one of the four 18-hole courses. Children have their own fishing pond near the visitor center. In winter, hiking turns to snowshoeing, cross-country, or backcountry skiing along the Dutch Hollow, Snake Creek, or Pine Creek trails winding up through stands of Gambel oak, aspen, and maple. ✉ *1281 Warm Springs Rd., Midway* ☎ *435/654–1791, 800/322–3770* 🌐 *stateparks.utah.gov* 🎟 *$7 per car.*

🍴 Restaurants

Café Galleria

$ | **PIZZA** | **FAMILY** | This family-friendly restaurant claims to have the best pizza and bagels in the state, and they may not be far off. The wood-fired pizza oven cooks to perfection, and bagel sandwiches, available throughout the day, hit the spot. **Known for:** casual atmosphere; bagels; wood-fired pizza. [$] *Average main: $11* ✉ *101 W. Main St., Midway* ☎ *435/657–2002* 🌐 *www.thecafegalleria.com.*

★ **Dairy Keen**

$ | **FAST FOOD** | **FAMILY** | A welcome respite from chain fast food, this family-owned drive-in is loved by all the locals and serves the best shakes and burgers for miles around. Railroad artifacts line the walls, and an electric train entertains children as it passes over the booths. **Known for:** signature burgers; vintage vibe. [$] *Average main: $5* ✉ *199 S. Main*

St. ☎ *435/654–5336* 🌐 *www.dairykeen.com.*

Fanny's Grill

$ | **AMERICAN** | **FAMILY** | Feed the ducks from the patio and enjoy the laid-back company of locals and golfers at one of Midway's original restaurants. Named in honor of Fanabelle Schneitter, whose father-in-law settled the Homestead in the 1800s, this simple eatery is open for breakfast and lunch through the spring, summer, and fall, serving burgers, salads, and sandwiches. **Known for:** great patio; postgame bite to eat. [$] *Average main: $12* ✉ *700 N. Homestead Dr., Midway* ☎ *435/654–1102* 🌐 *www.homesteadresort.com* 🕒 *Closed in winter.*

The Old Goat

$$ | **AMERICAN** | **FAMILY** | Executive Chef Ryan Estel created a family-friendly spot to gather for smoked backyard brisket and Heber Valley cheese curds battered in corn meal and fried. In this reimagined meat-and-potatoes American eatery, you can sit either inside or on the patio. **Known for:** all-you-can-eat taco Tuesday; "goat candy" (candied jalapeños); brownie skillet. [$] *Average main: $18* ✉ *650 W. 100 S, Heber* ☎ *435/657–9431* 🌐 *oldgoateatery.com.*

Tarahumara

$ | **MEXICAN** | Authentic art from the owner's Chihuahua hometown sets the genuine tone in this lively self-serve restaurant, where locals lap up the *carne asada,* seared sea scallops with passion fruit, and other Mexican specialties. Take in a televised soccer game, sip a margarita, and try to sample more than 20 fresh salsas. **Known for:** authentic Mexican cuisine; laid-back vibe; great margaritas. [$] *Average main: $11* ✉ *380 E. Main St., Midway* ☎ *435/654–3465* 🌐 *www.tarahumararestaurant.com* 🕒 *Closed Sun.*

Coffee and Quick Bites

The Bagel Den

$ | **AMERICAN** | Locals love this bagel shop, where they can pick up a latte and a New York-style bagel made fresh daily. Try the pumpernickel, French toast, or pretzel bagels and add a schmear like bacon scallion or blueberry cream cheese. **Known for:** New York-style bagels; local favorite; delicious smoothies. [$] *Average main: $8* ✉ *570 N. Main St., Heber* ☎ *435/654–3193* 🌐 *www.thebagelden.com.*

Hotels

Blue Boar Inn

$$ | **B&B/INN** | Wrought-iron balconies, mountain views, and an antique alpenhorn give this château-style inn a warm, romantic feel. **Pros:** hospitable staff; romantic ambience; full breakfast. **Cons:** not the ideal place for boisterous little ones; 20-plus minutes to the ski resorts; dark decor. [$] *Rooms from: $175* ✉ *1235 Warm Springs Rd., Midway* ☎ *435/654–1400, 888/650–1400* 🌐 *www.theblueboarinn.com* 🛏 *12 rooms* 🍴 *Free breakfast.*

Homestead Resort

$$ | **HOTEL** | **FAMILY** | Park City silver miners once soaked in the hot springs of this resort, which has been in operation since 1886. **Pros:** a Bruce Summerhays–designed golf course; natural hot springs; family-friendly. **Cons:** far from ski resorts; rooms are basic; a bit sleepy. [$] *Rooms from: $139* ✉ *700 N. Homestead Dr., Midway* ☎ *435/654–1102, 800/327–7220* 🌐 *www.homesteadresort.com* 🛏 *147 rooms* 🍴 *No meals.*

Zermatt Utah Resort & Spa

$$$ | **RESORT** | **FAMILY** | This charming Swiss-style hotel is a restful retreat tucked into the idyllic countryside. **Pros:** immaculate rooms; stellar views; plenty to do. **Cons:** far from restaurants and ski resorts; expensive resort fee; very quiet.

[$] *Rooms from: $215* ✉ *784 W. Resort Dr., Midway* ☎ *435/657–0180, 866/840–5087* 🌐 *www.zermattresort.com* 🛏 *427 rooms* 🍴 *No meals.*

Activities

GOLF

Homestead Golf Club

GOLF | This incredible course, in the heart of the Heber Valley on the Homestead Resort, offers views of the Wasatch Mountains and plenty of fresh mountain air. GPS-enabled cart paths mean you won't get lost while looking at the scenery. ✉ *700 N. Homestead Dr., Midway* ☎ *435/654–1102, 800/327–7220* 🌐 *playhomesteadgc.com* 🎫 *$45 for 18 holes Sun.–Thurs., $49 Fri. and Sat.* ⛳ *18 holes, 7040 yards, par 72* 🕒 *Closed Nov.–Mar.*

Soldier Hollow Golf Course

GOLF | Reflecting the Olympic heritage, the names of the two 18-hole courses are Gold and Silver. While on these greens, golfers enjoy the beauty of both the Heber Valley to the east and the stunning Mount Timpanogos to the west. The Gold course is considered a mountain course, with dramatic elevation changes within each hole. The Silver course is slightly shorter than Gold, but with longer and trickier greens. ✉ *1371 W. Soldier Hollow La., Midway* ☎ *435/654–7442* 🎫 *Gold: $50; Silver: $45 (includes cart)* ⛳ *Gold: 18 holes, 7598 yards, par 72; Silver: 18 holes, 7335 yards, par 72.*

★ Wasatch Golf

GOLF | The setting within the Wasatch Mountain State Park is spectacular, particularly at fall foliage time, and with the challenging Mountain Course as well as the gentler Lake Course, this is one of the most popular public courses in the state. The Mountain Course is designed around the natural contours of the surrounding Wasatch mountains, and motorized carts are mandatory. Sometimes you can even see deer and even moose while you golf. The easier Lake Course surrounds eight lakes and ponds, and is a favorite with high, low, and no handicappers. The course's café serves breakfast, lunch, and dinner. ✉ *975 W. Golf Course Rd., Midway* ☎ *435/654–0532* 🌐 *www.wasatchgolfcourse.com* 🎫 *$50 (includes cart)* ⛳ *Mountain course: 18 holes, 6459 yards, par 71; Lake course: 18 holes, 6942 yards, par 72.*

HIKING

The path connecting the towns of Heber and Midway is an easy walk with spectacular views of the Wasatch Range at a distance and, up close, the Provo River.

Jordanelle State Park

HIKING/WALKING | For a quiet experience, start your hike from the Rock Cliff Nature Center, under tall cottonwoods at the east end of Jordanelle State Park, which lies 10 miles east of Heber City. Hikers often report excellent wildlife viewing along this section of the upper Provo River. No dogs are allowed. ✉ *Hwy. 32, Heber* ☎ *435/782–3030* 🌐 *stateparks.utah.gov.*

Soldier Hollow

BICYCLING | **FAMILY** | Although the trail system here is more exposed than that in the northern end of Wasatch Mountain State Park, hikers will enjoy the stunning view of the east side of Mount Timpanogos as well as the vista of the Uinta Mountains to the east across the Heber Valley. Or, if you'd rather go faster than your feet can take you, rent an electric mountain bike at Soldier Hollow Lodge to zip down the trails. ✉ *2002 Soldier Hollow La., Midway* ☎ *435/654–2002* 🌐 *www.soldierhollow.com* ☞ *To rent an electric bike costs $75 for a half day and $105 for a full day.*

Wasatch Mountain State Park

HIKING/WALKING | Hikers will find lots of foliage and wildlife here, on any number of trails in Dutch Hollow, Pine Canyon, and along Snake Creek. ✉ *1281 Warm Springs Rd., Midway* ☎ *435/654–1791* 🌐 *stateparks.utah.gov.*

HORSEBACK RIDING
Rocky Mountain Outfitters
HORSEBACK RIDING | Visitors can enjoy the spectacular back country of the Wasatch Mountain State Park and surrounding areas on horseback year-round with Rocky Mountain Outfitters. Choose from a variety of ride durations and destinations with the nicest guides in the area. ☎ 435/654–1655 ⊕ www.rockymtnoutfitters.com ⊠ $79 for a 2-hr ride.

WATER SPORTS
Deer Creek State Park
FISHING | Consistently good fishing, mild canyon winds, and water warmer than you'd expect are responsible for Deer Creek State Park's popularity with windsurfers, sailors, swimmers, and those just kicking back in the mountain sunshine. The park is 5 miles south of Heber City. ⊠ U.S. 189, Heber ☎ 435/654–0174 ⊕ stateparks.utah.gov ⊠ $10 day-use fee.

Jordanelle State Park
WATER SPORTS | This park has three recreation areas on a large mountain reservoir. The Hailstone area, 10 miles north of Heber City via U.S. 40, offers day-use areas, boat ramps, playgrounds, and a marina store where water toys (wave runners and the like) can be rented. To the east, across the reservoir on Highway 32, the Rock Cliff area and facilities are near the Provo River. To the north, Ross Creek is where some of the best fishing in the area can be found. ⊠ Hwy. 32, Heber ☎ 435/649–9540 Hailstone Main Park ⊕ stateparks.utah.gov ⊠ Hailstone $10 per vehicle, Rock Cliff and Ross Creek $7 per vehicle.

Sundance Resort

35 miles south of Park City; 12 miles northeast of Provo.

As Thoreau had Walden Pond, so does Redford have Sundance. Lucky for the rest of us, the "Sundance Kid" shares his 5,000-acre bounty. Several miles up a winding mountain lane, Sundance Resort is a full-service ski resort with bustling slopes in winter, except during the Sundance Film Festival. In summer, it's a destination for filmmakers, writers, craftsmen, and artists of all sensibilities. It also caters to visitors looking to relax at spas, shop, or dine.

GETTING HERE AND AROUND
From Park City, take Highway 40 and 189 south. From Provo, head northeast on Highway 92.

Sights

★ Sundance Resort
RESORT—SIGHT | Set on the eastern slopes of the breathtaking 11,750-foot Mount Timpanogos, the 5,000-acre resort came into being when Robert Redford purchased the land in 1969. No matter the season, you'll find plenty of recreational opportunities, including hiking, biking, fly-fishing, horseback riding, alpine and cross-country skiing, snowboarding, snowshoeing, and zip lining. Relax with a body treatment in the Spa at Sundance or take one of many creative classes in the Art Studios. The Sundance Film Festival, based in nearby Park City each January, is an internationally recognized showcase for independent films. Festival screenings and summer workshops are held at the resort. ⊠ 8841 N. Alpine Loop Rd., Sundance ☎ 866/259–7468, 800/892–1600 ⊕ www.sundanceresort.com ⊠ Lift tickets $80 ⌖ 2,150-ft vertical drop; 450 skiable acres; 35% novice, 45% intermediate, 20% advanced; 3 quad lifts, 1 triple chair, 1 surface lift.

Restaurants

★ The Foundry Grill
$$$ | AMERICAN | Wood-oven pizzas, sizzling steaks, and spit-roasted chicken are among the hearty staples on the menu at this restaurant. Like the rest of Sundance, everything from the food

presentation to the interior design is beautiful, and fits right in with the eco-friendly, nature first concept established by Redford. **Known for:** Sunday brunch; open kitchen; wood-burning pizza oven. [$] *Average main: $30* ✉ *Sundance Resort, 8841 N. Alpine Loop Rd., Sundance* ☎ *866/932–2295* 🌐 *www.sundanceresort.com.*

★ The Tree Room

$$$$ | **AMERICAN** | It's easy to imagine that you're a personal guest of Robert Redford at this intimate, rustic restaurant with Western memorabilia from the actor's private collection. With its warm wood interior and natural light, this cozy restaurant is a great place to tuck into for hours to eat delicious food, listen to the creek nearby, and forget about your worries. **Known for:** fine dining; candlelit atmosphere; interesting art. [$] *Average main: $37* ✉ *Sundance Resort, 8841 N. Alpine Loop Rd., Sundance* ☎ *866/627–8313* 🌐 *www.sundanceresort.com* 🕒 *No lunch.*

Hotels

★ Sundance Resort

$$$$ | **RESORT** | With 11,750-foot Mount Timpanogos serving as a backdrop, Robert Redford's resort is tucked into a 5,000-acre swath of lush wilderness and is a genuine tribute to arts and the natural world. **Pros:** retreat from urban hubbub; glorious scenery; culinary magic. **Cons:** cell reception is spotty; far drive to other restaurants and nightlife; limited ski terrain compared to other Utah resorts. [$] *Rooms from: $285* ✉ *8841 N. Alpine Loop Rd., Sundance* ☎ *866/259–7468, 800/892–1600* 🌐 *www.sundanceresort.com* 🛏 *95 rooms* 🍴 *No meals.*

Nightlife

Owl Bar

BARS/PUBS | Whether you feel like a quiet midday chess game or more lively atmosphere at night, the Owl Bar is a good gathering space. Here you'll find live music on weekends and a wide selection of beers and spirits to accompany a limited but satisfying menu. Classic photographs of Paul Newman and Robert Redford as Butch Cassidy and the Sundance Kid hang on the walls, and with the worn plank floors, stone fireplace, and original 1890s rosewood bar (said to have been favored by Cassidy's Hole-in-the-Wall Gang) transported from Thermopolis, Wyoming, you might just feel like cutting loose. ✉ *Sundance Resort, 8841 N. Alpine Loop Rd., Sundance* ☎ *801/223–4222* 🌐 *www.sundanceresort.com.*

Performing Arts

Sundance Art Studio

ARTS CENTERS | The studios offer workshops in photography, jewelry making, wheel-thrown pottery, plein air acrylic and watercolor painting, and charcoal or pencil drawing. Mirroring the Sundance ethic, these classes blend the natural world with the artistic process. All workshops and classes are open to resort guests as well as day visitors and you'll go away with a finished piece of art ✉ *Sundance Resort, 8841 N. Alpine Loop Rd., Sundance* ☎ *801/225–4107* 🌐 *www.sundanceresort.com.*

Sundance Author Series

READINGS/LECTURES | For more than 15 years, the Sundance Author Series has brought literary and political icons like Sue Monk Kidd and Jimmy Carter to the Tree Room for an intimate brunch and lecture. As an added bonus, you'll walk away with a signed copy of the author's book. ✉ *Sundance Resort, 8841 N. Alpine Loop Rd., Sundance* ☎ *801/223–4567* 🌐 *www.sundanceresort.com* 🎟 *$85.*

Sundance Bluebird Café Concert Series

MUSIC | Each summer, Sundance brings a little Nashville to Utah with the Bluebird Café series. Singer-songwriters take the outdoor stage on select summer Fridays to share stories and music in the serene Utah mountains. ✉ *8841 N. Alpine Loop, Sundance* ☎ *866/734–4428* ⊕ *www. sundanceresort.com* ✉ *$30.*

★ Sundance Film Festival

FESTIVALS | Add this to your bucket list. Every January the Sundance Institute, a nonprofit organization supporting independent filmmaking, screenwriters, playwrights, composers, and other film and theater artists, presents the Sundance Film Festival. A world-renowned showcase for independent film, the 10-day festival is based in Park City, but has screenings and workshops at Sundance Resort, Salt Lake City, and Ogden. ✉ *Sundance* ☎ *435/658–3456* ⊕ *www. sundance.org/festival.*

Shopping

General Store

JEWELRY/ACCESSORIES | Step inside the Sundance catalog, which features distinctive home furnishings, clothing, and jewelry reflecting the rustically elegant Sundance style. Ask about many items that are organic or made of recycled materials. ✉ *Sundance Resort, 8841 N. Alpine Loop Rd., Sundance* ☎ *801/223–4250* ⊕ *www.sundanceresort.com.*

Sundance Deli

FOOD/CANDY | Selling foods from American cottage farmers and artisans as well as homemade oils, soaps, and bath salts, the Deli also has a juice bar and is a good place to get tea, coffee, shakes, pastries, deli meats, organic produce, and other tasty snacks. Stop here before your hike to pick up a fresh sandwich. ✉ *Sundance Resort, 8841 N. Alpine Loop Rd., Sundance* ☎ *801/223–4211* ⊕ *www. sundanceresort.com* ⊙ *Closed Sun.*

Activities

FLY-FISHING

The Provo River, minutes from Sundance Resort, is a fly-fishing catch-and-release waterway. Access to the rainbow, cutthroat, and German brown trout found in the river is year-round. Tours are provided by Wasatch Guide Service, and include all necessary gear and guides, and some may include drinks and snacks.

Wasatch Guide Service

FISHING | The preferred outfitter of Sundance Resort, Wasatch Guide Service provides access to some of the best fly-fishing in the state. Guides will take you to the world-class Provo River, right near Sundance Resort, or up to the Weber River to help you hook into fun runs of lively cuttroat or brown trout. They can even provide access to private waters and lesser-known streams. One guide to every two guests ensures personalized experiences, and they provide all necessary equipment. Half-day and full-day tours are available year-round, with lunch provided in the full-day tour. ✉ *Sundance* ☎ *801/830–3316* ⊕ *www. wasatchguideservice.com* ✉ *From $280 half-day; from $400 full day.*

HIKING

Hiking trails in the Sundance area vary from the easy 1.25-mile Nature Trail and the popular lift-accessed Stewart Falls Trail (3 miles) to the 7½-mile Big Baldy Trail, which leads past a series of waterfalls up steep, rugged terrain. You can access moderate- to expert-level trails from the resort base or chairlift. Select from three routes to summit the 11,000-foot Mount Timpanogos. Guided naturalist hikes are available.

MOUNTAIN BIKING

You'll find more than 25 miles of ski lift–accessed mountain-biking trails at Sundance Resort, extending from the base of Mount Timpanogos to Ray's Summit at 7,250 feet. High-tech gear rentals are available for full or half days, as is individual or group instruction.

Sundance Mountain Outfitters
BICYCLING | Rent all the gear you need for mountain biking, skiing, or snowboarding. ⊠ *8841 N. Alpine Loop Rd., Sundance* ☎ *801/223–4121* ⊕ *www. sundanceresort.com.*

SKIING
CROSS-COUNTRY
Enjoy terrain suitable for all skill levels on nearly 10 miles of groomed trails. Six miles of dedicated snowshoeing trails wind through mature aspen groves and pines. Lessons and equipment rentals, including telemark gear, are available for all techniques of cross-country skiing and snowshoeing at the Sundance Nordic Center.

DOWNHILL
Skiers and snowboarders at Sundance Resort will find 44 trails on 450 acres of varied terrain. Services include specialized ski workshops (including ladies' day clinics and personal coaching), a PSIA-certified ski school, and a ski school just for children, with programs that include all-day supervision, lunch, and ski instruction. Children as young as four are eligible for group lessons. Rentals are available for all skill levels. Night skiing is also available four nights a week.

Provo

45 miles southeast of Park City; 45 miles south of Salt Lake City; 14 miles south of Lehi.

With Mount Timpanogos to the east and Utah Lake to the west, Provo and the adjacent city of Orem make up one of the prettiest communities in the West. This two-city community is also one of the fastest growing.

GETTING HERE AND AROUND
Highway 189 from Park City or Interstate 15 from Salt Lake City both deposit you into Provo's tidy grid of easy-to-navigate streets. The sprawling Brigham Young University campus and historic downtown are at its center, with shopping malls scattered in all directions. Giant Utah Lake is to the west.

FESTIVALS
America's Freedom Festival
FESTIVALS | Each June and July, the America's Freedom Festival combines a series of patriotic activities and contests. The event peaks with a hot-air balloon festival, the state's biggest Independence Day parade, and fireworks at BYU's 65,000-seat LaVell Edwards Stadium. ⊠ *Provo* ☎ *801/818–1776* ⊕ *www.freedomfestival.org.*

ESSENTIALS
VISITOR INFORMATION **Utah County Convention and Visitors Bureau.** ⊠ *220 W. Center St., Suite 100* ☎ *801/851–2100, 800/222–8824* ⊕ *www.utahvalley.com.*

 # Sights

Brigham Young University
COLLEGE | Provo and the entire region are probably best known as the home of BYU. The university was established as the Brigham Young Academy in 1875. Heading up BYU attractions is a quartet of museums. A free guided university tour is offered weekdays on the hour, and reservations are recommended. ⊠ *BYU visitor center, Campus Dr.* ☎ *801/422–4678* ⊕ *www.byu.edu.*

Brigham Young University Museum of Art
MUSEUM | The permanent collection of more than 17,000 works here includes primarily American artists such as Maynard Dixon, Dorothea Lange, Albert Bierstadt, Minerva Teichert, and Robert Henri, and emphasizes the Hudson River School and the American impressionists. Rembrandt, Monet, and Rubens also turn up, along with some fine Far Eastern

pieces. The museum's café overlooks the sculpture garden. ✉ *N. Campus Dr., southeast of LaVell Edwards Stadium* ☎ *801/422–8287* 🌐 *moa.byu.edu* 🎟 *Free* 🕒 *Closed Sun.*

BYU Museum of Paleontology

MUSEUM | FAMILY | This museum, across from LaVell Edwards Stadium, features dinosaur bones, fossils, and tours for adults and children. Kids love the hands-on activities, which include several small tables of touchable artifacts. ✉ *1683 N. Canyon Rd.* ☎ *801/422–3680* 🌐 *geology.byu.edu/museum* 🎟 *Free.*

BYU's Museum of Peoples and Cultures

MUSEUM | A student-curated collection of artifacts relating to cultures from all over the world is housed here. Clothing, pottery, rugs, weapons, and agricultural tools of Utah's Native American cultures are often on display. A permanent display includes artifacts from the first Provo Tabernacle that BYU students dug up a couple of years ago. ✉ *2201 N. Canyon Rd.* ☎ *801/422–0020* 🌐 *mpc.byu.edu* 🎟 *Free* 🕒 *Closed weekends.*

Monte L. Bean Life Science Museum

MUSEUM | FAMILY | This museum at BYU, north of bell tower, has extensive collections of birds, mammals, fish, reptiles, insects, plants, shells, and eggs from around the world, as well as revolving nature-art exhibits. You'll also see current NASA satellite images, wildlife art, and various interactive ecology exhibits. If you bring a toddler, head for the play area themed around animal habitats. ✉ *645 E. 1430 N* ☎ *801/422–5050* 🌐 *mlbean.byu.edu* 🎟 *Free.*

Provo Pioneer Village

MUSEUM | This museum re-creates what life was like for the first settlers in the mid-19th century. Original cabins and shops furnished with period antiques are staffed by volunteer history buffs. ✉ *500 W. 600 N* ☎ *801/852–6609* 🌐 *www.provopioneervillage.org* 🎟 *Free* 🕒 *Closed Sept.–May.*

Seven Peaks Water Park

AMUSEMENT PARK/WATER PARK | FAMILY | There are 26 acres of waterborne fun here, with plenty of play areas and a wave pool. When you splash down from a water slide or rope swing, there won't be a temperature shock because the water is heated. ✉ *1330 E. 300 N* ☎ *801/373–4386* 🌐 *www.sevenpeaks.com* 🎟 *$25* 🕒 *Closed Sept.–May.*

Springville Museum of Art

MUSEUM | Springville, 10 miles south of Provo on I–15 or U.S. 89, is known for its support of the arts, and its museum is a must-stop for fine-arts fans. Built in 1937 to accommodate works by John Hasen and Cyrus Dallin, the museum now features mostly Utah artists, among them Gary Lee Price, Richard Van Wagoner, and James T. Harwood. It also has a collection of Soviet working-class impressionism and a sculpture garden with rotating exhibits. ✉ *126 E. 400 S, Springville* ☎ *801/489–2727* 🌐 *www.smofa.org* 🎟 *Free* 🕒 *Closed Mon. and Tues.*

🍴 Restaurants

★ Communal

$$$$ | AMERICAN | This cozy restaurant will feel a lot like a Sunday dinner around a large communal table, and you'll feel like you're part of the family. Meals are sourced from local food purveyors, like Payson Spring Ranch which supplies live trout to the restaurant just hours before you sit down to eat. **Known for:** locally sourced ingredients; communal dining; vibrant open kitchen. [$] *Average main: $38* ✉ *102 University Ave., Historic Downtown* ☎ *801/373–8000* 🌐 *www.communalrestaurant.com* 🕒 *Closed Sun. and Mon., no brunch weekdays.*

Guru's Café

$ | ECLECTIC | The vegetarian-friendly fare includes cilantro-lime quesadillas and rice bowls, and options for nonvegetarians include southwestern chipotle chicken wrap with a side of sweet-potato fries.

An art deco portrait of Gandhi decorates one wall of this downtown hippie refuge; elsewhere you'll find metal sculptures and blue skyscapes. **Known for:** eclectic decor; menu variety; vegetarian-friendly. $ *Average main: $10* ✉ *45 E. Center St.* ☎ *801/375–4878* ⊕ *www.guruscafe.com* ⊘ *Closed Sun.*

Pizzeria Seven Twelve

$ | PIZZA | With a name that comes from the ideal temperature for cooking pizza, the centerpiece of this bright, minimalist establishment is a wood-burning brick oven. Pizzas come topped with delectable items like *speck* (prosciutto) and *soppressata* (salami). **Known for:** varied pizza toppings; open kitchen. $ *Average main: $13* ✉ *320 S. State St., Orem* ☎ *801/623–6712* ⊕ *www.pizzeria712.com* ⊘ *Closed Sun. No lunch Sat.*

 Hotels

Hines Mansion Bed & Breakfast

$$ | B&B/INN | Quaint and charming, this bed-and-breakfast is located in an 1895 mansion, where much of the original woodwork, brick, and stained glass has been left intact. **Pros:** close to BYU; historic building with modern updates; unique and comfortable. **Cons:** bathtubs take up too much space; small rooms; inefficient layout in some rooms. $ *Rooms from: $165* ✉ *383 W. 100 S* ☎ *801/374–8400, 800/428–5636* ⊕ *www.hinesmansion.com* ➹ *9 rooms* ⅋ *Free breakfast.*

Hyatt Place Provo

$$ | HOTEL | Among the best lodging options in Provo, this dapper contemporary Hyatt boutique property is close to Brigham Young University and the city's many attractions while also providing convenience to Thanksgiving Point and mountains to the north and east. **Pros:** within walking distance of downtown Provo dining and sightseeing; mountain views from many rooms; convenient for exploring Mt. Timpanogos. **Cons:** at a busy intersection; books up during conventions and university events; 45-minute drive to downtown SLC. $ *Rooms from: $139* ✉ *180 W. 100 N* ☎ *801/609–2060* ⊕ *www.hyatt.com* ➹ *133 rooms* ⅋ *No meals.*

 Performing Arts

Because the university has a considerable interest in the arts, Provo is a great place to catch a play, dance performance, or musical production. BYU has a dozen performing groups in all. The BYU International Folk Dancers and Ballroom Dancers travel extensively, but also perform at home.

BYU Franklin S. Harris Fine Arts Center

ARTS CENTERS | Most performances at BYU are held in this center, which houses a concert hall, recital hall, and three theaters. The ticket office is on the third floor, near the south entrance, and is open weekdays 9–5; there's another ticket office on the north side of the Marriott Center, ground level, with more convenient parking. ✉ *N. Campus Dr.* ☎ *801/422–4322, 801/422–2981 tickets* ⊕ *arts.byu.edu.*

⊙ Shopping

Shopping in the Provo–Orem area centers around four primary areas. In addition to the malls, visitors find shopping opportunities at boutiques and galleries in downtown Provo, especially along Center Street.

Provo Towne Centre Mall

SHOPPING CENTERS/MALLS | On the south end of Provo, this mall has mainstream retailers like Dillard's, and specialty shops like Hallmark and Fanzz. It's open 10–9 Monday through Saturday and noon–6 on Sunday. ✉ *1200 S. University Ave.* ☎ *801/852–2400* ⊕ *www.provotownecentre.com.*

Shops at Riverwoods
SHOPPING CENTERS/MALLS | This mall is one of the newest in the area and home to upscale retailers like Jos. A. Banks, Victoria's Secret, and Williams-Sonoma. Sitting near Provo Canyon, enjoy outdoor dining amid fresh canyon breezes. ✉ *4801 N. University Ave.* ☎ *801/802–8430* ⊕ *www. shopsatriverwoods.com* ⊗ *Closed Sun.*

University Place
SHOPPING CENTERS/MALLS | Catering to the needs of BYU students with stores like Deseret Book and Simply Mac, this mall also has standard retailers like Macy's and H&M—more than 150 shops and restaurants in all. ✉ *575 E. University Pkwy., Orem* ☎ *801/224–0694* ⊕ *www. universityplaceorem.com* ⊗ *Closed Sun.*

 Activities

BICYCLING
In the Provo area, road cyclists may make a 100-mile circumnavigation of Utah Lake or tackle U.S. 189 through Provo Canyon or the Alpine Loop Scenic Byway. Mountain bikers can choose from a large selection of trails varying in degrees of difficulty.

Racer's Cycle Service
BICYCLING | For information about biking in the area, bicycle sales, and world-class service, call Racer's Cycle Service and talk to owner "Racer" Jared Gibson. Racer's Cycle Service is fully mobile with no brick-and-mortar store. ✉ *Provo* ☎ *801/375–5873* ⊕ *www.racerscycleservice.com* ☞ *By appointment only.*

FISHING
Utah Lake State Park
FISHING | Fishing is popular at Utah Lake, which, at 96,600 acres, is the state's largest freshwater lake. In spring and fall it gets some of the best wind in Utah for windsurfing and sailing. Powerboating and canoeing are also popular. ✉ *4400 W. Center St.* ☎ *801/375–0731* ⊕ *stateparks. utah.gov* ☜ *$10.*

GOLF
You'll find 10 public courses within Utah Valley, ranging from canyon or mountain settings to relatively flat and easy-to-walk terrain. Tee times are usually easy to get, and greens fees are reasonable.

Hobble Creek Golf Course
GOLF | The canyon setting at this affordable course east of Springville makes for a beautiful day, especially in fall when the hills explode with color. Golfers rave about the views and warn of tricky greens. This course is consistently rated a favorite among the public courses in Utah. The newly renovated Terrace Grill and full service pro shop are added conveniences. ✉ *5984 E. Hobble Creek Canyon Rd.* ☎ *801/489–6297* ⊕ *www. springville.org/golf* ☜ *$15 for 9 holes, $30 for 18 holes* ⅄ *18 holes, 6400 yards, par 71.*

Reserve at East Bay
GOLF | The 18-hole championship course wends around the beautiful shoreline of Utah Lake and wetlands, with excellent views of the Wasatch Mountains and the chance to spot birds along the way. The 7-hole Executive Course is great for beginners and juniors, and is walk-on only. The individual and group lessons, as well as clinics, provide personalized instruction with PGA professionals. ✉ *1860 S. East Bay Blvd.* ☎ *801/852– 7529* ⊕ *www.eastbaygolf.com* ☜ *$28 Mon.–Thurs.; $30 Fri., Sat., and holidays; $24 Sun.* ⅄ *18 holes, 6900 yards, par 73.*

HIKING
Visitors to the southern part of the Wasatch find many trails from which to choose.

Bonneville Shoreline Trail
HIKING/WALKING | The 100-mile Bonneville Shoreline Trail from Brigham City to Nephi spans the foothills of the Wasatch Front following the eastern shoreline of ancient Lake Bonneville. The section near Provo begins at the Rock Creek trailhead and continues south along the foothills,

The Alpine Loop Scenic Byway is especially gorgeous in the fall.

past the Y trailhead, to the Hobble Creek Parkway trailhead. ✉ *Provo.*

Bridal Veil Falls

HIKING/WALKING | The trailhead to Bridal Veil Falls is 2½ miles up Provo Canyon; after the moderate climb, hikers are rewarded with a cold mountain waterfall shower. ✉ *Provo.*

Provo Parkway

HIKING/WALKING | The easy, paved Provo Parkway meanders along the Provo River from the mouth of Provo Canyon and provides a good mix of shade and sun. ✉ *Provo.*

ICE-SKATING

Peaks Ice Arena

ICE SKATING | A 2002 Olympic Hockey venue, this arena includes two ice sheets, and is open throughout the year for figure skating, hockey, and parties. ✉ *100 N. Seven Peaks Blvd.* ☎ *801/852–7465* ⊕ *www.provo.org/community/peaks-ice-arena* ⊡ *$5.*

American Fork

14 miles north of Provo; 4 miles east of Lehi.

American Fork serves as a good base for exploring Timpanogos Cave National Monument as well as other sights throughout the canyon.

★ Alpine Loop Scenic Byway

MOUNTAIN—SIGHT | Beyond Timpanogos Cave, Highway 92 continues up American Fork Canyon before branching off to climb behind Mount Timpanogos itself. Designated the Alpine Loop Scenic Byway, this winding road offers stunning mountain views and fall foliage in the latter months before dropping into Provo Canyon to the south. The 14-mile round-trip Timpooneke Trail and the 14-mile round-trip Aspen Grove Trail, both off the byway, reach the summit of Mount Timpanogos. Also along this highway is the famed Sundance Resort. Closed, depending on snowfall, from late October to late May, the Alpine Loop is free to drive, but you need to purchase a National Forest pass ($6, good for three days) to park at any of the trailheads and recreation areas along the route. This is the roundabout way to get to scenic Provo Canyon and Deer Creek Resevoir from I–15 (if heading south from Salt Lake City); the more direct route is U.S. 189 east from near Orem and Provo (stop by Bridal Veil Falls on your way in). ⊠ *American Fork* ⊕ *www.utah.com/ scenic-drive/alpine-loop.*

Timpanogos Cave National Monument

CAVE | Soaring to 11,750 feet, Mount Timpanogos is the centerpiece of a wilderness area of the same name and towers over Timpanogos Cave National Monument along Highway 92 within American Fork Canyon. After a somewhat strenuous hike up the paved 1½-mile trail to the entrance, you can explore three caves connected by two man-made tunnels. Stalactites, stalagmites, and other formations make the three-hour round-trip hike and tour worth the effort. No refreshments are available on the trail or at the cave, and the cave temperature is 45°F throughout the year, so bring water and warm clothes. Although there's some lighting inside the caves, a flashlight will make your explorations more interesting; it will also come in handy if you're heading back down the trail after dusk. These popular tours often sell out; it's a good idea to book online in advance, especially on weekends. ⊠ *2038 W. Alpine Loop Rd., American Fork* ☎ *801/756–5239 cave info, 877/444–6777 tickets* ⊕ *www. nps.gov/tica* ⊠ *Cave tours $12* ☉ *Cave closed Nov.–Apr.*

Lehi

28 miles south of Salt Lake City.

One of the first towns settled in the Utah Valley, Lehi is home to Thanksgiving Point, a great place for the whole family to unwind, as well as for several historical museums and restored buildings.

GETTING HERE AND AROUND

From Salt Lake City, take Interstate 15 south for about 28 miles to Exit 282, then U.S. 89.

Sights

Thanksgiving Point

FARM/RANCH | **FAMILY** | Founded by the Ashton family (Alan Ashton founded WordPerfect computer software, which is now Orem-based Novell), Thanksgiving Point is an ever-evolving destination with a wealth of attractions. Wander among 60 dinosaur skeletons in the Museum of Ancient Life; explore a slew of oddities in the Museum of Natural Curiosity; play golf on an 18-hole Johnny Miller–designed course; or meditate in 55 acres of carefully landscaped and eminently Instagrammable gardens. There are also a petting zoo with cute farm animals, a butterfly biosphere, shops, restaurants, and a megaplex theater, and there are several hotels nearby. The museums are open year-round, but gardens and some other attractions are seasonal. ⊠ *3003 N. Thanksgiving Way* ☎ *801/768–2300* ⊕ *www.thanksgivingpoint.com* ⊠ *Museums, Butterfly Biosphere, and Ashton Gardens: $20 each. Farm Country: $10* ☉ *Closed Sun.*

Restaurants

Cubby's

$ | **AMERICAN** | **FAMILY** | Inspired by the Italian beef sandwiches with homemade relish that the owner couldn't get enough of while growing up in Chicago, this lively and fun Thanksgiving Point eatery creative comfort fare from morning through the evening. Lemon ricotta pancakes are a favorite way to start the morning, while mushroom-bacon-gouda burgers, apple-pecan chicken salads, and Chicago-style Italian sausage sandwiches are the draw later in the day. **Known for:** Chicago-style Italian beef sandwiches; plenty of veggie and vegan options;

fresh-berry milkshakes. $ *Average main: $10* ⊠ *3700 N. Thanksgiving Way* ☎ *801/766–8100* ⊕ *www.cubbys.co* ⊘ *Closed Sun.*

Porter's Place

$$ | **AMERICAN** | Belly up to the bar where the stools are made of old tractor seats, or sit down at one of the small tables and order a buffalo burger or a 20-ounce porterhouse steak, followed by a slice of pecan pie. The atmosphere is friendly in a rough-around-the-edges way, just like the early Mormon purported hit man Porter Rockwell after whom this place is named. **Known for:** Western vibe; divine burgers; local history. $ *Average main: $20* ⊠ *24 W. Main St.* ☎ *801/768–8348* ⊘ *Closed Sun.*

 ## Hotels

Best Western Timpanogos Inn

$ | **HOTEL** | Great views, convenient access, and clean updated rooms make this a good stopover. **Pros:** basic but comfortable. **Cons:** no frills. $ *Rooms from: $99* ⊠ *195 S. 850 E* ☎ *801/768–1400, 800/780–7234* ⊕ *www.bestwestern.com* ⤳ *59 rooms* ❍ *Free breakfast.*

Home2 Suites Lehi–Thanksgiving Point

$ | **HOTEL** | **FAMILY** | Within walking distance of the restaurants, shops, and attractions at Thanksgiving Point, this reasonably priced all-suites Hilton property has well-stocked kitchenettes and roomy accommodations. **Pros:** convenient for trips to Timpanogos Cave; in-room kitchenettes are nice for longer stays; in the heart of Thankgiving Point attractions. **Cons:** slightly dull suburban setting; can be packed with families on weekends; half-hour drive from downtown SLC. $ *Rooms from: $119* ⊠ *3051 W. Club House Dr.* ☎ *801/753–5430* ⊕ *www.hilton.com* ⤳ *103 rooms* ❍ *Free breakfast.*

 ## Activities

GOLF

Thanksgiving Point Golf Course

GOLF | The popular 18-hole Johnny Miller–designed golf course at Thanksgiving Point is a championship course geared toward intermediate and advanced players. Covering more than 200 acres, it is also the largest course in the state. The Jordan River winds around the perimeter and through the course, artistically used throughout the design of the holes. Wind is a factor when playing Thanksgiving Point, but many feel it adds to the personality of the course. ⊠ *3300 W. Clubhouse Dr.* ☎ *801/768–7400* ⊕ *thanksgivingpointgolfcourse.com* ⛳ *Peak Season: Mon.–Wed. $69, Thurs. $79, Fri. and Sat. $89, Sun. $54* ⚑ *18 holes, 7714 yards, par 72.*

Chapter 5

NORTHERN UTAH

Updated by
Andrew Collins

● Sights	🍴 Restaurants	🛏 Hotels	👜 Shopping	🍸 Nightlife
★★★★★	★★★★☆	★★★☆☆	★★★☆☆	★★★☆☆

WELCOME TO NORTHERN UTAH

TOP REASONS TO GO

★ **Ski Ogden:** Park City gets the accolades, but locals know that the snow is just as amazing, the slopes less crowded, and the prices much more reasonable at Snowbasin, Powder Mountain, and Nordic Valley.

★ **Hiking:** You'll find hiking adventures throughout Ogden Valley.

★ **Logan Canyon National Scenic Byway:** The magnificent, winding 39-mile stretch of U.S. 89 from Logan to Bear Lake is best enjoyed in the fall.

★ **Historic 25th Street, Ogden:** Once home to brothels and unsavory railside establishments, downtown Ogden's revitalized 25th Street and adjacent Nine Rails Creative District now abound with art galleries, museums, hip restaurants, and indie shops.

★ **Bear Lake:** A favorite retreat on the Utah-Idaho border during the hot summer months, this modestly developed lake has a reputation for azure-blue water and delicious raspberry milkshakes.

The region north of Salt Lake City stretches along the rugged Wasatch Range to the Idaho border and includes a couple of smaller cities with their own distinctive histories and personalities like Ogden and Logan, as well as the smaller community of Brigham City located between the two. Additionally, Ogden Valley and Garden City (with surrounding Bear Lake) are hubs of outdoor recreation.

1 Ogden. Not counting the sprawling suburbs around Salt Lake City, Ogden is Utah's second-largest metropolis, a once rough-and-tumble railroad and fur-trading hub whose vibrant and historic downtown now teems with cool dining, galleries, and retail; its outskirts abound with gorgeous hiking and mountain biking trails.

2 Ogden Valley. Just a 15-minute drive over the mountains from Ogden, this sweeping mile-high valley is home to the villages of Eden and Huntsville, which flank the shores of massive Pineview Reservoir. Ogden Valley is famed for its world-class ski resorts, Snowbasin and Powder Mountain.

3 Brigham City. The pleasant, all-American seat of Box Elder County makes a good stop en route between Ogden and Logan and a base for day trips to Golden Spike National Historical Park.

4 Logan. This picturesque collegiate community is home to Utah State University and offers a handsome downtown with some elegantly restored theaters where the Utah Festival Opera performs. There's also easy access to miles of breathtaking hiking trails, most of them off scenic U.S. 89, which winds through the sheer walls of nearby Logan Canyon.

5 Garden City. A tiny and mostly seasonal summer-vacation hub with a number of restaurants and hotels, Garden City hugs the western shore of enormous Bear Lake, which is half in Utah, half in Idaho.

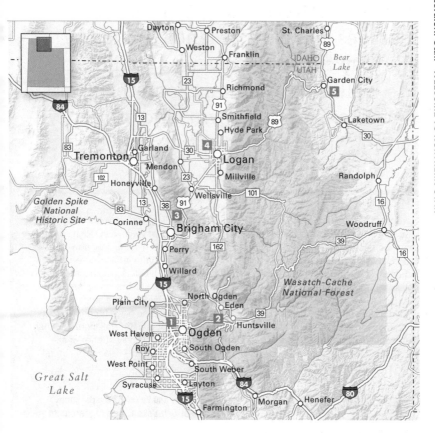

When you picture Utah, many envision the red-rock crags and canyons of the south, but the north, with its cattail marshes and pasture lands framed by the gray cliffs and towering conifers of the Wellsville Mountains and the Bear River Range, has its own kind of beauty—without the throngs of tourists you'll encounter in the south.

Here the Shoshones (Sacagawea's tribe) made their summer camps, living on roots, berries, and the plentiful game of the lowlands. In the 1820s and '30s mountain men came to trap beavers, foxes, and muskrats, taking time out for their annual rendezvous on the shores of Bear Lake. Some, like the famous Jim Bridger, married Native Americans and settled here; to this day, Cache, Rich, and Box Elder counties are collectively known as "Bridgerland." In the 1850s Mormon pioneers were sent by Brigham Young to settle here, and their descendants still populate this rugged land. In 1869 an event occurred here that would change the face of the West, and indeed the nation, forever: the completion of the Transcontinental Railroad was celebrated officially at Promontory Summit.

The region is characterized by alternating mountain ranges and valleys, typical of the Basin and Range geologic province that extends westward into Nevada and California. Much of the landscape has remained unspoiled, thankfully preserved as part of the Uinta-Wasatch-Cache National Forest, and offers a range of outdoor activities for all seasons: hiking, mountain biking, kayaking, skiing, snowmobiling, and birding among them. In more recent years, as Ogden has reimagined its historic downtown, the area has begun to attract more artists, foodies, and hipsters who appreciate the high quality of life and strong sense of community. With a large student population, Logan also has a burgeoning arts and maker scene. Overall, northern Utah enjoys an increasingly strong—if still slightly underrated—balance of natural and human-made attractions.

MAJOR REGIONS

Ogden City and Valley. The largest city north of Salt Lake City is Ogden, with more than 88,000 residents. Its growth was spurred by the coming of the railroads and Hill Air Force Base, but its 21st-century renaissance is oriented around the easygoing outdoorsy lifestyle here. Hiking, skiing, golf, kayaking, boating, and more are all available either within city limits or in the beautiful valley that lies 8 miles up the canyon.

The Golden Spike Empire. Heading north up I-15 from Ogden (or, if you're in no hurry, up U.S. 89, where you'll find plenty of farm stands), you'll come upon the Golden Spike Empire. Pleasant farmlands

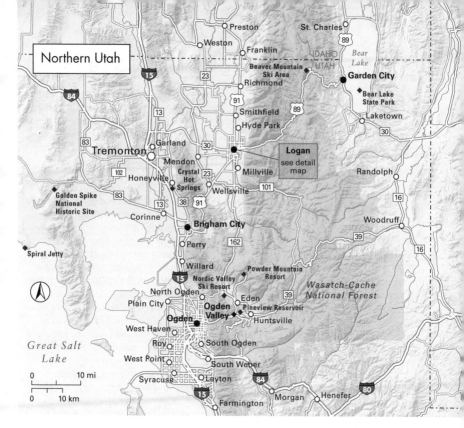

in the shadow of the Wellsvilles give way to rolling sagebrush-covered hills and eventually the desolate salt flats of the Great Salt Lake. Visit the Bear River Migratory Bird Refuge and the Golden Spike National Historic Site.

Cache Valley. North and roughly half the size of Ogden is the beautiful town of Logan, home to Utah State University and the Utah Festival Opera. You'll want to devote a day or two to the thriving college town, including the university's small but excellent museums and the spectacular drive through Logan Canyon along U.S. 89, which has lots of opportunities for hiking.

Bear Lake Country. It's almost incomprehensible that a lake as blue as the Mediterranean exists in the Intermountain West, but it does. Straddling the Utah–Idaho border, Bear Lake is relatively

undeveloped, with a quaint cluster of old-fashioned burger and shake shops on the southwest side in the town of Garden City, and only a few small motels and campgrounds. At 109 square miles, it will give you plenty to explore for a few days in the hot summer.

Planning

When to Go

Northern Utah offers four seasons of outdoor fun. Be prepared for hot summer days and extremely cold winter nights, especially in the mountains. Spring brings vistas of verdant pastures under the still snowcapped mountains. Hot summer afternoons prepare you for a dip in Bear Lake followed by an evening at Logan's Festival Opera. On crisp fall days, breathtaking hues of red scrub oak, orange maple, and bright yellow aspen rub shoulders with blue-green firs. Winter is the domain of skiers, snowshoers, and snowmobilers. This region drops dozens of inches of snow annually in the valleys and hundreds of inches in the mountains. You'll never battle hordes of tourists in this less-discovered part of the state, but you might have to wait in a line of locals for a raspberry shake at Bear Lake on a summer weekend.

Planning Your Time

You can get a good sense of the region's key draws over a long weekend, divided between Ogden, Logan, and perhaps Bear Lake. For a more intensive exploration of northern Utah, **Ogden** serves as a great base, offering plenty of urban and outdoor activities. Plan on a day in Ogden to check out **Historic 25th Street** and the area's several good museums and outdoor attractions. More ardent fans of recreation will want to add at least a day in **Ogden Valley,** with its abundance of hiking and boating opportunities and—in winter—world-class skiing and snowboarding at **Powder Mountain** and **Snowbasin.** The small city of **Brigham City** is worth a stop if you're planning to spend time at nearby **Golden Spike National Historic Site,** and perhaps for a soak at family-friendly **Crystal Hot Springs.** Heading north to the friendly college town of **Logan,** spend a day enjoying great opera in summer and some good museums and impressive hikes before venturing out on one of the state's most scenic drives through **Logan Canyon,** on your way to **Bear Lake State Park,** where boating, swimming, or lounging await at Rendezvous Beach.

Getting Here and Around

There are three main strategies for visiting the area north of Salt Lake City. By far the most popular and convienient is by car—Ogden is 45 minutes north of Salt Lake City via Interstate 15, and Logan is four hours southeast of Boise via Interstate 84 to U.S. 89. Although central Ogden and to a lesser extent Logan can be explored on foot or using local buses, you really need a car to fully appreciate the region's best attractions. A second option is to take a bus or commuter train to Ogden or Logan and rent a car once you arrive. Several major car rental agencies have offices in Ogden and there are a couple in Logan, too. The advantage with this strategy is that rental car rates are generally much lower at these local offices than at the Salt Lake International Airport. The least expensive but also least practical option is using public transit both to reach and explore the towns in the area—this works best in Ogden and Ogden Valley, which has a robust bus network. You could also use Lyft and Uber to get around in Ogden and Logan, but if you're making more than two or three trips a day, the cost may exceed that of renting a car.

BUS

The Utah Transit Authority (UTA) provides bus, FrontRunner commuter rail, and TRAX light-rail service throughout the Wasatch Front, and it can get you to a lot of places in Ogden and Brigham City and well as back and forth between Salt Lake City, but it's a slower and less flexible alternative to driving. Another option is using one of the region's shuttle bus companies. From Salt Lake City Airport, Express Shuttle can get you to Ogden and Ogden Valley, and from the airport and downtown, Salt Lake Express stops in Ogden, Brigham City, and Logan on its way north to Idaho.

BUS CONTACTS Express Shuttle.
☎ 800/397–0773 ⊕ www.expressshut-tleutah.com. **Salt Lake Express.**
☎ 208/656–8824 ⊕ www.saltlakeexpress.com. **Utah Transit Authority.** ☎ 801/743–3882 ⊕ www.rideuta.com.

CAR
The interstate cuts north from Salt Lake City through the region, joining U.S. 89, which winds up through Logan to Bear Lake, and also Interstate 84, which curves in a northwesterly direction to Idaho. U.S. 89 is also known as Logan Canyon Scenic Byway north of the city of Logan and is, as you might guess, stunning to drive. Off the main highways, roads range from well-paved multilane blacktop routes to barely graveled backcountry trails that may require high-clearance vehicles—if heading to trailheads or lakes in the national forest, it's a good idea to check websites or with local ranger offices for driving conditions, especially in winter or after rainy periods.

TRAIN
UTA's FrontRunner high-speed commuter train operates hourly Monday through Saturday, and every half-hour during weekday rush hour, between the downtowns of Ogden and Salt Lake City (and on south to Provo), with several stops in between. Fares are based on the distance traveled; it's $5.50 one way from Salt Lake City to Ogden.

TRAIN INFORMATION Utah Transit Authority. ☎ 801/743–3882 ⊕ www.rideuta.com.

Restaurants

Ogden has become a real dining destination in recent years; its historic downtown is rife with cool little indie eateries, gastropubs, international restaurants, and coffeehouses, along with a handful of craft-beer bars and micobreweries. Logan has a smattering of notable eateries too, but beyond these communities, you can mostly expect casual, Western-style grub (steaks, burgers, and the like). Note that many restaurants in this part of the state, especially beyond Ogden, don't serve alcohol and are closed on Sunday.

Hotels

Chain hotels are the most likely options in this part of the state, although you will find a handful of B&Bs in Logan and some of the small villages in Ogden Valley; the area also abounds with condo rentals that fill up—and can command steep rates—during ski season. Bear Lake, on the other hand, has very few hotels and virtually no chain properties but does have some family-friendly condos and vacation rentals (just remember that summer is high season in this area.)

Restaurant and hotel reviews have been shortened. For full information, visit Fodors.com.

What it Costs			
$	$$	$$$	$$$$
RESTAURANTS			
under $16	$16–$22	$23–$30	over $30
HOTELS			
under $125	$125–$175	$176–$225	over $225

Visitor Information

Bear Lake Convention and Visitors Bureau
✉ 69 N. Paradise Pkwy., Garden City ☎ 435/946–2197 ⊕ www.bearlake.org.

Cache Valley Visitors Bureau
✉ 199 N. Main St., Logan ☎ 435/755–1890 ⊕ www.explorelogan.com.

Ogden

35 miles north of Salt Lake City.

Even though it was settled several years prior to Salt Lake City's 1847 Mormon influx, Ogden has nonetheless been trumped by the capital city for most of its history.

GETTING HERE AND AROUND

Ogden lies about 40 minutes north of Salt Lake City on Interstate 15, with a few suburbs and the Hill Air Force Base in between. Slower but parallel U.S. 89 hugs the foothills of the Wasatch Mountains and offers an alternative route and a shortcut for drivers headed to Ogden Valley. Most visitors get here by car, but FrontRunner trains and UTA buses are public-transit options that make sense if you're planning to spend most of your time downtown, which is quite pedestrian-friendly.

ESSENTIALS

VISITOR INFORMATION Visit Ogden.

✉ *2411 Kiesel Ave., Suite 401* ☎ *800/255–8824, 801/778–6250* ⊕ *www.visitogden.com.*

Sights

Eccles Community Art Center

MUSEUM | Housed in an imposing 1893 Queen Anne mansion with soaring turrets, this vibrant community arts center with a focus on diversity and inclusion presents a permanent collection of works by regional and national artists. There are also rotating shows exhibited throughout the building's public spaces and a sculpture garden with flowers and a stunning fountain. The center also offers a wide range of performing and visual arts classes and special events. ✉ *2580 Jefferson Ave.* ☎ *801/392–6935* ⊕ *www.ogden4arts.org* ⊗ *Closed Sun.*

★ First Friday Art Stroll

MUSEUM | The first Friday of each month, 20 or so downtown galleries, shops, and restaurants showcase the work of local artists during a neighborhood stroll that stretches from the gallery inside Union Station to the Eccles Community Art Center, in the emerging Nine Rails Creative District. One of the most interesting stops is the Monarch, a multiuse business incubator and arts space housed in a restored 1920s parking garage and containing galleries as well as captivating murals. ✉ *Ogden* ⊕ *www.ogdencity.com/770/First-Friday-Art-Stroll.*

★ George S. Eccles Dinosaur Park

CITY PARK | FAMILY | This 6-acre park near the mouth of Ogden Canyon is the stomping ground for about 100 life-size dinosaur models and the delighted children who come to see them. A playground with dinosaurs to crawl on appeals to younger kids, and adults can brush up on their geology and paleontology inside two natural history museums. You can watch technicians working with excavated dinosaur bones in the paleontology lab. A particularly good gift shop brims with dinosaur toys and souvenirs. ✉ *1544 E. Park Blvd.* ☎ *801/393–3466* ⊕ *www.dinosaurpark.org* ⊠ *$7* ⊗ *Closed Sun. and Mon. in winter.*

Hill Aerospace Museum

MUSEUM | FAMILY | You can view the exteriors of nearly 100 military aircrafts dating from the early years of flight to the present at this impressive 30-acre indoor-outdoor museum at the north end of Hill Air Force Base, about 7 miles south of downtown Ogden. There are also missiles, military vehicles, munitions, uniforms, and thousands of other artifacts. ✉ *Hill Air Force Base, 7961 Wardleigh Rd., Roy* ☎ *801/825–5817* ⊕ *www.aerospaceutah.org* ⊗ *Closed Sun.*

★ Historic 25th Street

HISTORIC SITE | The centerpiece of downtown Ogden's highly successful renaissance, this broad, lively street with restaurants, bars, and shops set inside handsomely restored 19th-century buildings is a great spot for a stroll any time of day. Historical markers tell the story of the pubs, brothels, and gambling houses that thrived here a century ago, an anomaly in heavily Mormon Utah. The three-block stretch from Union Station to Washington Boulevard is especially vibrant, but the action continues a couple of blocks north to 23rd Street Street, where you'll find the Salomon Center (an indoor complex of gyms and fitness enterprises that includes a bowling alley, surfing and wakeboarding park, climbing wall, and indoor wind tunnel) and a big multiscreen movie theater at the corner of Kiesel Avenue. As you venture east, beyond Grant Avenue and between 24th and 26th streets, you'll encounter the rapidly emerging Nine Rails Creative District, a hub of galleries, start-up businesses, and creative endeavors that's anchored around the multiuse Monarch Building (*455 25th St.*), with its art studios and murals. ⊠ *25th St. at Washington Blvd.* ⊕ *www.historic25.com.*

Ogden Botanical Gardens

GARDEN | This tranquil 11-acre urban oasis set along the Ogden River Parkway is operated by the University of Utah and contains a series of themed gardens—rose, Oriental, water conservation, edible, cottage—connected by a network of meandering paths, some of which flank the river. One garden has been designed for people with mobility challenges, and an arboretum features trees that are ideal for planting beneath powerlines, as they never exceed 25 feet in height. On warm days, the conifer garden is a fragrant spot offering plenty of shade. There are also attractive picnic areas and lawns that invite relaxing. ⊠ *1750 Monroe Blvd.* ☏ *801/399–8080* ⊕ *www.ogdenbotanical-gardens.org.*

★ Ogden Nature Center

NATURE PRESERVE | FAMILY | Although close to Interstate 15 on the north side of the city, this quiet 152-acre center abounds with opportunities to view and interact with nature. It's home to thousands of trees, plus vibrant marshlands and ponds, with nature trails that are popular year-round (cross-country skiers take to them in winter). It's possible to view Canada geese, great blue herons, red foxes, mule deer, and porcupines roaming the grounds (you can get especially good views from a small observatory tower), as well as rescued bald eagles, owls, and other spectacular species. The eco-consciously designed visitor center has interesting exhibits as well as activities for kids while the education building shows rotating art exhibits and the excellent Nest gift shop sells nature-oriented goods. ⊠ *966 W. 12th St.* ☏ *801/621–7595* ⊕ *www.ogdennature-center.org* 🖃 *$5* 🕑 *Closed Sun.*

Treehouse Museum

MUSEUM | FAMILY | Offering a hands-on learning experience where children literally can step into a story, this downtown museum is filled with imaginative interactive exhibits geared generally those under 12. Visit Jack's Fairy Tale Diner, a Japanese House, the Jupiter Train Locomotive, or the German House Puppet Theater. Other fun activities include songs, theater, and art workshops. Admission is actually slightly higher ($8) for kids than adults. ⊠ *347 22nd St.* ☏ *801/394–9663* ⊕ *www.treehousemu-seum.org* 🖃 *$5* 🕑 *Closed Sun.*

★ Union Station

MUSEUM | FAMILY | Incorporating elements from Ogden's original 1870s train depot that was destroyed by a fire in 1923, the impressive Spanish Revival replacement has been developed into a landmark cultural center with two art galleries and four diverse museums. The **Browning Firearms Museum** celebrates the many achievements of the museum's namesake and showcases the sporting and military firearms that were popular in the Old West before Browning formed his own company. The **Browning–Kimball Classic Car Museum** pays tribute to the golden age of automobiles with a small but dazzling collection of restored cars from the first half of the 20th century. The **Utah State Railroad Museum** thrills train enthusiasts with its meandering exhibits detailing all phases of Utah's railroad history; a highlight is the outdoor Eccles Rail Center, which includes half a dozen restored train cars. The smallest museum of the bunch, the **Utah Cowboy & Western Heritage Museum,** features the Utah Cowboy Hall of Fame and honors artists, rodeo champions, entertainers, musicians, ranchers, and writers who have promoted the Western lifestyle. The Myra Powell Gallery mounts monthly photography exhibits while the Gallery at the Station showcases local art in an enclosed passenger platform. ✉ *2501 Wall Ave.* ☎ *801/629–8672* 🌐 *www.ogdencity.com/1562/Union-Station* 🎟 *$7 (combined admission for all museums)* 🕒 *Closed Sun.*

🍴 Restaurants

Harp & Hound
$ | **AMERICAN** | A hot spot among artists, hikers, musicians, LGBTQ folks, and college students, this festive gastropub serves up elevated comfort fare, like blackened salmon tacos, barbecue chicken pizzas, meatless "wings" with buffalo sauce, and garlic-mushroom-Swiss burgers. There's an excellent tap and cocktail list, and in the basement, you'll find the hip and diverse Funk and Dive speakeasy, an inviting spot for cocktails and live music. **Known for:** lots of vegan options; eclectic crowd and great people-watching; popular weekend brunch. [$] *Average main: $13* ✉ *2550 Washington Blvd.* ☎ *801/621–3483* 🌐 *www.harphound.com.*

Hearth on 25th
$$$ | **MODERN AMERICAN** | With an emphasis on wood-fired cooking and farm-to-table seasonality, the menu at this dapper but casual gem includes salmon and octopus with creative preparations and house-made pastas, breads, and dressings. On warm days, dine on the patio overlooking the historic district and the Wasatch Mountains while enjoying the wine on tap, a huge selection of whiskeys, and a seasonally changing array of fresh desserts. **Known for:** yak, rabbit, elk, and other wild game dishes; addictive truffle fries; market with pastas, olive oils, and gourmet groceries to go. [$] *Average main: $24* ✉ *195 25th St.* ☎ *801/399–0088* 🌐 *www.hearth25.com* 🕒 *Closed Mon. No lunch.*

★ **Pig & a Jelly Jar**
$ | **SOUTHERN** | **FAMILY** | This funky, down-home diner with graffiti-covered brick walls serves hearty Southern food throughout the day, starting with fried chicken and biscuits and ham hash in the morning and moving on to catfish and chips and brown sugar–and–maple barbecue pork sandwiches later in the day. Save room for the beignets or cinnamon biscuits for dessert, and snag a bottle of pineapple-lemon-rosemary or blueberry-lavender jam on your way out. **Known for:** shareable family-style platters; Nashville-style hot chicken; champagne cocktails mixed with house-made jams. [$] *Average main: $12* ✉ *227 25th St.* ☎ *801/605–8400* 🌐 *www.pigandajellyjar.com.*

Slackwater Pizzeria & Pub
$ | **PIZZA** | This casual stop along the Ogden River Parkway boasts hundreds of craft beers, mountain and river views, and a festive, friendly vibe. Try the boldly unorthodox pizza toppings, which are internationally inspired, verdant, and piled high; the gyro trip pie with a peppered-lemon base, shaved lamb, and tzatski drizzle is especially good. **Known for:** après-ski fun on the heated patio; live

Union Station houses four museums and two art galleries.

music and Ping-Pong; innovative brick-oven pizzas. $ *Average main: $15* ✉ *1895 Washington Blvd.* ☎ *801/399-0637* ⊕ *www.slackwaterpizzeria.com.*

★ Tona Sushi Bar and Grillog

$$ | **JAPANESE** | This chic little Japanese spot has a modern focus, offering much more than just sushi rolls (although the phenomenal rolls alone, such as the smokin hot machi with rosemary-smoked hamachi, fennel, Thai chili, orange slices, and citrus soy, would keep the doors open). Tona goes light on the sauce and heavy on the freshest ingredients, with an expansive menu that features artfully plated grilled mackerel with a raspberry-soy glaze, udon with chicken and tempura prawns, and flash-seared ahi with freshly cut pineapples. **Known for:** ocean-trout crudo and other creatively presented sashimi; extensive sake selection; house-made cheesecake with raspberry puree. $ *Average main: $18* ✉ *210 25th St.* ☎ *801/622-8662* ⊕ *www.tonarestaurant. com* ⊙ *Closed Sun. and Mon.*

★ WB's Eatery

$ | **MODERN AMERICAN** | Plush armchairs, exposed air ducts, rotating contemporary art, and brick walls create a salon ambience in this high-ceilinged space inside the Monarch Building in the trendy Nine Rails Creative District. Specializing in fine coffees and wines, WB's also turns out well-crafted café fare throughout the day, including brûléed grapefruit and ham-and-egg toasties at breakfast and grilled-shrimp bowls, Brussel sprouts tostadas, and fig-and-prosciutto bruschetta during the afternoon and evening hours. **Known for:** stunning, art-filled interior; delectable cheese and meat boards; craft beverages and snacks to go in the specialty market. $ *Average main: $12* ✉ *455 25th St.* ☎ *385/244-1471* ⊕ *www.wbseatery. com.*

☕ Coffee and Quick Bites

Wasatch Roasting Company

$ | **CAFÉ** | Tucked inside a narrow historic downtown building festooned with colorful murals and graffiti, this funky café has well-trained baristas and sources its coffee beans from small, high-quality growers. Choose from well-crafted espresso drinks, single-origin coffees by whatever brewing method you choose (chemex, French press, and so on), or one of the many nitro options, from on-tap cascara to kombucha. **Known for:** potent nitro cold brew (available by the can); affogato with premium ice cream; colorful "Aerosol Art Gallery" on the patio. $ *Average main: $6* ✉ *2436 Grant Ave.* ☎ *801/689–2626* ⊕ *www.wasatchroasting.com.*

 # Hotels

Courtyard Ogden
$$ | HOTEL | This eight-story chain property looks and feels a bit like any other Courtyard Marriott but stands out for its excellent downtown location a block from Historic 25th Street, its spacious rooms with sitting areas, and a wealth of fitness and leisure amenities, including an indoor pool, hot tub, and 24-hour gym. **Pros:** mountain views from even-number rooms; free parking; steps from 25th Street dining and retail. **Cons:** breakfast costs extra; cookie-cutter decor and design; in a busy part of downtown. $ *Rooms from: $144* ✉ *247 24th St.* ☎ *801/627–1190* ⊕ *www.marriott.com* ⇘ *193 rooms* ⦿ *No meals.*

★ Hampton Inn and Suites
$$ | HOTEL | Gray marble, bright bay windows, and soaring ceilings with ornate crown molding greet you in the lobby of this art deco beauty with airy guest rooms and gorgeous mountain and city views. **Pros:** elegant, historic architecture; suites are among the largest rooms downtown; steps from Historic 25th Street. **Cons:** frequently fills up with business travelers; no pool; on a very busy street. $ *Rooms from: $129* ✉ *2401 Washington Blvd.* ☎ *801/394–9400* ⊕ *www.hamptoninnogden.com* ⇘ *145 rooms* ⦿ *Free breakfast.*

Hilton Garden Inn
$$$ | HOTEL | A modern low-rise that's right in the heart of downtown and steps from attractions, restaurants, and shopping, this well-outfitted outpost of the reliable Hilton Garden brand has a slew of handy perks, including a full-service restaurant, an indoor pool and hot tub, a gym, and a striking glass-pavilion lobby with a bar and fireplace. **Pros:** some suites have jetted tubs or gas fireplaces; decent restaurant and lounge with room service; across from multiplex theater and Salomon Center fitness studios. **Cons:** a bit pricier than other downtown hotels; breakfast costs extra; rooms get some traffic noise. $ *Rooms from: $179* ✉ *2271 S. Washington Bd.* ☎ *801/399–2000* ⊕ *www.hilton.com* ⇘ *134 rooms* ⦿ *No meals.*

 # Nightlife

★ Angry Goat Pub
BARS/PUBS | With one of the best craft beer lists in Utah and a terrific selection of artisan spirts, this inviting gastropub with exposed-brick walls and a handful of sidewalk tables also turns out delicious comfort food, from lamb burgers to steamed mussels. It opens early on weekends for a very popular and boozy brunch. ✉ *2570 Washington Blvd.* ☎ *801/675–5757* ⊕ *www.angrygoatpk.com.*

Lighthouse Lounge
BARS/PUBS | A longtime favorite for drinks and live music (sometimes without a cover) amid the bustle of Historic 25th Street, the Lighthouse has comfy seating as well as a long old-fashioned bar and local art on the walls. ✉ *130 25th St.* ☎ *801/392–3901* ⊕ *lighthouseogden.com.*

Rooster's Brewing
BREWPUBS/BEER GARDENS | On Historic 25th Street, this long-time favorite brewpub (housed in a building from 1892) serves up an eclectic roster of house brews, including the popular O-Town Nut Brown ale, plus steak, sandwiches, and

pizzas with locally made cheeses. Hang on the patio on warm days or watch the weather from the glass-enclosed sunroom year-round. ✉ *253 25th St.* ☎ *801/627–6171* ⊕ *www.roostersbrewingco.com.*

★ UTOG Brewing

BREWPUBS/BEER GARDENS | With an industrial-chic vibe, retractable garage-door-style windows, and an impressively extensive selection of house brews, UTOG gives Salt Lake City's many acclaimed breweries a run for their money. The Mandarina Kolsch is a refreshing choice on a warm night, while the heady Red Eye Imperial Red Ale will warm your soul on a winter night. Brats, cheesesteaks, and other pub fare is served too. ✉ *2331 Grant Ave.* ☎ *801/689–3476* ⊕ *www.utogbrewing.com.*

The Yes Hell

BARS/PUBS | A dimly lit tavern and live-music lounge with an irreverent spirit—from its name to the beer taps with creepy doll heads—the Yes Hell brings in some great rock, blues, and soul performers. Order a few street food-style tacos (smoked carnitas and vegan soy chorizo) to go with your local IPA or craft cocktail. ✉ *2430 Grant Ave.* ☎ *801/903–3671* ⊕ *www.theyeshell.com.*

⬤ Performing Arts

Ogden Amphitheater

CONCERTS | **FAMILY** | Throughout the summer, you can attend free concerts and movie screenings at this open-air venue off Historic 25th Street, with gorgeous mountain views. ✉ *Municipal Gardens, 343 25th St.* ☎ *801/629–8309* ⊕ *www.ogdencity.com/709/Amphitheater.*

★ Peery's Egyptian Theater

CONCERTS | Built in the 1920s but then abandoned for many years, this restored art deco jewel with a working Wurlitzer pipe organ received a splendid restoration in 1997 and now hosts concerts ranging from world music to blues, jazz,

and country acts, as well as an ongoing film series and touring musicals. ✉ *2415 Washington Blvd.* ☎ *801/689–8700* ⊕ *www.egyptiantheaterogden.com.*

Val A. Browning Center for the Performing Arts

ARTS CENTERS | Theater, music, and dance performances by students and visiting artists are offered frequently at Weber State University's excellent performing arts center, home stage for the Ogden Symphony Ballet Association. ✉ *3950 W. Campus Dr.* ☎ *801/626–7015* ⊕ *www.weber.edu/browningcenter.*

Shopping

ARTWORK

Gallery 25

ART GALLERIES | More than 50 local and regional contemporary artists sell their art at this terrific co-op gallery that's been going strong along historic 25th Street since 2000. ✉ *268 25th St.* ☎ *801/334–9881* ⊕ *www.gallery25utah.com.*

Local Artisan Collective

ART GALLERIES | You can buy art and take classes at this vibrant community art space in the Junction district downtown. More than 60 artists working in pottery, glass, fiber, jewelry, toy-making, and several other disciplines create and sell here. ✉ *2371 Kiesel Ave.* ☎ *801/399–2787* ⊕ *www.localartisancollective.com.*

FOOD

★ Beehive Cheese

FOOD/CANDY | Just a 10-minute drive southeast of Ogden, this artisan creamery has become famous in recent years for its creamy yet nutty cheddars, including the signature lavender-coffee-rubbed Barely Buzzed variety, which appears on cheese platters at some of the country's top restaurants. Other flavored varieties of note include apple-walnut-smoked and Hatch chile. You can sample and buy them, along with other tasty products, at this friendly shop. ✉ *2440 E. 6600 S* ☎ *801/476–0900* ⊕ *www.beehivecheese.com.*

★ Farmers Market Ogden

FOOD/CANDY | FAMILY | Find an eye-opening selection of fresh local produce, gourmet goods, live music, and local art at one of Utah's largest and most popular farmers' markets. The main summer market runs late June through mid-September from 9 am to 2 pm along Historic 25th Street. There's also a shorter fall market from late September through late October, and a winter version of the market from mid-January to late February. ✉ *25th St. from Wall St. to Washington Blvd.* ☎ *385/389–1411* ⊕ *www.farmersmarketogden.com.*

SPORTING GOODS
Alpine Sports

CLOTHING | If you're in Utah for a ski vacation, you can't beat Alpine Sports for high-performance winter gear, stylish outdoor apparel, and design-conscious gadgets and accessories. The selection here is painstakingly curated by buyers who know their stuff, and you can't walk through the door without falling in love with something a little outside your budget. Rentals, tuning, and repair are also available. ✉ *1165 Patterson St.* ☎ *801/393–0066* ⊕ *www.alpinesportsutah.com.*

TEXTILES AND SEWING
Needlepoint Joint

TEXTILES/SEWING | Needlepointers, knitters, quilters, and crochet enthusiasts from miles around flock to this fantastic little shop to find patterns, yarn, thread, and instruction. ✉ *241 25th St.* ☎ *801/394–4355* ⊕ *www.needlepointjoint.com.*

🏃 Activities

More than 250 miles of trails for hiking, mountain biking, and horseback riding surround the Ogden area, and the scenic roads are perfect for biking enthusiasts. The Weber and Ogden rivers provide high-adventure rafting and kayaking while Olympic-caliber skiing is just up the canyon in Ogden Valley.

★ Lindquist Field

BASEBALL/SOFTBALL | One of the best minor-league ballparks in America, this "rookie ball" farm club of the Los Angeles Dodgers—known officially as the Ogden Raptors—plays from June to August. The mountain views are dazzling. ✉ *2330 Lincoln Ave.* ☎ *801/393–2400* ⊕ *www.ogden-raptors.com.*

BICYCLING
The Bike Shoppe

BICYCLING | Founded in 1976, this shop favored by serious bike enthusiasts sells and repairs top-of-the-line brands and offers bike rentals by the day. You can also rent snowshoes and wetsuits. ✉ *4390 Washington Blvd.* ☎ *801/476–1600* ⊕ *www.thebikeshoppe.com.*

GOLF
Mount Ogden Golf Course

GOLF | One of the most acclaimed municipal courses in the state, Mount Ogden is celebrated for its well-maintained greens and variety of elevation changes. ✉ *1787 Constitution Way* ☎ *801/629–0699* ⊕ *www.ogdencity.com/1687/Mt-Ogden* 💲 *$32* ⚑ *18 holes, 6342 yards, par 71.*

HIKING

With its numerous green spaces and proximity to rugged mountains and canyons east of downtown, Ogden is a terrific hiking destination. You can be out on an easy stroll along the river or a challenging trek to a lofty peak in no time. Most of the top hikes are mapped and described on the Ogden Trail Network and Trails Foundation Northern Utah websites. For less strenuous, family-friendly treks, consider venturing out along the 4½ mile Ogden River Parkway, which runs west to east on the north side of town. If you're up for a demanding but stunning adventure that will reward you with grand views from soaring outlooks, you might follow the Beus Canyon Trail to the 9,570-foot summit of Mount Ogden—this all-day hike is about 11 miles round trip. The North and South Skyline Trails are also favorite higher-elevation treks.

Pineview Reservoir resembles the shape of an airplane from above.

★ Ogden Trails Network

BICYCLING | The city's official and definitive hiking resource—with maps, details, and hiking etiquette and tips—details more than 25 adventures around the area, including local favorites like the Ogden River Parkway, Waterfall Canyon, Beus Canyon, and Bonneville Shoreline trails. Some of these destinations are also open to mountain biking. ✉ *Ogden* ☎ *801/629–8214* ⊕ *www.ogdencity. com/545/Ogden-Trails-Network.*

Trails Foundation Northern Utah

BICYCLING | This local nonprofit organization is dedicated to preserving and maintaining trails throughout Weber County. The online trail map includes detailed elevation information and covers adventures in Ogden but also well beyond into the Ogden Valley as well as north and south along the Wasatch Range ✉ *Ogden* ☎ *801/393–2304* ⊕ *www.tfnu.org.*

RECREATION CENTERS

★ WSU Outdoor Adventure & Welcome Center

CLIMBING/MOUNTAINEERING | Located on the campus of Weber State University, this outstanding outdoor recreation center has programs, guided tours, and many other resources available to the general public. Currently the university is constructing a 17,000-square-foot state-of-the-art center, slated to open by early 2021. Its features include a 55-foot climbing wall, a rooftop rappelling and rigging area, and an expanded equipment rental center, where you can pick up kayaking, rafting, winter sports, camping, mountain bikes, and lots of other gear. ✉ *Weber State University, 4022 Taylor Ave.* ☎ *801/626–6373* ⊕ *www.weber.edu/outdoor.*

Ogden Valley

8 miles east of Ogden City.

GETTING HERE AND AROUND

Most visitors approach the valley from Ogden via 12th Street, which becomes Highway 39. Pineview Reservoir lies at the center of the valley, and resembles an airplane with the nose pointing west, and wings (arms of the lake) extending north and south. You can drive around the reservoir in about 30 minutes without stops, and a car is definitely the best way to get around this area and visit the famed ski areas. From Salt Lake City, Trapper's Loop (Highway 167) is the scenic shortcut from I–84 to the south end of the reservoir. It's beautiful in spring and fall, and well maintained for access to the Snowbasin ski resort in the winter.

Sights

New World Distillery

WINERY/DISTILLERY | Set in a handsome barn-like building on the outskirts of the small ski town of Eden, this acclaimed small-batch distillery offers tastings as well as $20 tours, which include tastings. Known for bourbon, vodka, and barrel-conditioned gin, New World also makes a crisp tequila-like agave spirit and an agave liqueur flavored with Utah tart cherries. Tours are usually on Friday and Saturday only. ✉ *4795 E. 2600 N, Eden* ☎ *385/244–0144* 🌐 *www.newworld-distillery.com* 🕒 *Closed Sun. and Mon.*

Pineview Reservoir

BEACH—SIGHT | **FAMILY** | In summer, this 2,800-acre lake dotted with several marinas and sandy beaches is festooned with colorful umbrellas and the graceful arcs of water-skiers and wakeboarders. In winter it's a popular spot for ice-fishing. Middle Inlet, Cemetery Point, and Anderson Cove are the three developed beaches, and Anderson Cove also allows overnight camping. The Cove has a boat launch. The beaches at Pineview Trailhead, North Arm, and Spring Creek are free and have rest rooms but no other amenities. **Amenities:** parking (fee); toilets; water sports. **Best for:** swimming. ✉ *End of Cemetery Point Rd., Huntsville* ☎ *801/625–5112* 🎟 *$15–$17 day use; access to some beaches is free* 🕒 *Beach amenities closed Oct.–Apr.*

Restaurants

Carlos & Harley's

$$ | **MEXICAN** | Set inside the colorful 1890s Eden General Store, a few blocks from the north shore of Pineview Reservoir, this fun Tex-Mex restaurant specializes in the kind of food that effectively sustains the area's many skiers, hikers, boaters, and other outdoorsy sorts. Think big plates of chile con queso, bacon-wrapped jalapeño poppers, shrimp fajitas, pork tamales, and slow-roasted-pork carnitas tacos. **Known for:** buzzy, chatter-filled dining room; four types of fresh-made salsa; margaritas on the outdoor patio. [$] *Average main: $18* ✉ *5510 E. 2200 N, Eden* ☎ *801/745–8226* 🌐 *www.carlosandharleys.com.*

Gray Cliff Lodge Restaurant

$$$ | **AMERICAN** | Set in scenic Ogden Canyon, this romantic restaurant with lace tablecloths, linen napkins, and mountain and forest views is a time-honored destination for classic Continental fare, such as slow-roasted prime rib, grilled mountain trout, and sage-stuffed lamb chops with mint jelly. The fireplace makes this a fun gathering spot for pre or after-dinner drinks in winter. **Known for:** surf-and-turf combos; unabashed old-school vibe; leisurely Sunday brunches. [$] *Average main: $28* ✉ *508 Ogden Canyon, Ogden* ☎ *801/392–6775* 🌐 *www.grayclifflodge.com* 🕒 *Closed Mon. No lunch.*

Mad Moose Cafe

$ | **CAFÉ** | **FAMILY** | This super-chill, family-friendly eatery is a perfect stop for delicious flavored coffee drinks and traditional breakfast fare early in the day or burgers, panini sandwiches, and ice cream desserts after your outdoor adventures. It's even a good bet for an early dinner, but keep in mind that the Mad Moose closes nightly at 7 pm. **Known for:** Ivory Moose (white chocolate–hazelnut) lattes; burgers with lots of different topping combos; milkshakes, smoothies, and ice cream floats. [$] *Average main: $9* ✉ *2429 N. Hwy. 158, Eden* ☎ *801/452–7425* 🌐 *www.madmoosecafe.com.*

★ Shooting Star Saloon

$ | AMERICAN | The oldest remaining saloon in the state, in operation since the 1880s, is a beloved favorite hangout for skiers in winter and bikers in summer. The exterior looks straight out of a classic Western movie,while inside the rustic accoutrements draw the eye to every corner—think dollar bills pinned to the ceiling, comical signs, scruffy old boots, teapots, and rifles. **Known for:** the Star Burger (double cheeseburger topped with a Polish hot dog); Saint Bernard head mounted on the wall; decent selection of local craft brews. [$] *Average main: $9* ✉ *7350 E. 200 S, Huntsville* ☎ *801/745–2002.*

Hotels

There are no real hotels or motels in the Ogden Valley, but you will find a few tucked-away B&Bs and condos that accommodate groups of all sizes.

Alaskan Inn and Spa

$$ | HOTEL | Set along a scenic stretch of Hwy. 39 in Ogden Canyon, between Ogden and Pineview reservoirs, this rustic but upscale riverside lodge and cabins is perfect for a quiet getaway that's not too far from civilization yet offers easy access to hiking, boating, and Ogden Valley skiing. **Pros:** lush setting beneath craggy mountains peaks; next to Gray Cliff Lodge restaurant and a kayak and jet-ski rental agency; massage and spa services available. **Cons:** rooms facing road can get some traffic noise; 15-minute drive from downtown Ogden; log cabin vibe doesn't suit every taste. [$] *Rooms from: $159* ✉ *435 Ogden Canyon, Ogden* ☎ *801/621–8600* 🌐 *www.alaskaninn.com* 🛏 *23 rooms* 🍴 *Free breakfast.*

Atomic Chalet B&B

$$ | B&B/INN | With comfortable beds, cathedral ceilings, and three windows offering sweeping Ogden Valley views, each of the three rooms in this contemporary B&B near Pineview Reservoir is perfect for a good night's sleep during a weekend of skiing or hiking. **Pros:** 15- to 20-minute drive from Ogden Valley ski areas; friendly, helpful hosts; picturesque, tranquil grounds. **Cons:** in a small, quiet town; not suitable for kids under 16; two-night minimum on ski-season weekends. [$] *Rooms from: $139* ✉ *6917 E. 100 S, Huntsville* ☎ *801/425–2813* 🌐 *www.atomicchalet.com* 🛏 *3 rooms* 🍴 *Free breakfast.*

★ Compass Rose Lodge

$$$ | B&B/INN | The gorgeous contemporary design, charming small-town location, hip coffeehouse, welcoming hosts, and light-filled sitting areas are—amazingly—not even the coolest thing about this stylish boutique inn: that honor belongs to the silo-shaped Huntsville Astronomic and Lunar Observatory, which adjoins the inn and offers unforgettable viewing experiences of the cosmos. **Pros:** stunning steampunk–meets–ski lodge design; steps from Utah's oldest bar, the Shooting Star Saloon; half-price "star walk" observatory tours for guests. **Cons:** fills up on weekends, especially in ski season; not too many dining options in town; slightly spendy for the area. [$] *Rooms from: $199* ✉ *198 S. 7400 E, Huntsville* ☎ *385/279–4460* 🌐 *www.compassroselodge.com* 🛏 *15 rooms* 🍴 *Free breakfast.*

Moose Hollow at Wolf Creek Resort

$$ | RENTAL | FAMILY | The individually decorated condos at Wolf Creek's Moose Hollow property—all with full kitchens, stone fireplaces, decks or patios, vaulted ceilings, and massive log beams—are just a few miles from Powder Mountain and within walking distance of Wolf Creek's scenic 18-hole golf course. **Pros:** spacious units with kitchens; outdoor pool; gorgeous views of the lake and mountains. **Cons:** two-night minimum stay during busy times; no pets; no housekeeping during stay. [$] *Rooms from: $150* ✉ *N. Huntsman Path at Moose Hollow Dr., Eden* ☎ *801/745–3737* 🌐 *www.wolfcreekrentals.com* 🛏 *30 units* 🍴 *No meals.*

Activities

HIKING

★ Snowbasin

HIKING/WALKING | Beginning at an elevation of 6,500 feet, Snowbasin offers 26 miles of hiking and mountain-biking trails of varying degrees of difficulty, many of them ascending through bowls filled with summer wildflowers to the dramatic 9,350-foot summit of Mount Ogden. On weekends, you can ride the gondola ($16) to Needles lodge, eat lunch, and then hike along the ridge to the peak. June through September, the resort hosts the popular Blues, Brews & BBQ every Sunday, bringing free musical acts to the base of the mountain. ✉ *3925 Snowbasin Rd., Huntsville* ☎ *801/620–1000* 🌐 *www.snowbasin.com.*

SKIING

If you're staying in Ogden and want to head for the mountains for a day of skiing or snowboarding, you can catch the Ski Bus (🌐 *www.rideuta.com*), which runs between several downtown Ogden hotels and the ski resorts in the Ogden Valley. Black Diamond Shuttle (🌐 *www.blackdiamondshuttle.com*) also offers taxi service from hotels and Salt Lake City International Airport.

Nordic Valley

SKIING/SNOWBOARDING | **FAMILY** | Utah's smallest ski resort was used for downhill training for the 2002 Olympics. A great place to learn, this charming family-oriented resort is one of the most affordable in the state, and the whole mountain is lighted for night skiing and boarding. ✉ *3567 E. Nordic Valley Way, Eden* ☎ *801/745–3511* 🌐 *www.nordicvalley.com* 🎫 *Lift tickets $50* ☞ *965-ft vertical drop; 140 skiable acres; 36% beginner, 45% intermediate, 18% advanced; 2 double chairs, 1 triple chair, 1 surface lift.*

North Fork Park

SKIING/SNOWBOARDING | The 14 well-maintained miles of cross-country trails here, plus 6 miles of snowshoe trails, are perfect for all experience levels and also popular in summer for hiking and biking. Cross-country ski and snowshoe rentals are available, and day passes cost $10 for hiking, $8 for biking, and $5 for snowshoeing. ✉ *4150 E. 5950 N, Eden* ☎ *801/648–9020* 🌐 *www.ogdennordic.com.*

★ Powder Mountain

SKIING/SNOWBOARDING | This classic ski resort offers huge terrain—more skiable acres than any other resort in North America— even though it doesn't have as many lifts (nine all together) as some of Utah's destination resorts. Two terrain parks and a half-pipe are popular with snowboarders. Snowcat skiing (for an additional $25) and night skiing are also popular. Although plenty challenging, the intermediate options (40 percent of the 154 runs) are heavenly in contrast to nearby Snowbasin, which is generally steeper and more exposed. You won't find fancy lodges or haute cuisine here, but with caps on passes (3,000 per season and 1,500 per day), crowds are nonexistent, and the laid-back slope-side eateries serve everything from scones and hot soup to flame-broiled burgers at the Powder Keg. ✉ *6965 E. Hwy. 158, Eden* ☎ *801/745–3772* 🌐 *www.powdermountain.com* 🎫 *Lift tickets $96* ☞ *2,205-ft vertical drop; 8,464 skiable acres; 25% beginner, 40% intermediate, 35% advanced; 4 quad chairs, 1 triple chair, 3 surface lifts.*

At Golden Spike National Historic Site, visitors can see replicas of famed locomotives.

★ Snowbasin

SKIING/SNOWBOARDING | A vertical drop of 2,959 feet and a dramatic start at the pinnacle of Mount Ogden made this resort just 17 miles from Ogden the perfect site for the downhill ski races during the 2002 Olympic Winter Games. With nine lifts accessing more than 3,000 acres with 104 runs of steep, skiable terrain, this is one of Utah's largest resorts. It also offers miles of Nordic trails for cross-country skiing. Served in spectacular lodges, the on-mountain food consistently ranks among the best in the state, and the resort also scores high marks for service, lifts, and grooming. ⊠ *3925 E. Snowbasin Rd. (Hwy. 226), Huntsville* ☎ *801/620–1000, 888/437–5488* ⊕ *www. snowbasin.com* ☜ *Lift tickets $125* ☞ *2,959-ft vertical drop; 3,000 skiable acres; 20% beginner, 50% intermediate, 30% advanced; 2 high-speed gondolas, 1 tram, 1 high-speed six-pack chair, 2 high-speed quad chairs, 3 triple chairs, 2 surface lifts.*

SNOWMOBILING

Club Rec

BOATING | This outdoor recreation shop rents Jet Skis, speed boats, double-decker pontoon boats, and other watercraft so you can enjoy Pineview Reservoir to the fullest. In the winter time, a guided tour of Monte Cristo is one of the best snow adventures in the West. In addition to the main store, there are a few satellite locations in the area. ⊠ *3718 N. Wolf Creek Dr., Eden* ☎ *801/614–0500* ⊕ *www.clubrecutah.com.*

Brigham City

21 miles north of Ogden.

People passing through Brigham City are charmed by its sycamore-lined Main Street and old-fashioned downtown, but may not realize they are in one of Utah's most progressive towns.

GETTING HERE AND AROUND

Brigham City lies just to the east of I-15 on Highway 89/91. Like many cities settled by LDS pioneers, it's laid out on a grid system, with Main Street running north–south and each street numbered by 100s as you head in all four directions. Head north on Main to get to the quaint center of town. Highway 89/91 to Logan bypasses the town.

ESSENTIALS

VISITOR INFORMATION Box Elder Chamber of Commerce. ✉ *6 N. Main St.* ☎ *435/723–3931* ⊕ *www.boxeldercham-ber.com.*

Sights

★ Bear River Migratory Bird Refuge

NATURE PRESERVE | Established in 1928 to conserve the Bear River habitat for migratory waterfowl and wildlife, this 80,000-acre U.S. Fish and Wildlife Service refuge is just west of Brigham City. You can observe wildlife along a 12-mile driving route and 1½ miles of walking trails, with ducks, geese, pelicans, herons, swans, shore birds, and more than 200 other kinds of birds arriving in various seasons. The Wildlife Education Center contains interactive displays and observation decks. ✉ *2155 W. Forest St.* ☎ *435/734–6425* ⊕ *www.fws.gov* ⊘ *Wildlife Education Center closed Sun. and Mon.*

Brigham City Museum of Art & History

MUSEUM | More than 10,000 objects from Box Elder County's 170-year history tell the story of the area's early settlement and Mormon cooperative periods. This well-designed, modern museum also includes a permanent collection of more than 300 works of art, with several rotating exhibitions throughout the year. ✉ *24 N. 300 W.* ☎ *435/723–6769* ⊕ *www.brighamcitymuseum.org* ⊘ *Closed Sun. and Mon.*

Crystal Hot Springs

HOT SPRINGS | FAMILY | Originally used as a winter camp by the Shoshones, this popular recreation area has one of the world's largest natural hot and cold springs. Mixing water from the two springs allows for a variety of pools with temperatures ranging from 80°F to 105°F. The complex in Honeyville, about 11 miles north of Brigham City, has its own campground, hot tubs, a large soaker pool, a cold freshwater swimming pool, two water slides, and a lap pool. ✉ *8215 N. Hwy. 38, Honeyville* ☎ *435/279–8104* ⊕ *www.crystalhotsprings.net* ☜ *$12 pool; $14 pool and slide.*

★ Golden Spike National Historic Site

HISTORIC SITE | The Union Pacific and Central Pacific railroads met here at Promontory Summit on May 10, 1869, to celebrate the completion of the first transcontinental rail route. Today, the national park service runs the site, which includes a visitor center and two beautifully maintained locomotives that are replicas of the originals that met here for the "wedding of the rails." Every May 10 (and on Saturday and holidays in summer), a reenactment of the driving of the golden spike is held, and throughout summer you can watch the trains in action on demonstration runs a few times a day. You can also walk a 1½-mile trail around the site and drive two scenic auto tour routes that reveal the terrain and engineering feats involved in creating this remote stretch of the rail line. In August, boiler stoking, rail walking, and buffalo-chip throwing test participants' skills at the Railroader's Festival. The Winter Steam Festival around Christmas gives steam buffs opportunities to photograph the locomotives in the cold, when the steam from the smokestacks forms billowing clouds. To get here, it's about a 40-minute drive west from Brigham City and a 90-minute drive north of Salt Lake City. ✉ *Golden Spike Rd., off Hwy. 83, Promontory* ☎ *435/471–2209* ⊕ *www.nps.gov/gosp* ☜ *$10 per vehicle.*

Spiral Jetty

PUBLIC ART | This 1,500-foot-long, 15-foot-wide earthen creation that juts in a spiral out into Great Salt Lake was created by artist Robert Smithson in 1970 and is often photographed by passengers in planes flying overhead. The jetty, 16 miles from the Golden Spike site via a dirt road, was submerged for much of the subsequent 30 years, before the lake level fell precipitously in 2002 revealing the structure again. The snail shell–shape land art structure is considered one of the most remote sculptures in modern American art history, and it is Utah's state work of art. ⊠ *N. Rozel Flats Rd. W, Rozel Point* ☎ *212/989–5566* 🆓 *Free.*

 Restaurants

★ Idle Isle Café

$ | **AMERICAN** | **FAMILY** | It feels like you've wandered onto the set of *The Andy Griffith Show* at this quaint 1921 café with a menu specializing in old-fashioned comfort foods like pot roast and au gratin potatoes, chicken-fried steak, and hot turkey sandwiches with gravy. Save room for ice cream or a shake—or perhaps some sweet treats from the Idle Isle candy factory across the street. **Known for:** hefty sandwiches; authentic 1920s soda fountain; idleberry pie (with blueberries, blackberries, and boysenberries). $ *Average main: $12* ⊠ *24 S. Main St.* ☎ *435/734–2468* ⊕ *www.idleislecafe. com* ⊗ *Closed Sun.*

Maddox Ranch House

$$ | **AMERICAN** | **FAMILY** | Just a little south of Brigham City, this down-home log-cabin-style eatery is one of the most celebrated family-owned restaurants in Utah, a favorite since the late 1940s. The Maddox family serves stick-to-your-ribs Western fare—the fried chicken, Porterhouse steaks, and bison rib-eyes are big enough to satisfy a ranch hand, especially if you factor in generous sides of vegetables, potatoes, homemade soups, and fresh-baked dinner rolls served with raspberry honeybutter. **Known for:** attached retro burger drive-in with car hop service; fresh peach pie; no alcohol. $ *Average main: $21* ⊠ *1900 S. U.S. 89, Perry* ☎ *435/723–8545, 800/544–5474* ⊕ *www.maddoxfinefood.com* ⊗ *Closed Sun. and Mon.*

Hotels

Best Western Brigham City

$ | **HOTEL** | Less than two miles off Interstate 15 on the edge of downtown Brigham City, this two-story Best Western with views of the mountains is a convenient, affordable base for exploring the area, from Bear Lake to Promontory. **Pros:** good prices; pet-friendly; less than 30 minutes from Logan and Ogden. **Cons:** ho-hum design; no elevator; nothing much within walking distance. $ *Rooms from: $107* ⊠ *480 Westland Dr.* ☎ *435/723–0440* ⊕ *www.bestwestern. com* 🛏 *53 rooms* ¶⊙¶ *Free breakfast.*

Logan

25 miles northeast of Brigham City.

Mormon pioneers created the permanent settlement of Logan in 1859, but the town didn't become prominent until 1888, when it was chosen as the site for Utah's land-grant agricultural college, now called Utah State University (USU). Logan is now the hub of the dramatic Cache Valley.

GETTING HERE AND AROUND

Head up U.S. 89 from Brigham City through Sardine Canyon and you'll arrive at the beautiful Cache Valley and the city of Logan. Although downtown is quite walkable, you'll find a car the most convenient way to get here and explore the scenic attractions in the vicinity.

VISITOR INFORMATION

Cache Valley Visitors Bureau
⊠ *199 N. Main St.* ☎ *435/755–1890* ⊕ *www.explorelogan.com.*

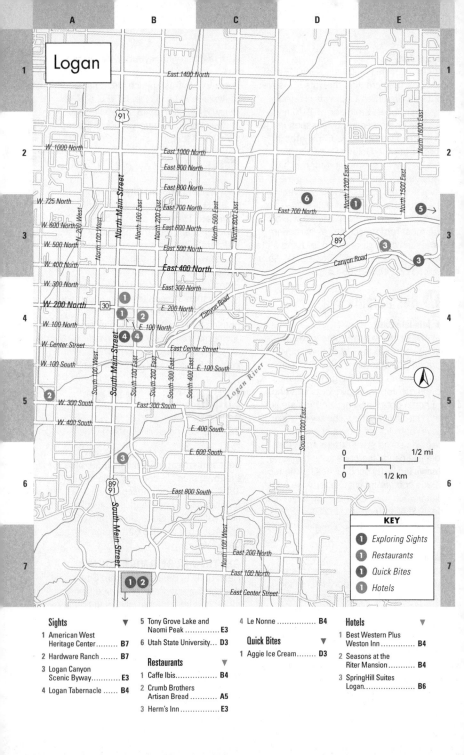

Logan

A   B   C   D   E

Sights ▼

1 American West
  Heritage Center......... **B7**
2 Hardware Ranch **B7**
3 Logan Canyon
  Scenic Byway............ **E3**
4 Logan Tabernacle **B4**
5 Tony Grove Lake and
  Naomi Peak **E3**
6 Utah State University... **D3**

Restaurants ▼

1 Caffe Ibis.................. **B4**
2 Crumb Brothers
  Artisan Bread **A5**
3 Herm's Inn **E3**
4 Le Nonne **B4**

Quick Bites ▼

1 Aggie Ice Cream........ **D3**

Hotels ▼

1 Best Western Plus
  Weston Inn **B4**
2 Seasons at the
  Riter Mansion........... **B4**
3 SpringHill Suites
  Logan..................... **B6**

KEY

1 Exploring Sights
1 Restaurants
1 Quick Bites
1 Hotels

◉ Sights

American West Heritage Center

FARM/RANCH | FAMILY | On U.S. 89/91 enroute to Logan from points south, this 160-acre living history museum interprets Cache Valley's development from 1820 to 1920. At the farm, antique implements are on display, draft horses still pull their weight, pony and train rides entertain the kids, and docents dressed in period clothing demonstrate sheep shearing and carding and offer bison tours. Baby Animal Days is popular in the spring, and the fall corn maze is actually quite challenging. Late July's Pioneer Festival features additional displays and reenactments, along with food booths, cowboy poetry readings, ice-cream making, and concerts. ⊠ *4025 S. U.S. 89/91, Wellsville* ☎ *435/245–6050* ⊕ *www.awhc.org* ☜ *$8* ⊙ *Closed Sun.*

Hardware Ranch

NATURE PRESERVE | FAMILY | In winter, it's worth taking the picturesque mountain drive about 25 miles east of Logan to Blacksmith Fork Canyon, where the State Division of Wildlife Resources feeds 500 to 600 elk during the snowy months. A 20-minute sleigh ride takes you up close to the majestic creatures. Dress warmly in layers. The visitor center is only open December through early February, when tours are offered, but from spring through fall, the area is also popular for hiking and wildlife viewing. ⊠ *Off Hwy. 101, Hyrum* ☎ *435/753–6206, 435/753–6168* ⊕ *wildlife.utah.gov/hardware-visit. html* ☜ *Sleigh rides $5* ⊙ *Visitor center closed mid-Feb.–early Dec.*

★ Logan Canyon Scenic Byway

SCENIC DRIVE | Connecting the Cache Valley and Logan to Bear Lake, the Logan Canyon Scenic Byway (U.S. 89) is perhaps best known for its vibrant fall colors. A photographer's dream in autumn, the canyon also thrills snowmobilers in the winter and wildflower watchers in spring.

Towering limestone walls follow the path of the Logan River through the Bear River Mountains and provide ample opportunity for rock climbing. Hiking, fishing, biking, and horseback riding are also popular all along this route. High in the canyon's mountains, Tony Grove Lake and its campground provide a serene escape, and a trail from the lake leads to Naomi Peak, the highest point in the Bear River Mountains. ⊠ *U.S. 89.*

Logan Tabernacle

RELIGIOUS SITE | It took Mormon settlers 27 years to build the tabernacle, which they completed in 1891. Today's tabernacle is a venue for concerts and lectures. You can also tour the building or search for information about your family history at the genealogical research facility. ⊠ *50 Main St.* ☎ *435/755–5598.*

★ Tony Grove Lake and Naomi Peak

SCENIC DRIVE | From Logan, U.S. 89 continues for 30 miles up Logan Canyon before topping out at the crest of the Bear River Range (from which it continues another 10 miles to Bear Lake). For a particularly satisfying excursion that leads to awesome hiking and mountain biking, drive the well-signed 7-mile side road to Tony Grove Lake. At more than 8,000 feet, this subalpine jewel is surrounded by cliffs and meadows filled in summer with a stunning profusion of wildflowers. A short trail circles the lake. Mountain bikers and hikers alike can access a prime wilderness area via the 3.3-mile one-way route from the lake to the 9,984-foot summit of Naomi Peak, which offers 80-mile views on clear days. With a gain almost 2,000 feet in elevation, the hike passes through conifer forests and open meadows and along subalpine basins and rocky ledges. A shorter hike to White Pine Lake, which begins on the same trail and splits after a quarter of a mile, is also lovely. ⊠ *Tony Grove Rd.* ⊕ *www. fs.usda.gov/uwcnf* ☜ *$7 per vehicle.*

★ Utah State University

COLLEGE | Established in 1888 as a small agricultural school, USU now enrolls around 27,000 students and is an intellectual and technological leader in land, water, space, and life enhancement. The scenic, 400-acre campus is best toured by starting at the historic Old Main administration building east of downtown Logan—look for the bell tower. Inside the building you'll find the **Museum of Anthropology,** which contains an impressive collection of prehistoric and contemporary Native American artifacts and cultural works. The first Saturday of each month features family-friendly exploration of a specific country through its food, arts and crafts, and music. Also worth a stop is the **Nora Eccles Harrison Museum of Art,** which is in a striking contemporary building a few blocks northeast of the campus Quad and contains a permanent collection as well as mounting rotating shows. You can also pick up a map here of sculptures and public art visible throughout the campus. ✉ *Old Main Hill at Champ Dr.* ☎ *435/797–1000* 🌐 *www.usu.edu.*

🍴 Restaurants

Caffe Ibis

$ | **CAFÉ** | Inside this handsome café with ample seating and live music on weekend evenings, you'll see shiny brass canisters brimming with shade-grown, organic, fair-trade coffee beans ground daily at the local off-site roastery. In addition to tasty drinks, Ibis serves a nice array of breakfast and lunch entrées, such as avocado toast with farm eggs and roasted-veggie sandwiches. **Known for:** superbly crafted coffee drinks; hip and down-to-earth crowd; weekend brunch. [$] *Average main: $11* ✉ *52 Federal Ave.* ☎ *435/753–4777* 🌐 *www.caffeibis.com* 🕘 *No dinner.*

★ Crumb Brothers Artisan Bread

$ | **BAKERY** | The thick-crusted artisan breads served in this airy, verdant, and much-beloved bakery are fantastic on their own or in an impressive roster of freshly prepared sandwiches, like the bacon, avocado, egg, and provolone on ciabatta or the banh mi on a crisp baguette, available vegan or with pork belly. Some of the most creative fare incorporates house-made organic bread as an ingredient, from bread pudding to panzanella, and there's an ever-changing array of ethereal pastries. **Known for:** daily-rotating pizzettas with inventive toppings; pretty garden patio; beer, wine, and champagne cocktails. [$] *Average main: $9* ✉ *291 S. 300 W* ☎ *435/753–0875* 🌐 *www.crumbbrothers.com* 🕘 *Closed Mon. No dinner.*

★ Herm's Inn

$ | **AMERICAN** | Famous for its pizza-size cinnamon swirl pancakes, this popular breakfast and lunch spot is often jam-packed with students from Utah State University or hikers headed to Logan Canyon, but it's worth the wait. The meat-lover's breakfast skillet with eggs, toast, ham, bacon, sausage, and cheddar will fuel you up before a big hike, while the burger on marble rye topped with caramelized garlic and onions, Swiss cheese, and garlic mayo is a lunchtime specialty. **Known for:** patio with fireplace overlooking Logan Canyon; killer breakfasts; open Sunday (which is rare for the area). [$] *Average main: $10* ✉ *1435 Canyon Rd.* ☎ *435/792–4321* 🌐 *www.hermsinn.com* 🕘 *No dinner.*

Le Nonne

$$ | **ITALIAN** | Housed in a courtly converted Victorian home, this sophisticated restaurant features Northern Italian cuisine—such as rigatoni amatriciana, sweet-potato ravioli, and thinly sliced, oven-baked steak tagliata with sun-dried tomatoes—crafted by a chef born and raised in Tuscany. Live jazz some evenings wafts through the cozy dining room and the outdoor patio nestled in a garden. **Known for:** romantic dining room with attentive service; pre-theater dining; nicely curated wine

list. $ *Average main: $22* ⊠ *129 N. 100 E* ☎ *435/752–9577* ⊕ *www.lenonne.com* ⊗ *Closed Sun. No lunch.*

Coffee and Quick Bites

★ Aggie Ice Cream

$ | **CAFÉ** | **FAMILY** | The pride and joy of Utah State University dairy students, this historic ice cream shop on campus makes luscious creations using milk from cows that live on the USU's farm and a recipe and production process that's been perfected over more than a century. Savor a scoop or two of lemon custard, blue mint, praline pecan, or huckleberry to fully grasp what all the fuss is about. **Known for:** lines out the door on hot days; Aggie Blue Mint–flavored ice cream; thick shakes and malts. $ *Average main: $5* ⊠ *Nutrition & Food Science Bldg., USU, 750 N. 1200 E* ☎ *435/797–2109, 888/586–2735* ⊕ *www.aggieicecream. usu.edu* ▭ *No credit cards* ⊗ *Closed Sun.*

🛏 Hotels

Best Western Plus Weston Inn

$$ | **HOTEL** | This reasonably priced, centrally located Best Western is ideal for being close to downtown dining and attractions, and with free parking and a hot breakfast, it's a good value. **Pros:** walking distance to theaters and restaurants; good-size indoor pool; free parking in front of or near your room. **Cons:** standard chain furnishings; small bathrooms; some street noise. $ *Rooms from: $149* ⊠ *250 N. Main St.* ☎ *435/752–5700* ⊕ *www.bestwestern.com* ⊃ *89 rooms* ⏃ *Free breakfast.*

★ Seasons at the Riter Mansion

$$ | **B&B/INN** | In a quiet residential area just a short walk from Main Street, this beautifully restored Greek Revival–Georgian mansion is perfect for a romantic getaway or as a cozy retreat, its suites warmly decorated and outfitted with whirlpool baths and, in many cases, fireplaces. **Pros:** surrounded by fragrant gardens and mature shade trees; within walking distance of downtown; fantastic breakfasts. **Cons:** sometimes booked for weddings and events; not a good option for kids; antique-y aesthetic may not please modernists. $ *Rooms from: $149* ⊠ *168 N. 100 E* ☎ *435/752–7727* ⊕ *www. theritermansion.com* ⊃ *6 rooms* ⏃ *Free breakfast.*

Springhill Suites Logan

$$ | **HOTEL** | Logan's most upscale hotel offers bright and modern all-suite accommodations that are nicely outfitted for families and for longer stays, each with separate sitting areas, refrigerators and microwaves, high-end pull-out sleeper sofas, and flat-screen TVs. **Pros:** very nice indoor pool and fitness center; substantial complimentary breakfast buffet; quiet but fairly central location. **Cons:** sometimes books up with conventioneers; 15-minute walk to city center; no pets. $ *Rooms from: $159* ⊠ *635 S. Riverwoods Pkwy.* ☎ *435/750–5180* ⊕ *www. marriott.com* ⊃ *115 suites* ⏃ *Free breakfast.*

🎫 Performing Arts

★ Ellen Eccles Theatre

DANCE | This European-style theater, with ornate balconies, murals, and frescoes, was built in 1923 and restored to its original grandeur in 1993. Cache Valley Center for the Arts brings about a dozen national touring productions here each year, including musicals, dance, comedy, and concerts. ⊠ *43 S. Main St.* ☎ *435/752–0026* ⊕ *www.cachearts.org.*

★ Utah Festival Opera & Musical Theatre

OPERA | Each summer this highly respected company presents a five-week season at Logan's Utah Theatre, Ellen Eccles Theatre, and Dasante Building. Featuring nationally renowned performers from across the country, the productions dazzle. ⊠ *59 S. 100 W* ☎ *435/750–0300, 800/262–0074* ⊕ *www.utahfestival.org.*

Shopping

FOOD

Cox Honeyland and Gifts

FOOD/CANDY | Specializing in honey products, this Logan landmark, operated by the Cox family for four generations, offers pure raw honey, fresh fudge and candy, gift baskets, and skin and body items. ⊠ *1780 S. Hwy. 89* ☎ *435/752–3234* ⊕ *www.coxhoney.com.*

★ Rockhill Creamery and Harvest Market

FOOD/CANDY | At this renowned artisan cheesemaker 12 miles north of Logan in the small town of Richmond, you can sample and purchase creamy raw milk, alpine-style cheeses of exceptional quality in a rustic, handsome barn. On the first and third Saturdays from June through September, the creamery also hosts Richmond's endearing Harvest Market, featuring local farm and food vendors and live music. ⊠ *563 S. State St., Richmond* ☎ *435/258–1278* ⊕ *www.rockhillcheese.com.*

GIFTS

★ The Spirit Goat

LOCAL SPECIALTIES | Just steps from Main Street, this family-owned shop specializes in skin care products made from goat's milk. Filled with aromatic fragrances like cranberry orange, citrus, and lavender, the quaint shop has an in-store workshop and brims with more than 80 varieties of soaps, plus body lotions and other gifts. ⊠ *28 Federal Ave.* ☎ *435/512–9040* ⊕ *www.spiritgoat.com.*

MARKETS

Cache Valley Gardeners' Market

OUTDOOR/FLEA/GREEN MARKETS | From early May through mid-October, Utah's oldest local farmers' market is held every Saturday from 9 to 1, outside the Cache Historic Courthouse. The market features regional produce vendors, locally made goods, and live music. ⊠ *199 N. Main St.* ⊕ *gardenersmarket.org.*

Activities

BICYCLING AND HIKING

★ Logan Canyon

BICYCLING | You'll find some gorgeous hikes just a few miles up Logan Canyon from town, starting with the popular and easy **Logan River Trail,** which meanders along the river for nearly 4 miles and is suitable for all skill levels. The wide passageway accommodates dogs and even strollers, and it passes both the family-friendly Stokes Nature Center and picturesque Second Dam, which has a lovely picnic area. A few miles' drive farther east of the Logan River Trailhead, you'll reach the parking lot for the **Crimson Trail,** a more rugged but also rewarding 5-mile loop along the dramatic China Wall crag that offers eye-popping views throughout the canyon. Note that it entails an elevation gain of about 1,345 feet, and it is a bit steep in places. Just a mile farther up U.S. 89, park near Guinavah-Malibu Campground to access the famed **Wind Caves Trail,** which a 3½-mile hike that's only moderately challenging and ascends about 1,000 feet through wildflower-strewn meadows and conifer forests to a fanciful triple-arch rock formation sometimes nicknamed the "Witch's Castle." ⊠ *Logan River Trailhead, 2696 U.S. 89* ⊕ *www.fs.usda.gov/uwcnf.*

SKIING

Cherry Peak

SKIING/SNOWBOARDING | **FAMILY** | Twenty minutes from Logan, Utah's newest ski area, is also the state's most affordable place to board or ski. Night skiing and tubing make this a fun place for families, as do summertime concerts, mountain biking, and a water slide. ⊠ *3200 E. 11000 N, Richmond* ☎ *435/200–5050* 🎿 *Lift ticket $39* ⚡ *1,265-ft vertical drop; 400-plus skiable acres; 30% beginner, 35% intermediate, 35% advanced; 3 triple chair lifts, 1 surface lift.*

Garden City

41 miles northeast of Logan.

Nearly 6,000 feet above sea level and quite remote, Bear Lake straddles the Utah–Idaho border. Known for its vibrant blue water rivaling Lake Tahoe, it's one of the most beautiful alpine lakes in America. Garden City (population 615), on the lake's western shore and reached via scenic U.S. 89 from Logan, offers most of lake area's few dining and and lodging options, which tend to book up quickly during the warmer months (some are closed in winter). From here, it can take 90 minutes to circle the 109-square-mile lake by car, especially if it's a busy summer weekend (and in winter, the road around the lake is sometimes closed due to snow).

GETTING HERE AND AROUND

Garden City is where you'll find most of the services and businesses in the Bear Lake region. It has a walkable downtown, but you need a car to get around the area.

VISITOR INFORMATION

CONTACTS Bear Lake Convention and Visitors Bureau. ✉ *69 N. Paradise Pkwy., Garden City* ☎ *435/946–2197* 🌐 *www.bearlake.org.*

Sights

★ Bear Lake State Park
BODY OF WATER | FAMILY | Eight miles wide and 20 miles long, Bear Lake is an unusually radiant shade of blue, thanks to limestone particles suspended in the water. The Utah half of the lake is a state park. Along the south shore of Bear Lake, Highway 30 traces an old route used by Native Americans, mountain men, and settlers following the Oregon Trail. Harsh winters persuaded most settlers to move on before the first snows, but hardy Mormon pioneers settled in the area and founded Garden City. From town you can stroll along a ¼-mile boardwalk through a small wetlands preserve to the lakeshore, and there's a large marina just to the north. The park operates a few other recreation areas along other parts of the shore, including **Rendezvous Beach** to the south, which has a marina and burger stand, and **Cisco Beach** on the lake's quieter eastern shore, where the lake bottom drops off quickly, making it a favorite spot among anglers and scuba divers. The lake is home to four species of fish found nowhere else, including the Bonneville cisco, which draws anglers during the January spawning season. ✉ *U.S. 89 at Hwy. 30, Garden City* ☎ *435/946–3343* 🌐 *stateparks.utah.gov/parks/bear-lake* 🎫 *$8–$15 per vehicle.*

Restaurants

Campfire Grill
$$$ | MODERN AMERICAN | FAMILY | Located within Garden City's distinctive Conestoga Ranch glamping resort, this rambling and scenic seasonal restaurant (set in a tent with a firepit overlooking the property's covered wagons) is the most distinctive dining destination in town, and one of the most upscale too. Serving creative American fare throughout the day—including a popular brunch on Sundays—this open-air eatery offers delicious pancakes with maple-macerated berries, shrimp with smoked-cheddar grits, an array of wood-fired pizzas, and other enticing dishes. **Known for:** Wagyu burgers and meat loaf; open-air dining with glorious lake views; s'mores and ice cream. [$] *Average main: $25* ✉ *427 N. Paradise Pkwy., Garden City* ☎ *385/626–7394* 🌐 *www.campfiregrillrestaurant.com* 🕒 *Closed Oct.–mid-May.*

LaBeau's Drive-in
$ | FAST FOOD | The Bear Lake region is well known for its locally grown raspberries, and this is the most popular spot in town to enjoy a thick and creamy raspberry shake. Choose from 45 other shake flavors along with

a menu of old-fashioned hamburgers, hot dogs, and chicken sandwiches, and if you haven't tried Utah's signature condiment, "fry sauce" (i.e., ketchup and mayo), LaBeau's is a good place for that too. **Known for:** pastrami burgers; people-watching at outdoor picnic tables; famous milkshakes in dozens of flavors. [$] *Average main: $9* ✉ *69 N. Bear Lake Blvd., Garden City* ☎ *435/946–8821* 🌐 *www.labeaus.com* 🕒 *Closed Sun. and mid-Oct.–late Apr.*

★ Ruca's

$ | CAFÉ | Specializing in *aebleskivers* (fluffy, round Danish pancakes) topped with Nutella and strawberries and any number of other sweet toppings along with overstuffed sandwiches, this cute counter-service eatery is a fun spot for breakfast or lunch all summer long. This is also Bear Lake's go-to for espresso and coffee drinks, and there's an extensive menu of gourmet milkshakes, too. **Known for:** Danish aebleskivers; raspberry milkshakes; outdoor seating overlooking the lake. [$] *Average main: $10* ✉ *284 S. Bear Lake Blvd., Garden City* ☎ *435/946–3691* 🌐 *www.rucasbearlake.com* 🕒 *Closed Thurs. and mid-Oct.–mid-May.*

Hotels

★ Bluebird Inn

$$ | B&B/INN | The most charming lodging on the western shore of Bear Lake happens to be just over the border in Idaho, set on a grassy bluff near Bear Lake West Golf Course and offering five rooms and a larger apartment decorated with country furnishings and colorful quilts. **Pros:** grand lake and mountain views; hearty full breakfast included; 10-minute drive to downtown Garden City. **Cons:** only one restaurant within walking distance; not able to accommodate kids (except in apartment unit); some may find decor too frilly. [$] *Rooms from: $170* ✉ *423 U.S. 89* ☎ *208/945–2571* 🌐 *www.thebluebirdinn.com* 🛏 *6 rooms* 🍴 *Free breakfast.*

Ideal Beach Resort

$$$$ | RESORT | FAMILY | A private beach awaits at this traditional family-friendly condo resort offering two- to four-bedroom accommodations that vary in size and amenities, but all have fully equipped kitchens and offer easy access to pools, hot tubs, saunas, tennis, miniature golf, a children's playground, and a kids' activity center. **Pros:** tons of activities for families; 5-minute drive from Garden City dining; direct beach access. **Cons:** with so many kids around, it can get a little loud; some units could use updating; expensive in summer high season. [$] *Rooms from: $244* ✉ *2176 S. Bear Lake Blvd., Garden City* ☎ *435/946–3364* 🌐 *www.idealbeachresort.com* 🛏 *60 units* 🍴 *No meals.*

Activities

SKIING

Beaver Mountain Ski Area

SKIING/SNOWBOARDING | FAMILY | Family-owned and operated since 1939, this locals' favorite is a 20-minute drive from Garden City and offers skiing like it was before it became an expensive sport. See aerial tricks or try night skiing (until 9 pm) at the two terrain parks. There aren't any trendy nightspots at the foot of this mountain, just an old-fashioned A-frame lodge with burgers and chili. ✉ *40000 E. U.S. 89, Garden City* ☎ *435/946–3610* 🌐 *www.skithebeav.com* 🎫 *Lift tickets $55* ☞ *1,700-ft vertical drop; 828 skiable acres; 48 runs; 35% beginner, 40% intermediate, 25% advanced; 3 triple chairs, 1 double chair.*

Chapter 6

DINOSAURLAND AND EASTERN UTAH

6

Updated by
Stina Sieg

👁 Sights	🍴 Restaurants	🛏 Hotels	🛍 Shopping	🍸 Nightlife
★★★★☆	★★☆☆☆	★★☆☆☆	★☆☆☆☆	☆☆☆☆☆

WELCOME TO DINOSAURLAND AND EASTERN UTAH

TOP REASONS TO GO

★ **One great gorge:** The most jaw-dropping spot in northeastern Utah is the Flaming Gorge National Recreation Area.

★ **Famous fossils:** Come to Dinosaur National Monument to see the famous dinosaur fossils or just to explore some truly remote country.

★ **Ancient art:** The cliffs near Vernal and Price are striking not only for their interesting rock formations, but also for numerous displays of ancient petroglyphs and pictographs, drawn once upon a time by members of the Fremont tribe.

★ **Bike Vernal:** In the last decade, almost 200 miles of former cow trails around Vernal have been converted for use by mountain bikes.

★ **Alone in the swell:** The San Rafael Swell is one of the least crowded spots in a region that's already known for its sparse population.

This section of Utah is large, but it's easy to get around. With few towns in the area, traffic is almost always light. The main highways to explore this area are U.S. 191 and U.S. 40, which run north–south. The biggest towns are Vernal and Price, both of which make comfortable bases for the backcountry.

1 Helper. A sleepy former mining town in the middle of a resurgence.

2 Price. Home to several major dinosaur sites and the San Rafael Swell.

3 Duchesne. A good stopping point for visits to Fred Hayes State Park at Starvation.

4 Roosevelt. A small town close to the Uintah and Ouray Reservation.

5 Vernal. The largest town in the region and a major hub for Dinosaurland.

6 Dinosaur National Monument. Home to ancient dinosaur fossils and stunning landscapes.

7 Flaming Gorge National Recreational Area. An astounding reservoir and 91-mile-wide canyon with excellent fishing and boating.

8 Mirror Lake Scenic Byway. A gorgeous road that takes you through the Uinta Mountains.

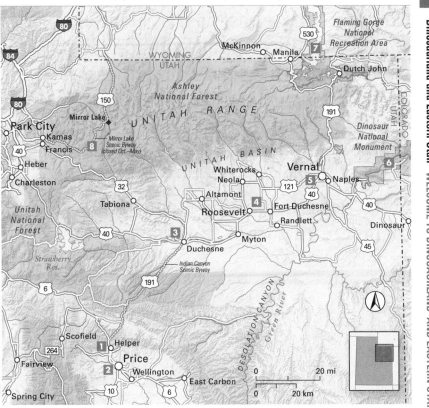

The rugged beauty of Utah's northeastern corner, wedged neatly between Wyoming to the north and Colorado to the east, is the reward for those willing to take the road less traveled. Neither I–80 nor I–70 enters this part of the state, so most visitors who pass through the western United States never even see it—that is part of its appeal. Small towns, rural attitudes, and a more casual and friendly approach to life are all part of the eastern Utah experience.

Northeastern Utah is home to superb boating and fishing at Flaming Gorge, Red Fleet, and the Steinaker reservoirs. Hundreds of miles of hiking and mountain-biking trails (available to cross-country skiers, snowmobilers, or snowshoers in winter) crisscross the region. The Green and Yampa rivers entice white-water rafters as well as less ambitious float-trippers. The pine- and aspen-covered Uinta Mountains offer campers and hikers hidden, pristine lakes and streams surrounded by amazing mountain views. Even if you don't get out of the car, exploring this region on the road takes you through vast red-rock basins, over high mountain passes, and between geologic folds in the earth.

Dinosaurs once dominated this region, and in many ways, they still do. Excavation sites such as Dinosaur National Monument make northeastern Utah one

of the most important paleontological research areas in the world. Paleontology labs and fossil displays can be found at roadside stops and on off-road adventures, along with kitschy dino statues and impressive life-size skeleton casts.

Ancient Native American cultures also left their marks throughout the region. Cliff walls and boulders are dotted with thousands of examples of rock art of the Fremont people (AD 600 to 1300), so called because they inhabited the region near the Fremont River. Today, the Uintah and Ouray Reservation is the second largest in the United States. It covers a significant portion of eastern Utah, though much of the reservation's original land grant was reclaimed by the U.S. government for its mineral and timber resources. The Ute Tribe, whose 3,000-some members inhabit the land, hold powwows and host other cultural ceremonies available to the public.

Museums throughout the region are full of fascinating pioneer relics, and there are a number of restored homesteads in and around Vernal. The rich mining and railroad history of the Price–Helper area fuels the tall tales you're certain to hear of outlaws, robberies, mine disasters, and heroes of the past.

MAJOR REGIONS

Northeast–Central Utah (Castle Country). Nicknamed for the impressive castle-like rock formations that dot the landscape, Castle Country is one of those secret spots that many vacationers miss out on. Most of the attractions are near the town of Price, such as the huge crop of petroglyphs at Nine Mile Canyon. The San Rafael Swell, one of the largest and wholly unvisited natural wonders, lies 25 miles south of Price.

The Uinta Basin (Dinosaurland). Dubbing the Uinta Basin "Dinosaurland" is no overstatement. Named in honor of the large quantity of dinosaur fossils in the area (and especially the 1909 discovery of a huge cache of dino fossils in what is now Dinosaur National Monument), this slice of Utah boasts about its paleontological history whenever possible. Here you can see the ancient bones at the monument and get a crash course in dinosaur history at Vernal's Utah Field House of Natural History State Park. The breathtaking Flaming Gorge National Recreation Area is an excellent place to fish, boat, swim, and catch up-close glimpses of wildlife such as bighorn sheep and wild turkeys. The region encompasses Daggett, Duchesne, and Uintah counties.

Camping

Wilderness makes up the majority of this beautifully undeveloped region. Many visitors choose to immerse themselves in the outdoors by camping for at least part of their stay. For campground information contact **Dinosaur National Monument Quarry Visitor Center** (☎ 435/781–7700 ⊕ www.nps.gov/dino), the state government's recreation department (☎ 877/444–6777 ⊕ www.recreation.gov), or **Utah State Parks** (☎ 800/322–3770 ⊕ stateparks.utah.gov).

Planning

When to Go

In northeastern Utah most museums, parks, and other sights extend their hours from Memorial Day to Labor Day or through the end of September. (Some museums and parks are open only in summer.) Summer (when temperatures can reach 100°F) also brings art festivals, pioneer reenactments, rodeos, and other celebrations. Spring and autumn are cooler and less crowded. Some campgrounds are open year-round, but the drinking water is usually turned off after Labor Day. In winter you can cross-country ski or snowshoe on many of the hiking trails.

Planning Your Time

The two biggest draws in this area are **Flaming Gorge National Recreation Area** and **Dinosaur National Monument.** While it's reasonable to see the fossils on display at Dinosaur in just a day, you'll get a better sense of the park's untouched natural beauty if you stay overnight. Likewise, you can spend a day or several hiking the trails and playing in the water at Flaming Gorge. Many of the towns in the area can be driven through or stopped in without spending the night. A good base for your adventures is **Price,** a pleasant town that's less than two hours from the stunning **San Rafael Swell,** a huge, oval-shape, geologic dome that's far from everything but worth the trek. You could easily spend a few days exploring these unique areas. If you can make the time, a one or multiday excursion on the **Green, White,** or **Yampa River** would be an unforgettable—and occasionally heart-pounding—addition to your stay.

Getting Here and Around

AIR

The closest major airport is Salt Lake City International Airport—two hours from Price and three hours from Vernal; it's served by most major airlines.

CAR

Both U.S. 40 and U.S. 191 are well maintained but have some curvy, mountainous stretches, and away from major towns, be prepared for dirt roads. Keep your vehicle fueled up because gas stations can be far apart, and some are closed on Sunday. Watch for wildlife on the road, especially at night. Price is the largest city on U.S. 6, the major route between the Wasatch Front and the southeastern part of the state. Dinosaur National Monument (which spans the Utah–Colorado border) is about 3½ hours east of Salt Lake City on U.S. 40, or 2½ hours northeast of Price via U.S. 191 and U.S. 40. Flaming Gorge is 40 miles north of Vernal via U.S. 191. The Uinta Mountains and the High Uintas Wilderness Area are about 1½ hours east of Salt Lake City, first via I–80, U.S. 40, and Highway 248 to Kamas and then via Highway 150.

INFORMATION Road Conditions.
☎ *866/511–8824* ⊕ *www.udottraffic.utah. gov.*

Restaurants

Because the towns in eastern Utah are small, dining options are generally more casual and less innovative than you may find in cities. The best dining in this part of the state can be found in upscale lodges—Falcon's Ledge Lodge, between Duchesne and Roosevelt, and Red Canyon Lodge and Flaming Gorge Resort, both near Flaming Gorge—which pride themselves on gourmet menus. Vernal, historically a farming and ranching town, has good steak houses and tasty diner eats. Price has a mix of diverse restaurants (with surprisingly low prices) that represents its immigrant railroad and mining history. Bear in mind that most locally owned restaurants are closed on Sunday.

The area also has two brewpubs: the refreshingly trendy Vernal Brewing Company, located off Vernal's Main Street, and Grogg's Pinnacle Brewing Co., between Helper and Price. Grogg's no longer makes its own beer but is still a great spot to sip some local brews.

Hotels

Most hotels and motels in eastern Utah are chains, and you can expect clean, comfortable rooms and standard amenities. The area's lodges make for a nice change of pace when desired, surrounding you with natural beauty and more individualized rooms and services. Though it goes against logic, many hotels here offer cheaper rates on weekends than weekdays, due to the high number of workers who stay during the week. On weekends, hotels and motels do their best to attract tourists.

Restaurant and hotel reviews have been shortened. For full information, visit Fodors.com.

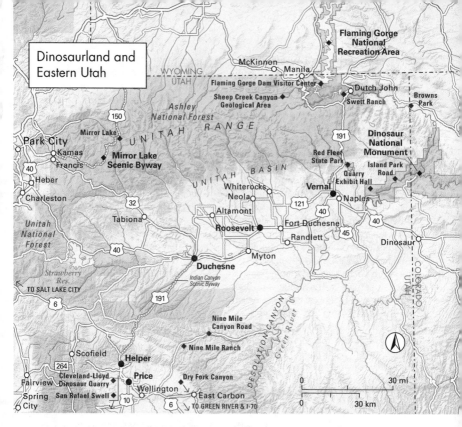

Dinosaurland and Eastern Utah

Dinosaurland and Eastern Utah

What it Costs

	$	$$	$$$	$$$$
RESTAURANTS				
	under $16	$16–$22	$23–$30	over $30
HOTELS				
	under $125	$125–$175	$176–$225	over $225

Visitor Information

VISITOR INFORMATION Bureau of Land Management. ✉ 125 S. 600 W, Price ☎ 435/636–3600 ⊕ www.blm.gov/ut ✉ 170 S. 500 E, Vernal ☎ 435/781–4400 ⊕ www.blm.gov/ut. **Visit Dinosaurland.** ✉ 152 E. 100 N, Vernal ☎ 435/781–6765 Uintah County Travel and Tourism, 800/477–5558 visits and more info ⊕ www.dinoland.com.

Helper

110 miles southeast of Salt Lake City.

If you stroll Helper's main street, you'll be greeted by art galleries sprinkled between closed-down shop fronts. You might even see one of the bumper stickers dedicated to the sleepy spot's resurgence: "Been There, Done That/ Now We're Doing it Again," they read. This phrase represents a slow but hopeful shift in Helper's culture and a desire to escape the fate that swallowed the ghost towns up Spring Canyon Road to the west.

Helper has never fit the small-town Utah mold. Unlike most places in the state, it wasn't settled by Mormons but instead grew out of necessity in the late 1880s due to its proximity to the rail line. Designed to be the division point between the eastern and western terminals of the Denver & Rio Grande Western Railroad, it was named after the "helper" locomotives used to get the trains up the steep, nearby mountain and into the Salt Lake City valley. It quickly became a hub for the various settlers. Miners converged here to drink and visit houses of ill repute, and immigrants arrived to set up shops, bars, and restaurants. From the beginning, it had a diversity that's still uncommon in the state. Sandwiched between several mining camps, Helper remained a supply and service town for decades, and continued strong until the 1960s. By the 1970s, however, mining started to decline, and the town began to lose its usefulness. The 1980s and 1990s were especially rough, a period to which the shuttered stores and abandoned houses are still a testament. These days Helper is trying to slough off those years of hibernation. Each year its biggest surge of vitality comes in the summer, during the popular Helper Arts and Music Festival.

GETTING HERE AND AROUND

From Salt Lake City, travel south on I–15 for 50 miles, then southeast on Highway 6.

FESTIVALS

Helper Arts and Music Festival

ARTS FESTIVALS | **FAMILY** | The big event in town is this annual festival, spread over several days in mid-August, which celebrates Helper's local artists via street performances, concerts, outdoor galleries, and sculptures, plus a children's art yard to explore. ✉ *Helper* 🌐 *www.helperartsfest.com.*

Sights

Western Mining & Railroad Museum

MUSEUM | **FAMILY** | Located within the old Hotel Helper in the town's National Historic District, this excellent museum doubles as a visitor center. A labyrinth of rooms spread over four floors depict everyday activities of Helper's past, and include uncountable trinkets, toys, clothing, and tools from the various businesses and homes here. Some visitors come just for the incredible historic photographs, including several by Dorthea Lange of a nearby coal camp in the 1930s. The museum also features one of the best collections in the state of WPA paintings from Utah artists, including Price's own Lynn Fausett. An exhibit on railroad and mining equipment is located outdoors. ✉ *294 S. Main St.* ☎ *435/472–3009* 🌐 *www.facebook.com/helperutahmuseum* 🎟 *$5 suggested donation* 🕒 *Closed Sun. year-round and Mon. Sept.–May.*

Spring Canyon

GHOST TOWN | The Helper area—in particular the area around Spring Canyon, 4 miles to the west—probably holds the state's best concentration of ghost towns. Spring Canyon Road winds past the remnants of several, including the towns of Spring Canyon, Standardville, Latuda, and Mutual. If you're lucky, you might catch a glimpse of "the White Lady"—a ghost rumored to haunt the Latuda mine office. You can get a map of all the ghost towns in the Helper area at the Western Mining & Railroad Museum's information desk. ✉ *Spring Canyon Rd.* ☎ *435/637–3009.*

Restaurants

Balance Rock Eatery

$ | **AMERICAN** | Broad white walls, two-story ceilings, a white railing around the second-floor mezzanine, and paddle fans give this American-fare pub a light and airy feeling. Try a better-than-home-cookin' breakfast, or enjoy a burger and quaff Utah-made microbrews while you browse the eclectic assortment of gift items for sale on the upper level. **Known for:** homemade potato chips; all-day breakfast; live music by local bands. [$] *Average main: $11* ✉ *148 S. Main St.* ☎ *435/472–0403* 🕒 *No dinner Sun.*

Grogg's Pinnacle Brewing Company

$ | **AMERICAN** | This casual pub on a side road between Helper and Price serves a hefty spectrum of burgers, pizzas, salads, and steaks. Top your meal off with a draft pint of freshly brewed beer, and take a seat on the outdoor deck if the weather's nice. **Known for:** tasty burgers in more than a dozen varieties; good selection of beers on-tap; family-friendly vibe. $ *Average main: $13* ⊠ *1653 N. Carbonville Rd.* ☎ *435/637–2924* ⊕ *www.groggspinnacle-brewing.com.*

Marsha's Sammich Shop-N-Bakery

$ | **CAFÉ** | This casual gathering spot downtown is a great place to get a sense of what's going on in Helper, plus a cup of coffee and a homebaked treat (the cinnamon rolls, in particular, sell out early). Marsha, one of the town's many colorful characters, serves breakfast until noon on weekdays and until 3 pm on Saturday. **Known for:** delicious cinnamon rolls (especially when heated up); homemade soups; local hang-out. $ *Average main: $8* ⊠ *69 S. Main St.* ☎ *435/472–2253* ⊘ *Closed Sun. and Mon. No dinner Sat.*

Price

120 miles southeast of Salt Lake City.

Thousands of visitors travel to Price every year to experience Utah's past through fossils, exhibits, and preservation sites at the Prehistoric Museum, USU Eastern. For being a quite small, mostly blue-collar town, one may not expect to find much excitement here, but they'd be wrong. While Price began as a Mormon farming settlement in the late 1800s, in 1883 the railroad arrived, bringing with it immigrants from around the world to mine coal reserves. As the town expanded, coal became the cash crop of the area, and mining remains the town's primary industry to this day.

GETTING HERE AND AROUND

To get to Price from Salt Lake City, travel on I–15 South for 50 miles, and then take U.S. 6 for 70 miles toward the southeastern corner of the state. This drive contains many of the area's breathtaking views and rock formations. Be aware that mountain and canyon roads can seem unpredictable if you're not used to them.

If you're heading to Price from Green River or the surrounding area, take U.S. 191 north for 65 miles. The town is easy to navigate, with most of the main attractions on or close to Main Street.

FESTIVALS

Greek Festival Days

FESTIVALS | **FAMILY** | A sizable number of Greek immigrants arrived in the area of Price to work in the mines throughout the early 1900s. This annual festival in mid-July celebrates that heritage with two days of traditional Greek food, dance, and music. ⊠ *Assumption Greek Orthodox Church, 61 S. 200 E* ☎ *435/636–3701* ⊕ *www.castlecountry.com/greek-festival-days.*

Price City International Days

FESTIVALS | **FAMILY** | Held annually at the end of July, this three-day festival uses music, dance, and food to celebrate the many nationalities and cultures that make up the Price community. It's right on the heels of the statewide Pioneer Days festivities, always on July 24. ⊠ *Pioneer Park, 100 E. 550 N* ☎ *435/636–3701* ⊕ *www.castlecountry.com.*

ESSENTIALS

VISITOR INFORMATION Carbon County Office of Tourism and Visitors Center. ⊠ *751 E. 100 N #2100* ☎ *435/636–3701* ⊕ *www.castlecountry.com.*

Sights

Cleveland-Lloyd Dinosaur Quarry

NATURE SITE | **FAMILY** | Paleontologists and geologists have excavated more than 12,000 dinosaur bones from

The San Rafael Swell looks otherworldly at sunset.

the Cleveland-Lloyd Dinosaur Quarry, making this "predator trap" the densest concentration of Jurassic fossils ever found. The center is 15 miles on a gravel road from the nearest services, so bring food and water and dress for desert conditions. It's 33 miles south of Price: take Highway 10 south to the Cleveland/Elmo turnoff and follow the signs. Free admission for ages 15 and younger. ✉ Off Hwy. 10 ☎ 435/636–3600 ⊕ www.blm.gov/ut ✉ $5 ⊙ Closed Mon.–Wed. and Nov.–Mar.

Indian Canyon Scenic Byway

SCENIC DRIVE | This section of U.S. 191 climbs north from the Price and Helper vicinity, cresting at Indian Creek Pass at an elevation of 9,100 feet. It then begins a long descent into the Uinta Basin area, ending at Duchesne. The winding, 43-mile route takes you through canyons, over plateaus, and into the heart of the geology and natural beauty that define this part of Utah. Take it slow and watch for fallen rocks and rockslides, which

often litter the road. There are plenty of scenic viewpoints along the way. ✉ U.S. 191, Helper.

★ Nine Mile Canyon

NATIVE SITE | The hundreds of petroglyphs etched into the boulders and cliffs of Nine Mile Canyon may be one of the world's largest outdoor art galleries. They're the work of the Fremont people, who lived in much of what is now Utah from AD 600 to 1300. The canyon also shelters the remnants of many early homesteads, stage stops, and ranches. It's important not to touch the fragile rock art because oils from your fingers can damage them. The scenic drive through Nine Mile Canyon spans about 100 miles round trip. ✉ Nine Mile Canyon Rd. ✛ To reach canyon, go 7½ miles southeast of Price on U.S. 6 and then turn north on Soldier Creek Rd., which eventually connects with Nine Mile Canyon Rd. ☎ 435/637–3701 ⊕ www.castlecountry.com/nine-mile-canyon.

The Prehistoric Museum, USU Eastern

MUSEUM | **FAMILY** | Miners working in the coal pits around Price in the late 1800s often saw and excavated rare treasures that most scientists could only dream of finding—dinosaur bones, eggs, skeletons, and fossilized tracks. These are all on exhibit at the Prehistoric Museum, USU Eastern. For families, this museum offers a small but excellent kids' discovery area where children can experiment with excavating dino bones all on their own. A second hall is devoted to early humans, with displays of beadwork, clay figurines, a walk-in teepee, and other area artifacts. You can't miss the museum's gigantic wooly mammoth and saber-toothed tiger replicas. ✉ *155 E. Main St.* ☎ *435/613–5060, 800/817–9949* 🌐 *www.usueastern.edu/museum* 🎟 *$6* 🕒 *Closed Sun.*

Price Mural

PUBLIC ART | The 200-foot-long mural inside the Price Municipal Building is a visual narration of the history of the town and of Carbon County, beginning with the first trappers and white settlers. The painting took artist Lynn Fausett almost four years to complete back in the late 1930s. ✉ *200 E. Main St.* ☎ *435/637–5010* 🎟 *Free.*

★ San Rafael Swell Recreation Area

NATURE SITE | **FAMILY** | Tremendous geological upheavals pushed through the Earth's surface eons ago, forming a giant oval-shape dome of rock about 80 miles long and 30 miles wide, giving rise to the name "swell." Over the years, the harsh climate beat down the dome, eroding it into a wild array of multicolor sandstone and creating buttes, pinnacles, mesas, and canyons that spread across more than 600,000 acres. In the northern Swell, the Wedge Overlook peers into the Little Grand Canyon and the San Rafael River below. The strata at the edges of the southern Swell are angled near vertical, creating the San Rafael Reef. Both are known for fantastic hiking, canyoneering, and mountain biking. ⚠ **Bring plenty of water, food, and a spare tire. Always keep your wits about you, as flash flooding can be deadly, especially in the Swell's narrow slot canyons.** ✉ *BLM Field Office, 125 S. 600 W* ☎ *435/636–3600* 🌐 *www.blm.gov.*

🍴 Restaurants

Farlaino's Café

$ | **AMERICAN** | Found in a historic building along Main Street, this casual restaurant attracts locals with large portions of American diner fare for breakfast, lunch, and early dinners (it closes at 7 pm). **Known for:** hand-cut curly fries; homemade soups (on weekdays); giant pancakes. [$] *Average main: $10* ✉ *87 W. Main St.* ☎ *435/637–9217* 🕒 *Closed Sun.*

Greek Streak

$ | **GREEK** | In what used to be a Greek coffeehouse in the early 1900s, this low-key café is a reminder of Price's strong Greek heritage. The menu includes traditional recipes from Crete, like gyros and dolmades. **Known for:** long-time local favorite; baklava and other Greek pastries; delicious lemon-rice soup. [$] *Average main: $11* ✉ *84 S. Carbon Ave.* ☎ *435/637–1930* 🕒 *Closed Sun.*

★ Sherald's

$ | **FAST FOOD** | **FAMILY** | If you hanker for the nostalgia, and the prices, of an old-fashioned hamburger stand, you're in luck. Order at the window and eat outside at picnic tables, or use the car-side service. **Known for:** very thick milkshakes; delicious burgers and fries; long lines. [$] *Average main: $6* ✉ *434 E. Main St.* ☎ *435/637–1447* 🕒 *Closed Sun.*

🛏 Hotels

Greenwell Inn & Convention Center

$ | **HOTEL** | **FAMILY** | With more amenities than most of the area's hotels but still reasonably priced, the Greenwell is a great choice for most travelers. **Pros:**

convenient downtown location; nice pool; good value, especially in quieter months. **Cons:** older property with basic rooms; fitness center is large but is in lobby/pool area; motel-style room entrances are a downside in inclement weather. [$] *Rooms from: $90* ✉ *655 E. Main St.* ☎ *435/637–3520, 800/666–3520* 🌐 *www.greenwellinn.com* 🛏 *136 rooms* 🍴 *No meals.*

Legacy Inn

$ | **HOTEL** | If you want to save a bit of cash, but not scrimp on amenities, this simple, updated motel is perfect. **Pros:** great value; easy access to freeway; free continental breakfast. **Cons:** not all rooms are remodeled; some rooms don't have strong Wi-Fi; rooms are a little small and dark. [$] *Rooms from: $65* ✉ *145 N. Carbonville Rd.* ☎ *435/637–2424* 🌐 *www.legacyinnutah.com* 🛏 *33 rooms* 🍴 *Free breakfast.*

Nine Mile Ranch

$ | **B&B/INN** | Ben Mead grew up in beautiful Nine Mile Canyon, and now runs this "bunk and breakfast" establishment on his working cattle ranch, where guests can stay in the comfy house or rent one of the rustic cabins. **Pros:** a true cowboy experience; beautiful setting with dark-as-can-be nighttime skies; cabins are an affordable, no-frills choice for groups. **Cons:** breakfast for guests in the main house is continental (and not included with cabin rental); cabins are rustic, with bathrooms located behind the buildings; bedding not included with cabin rental. [$] *Rooms from: $90* ✉ *Nine Mile Canyon Rd., Mile Post 24, Wellington* ✥ *To reach ranch, travel 7 miles southeast of Price to Wellington via Hwy. 6, then make left onto Soldier Creek Canyon Rd., which will become Nine Mile Canyon Rd., and drive north for 25 miles* ☎ *435/637–2572* 🌐 *9mileranch.com* 🛏 *4 rooms* 🍴 *Free breakfast.*

Ramada by Wyndham Price

$ | **HOTEL** | **FAMILY** | This stylishly decorated hotel has a large atrium surrounding the pool area; rooms are clean and comfortable, with suites offering kitchenettes. **Pros:** many amenities, including a restaurant that serves alcohol; pleasant and well-lit interiors; large pool. **Cons:** few electrical outlets in rooms; a bit expensive for the area; older property. [$] *Rooms from: $109* ✉ *838 Westwood Blvd.* ☎ *435/637–8880, 877/492–4803* 🌐 *www.ramada.com* 🛏 *151 rooms* 🍴 *Free breakfast.*

Nightlife

Sports Page Bar

BARS/PUBS | Inside Price's Ramada hotel, this bar offers pool and big-screen TVs to watch the night's game. But that's not what makes the Sports Page Bar special; karaoke and a live DJ on Wednesday and Saturday offer plenty of entertainment alongside the drinks and bar food. ✉ *Ramada by Wyndham Price, 838 Westwood Blvd.* ☎ *435/637–8880, 877/492–4803* 🌐 *www.ramada.com.*

The Vault at the Tuscan

BARS/PUBS | This club's classy atmosphere renders it a pleasant place to park for the evening. Come early for dinner; it's attached to a tasty fine dining restaurant with extremely reasonable prices. Afterwards, step across the hall for a drink and maybe a game of pool. The atmosphere livens up on the weekends, when the doors stay open until 2 am and a live DJ brings the dance floor to life. ✉ *23 E. 100 N* ☎ *435/613–2582.*

Wooly's Lounge

BARS/PUBS | Downstairs at the Greenwell Inn, Wooly's is a little hideout where you can watch the game on the big-screen TV, throw some darts, or play a game of pool. This casual lounge is a great stop for weary travelers. Find your own taste of local brews here, and enjoy the local chit-chat you'll find along the barstools and booths. ✉ *655 E. Main St.* ☎ *435/637–2020* 🌐 *www.greenwellinn.com.*

Activities

Carbon County covers a wide range of geography, from mountains to gorges to plateaus. Hundreds of miles of hiking and biking trails crisscross the region.

GOLF

Carbon Country Club

GOLF | The 18-hole championship course at the Carbon Country Club is open to the public. Along with its quality atmosphere, this course has a pleasant, relaxing feel that will make even the most novice of players feel welcome. And if you happen to be a little over par, the sandstone cliffs, waterfall, and Native American petroglyphs will be enough to distract you from an off game day. ⊠ 3055 N. U.S. 6 ☎ 435/637–2388 ⊕ www.carbon-countryclub.com ☞ $27.50 🏌. 18 holes, 6159 yards, par 70.

HIKING AND MOUNTAIN BIKING

The canyons and surrounding landscapes of Price include trails that rival the slickrock of Moab, minus the crowds. The visitor center in Price has a mountain biking guide that shows several trails you can challenge yourself on, including Nine Mile Canyon. Adventurous hikers can use many of these trails as well. Bicyclewerks is a great source of information for those looking to explore.

Bicyclewerks

BICYCLING | This is Price's go-to bike shop for trail details, repairs, and area information. ⊠ 82 N. 10 W ☎ 435/637–2453.

Duchesne

54 miles northeast of Price.

A small town in a small county of the same name, Duchesne is probably best known for its proximity to Fred Hayes State Park at Starvation and the park's fishing-friendly reservoir.

GETTING HERE AND AROUND

From Price, take U.S. 191 north, and then go a mile west on U.S. 40.

ESSENTIALS

VISITOR INFORMATION Duchesne County Chamber of Commerce. ⊠ 50 E. 200 S, Roosevelt ☎ 435/722–4598 ⊕ www.uintabasin.org.

⊙ Sights

Fred Hayes State Park at Starvation

NATIONAL/STATE PARK | FAMILY | This state park's original name, Starvation State Park, was most likely in recognition of the early homesteaders and cattlemen who battled bitter winters, short growing seasons, and other hardships in the area. It was recently renamed in memory of a beloved director of the Utah Divison of Parks and Recreations. Now boaters and anglers come to cast for walleye, yellow perch, and smallmouth bass in the park's 3,500-acre reservoir. There are six campgrounds within the park, two of which are developed. Bring sunscreen, as there is little natural shade on-site. ⊠ Hwy. 311 ☎ 435/738–2326 ⊕ stateparks.utah.gov ☞ $10 per vehicle.

Roosevelt

80 miles northeast of Price.

Roosevelt, a small town named for President Theodore Roosevelt, lies between blocks of the sovereign land of the Uintah and Ouray Indian Reservation. Its tiny main street is pure Americana, and resembles any number of the other little towns in the area. It's a good place to stop for a cup of coffee or a meal, or to spend the night on the way to somewhere else.

GETTING HERE AND AROUND

Roosevelt is more of a place you end up than a planned destination. Its location between Price and Vernal on U.S. 40 makes it an ideal place to get out and stretch your legs while driving through the region's beautiful countryside. If you're headed here from Price, go north on U.S. 191, then east on U.S. 40.

Sights

Northern Ute Pow Wow

FESTIVAL | Each July 4 weekend, the Northern Ute Pow Wow has drumming, dancing, and singing competitions featuring top performers from throughout North America. The powwow is one of the largest in the West and is free to the public. All are welcome to attend and camp on the grounds. Other attractions include a rodeo, golf and softball tournaments, and an arts-and-crafts fair. The tribe also celebrates Ute Bear Dances in spring, Sundances in July and August, and a smaller powwow held over Thanksgiving weekend at the tribal gymnasium in Fort Duchesne. ✉ *U.S. 40, Fort Duchesne* ✣ *8 miles east of Roosevelt* ☎ *435/722–5141* 🌐 *www.utetribe.com.*

Ouray National Wildlife Refuge

NATURE PRESERVE | Established in 1960, this refuge consists of 11,987 acres of land along the Green River. Here you can see more than 200 species of migratory birds in spring and fall, mule deer and golden eagles year-round, and bald eagles in early winter. An information kiosk at the refuge has a bird checklist and other leaflets. Best times to visit are in the early morning and early evening. ✉ *Wildlife Refuge Rd., off Hwy. 88, Ouray* ✣ *15 miles east of Roosevelt on U.S. 40, then 13 miles south on Rte. 88* ☎ *435/545–2522* 🌐 *www.fws.gov/ouray* 🎟 *Free.*

Uintah and Ouray Reservation

NATIVE SITE | The over 4.5 million acres of the reservation is spread out in a patchwork-like fashion across the Uinta Basin and northeastern Utah, all the way to the eastern edge of the state. Fort Duchesne is the tribal headquarters for the Uintah and Ouray branch of the Ute Tribe. Because it's sometimes difficult to tell whether you're on reservation land, public land, or private land, you should stay on main roads unless you have permission to be on the reservation lands. ✉ *Fort Duchesne* 🌐 *www.utetribe.com.*

Hotels

Best Western Plus Landmark Hotel

$$ | **HOTEL** | **FAMILY** | Ample amenities, including one of the few indoor pools in the region, make this chain hotel a reliable choice. **Pros:** hot breakfast; large rooms; indoor pool open year-round. **Cons:** rates are high for the area; rooms nearest the highway can be noisy; few nearby attractions. [$] *Rooms from: $145* ✉ *2477 E. U.S. 40, Ballard* ☎ *435/725–1800, 800/780–7234* 🌐 *www.bestwestern.com* 🛏 *96 rooms* 🍴 *Free breakfast.*

★ **Falcon's Ledge Lodge**

$$$ | **B&B/INN** | With an emphasis on escaping the workday world, this small and comfortable lodge is found on a 600-acre private ranch, and caters to fly-fishers and hunters. **Pros:** gorgeous setting with dark skies; exquisite food; great fishing. **Cons:** location is quite remote; no TVs in rooms; expensive for the area. [$] *Rooms from: $195* ✉ *Hwy. 87, Altamont* ✣ *15 miles north of Duchesne or 25 miles west of Roosevelt* ☎ *435/253–7336* 🌐 *www.falconsledge.com* 🛏 *9 rooms* 🍴 *Free breakfast* ☞ *No children under 12 allowed.*

Frontier Grill & Motel

$ | **HOTEL** | Accommodations at this downtown motel are simple, but adequate and inexpensive. **Pros:** convenient downtown location; adjacent restaurant is considered the best in Roosevelt; updated rooms. **Cons:** aging facilities and interior design; breakfast is not included (but you do receive a small voucher for the restaurant); there isn't much to do in Roosevelt. [$] *Rooms from: $80* ✉ *75 S. 200 E* ☎ *435/722–2201* 🛏 *54 rooms* 🍴 *No meals.*

Performing Arts

CINEMAS

Echo Drive-In

THEATER | FAMILY | For a nostalgic dose of Americana, catch a show at the Echo Drive-In on summer evenings. ⊠ *250 W. Hwy. 40* 🕾 *435/722–2095* ⊕ *www. rooseveltmovies.com.*

🏃 Activities

FISHING

Ute Tribe Fish & Wildlife Department

FISHING | Information about camping, sporting, and photo safaris on the Uintah and Ouray Reservation is available from the Ute Tribe Fish & Wildlife Department. You can purchase fishing permits from Fort Duchesne's Ute Plaza Supermarket, as well as Ute Petroleum, a gas station in Myton. ⊠ *Fort Duchesne* 🕾 *435/722–5511* ⊕ *www.utetribe.com.*

Vernal

22 miles east of Fort Duchesne.

Vernal is the hub of Dinosaurland, mixing the region's ancient heritage with a certain kitschy charm—think down-home diners and giant dino statues. Dinosaurs aren't the only things they're proud of in Vernal, though. The town claims a connection to the ancient Fremont people, a rowdy ranching past, and more than a passing acquaintance with outlaws like Butch Cassidy, who frequented the area whenever he felt it was safe to be seen around town.

Legend has it that the saloonkeepers of Vernal gave Butch's gang the name "Wild Bunch," muttering "There goes that wild bunch" whenever the outlaws rolled in. Now the largest town (population 10,000) in the northeast corner of the state, this cattle-ranching and oil-and-gas community is one of the few Utah towns founded by non-Mormons. However, it was its

remote location, far from government authorities, that led to its early reputation as a wild and lawless place. These days it's more of a tame, friendly spot to cool your heels between trips to outlying areas; it's also full of opportunities for biking and river adventures.

GETTING HERE AND AROUND

Though secluded, it's easy to get to Vernal. From Salt Lake City, head 25 miles via I–80, then 145 miles east via U.S. 40/U.S. 191; from Price go east on U.S. 40. Most of Vernal's attractions are right on Main Street. From Vernal, take U.S. 40 east to reach Dinosaur National Monument, or head north on U.S. 191 to explore Flaming Gorge National Recreation Area.

ESSENTIALS

VISITOR INFORMATION Vernal Area Chamber of Commerce. ⊠ *134 W. Main St.* 🕾 *435/789–1352* ⊕ *www.vernalchamber. com.* **Visit Dinosaurland.** ⊠ *152 E. 100 N* 🕾 *435/781–6765 Uintah County Travel and Tourism, 800/477–5558 visits and more info* ⊕ *www.dinoland.com.*

Sights

Browns Park

HISTORIC SITE | FAMILY | Along a quieter stretch of the Green River and extending into Colorado, this area features plenty of high-desert scenery, a national waterfowl refuge. Explore several buildings on the **John Jarvie Ranch.** Buildings date from 1880 to the early 1900s, and there's also a cemetery with graves of a few men who met violent ends nearby. Jarvie also ran a post office, store, and river ferry, and his spread was a major hideout on the so-called Outlaw Trail. In late May, **Jarvie Fest** celebrates this past with mountain men, wagon rides, pioneer demonstrations, rope- and leather-making, and live music. A similar festival takes place the last Saturday of October. Reach the park and ranch by driving 65 miles north of Vernal on U.S. 191, then 22 miles east on a gravel road. ⊠ *Browns Park Rd., Browns Park* ☎ *435/885–3307 John Jarvie Ranch* ⊕ *www.blm.gov/utah* ☞ *Free.*

Daughters of Utah Pioneers Museum

MUSEUM | FAMILY | This museum provides a window into the daily lives of the pioneers. The large collection of artifacts (most donated by descendents of the area's early settlers) range from a working loom to guns to a mortician's tools. Most everything is displayed in period rooms, including a shop, a house, and a doctor's office. ⊠ *186 S. 500 W* ☞ *Free* ☉ *Closed Sept.–May and Sun.–Tues.*

Dry Fork Canyon

NATIVE SITE | FAMILY | An impressive array of Native American petroglyphs and pictographs adorn the 200-foot-high cliffs in Dry Fork Canyon, making the 22-mile round-trip drive from Vernal well worth your time. Two trails leading to the rock art are on **McConkie Ranch,** a privately owned property that asks only for a $5 per vehicle donation and respect for the site. Make sure to bring sturdy shoes, because both short paths have steep and rough spots. If you call the ranch's number, Jean McConkie McKenzie, who was born and still lives here, will show you her collection of arrowheads and antiques. Her mother, Sadie, first opened the rock art to the public in 1930. ⊠ *3500 Dry Fork Canyon Rd.* ☎ *435/789–6733* ☞ *$5 per vehicle donation requested.*

Flaming Gorge-Uintas National Scenic Byway

SCENIC DRIVE | Past Red Fleet Reservoir north of Vernal, U.S. 191 begins to ascend the eastern flank of the Uinta uplift as you head toward Flaming Gorge. The section of U.S. 191 and Highway 44 between Vernal and Manila, Utah, is known as the Flaming Gorge-Uintas National Scenic Byway. Within a distance of 30 miles the road passes through 18 uptilted geologic formations, including the billion-year-old exposed core of the Uinta Mountains, with explanatory signs. The route also provides plenty of opportunity for wildlife-watching and fossil hunting, with several nature trails. Before setting out, pick up a guide at the Utah Field House of Natural History. ⊠ *U.S. 191.*

Uintah County Heritage Museum

MUSEUM | FAMILY | Inside the Uintah County Heritage Museum are collections of Fremont and Ute Indian artifacts, including baskets, water jugs, and beadwork, as well as pioneer items like carriages, guns, saddles, and old-fashioned toys. Kids can try out interactive exhibits that let them tap out telegrams and dial a rotary phone, while their parents check out the most off-beat installation: a collection of kitschy handmade porcelain dolls modeled after the nation's First Ladies, from Martha Washington to Nancy Reagan. ⊠ *155 E. Main St.* ☎ *435/789–7399* ⊕ *www.uintahmuseum.org* ☞ *Free* ☉ *Closed Sun.*

★ Utah Field House of Natural History State Park

MUSEUM | FAMILY | Around 150 million years ago, this was the stomping ground of dinosaurs, and you can see rock samples, fossils, Fremont and Ute nation artifacts, and a viewing lab where you can watch paleontologists restore actual fossils. The biggest attraction for kids is undoubtedly the outdoor Dinosaur Garden with its 18 life-size models of prehistoric creatures, including a T. rex and a woolly mammoth. The Field House also doubles as a visitor center for all of Dinosaurland, so stop here for maps and guides for the entire area. ⊠ *496 E. Main St.* ☎ *435/789–3799* ⊕ *stateparks.utah.gov* ☞ *$7* ☉ *Closed Sun. Nov.–Mar.*

🍴 Restaurants

Betty's Café

$ | AMERICAN | This friendly, no-frills greasy spoon brings in locals and tourists alike for meals that will leave you full all day. While lunch is tasty here, too, this is the best spot in Vernal for breakfast. **Known**

for: giant portions; the Betty Omelet, filled with everything but the kitchen sink; homemade items, including strawberry jam, biscuits, and scalloped-cut home fries. [$] *Average main: $10* ✉ *416 W. Main St.* ☎ *435/781–2728* 🕑 *No dinner.*

Dinosaur Brew Haus

$ | **AMERICAN** | This friendly joint serves higher quality food than your average sports pub, including hand-cut fries (try them Cajun-style), house-smoked meats, and grilled salmon. Snack on peanuts and watch a game on one of the TVs while you wait for your food, or drop a coin in the jukebox and shoot some pool. **Known for:** tasty, affordable burgers; good selection of local microbrews on tap; sweet potato fries. [$] *Average main: $12* ✉ *550 E. Main St.* ☎ *435/781–0717.*

Plaza Mexicana

$$ | **MEXICAN** | Festive, colorful interiors and authentic Mexican specialties make Plaza Mexicana a sure bet if you need a break from Vernal's ubiquitous diner eateries. There are 22 varieties of burritos to choose from, as well as a large selection of seafood options. **Known for:** huge portions; fantastic homemade salsas; extensive menu. [$] *Average main: $16* ✉ *55 E. Main St.* ☎ *435/781–2931.*

★ Vernal Brewing Company

$$ | **MODERN AMERICAN** | One of the rare breweries in this corner of the state, this gastropub also stands out for its creative, modern takes on burgers, pizza, and sandwiches. Choose from several of VBC's craft beers brewed on-site, and even get a growler to go. **Known for:** large burger selection; chicken skillet pie; hip atmosphere. [$] *Average main: $16* ✉ *55 S. 500 E* ☎ *435/781–2337* 🌐 *www.vernalbrewingcompany.com* 🕑 *Closed Sun.*

Hotels

Dinosaur Inn & Suites

$$ | **HOTEL** | **FAMILY** | Remodeled rooms and a delicious pizza restaurant spruce up this comfortable Best Western motel located within blocks of all downtown attractions. **Pros:** pool makes it a good choice for families; central location; tasty, hot breakfast included. **Cons:** traffic noise in some rooms; pricey considering that it's a basic chain offering; not a lot of natural light in rooms. [$] *Rooms from: $160* ✉ *251 E. Main St.* ☎ *435/789–2660* 🌐 *www.bestwestern.com* 🛏 *60 rooms* 🍴 *Free breakfast.*

Ledgestone Hotel Vernal

$ | **HOTEL** | **FAMILY** | This modern, centrally located hotel is one of the most comfortable places in Vernal to spend a night, with a dining table/desk and a fully furnished kitchen in each room. **Pros:** every room is a comfortable suite with a full kitchen; luxurious touches at an affordable price; one the newer hotels in town. **Cons:** no pool; no breakfast; only single-queen rooms have sleeper sofas (double-queen rooms have armchairs). [$] *Rooms from: $89* ✉ *679 W. Main St.* ☎ *435/789–4200* 🌐 *ledgestonehotel.com* 🛏 *78 rooms* 🍴 *No meals.*

Performing Arts

THEATER

Outlaw Trail Theater

ARTS VENUE | In late June and early July, enjoy musicals, melodramas, or comedies under the stars. Shows typically run Monday through Saturday. ✉ *Western Park Outdoor Amphitheater, 302 E. 200 S* ☎ *888/240–2080* 🌐 *www.outlawtrailtheater.com.*

Shopping

Ashley Trading Post

LOCAL SPECIALTIES | Dinosaur memorabilia, rocks, fossils, and Native American jewelry and baskets sold here make great souvenirs. ✉ *236 E. Main St.* ☎ *435/789–8447.*

Fullbright Studios

LOCAL SPECIALTIES | Stop here to enjoy artist Randy Fullbright's collection of gorgeous Dinosaur National Monument photographs. His paper castings of petroglyphs make nice mementos, too. ✉ *216 E. Main St.* ☎ *435/789–2451* ⊕ *www.randyfullbright.com.*

Activities

BICYCLING

Because Dinosaurland is lesser-known than other parts of the state, bikers can often escape the crowds and enjoy some scenic solitude. The Uinta Basin has some 100 miles of trails. Bring plenty of water and sunblock.

Altitude Cycle

BICYCLING | To talk to knowledgeable cyclists about local trails off-the-beaten path, stop in here; they can set you up with trail guides, repairs, and accessories. Ask for a map of biking hot spot **McCoy Flats,** just 6½ miles west of the shop, off Highway 40. There you'll find 35 miles of trails to explore. ✉ *580 E. Main St.* ☎ *435/781–2595* ⊕ *www.altitudecycle.com.*

BOATING

Red Fleet State Park

BOATING | Like the other reservoirs in the region, this one, just 10 miles north of Vernal, is great for boating and fishing. Visitors come to see the colorful sandstone formations surrounding the lake, and the section of 200-million-year-old dinosaur tracks reachable by a short hike or by boat. Enjoy the scenery, the trails, and more at your leisure when you camp in the park. ✉ *Off U.S. 191* ☎ *435/789–4432* ⊕ *stateparks.utah.gov* 🎫 *$10 day use.*

Steinaker State Park

BOATING | Boating and waterskiing enthusiasts love Steinaker State Park, 7 miles north of Vernal. With 825 surface acres, Steinaker Reservoir relinquishes a fair number of largemouth bass and rainbow trout. There's a sandy swimming beach, hiking trails begin at the park, and wildlife-viewing areas are nearby. A campground and covered group pavilions make this a popular park. ✉ *U.S. 191* ☎ *435/789–4432* ⊕ *stateparks.utah.gov* 🎫 *$10 day use.*

HIKING

Dinosaur National Monument Quarry Visitor Center

HIKING/WALKING | Check with the rangers at this visitor center, 20 miles east of Vernal, for information about the numerous hiking trails in the area. ✉ *Hwy. 149, Dinosaur National Monument* ☎ *435/781–7700* ⊕ *www.nps.gov/dino.*

Jones Hole Creek

HIKING/WALKING | One of the most beautiful hikes in the area begins at the Jones Hole National Fish Hatchery, 40 miles northeast of Vernal on the Utah–Colorado border, and follows Jones Hole Creek through riparian woods and canyons, past petroglyphs and wildlife. The full trail is a moderate 8½-mile round trip to the Green River and back, but you can stop halfway at Ely Creek and return for an easier, but still lovely, 4¼-mile hike. There are numerous trails in this area that are unmarked and not maintained, but easy to follow if you use reasonable caution. ✉ *24495 E. Jones Hole Hatchery Rd.* ☎ *435/789–4481.*

SCENIC FLIGHTS

Dinaland Aviation

TOUR—SPORTS | For a bird's-eye view of Dinosaurland's deep canyons, wide-open deserts, and blue reservoirs, take to the air with Dinaland Aviation. They offer flight-seeing tours from 30 minutes to more than an hour. ✉ *830 E. 500 S* ☎ *435/789–4612* ⊕ *dinalandaviation.com.*

Get close to Dinosaur National Monument by rafting down Green or Yampa river.

Dinosaur National Monument

20 miles east of Vernal.

Dinomania rules at this 330-square-mile park that straddles the Utah–Colorado border. Although the main draw is obviously the ancient dinosaur fossils, the park's setting is something to savor as well, from craggy rock formations to waving grasslands to the Green and Yampa rivers. The best part is that complete solitude is easy to find, as desolate wilderness surrounds even the busiest spots within the park.

GETTING HERE AND AROUND

Coming from Vernal, go east about 10 miles to the town of Jensen, via U.S. 40. Once there, be on the lookout for Utah Highway 149 on your left and then follow the signs to the park. Note that the dinosaur fossils and Quarry Exhibit Hall are both on the Utah side of the monument.

Sights

Cub Creek Road

SCENIC DRIVE | This scenic 20-mile round-trip drive goes from the Quarry Visitor Center east to the Josie Morris Cabin. Josie's sister, Ann Bassett, was reputedly the "Etta Place" of Butch Cassidy legends. Morris lived alone for 50 years at her isolated home. Along the drive, watch for ancient rock art, geological formations, views of Split Mountain, the Green River, and hiking trails. The route is dubbed the "Tour of the Tilted Rocks" on the $1 guidebook sold at the visitor center. ⊠ *Dinosaur National Monument.*

Island Park Road

SCENIC DRIVE | A scenic drive on the unpaved Island Park Road, along the northern edge of the park, not only passes some impressive Fremont petroglyph panels but also Rainbow Park Campground, a beautiful place to spend a night or two on the banks of the Green River. Be sure to check with the visitor center about road conditions, as it can be impassable when wet and there is no winter maintenance. ✉ *Dinosaur National Monument.*

★ Quarry Exhibit Hall

MUSEUM | FAMILY | Here you can view more than 1,500 genuine fossils, displayed in their original burial positions in an excavated river bed, several stories high, 150-feet long, and now enclosed by a large, airy museum. ✉ *Hwy. 149, 20 miles east of Vernal* ☎ *435/781–7700* 🌐 *www.nps.gov/dino* 🎟 *$25 per vehicle to enter monument.*

Hotels

★ The Jensen Inn

$ | B&B/INN | Tucked just off the road to Dinosaur National Monument, this is a bright, cheery bed-and-breakfast with friendly owners and tasteful modern interiors. **Pros:** close to Dinosaur National Monument; excellent breakfasts; welcoming atmosphere. **Cons:** far from stores or restaurants; closed December through February; no TVs in rooms. [$] *Rooms from: $100* ✉ *5056 S. 9500 E, Jensen* ☎ *435/789–5905* 🌐 *www.thejenseninn.com* ⏲ *Closed Dec.–Feb.* 🛏 *6 rooms* 🍴 *Free breakfast.*

Activities

HIKING

When embarking on any hike in Dinosaur, bring plenty of water and sun protection, as most trails have little to no shade. Dehydration is a real concern (especially in summer) with the dry air and elevation changes. Pets are not allowed on most trails.

Desert Voices Nature Trail

HIKING/WALKING | Four miles past the Quarry Visitor Center, the moderate 1½-mile trail has interpretive signs that describe the arid environment you're hiking through. You can make a longer hike by using the Connector Trail to link up with the Sound of Silence Trail. ✉ *Dinosaur National Monument.*

Sound of Silence Trail

HIKING/WALKING | More challenging than the Desert Voices trail, this 3-mile trail begins 2 miles past the Dinosaur Quarry, and delivers excellent views of Split Mountain. To hike both trails without returning to your car, use the easy ¼-mile **Connector Trail,** which links the two, making a trek of about 5 miles total. ✉ *Dinosaur National Monument.*

RAFTING

The best way to experience the geologic depths of Dinosaur National Monument is to take a white-water rafting trip on the Green or Yampa River. Joining forces near Echo Park in Colorado, the two waterways have each carved spectacular canyons through several eons' worth of rock, and contain thrilling white-water rapids. River-running season is typically May through September. ■ **TIP→ Permits are required for all boaters.**

Adrift Adventures

WHITE-WATER RAFTING | FAMILY | The closest guide service to the Dinosaur National Monument, this outfitter offers one-day or multiday rafting trips on the Green and Yampa rivers. Note that a pass to Dinosaur National Monument must be purchased separately beforehand. ✉ *9500 E. 6000 S, Jensen* ☎ *435/789–3600, 800/824–0150* 🌐 *www.adrift.com* 🎟 *From $109 (day trip, including lunch).*

Dinosaur River Expeditions

WHITE-WATER RAFTING | FAMILY | The only locally owned outfitter in Dinosaur National Monument, this company offers daily and multiday whitewater trips on the Green and Yampa rivers. Guided hikes are also offered that can take you to petroglyths, rock formations, and dinosaur footprints, depending on the route. ✉ *2279 N. Vernal Ave., Vernal* ☎ *800/345–7238* 🌐 *www.dinosaurriverexpeditions.com* 🎟 *From $95.*

OARS Dinosaur

WHITE-WATER RAFTING | FAMILY | In operation since 1969, OARS offers one-day and multiday rafting trips on both calm and white waters on the Green and Yampa rivers. ✉ *221 N. 400 E, Vernal* ☎ *800/342–8243* ⊕ *www.greenriverrafting.com* 🖥 *From $109.*

Flaming Gorge National Recreation Area

40 miles north of Vernal (to Flaming Gorge Dam).

If you are standing in front of the Flaming Gorge or its reservoir with a crowd of people, you'll likely hear gasps and exclamations of amazement. The sheer size of these bodies of water is astounding, as are the red, narrow walls on either side of the gorge. Though not far from the suburban town of Vernal, the Flaming Gorge area offers a lesson in stillness and serenity. The lake and 91-mile gorge also has some of the best boating and fishing in the state. The Flaming Gorge Reservoir stretches north into Wyoming, but most facilities lie south of the state line in Utah.

GETTING HERE AND AROUND

From Vernal, getting to the gorge is a straight shot north via U.S. 191. Follow the highway for about 38 miles, which will take you into some magnificent country at high elevations. Then, simply follow the signs to the gorge. The road will veer downward for a few miles before you reach it. From Salt Lake City, go 30 miles east via I–80 past Evanston, Wyoming. Take the Fort Bridge exit, and drive to Manila via Highway 414, which becomes Highway 43. Once in Manila, turn right on Highway 44 for 38 miles until you reach U.S. 191 and follow signs.

ESSENTIALS

Flaming Gorge Dam Visitor Center
The main information center for the Utah side of the gorge, 2 miles north of Greendale Junction, includes displays and an explanatory movie. Depending on the weather, this engineering marvel may be open for free guided tours. ✉ *U.S. 191* ☎ *435/885–3135* ⊕ *www.flaminggorge-country.com.*

Red Canyon Visitor Center
Displays here explain the geology, flora and fauna, and human history of the Flaming Gorge area. But the best thing has to be the clifftop location 1,300 feet above the lake. The views are outstanding, and you can enjoy them while having a picnic. To get here, head west from the Greendale Junction of U.S. 191 and Highway 44, and follow the signs. ✉ *Hwy. 44* ☎ *435/889–3713* ⊕ *www.flaminggorge-country.com.*

 ## Sights

Sheep Creek Canyon Geological Area
NATURE SITE | A scenic 13-mile drive on paved and gravel roads crosses the Sheep Creek Canyon Geological Area, which is full of upturned layers of rock, craggy pinnacles, and hoodoos. Watch for a herd of bighorn sheep, as well as a popular cave alongside the road. In the fall, salmon return to Sheep Creek to spawn; a kiosk and several bridges provide unobtrusive viewing. The area, 28 miles west of Greendale Junction off U.S. 191 and Highway 44, is open from May to October. ✉ *Forest Service Rd. 218* ☎ *435/784–3445* ⊗ *Closed Nov.–Apr.*

Spirit Lake Scenic Backway
SCENIC DRIVE | This 17-mile round-trip add-on to the Sheep Creek Canyon Loop road leads past the **Ute Lookout Fire Tower,** which was in use from the 1930s through the 1960s. ✉ *Flaming Gorge National Recreation Area.*

Flaming Gorge was named by explorer John Wesley Powell for its "flaming, brilliant red" color.

Swett Ranch

HISTORIC SITE | This isolated homestead belonged to Oscar and Emma Swett and their nine children through most of the 1900s. The U.S. Forest Service has turned the ranch into a working historical site, complete with restored and decorated houses and buildings. ✉ *Off U.S. 191* ✣ *At Greendale Junction of U.S. 191 and Hwy. 44, stay on U.S. 191; about ½ mile north of junction there's a sign for 1½-mile dirt road to ranch* ☎ *435/784–3445* 🌐 *www.flaminggorgecountry.com* 🎟 *Free* 🕒 *Closed early Sept.–Memorial Day.*

Hotels

Flaming Gorge Resort

$$ | **HOTEL** | With motel rooms and condo-style suites, a good American-cuisine restaurant, and a store just a short drive from the water, this is a practical home base for activities. **Pros:** plenty of amenities and recreational options; good restaurant; great fishing. **Cons:** rooms need updating; most rooms don't have air-conditioning; can be very busy in summer and too quiet in winter. [$] *Rooms from: $139* ✉ *1100 E. Flaming Gorge Resort Rd., off U.S. 191, Dutch John* ☎ *435/889–3773* 🌐 *www.flaminggorgeresort.com* 🛏 *46 rooms* 🍴 *No meals.*

★ Red Canyon Lodge

$$ | **RESORT** | **FAMILY** | A pleasant surprise in the woods, this lodge is surrounded by well-built, handcrafted log cabins with kitchenettes (some with wood-burning stoves) that face a private trout-stocked lake. **Pros:** beautiful setting; cabins are comfortable for families or groups (up to 6 people per cabin); lots of recreation opportunities. **Cons:** must book a year in advance for summer months; Wi-Fi only in restaurant; no air-conditioning. [$] *Rooms from: $145* ✉ *2450 W. Red Canyon Lodge, Dutch John* ☎ *435/889–3759* 🌐 *www.redcanyonlodge.com* 🛏 *18 cabins* 🍴 *No meals.*

⚡ Activities

BICYCLING

Because it mixes high-desert vegetation—blooming sage, rabbit brush, cactus, and wildflowers—and red-rock terrain with a cool climate, Flaming Gorge is ideal for road and trail biking. The 3-mile round-trip **Bear Canyon–Bootleg** ride begins south of the dam off U.S. 191 at the Firefighters' Memorial Campground, and runs west to an overview of the reservoir. For the intermediate rider, **Dowd Mountain Hideout** is a 10-mile ride with spectacular views through forested single-track trail, leaving from Dowd Springs Picnic Area off Highway 44. Fliers describing cycling routes are at area visitor centers or online at ⊕ *www.dinoland. com.* Several local lodges rent bikes.

BOATING AND FISHING

Flaming Gorge Reservoir provides ample opportunities for boating and water sports of all kinds. Most boating facilities close from October through mid-March.

Old-timers maintain that Flaming Gorge provides the best lake fishing in the state, yielding rainbow and lake trout, smallmouth bass, and Kokanee salmon. The Green River below Flaming Gorge Dam has been identified as one of the best trout fisheries in the world. Rainbow and brown trout are plentiful and big, but only artificial lures and fly-fishing are permitted; bait fishing isn't allowed. Fed by cold water from the bottom of the lake, this stretch is a calm, scenic stretch of water, ideal for risk-averse folk or for families who want to take smaller children on rafting trips but don't want to worry about them falling into white water.

Cedar Springs Marina

BOATING | If you have your own boat, this is your one-stop shop. You can launch, fuel up, or rent a slip here. You can also rent a boat or hire a fishing guide. The marina is approximately 2 miles southwest of Flaming Gorge Dam. ✉ *2675 N. Cedar Springs Rd., Dutch John* ☎ *435/889–3795* ⊕ *www.cedarspringsmarina.com.*

Dutch John Resort

BOATING | Boat rentals, guided fishing trips, and daily float trips on the Green River are available here. ✉ *1050 South Blvd., Dutch John* ☎ *435/885–3191* ⊕ *dutchjohnresort.com.*

Lucerne Valley Marina

BOATING | Seven miles east of Manila you'll find this marina, with just about any amenity you may need for your watertop adventure. With a boat launch, slips, boat rentals, fishing licenses, mechanical services, gas, and houseboat and floating-cabin rentals, you can't ask for much more. ✉ *5570 E. Lucerne Valley Rd.* ☎ *435/784–3483, 888/820–9225* ⊕ *www. flaminggorge.com.*

HIKING

There's plenty of hiking in the Flaming Gorge area and any of the local visitor centers or lodges can recommend hikes. From the Red Canyon Visitor Center, three different hikes traverse the **Canyon Rim Trail** through the pine forest: an easy ½-mile round-trip trek leads to the Red Canyon Rim Overlook (above 1,300-foot cliffs), a moderate 3½-mile round-trip hike finds you at the Swett Ranch Overlook, and a 7-mile round-trip hike winds through brilliant layered colors to the Green River at the canyon's bottom below the dam. In the Sheep Creek Canyon Geological Area, the 4-mile **Ute Mountain Trail** leads from the Ute Lookout Fire Tower down through pine forest to Brownie Lake, and back the same way. The **Tamarack Lake Trail** begins at the west end of Spirit Lake (on Highway 44, go past the Ute Lookout Fire Tower turnoff and take F.S. Road 221 to Spirit Lake) and goes to Tamarack Lake and back for a moderate 3-mile trek, round trip.

Mirror Lake Scenic Byway

Kamas is 42 miles from Salt Lake City.

Although the Wasatch may be Utah's best-known mountain range, the Uinta Mountains, the only major east–west mountain range in the United States, are its tallest, topped by 13,528-foot Kings Peak. This area, particularly in the High Uintas Wilderness where no vehicles are allowed, is great for pack trips, horseback day rides, hiking, and overnight backpacking in summer. The Uintas are ribboned with streams and dotted with small lakes set in rolling meadows.

GETTING HERE AND AROUND

From Salt Lake City, take I–80 and Highway 32 south to Kamas. You can access the Uinta Mountains either from Kamas or Evanston, Wyoming. From Kamas, go 65 miles east via Highway 150. From Evanston, travel 30 miles south on the same highway.

Sights

Mirror Lake

VIEWPOINT | A mile north of the crest of Bald Mountain Pass on Highway 150, this is arguably the best-known lake in the High Uintas Wilderness. At an altitude of 10,000 feet, it offers a cool respite from summer heat. It's easy to reach by car, and families enjoy fishing, hiking, and camping along its rocky shores. Its campgrounds provide a base for hikes into the surrounding mountains, and Highline Trail accesses the 460,000-acre High Uintas Wilderness Area to the east. There's a $6 day-use fee for Mirror Lake, but it's good for three days. ✉ *Hwy. 150, mile marker 32.*

★ Mirror Lake Scenic Byway

SCENIC DRIVE | This scenic road begins in Kamas and winds its way up to the High Uinta country. The 65-mile drive follows Highway 150 through heavily wooded canyons past mountain lakes and peaks, cresting at 10,687-foot Bald Mountain Pass. Because of heavy winter snows, much of the road is closed from October to June. A three-day pass is required to use facilities in the area. You can purchase a pass at self-serve sites along the way, or at the Chevron, Kamas Food Town, or Samak Smoke House in Kamas. You can buy a guide to the Byway from the Wasatch-Cache National Forest's Kamas Ranger District office in Kamas (50 E. Center St. ☎ *435/783–4338*). ✉ *Kamas* 🎟 *$6 for 3-day pass.*

Upper Provo Falls

TRAIL | This is a good place to stop en route, near mile marker 24, where you can stroll the boardwalk to the terraced falls cascading with clear mountain water.

Hotels

The Cabins at Bear River Lodge

$$$$ | **RENTAL** | Log cabins in the forest let you reconnect with nature via a range of on-site activities without giving up creature comforts. **Pros:** peaceful getaway in beautiful setting; plenty of activities; comfortable cabins. **Cons:** prices seem high for the level of amenities; no other restaurants within 30 miles; lower-level floors can be noisy. [$] *Rooms from: $229* ✉ *Mirror Lake Hwy., mile marker 49* ☎ *435/642–6289* 🌐 *www.bearriverlodge.com* 🛏 *16 cabins* 🍴 *No meals.*

Chapter 7

CAPITOL REEF
NATIONAL PARK

7

Updated by
Shelley Arenas

◉ Sights	🍴 Restaurants	🛏 Hotels	🛍 Shopping	🍸 Nightlife
★★★★★	★★★☆☆	★★★★★	★★★★☆	★★☆☆☆

WELCOME TO
CAPITOL REEF NATIONAL PARK

TOP REASONS TO GO

★ **The Waterpocket Fold:** See an excellent example of a monocline—a fold in the Earth's crust with one very steep side in an area that is otherwise horizontal. This one's almost 100 miles long.

★ **Fewer crowds:** Although visitation has nearly doubled (to more than 1.2 million per year) since 2011, Capitol Reef is less crowded than nearby parks, such as Zion and Bryce Canyon.

★ **Fresh fruit:** Pick apples, pears, apricots, and peaches in season at the pioneer-planted orchards at historic Fruita. These trees still produce plenty of fruit.

★ **Rock art:** View pictographs and petroglyphs left by Native Americans who lived in this area from AD 300 to 1300.

★ **Pioneer artifacts:** Buy tools and utensils similar to those used by Mormon pioneers at the Gifford Homestead.

At the heart of this 378-square-mile park is the massive natural feature known as the Waterpocket Fold, which runs roughly northwest to southeast along the park's spine. Capitol Reef itself is named for a formation along the fold near the Fremont River. A historic pioneer settlement, the green oasis of Fruita is easily accessed by car, and the 8-mile Scenic Drive provides a good overview of the canyons and rock formations that populate the park. Colors here range from deep, rich reds to sage greens to crumbling gray sediments. The absence of large towns nearby ensures that night skies are brilliant starscapes.

1 Fruita. This historic pioneer village is at the heart of what most people see of Capitol Reef. The one and only park visitor center nearby is the place to get travel and weather information and maps. Scenic Drive, through Capitol Gorge, provides a view of the Golden Throne.

2 Scenic Drive. Winding 8 miles through the park, this aptly named road is the best way to get an overview of Capitol Reef's highlights, and it's the most accessible for all vehicles. It takes about 90 minutes to drive to the end and back, but you'll want to take your time with so many interesting sights to see along the way.

3 Cathedral Valley. The views are stunning and the silence deafening in the park's remote northern section. High-clearance vehicles are required, as is crossing the Fremont River. Driving in this valley is next to impossible when the Cathedral Valley Road is wet, so ask at the visitor center about current weather and road conditions.

4 Muley Twist Canyon. At the southern reaches of the park, this canyon is accessed via Notom-Bullfrog Road from the north, and Burr Trail Road from the west and southeast. High-clearance vehicles are required for Upper Muley and Strike Valley Overlook.

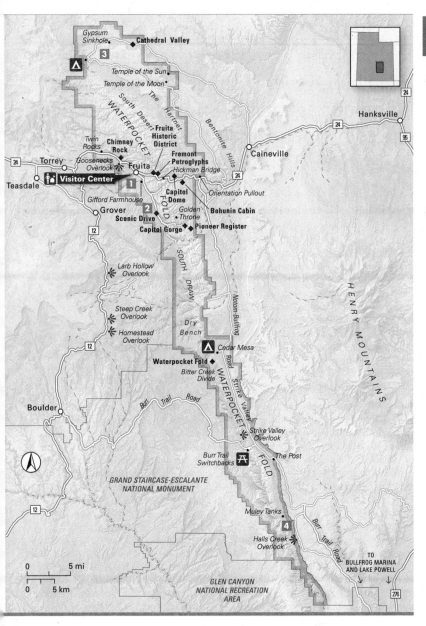

Gypsum Sinkhole

Cathedral Valley

3

Temple of the Sun

Temple of the Moon

The Hartnet

Bentonite Hills

Hanksville

24

95

WATERPOCKET South Desert

Fruita Historic District

Fremont Petroglyphs

Caineville

Twin Rocks

Chimney Rock

Goosenecks Overlook

Fruita

Hickman Bridge

24

Torrey

24

Visitor Center

1

Teasdale

Gifford Farmhouse

Capitol Dome

Orientation Pullout

Grover

2

Scenic Drive

Golden Throne

Behunin Cabin

Capitol Gorge

Pioneer Register

12

FOLD

SOUTH DRAW

Larb Hollow Overlook

Steep Creek Overlook

Dry Bench

Notom-Bullfrog Road

Strike Valley Road

H E N R Y   M O U N T A I N S

12

Homestead Overlook

Cedar Mesa

Waterpocket Fold

Bitter Creek Divide

WATERPOCKET

Boulder

Burr Trail Road

Strike Valley Overlook

Burr Trail Switchbacks

The Post

FOLD

GRAND STAIRCASE-ESCALANTE NATIONAL MONUMENT

12

Muley Tanks

4

Burr Trail Road

Halls Creek Overlook

TO BULLFROG MARINA AND LAKE POWELL

0   5 mi

0   5 km

GLEN CANYON NATIONAL RECREATION AREA

276

Capitol Reef National Park is a natural kaleidoscopic feast for the eyes, with colors more dramatic than anywhere else in the West. The Moenkopi rock formation is a rich, red-chocolate hue; deep blue-green juniper and pinyon stand out against it. Sunset brings out the colors in an explosion of copper, platinum, and orange, then dusk turns the cliffs purple and blue.

The park, established in 1971, preserves the Waterpocket Fold, a giant wrinkle in the earth that extends 100 miles between Thousand Lake Mountain and Lake Powell. When you climb high onto the rocks or into the mountains, you can see this remarkable geologic wonder and the jumble of colorful cliffs, massive domes, soaring spires, and twisting canyons that surround it. It's no wonder early pioneers called this part of the country the "land of the sleeping rainbow."

Beyond incredible sights, the fragrance of pine and sage rises from the earth, and canyon wrens serenade you as you sit by the water. Flowing across the heart of Capitol Reef is the Fremont River, a narrow little creek that can turn into a swollen, raging torrent during desert flash floods. The river sustains cottonwoods, wildlife, and verdant valleys rich with fruit. During the harvest, your sensory experience is complete when you bite into a perfect ripe peach or apple from the park's orchards. Your soul, too, will be gratified here. You can walk the trails in relative solitude and—except during busier periods—enjoy the beauty

without confronting significant crowds on the roads or paths. All around you are signs of those who came before: ancient Native Americans of the Fremont culture, Mormon pioneers who settled the land, and other courageous explorers who traveled the canyons.

The best home base for exploring Capitol Reef, the pretty town of **Torrey,** just west of the park, has lots of personality. Giant old cottonwood trees make it a shady, cool place to stay, and the townspeople are friendly and accommodating. A little farther west on Highway 24, tiny **Teasdale** is a charming settlement cradled in a cove of the Aquarius Plateau. The homes look out onto brilliantly colored cliffs and green fields. Quiet **Bicknell** lies another few miles west of Torrey. The Wayne County seat of **Loa,** 10 miles west of Torrey, was settled by pioneers in the 1870s. If you head south from Torrey instead of west, you can take a spectacular 32-mile drive along Highway 12 (see the Bryce Canyon National Park chapter for more details)' to **Boulder,** a town so remote that its mail was carried on horseback until 1940. Nearby is Anasazi

Capitol Reef in One Day

Pack a picnic lunch, snacks, and cold drinks to take with you (there are no restaurants in the park). As you enter the park from the west, look to your left for Chimney Rock; in a landscape of spires, cliffs, and knobs, this deep-red landmark is unmistakable. Start your journey at the **visitor center**, where you can study a three-dimensional map of the area, peruse exhibits, watch a short film, and browse the many books and maps related to the park. Then, head for Scenic Drive, stopping at the **Fruita Historic District** to see some of the sites associated with the park's Mormon history. Visit **Gifford Homestead** to browse the gift shop. Enjoy that lunch you packed at picnic tables on rolling green lawns lining both sides of the road by the Gifford House.

Check out the **Fremont Indian Petroglyphs**, and if you feel like some exertion, take a hike on the Hickman Bridge Trail. From the trail (or 2 miles east of the visitor center from Highway 24 if you skip the hike), you'll see **Capitol Dome**. Along this stretch of Highway 24 stop to see the old one-room **Fruita Schoolhouse**, the **petroglyphs**, and the **Behunin Cabin**. Next you'll have to backtrack west a few miles on Highway 24 to find the **Goosenecks Trail**. At the same parking lot you'll find the trailhead for **Sunset Point Trail**; take this short hike in time to watch the setting sun hit the colorful cliffs.

7

Capitol Reef National Park PLANNING

AVERAGE HIGH/LOW TEMPERATURES					
JAN.	**FEB.**	**MAR.**	**APR.**	**MAY**	**JUNE**
41/20	47/26	58/34	66/40	75/48	87/59
JULY	**AUG.**	**SEPT.**	**OCT.**	**NOV.**	**DEC.**
91/65	88/63	80/55	66/44	51/31	41/21

State Park. In the opposite direction, 51 miles east, **Hanksville** is a place to stop for food and fuel—the small wayside en route to Moab also has a couple of decent budget motels.

Planning

When to Go

Spring and early summer are the most bustling seasons. Some folks clear out in the midsummer heat, and then return for the apple harvest and crisp temperatures of autumn. Although the park is less crowded than nearby Zion, Bryce Canyon, and Arches, visitation has increased dramatically in recent years, and the campground fills quickly (and is by reservation only). Annual rainfall is scant, but when it does rain, flash floods can wipe out park roads. Snowfall is usually light. Sudden, short-lived snowstorms—and thunderstorms—are not uncommon in the spring.

FESTIVALS AND EVENTS

Harvest Time Scarecrow Festival. Events for this month-long celebration marking the end of another busy season are held throughout Wayne County. In addition to a scarecrow contest, there are plenty of family-friendly events, including live music, arts and crafts, pumpkin carving, and a Halloween party. ⊕ *www.entradain-stitute.org.*

Wayne County Fair. The great American county fair tradition is at its finest in Loa in mid-August. A demolition derby, rodeo, horse shows, and a parade are all part of the fun. You'll also find crafts such as handmade quilts, agricultural exhibits, children's games, and plenty of good food. ⊕ *waynecountyutah.org.*

Getting Here and Around

AIR
The nearest major airports are in Salt Lake City and Las Vegas, about 3½ and 5½ hours away by car, respectively. St. George Regional Airport (3½ hours away) is a handy, smaller airport with direct flights from several major cities in the West, Cedar City Municipal Airport (2¾ hours) has direct daily service on Delta from Salt Lake City, and Canyonlands Field Airport in Moab (2 hours away) has direct daily service on United Airlines from Denver.

CAR
You can approach Capitol Reef country from several approaches, including highways 24 and 72 from Interstate 70 (and Moab), Highway 12 from Bryce Canyon National Park, and Highway 20 to U.S. 89 to Highway 62 from Interstate 15. All are well-maintained, safe roads that bisect rich agricultural communities steeped in Mormon history (especially in the nearby towns of Bicknell and Loa). Highway 24 runs across the middle of Capitol Reef National Park, offering scenic views the entire way.

Hotels

There are no lodging options within Capitol Reef, but clean and comfortable accommodations for all budgets exist just west in nearby Torrey, and not far beyond in Bicknell and Loa. There are also a couple of options east of the park, in Hanksville. Book well ahead if visiting March through October. *Hotel reviews have been shortened. For full information, visit Fodors.com.*

What It Costs			
$	$$	$$$	$$$$
RESTAURANTS			
under $16	$16–$22	$23–$30	over $30
HOTELS			
under $125	$125–$175	$176–$225	over $225

Park Essentials

ACCESSIBILITY
Capitol Reef doesn't have many trails that are accessible to people in wheelchairs. The visitor center, museum, film, and restrooms are all accessible, as is the campground amphitheater where evening programs are held. The Fruita Campground Loop C restroom is accessible; so is the boardwalk to the petroglyph panel on Highway 24, 1.2 miles east of the visitor center.

PARK FEES AND PERMITS
There is no fee to enter the park, but it's $20 per vehicle (or $10 per bicycle and $15 per motorcycle) to travel on Scenic Drive beyond Fruita Campground; this fee is good for one week, paid via the "honor system" at a drop box versus a staffed entry gate. Backcountry camping permits are free; pick them up at the visitor center. An annual pass that allows unlimited access to Scenic Drive is $35.

PARK HOURS
The park is open 24/7 year-round. It's in the Mountain time zone.

CELL PHONE RECEPTION

Cell phone reception is nearly nonexistent in the park, although you may pick up a weak signal in a few spots. Pay phones are at the visitor center and at Fruita Campground.

Restaurants

Inside Capitol Reef you won't find any restaurants, though in summer there's a small store selling baked goods and ice cream. More dining options exist close by in Torrey, where you can find everything from creative Southwestern fusion cuisine to basic hamburger joints serving consistently good food.

Visitor Information

PARK CONTACT INFORMATION Capitol Reef National Park. ⊠ *Off Hwy. 24* ☎ *435/425–3791* ⊕ *www.nps.gov/care.*

Fruita

In the 1880s Nels Johnson became the first homesteader in the Fremont River Valley, building his home near the confluence of Sulphur Creek and the Fremont River. Other Mormon settlers followed and established small farms and orchards, creating the village of Junction. The orchards thrived, and by 1900 the name was changed to Fruita. The orchards, less than a mile from the visitor center, are preserved and protected as a Rural Historic District.

 Sights

GEOLOGICAL LANDMARKS

Capitol Dome

NATURE SITE | One of the rock formations that gave the park its name, this giant sandstone dome is visible in the vicinity of the Hickman Bridge trailhead, 1.9 miles east of the visitor center. ⊠ *Hwy. 24.*

Chimney Rock

NATURE SITE | Even in a landscape of spires, cliffs, and knobs, this deep-red landform, 3.9 miles west of the visitor center, is unmistakable. ⊠ *Hwy. 24.*

HISTORIC SIGHTS

Behunin Cabin

BUILDING | FAMILY | Elijah Cutlar Behunin used blocks of sandstone to build this cabin in 1882. Floods in the lowlands made life too difficult, and he moved before the turn of that century. The house, 5.9 miles east of the visitor center, is empty, but you can peek through the window to see the interior. ⊠ *Hwy. 24.*

Fremont Petroglyphs

NATIVE SITE | Between AD 300 and 1300 the Capitol Reef area was occupied by Native Americans who were eventually referred to by archaeologists as the Fremont, named after the Fremont River that flows through the park. A nice stroll along a boardwalk bridge, 1.1 miles east of the visitor center, allows close-up views of ancient rock art, which can be identified by the large trapezoidal figures often depicted wearing headdresses and ear baubles. ⊠ *Hwy. 24.*

TRAILS

★ Chimney Rock Trail

TRAIL | You're almost sure to see ravens drifting on thermal winds around the deep-red Mummy Cliff that rings the base of this trail. This loop trail begins with a steep climb to a rim above dramatic Chimney Rock. The trail is 3.6 miles round-trip, with a 590-foot elevation change. No shade. Use caution during monsoon storms due to lightning hazards. Allow three to four hours. *Moderate–Difficult.* ⊠ *Capitol Reef National Park* ⊹ *Trailhead: Hwy. 24, about 3 miles west of visitor center.*

Fremont River Trail

TRAIL | What starts as a quiet little stroll beside the river turns into an adventure. The first ½ mile of the trail wanders past

Did You Know?

The 3.5-mile round-trip trek up to Chimney Rock has some steep switchbacks, but the journey yields panoramic views. The trailhead is 3 miles from the park visitor center, near the entrance. It is forbidden to rock climb on it.

orchards next to the Fremont River. After you pass through a narrow gate, the trail changes personality and you're in for a steep climb on an exposed ledge with drop-offs. The views at the top of the 480-foot ascent are worth it. It's 2 miles round-trip; allow two hours. *Moderate.* ⊠ *Capitol Reef National Park* ⚓ *Trailhead: near amphitheater off Loop C of Fruita Campground, about 1 mile from visitor center.*

Golden Throne Trail

TRAIL | As you hike to the base of the Golden Throne, you may be lucky enough to see one of the park's elusive desert bighorn sheep, but you're more likely to spot their split-hoof tracks. The trail is about 2 miles of gradual rise with some steps and drop-offs. The Golden Throne is hidden until you near the end of the trail, then suddenly you see the huge sandstone monolith. If you hike near sundown the throne burns gold. The round-trip hike is 4 miles and takes two to three hours. *Difficult.* ⊠ *Capitol Reef National Park* ⚓ *Trailhead: at end of Capitol Gorge Rd., 10 miles south of visitor center.*

Goosenecks Trail

TRAIL | This nice little walk gives you a good introduction to the land surrounding Capitol Reef. You'll enjoy the dizzying views from the overlook. It's only 0.2 miles round trip to the overlook and a very easy walk. *Easy.* ⊠ *Hwy. 24, about 3 miles west of visitor center.*

Hickman Bridge Trail

TRAIL | This trail leads to a natural bridge of Kayenta sandstone, with a 133-foot opening carved by intermittent flash floods. Early on, the route climbs a set of steps along the Fremont River. The trail splits, leading along the right-hand branch to a strenuous uphill climb to the Rim Overlook and Navajo Knobs. Stay to your left to see the bridge, and you'll encounter a moderate up-and-down trail. Up the wash on your way to the bridge is a Fremont granary on the right side of the small canyon. Allow about two hours for the 1.8-mile round trip. Expect lots

of company. *Moderate.* ⊠ *Capitol Reef National Park* ⚓ *Trailhead: Hwy. 24, 2 miles east of visitor center.*

Sunset Point Trail

TRAIL | The trail starts from the same parking lot as the Goosenecks Trail, on your way into the park about 3.3 miles west of the visitor center. Benches along this easy, 0.8-mile round trip invite you to sit and meditate surrounded by the colorful desert. At the trail's end, you will be rewarded with broad vistas into the park; it's even better at sunset. *Easy.* ⊠ *Hwy. 24.*

SCENIC DRIVES

★ Utah Scenic Byway 24

SCENIC DRIVE | For 75 miles between Loa and Hanksville, you'll cut right through Capitol Reef National Park. Colorful rock formations in all their hues of red, cream, pink, gold, and deep purple extend from one end of the route to the other. The closer you get to the park the more colorful the landscape becomes. The vibrant rock finally gives way to lush green hills and the mountains west of Loa.

VISITOR CENTERS

Capitol Reef Visitor Center

INFO CENTER | **FAMILY** | Watch a park movie, talk with rangers, or peruse the many books, maps, and materials for sale in the bookstore. Towering over the center (11 miles east of Torrey) is the Castle, one of the park's most prominent rock formations. ⊠ *Scenic Dr. at Hwy. 24* ☎ *435/425–3791* ⊕ *www.nps.gov/care.*

Scenic Drive

This 8-mile road, simply called Scenic Drive, starts at the visitor center and winds its way through the Fruita Historic District and colorful sandstone cliffs into Capitol Gorge; a side road, Grand Wash Road, provides access into the canyon. At Capitol Gorge, the canyon walls become steep and impressive but the route becomes unpaved for about the last 2 miles, and road conditions may vary due to weather and usage. Check with the visitor center before setting out.

Sights

GEOLOGICAL LANDMARKS
The Waterpocket Fold

NATURE SITE | A giant wrinkle in the earth extends almost 100 miles between Thousand Lake Mountain and Lake Powell. You can glimpse the fold by driving south on Scenic Drive after it branches off Highway 24, past the Fruita Historic District. For complete immersion enter the park via the 36-mile Burr Trail from Boulder. Roads through the southernmost reaches of the park are largely unpaved. The area is accessible to most vehicles during dry weather, but check with the visitor center for current road conditions. ⊠ *Capitol Reef National Park*.

HISTORIC SIGHTS
Gifford House Store and Museum

NATIONAL/STATE PARK | One mile south of the visitor center in a grassy meadow with the Fremont River flowing by, this is an idyllic shady spot in the Fruita Historic District for a sack lunch, complete with tables, drinking water, grills, and a convenient restroom. The store sells reproductions of pioneer tools and items made by local craftspeople; there's also locally made fruit pies and ice cream to enjoy with your picnic. ⊠ *Scenic Dr.*

Pioneer Register

HISTORIC SITE | Travelers passing through Capitol Gorge in the 19th and early 20th centuries etched the canyon wall with their names and the date. Directly across the canyon from the Pioneer Register and about 50 feet up are signatures etched into the canyon wall by an early United States Geologic Survey crew. Though it's illegal to write or scratch on the canyon walls today, plenty of damage has been done by vandals over the years. You can reach the register via an easy hike from the sheltered trailhead at the end of Capitol Gorge Road, 10.3 miles south of the visitor center; the register is about 10 minutes along the hike to the sandstone "tanks." ⊠ *Off Scenic Dr.*

SCENIC DRIVES
★ Capitol Gorge

SCENIC DRIVE | Eight miles south of the visitor center, Scenic Drive ends, at which point you can drive an unpaved spur road into Capitol Gorge. The narrow, twisting road on the floor of the gorge was a route for pioneer wagons traversing this part of Utah starting in the 1860s. After every flash flood, pioneers would laboriously clear the route so wagons could continue to go through. The gorge became the main automobile route in the area until 1962, when Highway 24 was built. The short drive to the end of the road has striking views of the surrounding cliffs and leads to one of the park's most popular walks: the hiking trail to the water-holding "tanks" eroded into the sandstone. ⊠ *Scenic Dr.*

TRAILS
★ Capitol Gorge Trail and the Tanks

NATIONAL/STATE PARK | Starting at the Pioneer Register, about a ½ mile from the Capitol Gorge parking lot, is a ½-mile trail that climbs to the Tanks—holes in the sandstone, formed by erosion, that hold water after it rains. After a scramble up about ¼ mile of steep trail with cliff drop-offs, you can look down into the Tanks and see a natural bridge below the lower tank. Including the walk to the Pioneer Register, allow an hour or more for this interesting hike, one of the park's most popular. *Moderate.* ⊠ *Capitol Reef National Park* ✛ *Trailhead: at end of Scenic Dr., 10 miles south of visitor center.*

Cohab Canyon Trail

TRAIL | Find rock wrens and Western pipistrelles (canyon bats) on this trail. One end is directly across from the Fruita Campground on Scenic Drive; the other is across from the Hickman Bridge parking lot. The first ¼ mile from Fruita is strenuous, but the walk becomes easier except for turnoffs to the overlooks, which are short. You'll find miniature arches, skinny side canyons, and honeycombed patterns on canyon walls where the wrens make nests. The trail is 3.2 miles round trip to the Hickman Bridge parking lot (two to three hours). The Overlook Trail adds 1 mile. Allow two hours to overlooks and back. *Moderate.* ⊠ *Capitol Reef National Park ✣ Trailheads: Scenic Dr., about 1 mile south of visitor center, or Hwy. 24, about 2 miles east of visitor center.*

Grand Wash Trail

TRAIL | At the end of unpaved Grand Wash Road you can continue on foot through the canyon to its end at Highway 24. This flat hike takes you through a wide wash between canyon walls, and is an excellent place to study the geology up close. The round-trip hike is 4.4 miles; allow two to three hours for your walk. Check at the ranger station for flash-flood warnings before entering the wash. *Easy.* ⊠ *Capitol Reef National Park ✣ Trailhead: at Hwy. 24, east of Hickman Bridge parking lot, or at end of Grand Wash Rd., off Scenic Dr. about 5 miles from visitor center.*

Cathedral Valley

This primitive, rugged area was named for its sandstone geological features that are reminiscent of Gothic cathedrals. Visiting is quite the backroad adventure, so not many people make the effort to drive on roads that some have called brutal. But if you have the right vehicle and an adventurous spirit, the rewards of seeing ancient natural wonders should be worth it. The selenite crystals of Glass Mountain attract rockhounds for a closer look, but no collecting is allowed. Sunset and sunrise at the Temple of the Sun and Temple of the Moon monoliths are especially colorful and photogenic.

Sights

SCENIC DRIVES

Cathedral Valley/North District Loop

TRAIL | The north end of Capitol Reef, along this backcountry road, is filled with towering monoliths, panoramic vistas, water crossings, and a stark desert landscape. The area is remote and the road through it unpaved, so do not enter without a suitable mountain bike or high-clearance vehicle, some planning, and a cell phone (although reception is virtually nonexistent). The trail through the valley is a 58-mile loop that you can begin at River Ford Road, 11¾ miles east of the visitor center off Highway 24; allow half a day. If your time is limited, you can tour only the Caineville Wash Road, which takes about two hours by ATV or four-wheel drive vehicle. If you are planning a multiday trip, there's a primitive campground about halfway through the loop. Pick up a self-guided tour brochure at the visitor center. ⊠ *River Ford Rd., off Hwy. 24.*

Muley Twist Canyon

This long canyon runs 12 miles north to south at the south end of park. It was used as a pass by pioneers traveling by wagon through the Waterpocket Fold and got its name because it was so narrow that it could "twist a mule." Park visitors typically explore Lower Muley Twist Canyon on long day hikes or overnight (a permit is required for overnight camping). Upper Muley Twist Canyon has some shorter trails, including a one-mile hike to an overlook. Trails are not maintained, so bring a map, along with plenty of water as the area is quite hot in summer. High-clearance vehicles are necessary for most of the roads.

7

Capitol Reef National Park   MULEY TWIST CANYON

Activities

BIKING

Bicycles are allowed only on established roads in the park. Highway 24 is a state highway and receives a substantial amount of through traffic, so it's not the best place to pedal. Scenic Drive is better, but the road is narrow, and you have to contend with drivers dazed by the beautiful surroundings. In fact, it's a good idea to traverse it in the morning or evening when traffic is reduced, or in the off-season. Four-wheel-drive roads are certainly less traveled, but they are often sandy, rocky, and steep. The Cathedral Valley/North District Loop is popular with mountain bikers (but also with four-wheelers). You cannot ride your bicycle in washes or on hiking trails.

South Draw Road

BICYCLING | This is a very strenuous but picturesque ride that traverses dirt, sand, and rocky surfaces, and crosses several creeks that may be muddy. It's not recommended in winter or spring because of deep snow at higher elevations. The route starts at an elevation of 8,500 feet on Boulder Mountain, 13 miles south of Torrey, and ends 15¾ miles later at 5,500 feet in the Pleasant Creek parking area at the end of Scenic Drive. ⊠ *Bowns Reservoir Rd. and Hwy. 12.*

CAMPING

Campgrounds—both the highly convenient Fruita Campground and the backcountry sites—in Capitol Reef fill up fast between March and October. Most of the area's state parks have camping facilities, and the region's two national forests offer many wonderful sites.

Cathedral Valley Campground. This small (just six sites), basic (no water, pit toilet), no-fee campground in the park's remote northern district touts sprawling views, but the bumpy road there is hard to navigate. ⊠ *Hartnet Junction, on Caineville Wash Rd.* ☎ *435/425–3791.*

Cedar Mesa Campground. Wonderful views of the Waterpocket Fold and Henry Mountains surround this primitive (pit toilet, no water), no-fee campground with five sites in the park's southern district. ⊠ *Notom-Bullfrog Rd., 22 miles south of Hwy. 24* ☎ *435/425–3791.*

Fruita Campground. Near the orchards and the Fremont River, the park's developed (flush toilets, running water), shady campground is a great place to call home for a few days. The sites require a $20 nightly fee and those nearest the Fremont River or the orchards are the most coveted. ⊠ *Scenic Dr., about 1 mile south of visitor center* ☎ *435/425–3791* ⊕ *www.recreation.gov.*

FOUR-WHEELING

You can explore Capitol Reef in a 4X4 on a number of exciting backcountry routes, but note that all vehicles must remain on designated roadways. Road conditions can vary greatly depending on recent weather patterns. The Cathedral Valley/North District Loop is popular with four-wheelers (and also with mountain bikers).

HIKING

Many park trails in Capitol Reef include steep climbs, but there are a few easy-to-moderate hikes. A short drive from the visitor center takes you to a dozen trails near the Fruita Historic District, but there are more challenging hikes in the other areas.

HORSEBACK RIDING

Many areas in the park are closed to horses and pack animals, so it's a good idea to check with the visitor center before you set out with your animals. Day use does not require a permit, but you need to get one for overnight camping with horses and pack animals.

Hondoo Rivers & Trails in Torrey (⇨ *see Southeastern Utah*) runs horseback tours into the national park. Unless you ride with a park-licensed outfitter, you have to bring your own horse, as no rentals are available.

Chapter 8

ZION NATIONAL PARK

8

Updated by
Shelley Arenas

⊙ Sights   🍴 Restaurants   🛏 Hotels   🛍 Shopping   🍸 Nightlife

★★★★★   ★★★☆☆   ★★★★★   ★★★★☆   ★★☆☆☆

WELCOME TO ZION NATIONAL PARK

TOP REASONS TO GO

★ **Eye candy:** Pick just about any trail in the park and it's all but guaranteed to culminate in an astounding viewpoint full of pink, orange, and crimson rock formations.

★ **Peace and quiet:** From February through November, cars are generally not allowed on Zion Canyon Scenic Drive, allowing this section of the park to remain relatively quiet and peaceful.

★ **Botanical wonderland:** Zion Canyon is home to more than 1,000 species of plants, more than anywhere else in Utah.

★ **Animal tracks:** Zion has expansive hinterlands where furry, scaly, and feathered residents are common. Hike long enough and you'll encounter deer, elk, rare lizards, birds of prey, and other zoological treats.

★ **Unforgettable canyoneering:** Zion's array of rugged slot canyons is the richest place on Earth for scrambling, rappelling, climbing, and descending.

The heart of Zion National Park is Zion Canyon, which follows the North Fork of the Virgin River for 6½ miles beneath cliffs that rise 2,000 feet from the river bottom. The Kolob Canyons area is considered by some to be superior in beauty, and because it's isolated from the rest of the park, you aren't likely to run into any crowds here. Both sections hint at the extensive back-country beyond, open for those with the stamina, time, and courage to go off the beaten path.

1 Zion Canyon. This area defines Zion National Park for most people. Free shuttle buses are the only vehicles allowed February through November, the busiest months in the park. The backcountry is accessible via the West Rim Trail and the Narrows, and 2,000-foot cliffs rise all around.

2 Kolob Canyons. The northwestern corner of Zion is a secluded 30,000-acre wonderland that can be reached only via a special entrance. Don't miss the West Temple and the Kolob Arch, and keep looking up to spot Horse Ranch Mountain, the park's highest point.

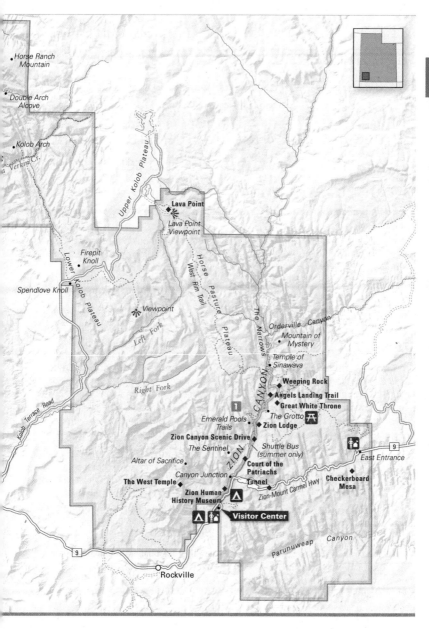

The walls of Zion Canyon soar more than 2,000 feet above the valley. Bands of limestone, sandstone, and lava in the strata point to the distant past. Greenery high in the cliff walls indicate the presence of water seepage or a spring. Erosion has left behind a collection of domes, fins, and blocky massifs bearing the names of cathedrals and temples, prophets and angels.

Trails lead deep into side canyons and up narrow ledges to waterfalls, serene spring-fed pools, and shaded spots of solitude. So diverse is this place that 85% of Utah's flora and fauna species are found here. Some, like the tiny Zion snail, appear nowhere else in the world.

The Colorado River helped create the Grand Canyon, while the Virgin River—the Colorado's muddy progeny—carved Zion's features. Because of the park's unique topography, distant storms and spring runoff can transform a tranquil slot canyon into a sluice, and flood damage does sometimes result in extended trail closures, as happened in summer 2018 to three trails near the Grotto and Zion Lodge sections of Zion Canyon.

Planning

When to Go

Zion is the most heavily visited national park in Utah, receiving 4.5 million visitors each year. Locals used to call the spring and fall the shoulder seasons because traffic would drop off from the highly visited summer months. Not so much anymore. These days the park is busy from March through November.

Summer in the park is hot and dry, punctuated by sudden cloudbursts that can create flash flooding and spectacular waterfalls. Expect afternoon thunderstorms between July and September. Whether the day starts out sunny or not, wear sunscreen and drink lots of water, even if you aren't exerting yourself or spending much time outside. The sun is very powerful at this elevation.

Winters are mild at lower desert elevations. You can expect to encounter winter driving conditions from November to mid-March, and although most park programs are suspended in winter, it is a wonderful and solitary time to see the canyons.

■ TIP→ The temperature in Zion often exceeds 100°F in July and August.

Zion in One Day

Begin your visit at the **Zion Canyon Visitor Center,** where outdoor exhibits inform you about the park's geology, wildlife, history, and trails. Get a taste of what's in store by viewing the far off Towers of the Virgin, then head to the **Court of the Patriarchs** viewpoint to take photos and walk the short path. Take the shuttle (or your car, if it's December or January) to **Zion Lodge,** where you can hike a trail to one of the park's most beautiful spots, the **Emerald Pools.** The Lower Pool Trail is the second most popular walk at Zion; the trail branches off into Middle Pool and Upper Pool trails for those with more time. Ride the next shuttle to the end of the road, where the paved,

accessible **Riverside Walk,** Zion's most popular path, will deliver you to the gateway of the canyon's **Narrows.**

Reboard the shuttle to return to the Zion Canyon Visitor Center to pick up your car (or continue driving December–January). Head out onto the beautiful **Zion–Mount Carmel Highway,** with its long, curving tunnel, keeping your camera at the ready for stops at viewpoints along the road. Once you reach the park's east entrance, turn around, and on your return trip stop to take the short hike up to **Canyon Overlook.** In the evening, you might want to attend a ranger program at one of the campground amphitheaters or at Zion Lodge.

Zion National Park PLANNING

8

AVERAGE HIGH/LOW TEMPERATURES.

JAN.	FEB.	MAR.	APR.	MAY	JUNE
52/29	57/31	63/36	73/43	83/52	93/60
JULY	AUG.	SEPT.	OCT.	NOV.	DEC.
100/68	97/66	91/60	78/49	63/37	53/30

Getting Here and Around

AIR

The nearest commercial airport, with direct flights from a number of western U.S. hubs, is an hour away in St. George, Utah. It's about a three-hour drive to the nearest major airport, McCarran in Las Vegas, Nevada, and a 4½-hour drive Salt Lake City's airport.

CAR

Zion National Park lies east of Interstate 15 in southwestern Utah. From the interstate, head east on Highway 9. After 21 miles you'll reach Springdale, which abuts the main entrance.

From February through November, you can drive on Zion Canyon Scenic Drive only if you have reservations at the Zion Lodge. Otherwise, you must park your car in Springdale or at the Zion Canyon Visitor Center and take the shuttle. There are no car restrictions in December and January.

The Zion Canyon Visitor Center parking lot fills up quickly. You can avoid parking heartburn by leaving your car in Springdale and riding the shuttle to the park entrance. Shuttles are accessible for people with disabilities and have plenty of room for gear. Consult the print park guide or check online at ⊕ www.nps.gov/zion/planyourvisit/shuttle-system.htm for the town shuttle schedule.

Park Essentials

ACCESSIBILITY

Both visitor centers, all shuttle buses, and Zion Lodge are fully accessible to people in wheelchairs. Several camp-sites (sites A24 and A25 at Watchman Campground and sites 103, 114, and 115 at South Campground) are reserved for people with disabilities, and two trails—Riverside Walk and Pa'rus Trail—are accessible with some assistance.

PARK FEES AND PERMITS

Entrance to Zion National Park costs $35 per vehicle for a seven-day pass. People entering on foot or by bicycle pay $20 per person for a seven-day pass; those on motorcycle pay $30.

Permits are required for backcountry camping and overnight hikes. Depending on which parts of the trails you intend to explore, you'll need a special permit for the Narrows and Kolob Creek or the Subway slot canyon. Climbing and can-yoneering parties need a permit before using technical equipment.

Zion National Park limits the total number of overnight and canyoneering permits issued per day and has a reservation system with most of the permits now issued in an online lottery to apportion them fairly. Permits to the Subway, Mystery Canyon, the Narrows through-hikes, and West Rim are in short supply during high season. The maximum size of a group hiking into the backcountry is 12 people. Permits cost $15 for one or two people; $20 for three to seven; and $25 for eight or more. Permits are available at the visitor centers.

PARK HOURS

The park, open daily year-round, 24 hours a day, is in the Mountain time zone.

AUTOMOBILE SERVICE STATIONS

Just outside the park and in nearby Kanab and Springdale, you can fuel up, get your tires and oil changed, and have auto repairs done.

CELL PHONE RECEPTION

Cell phone reception is good in Spring-dale but spotty in the park. Public telephones can be found at Zion Canyon Visitor Center, Zion Lodge, and Zion Human History Museum.

EMERGENCIES

In the event of an emergency, dial 911, report to a visitor center, or contact a park ranger at ☎ *435/772–3322*. The near-est hospitals are in St. George, Cedar City, and Kanab.

Hotels

The Zion Lodge is rustic, designed in 1920s period style, and comfortable. Most lodging is located outside the park. Springdale has dozens of lodging options, from quaint bed-and-breakfasts to mod-est motels to chain hotels with riverside rooms, and farther west you'll find more options (and usually better values) in Hurricane and St. George. To the east and north, you'll find a smaller number of hotels and motels, from Kanab up to Panguitch, both of which are good bases if you're continuing on to Bryce or, in the case of Kanab, the Grand Canyon *(see chapter 10, Southwestern Utah, for these listings). Hotel reviews have been shortened. For full information, visit Fodors.com.*

What It Costs			
$	$$	$$$	$$$$
RESTAURANTS			
under $16	$16–$22	$23–$30	over $30
HOTELS			
under $125	$125–$175	$176–$225	over $225

Restaurants

Only one full-service restaurant operates within the park, at the famed Zion Lodge, but in Springdale, just outside the park's South Entrance, you'll find a growing number of both casual and sophisticated eateries *(see chapter 10, Southwestern Utah)*. To the east, options are limited, but there are a handful of options within an hour's drive. *Restaurant reviews have been shortened. For full information, visit Fodors.com.*

Visitor Information

PARK CONTACT INFORMATION Zion National Park. ✉ *Hwy. 9, Springdale* ☎ *435/772–3256* ⊕ *www.nps.gov/zion.*

VISITOR CENTERS

Kolob Canyons Visitor Center

INFO CENTER | Make this your first stop as you enter this remote section of the park. There are books and maps, a small gift shop, and clean restrooms here, and rangers are on hand to answer questions about Kolob Canyons exploration. ✉ *3752 E. Kolob Canyons Rd., Exit 40 off I–15* ☎ *435/772–3256* ⊕ *www.nps.gov/zion.*

Zion Canyon Visitor Center

INFO CENTER | Learn about the area's geology, flora, and fauna at an outdoor exhibit next to a gurgling stream. Inside, a large shop sells everything from field guides to souvenirs. Zion Canyon shuttle buses leave regularly from the center and make several stops along the canyon's beautiful Scenic Drive; ranger-guided shuttle tours depart once a day from Memorial Day to late September. ✉ *Zion Park Blvd. at south entrance, Springdale* ☎ *435/772–3256* ⊕ *www.nps.gov/zion.*

Zion Canyon

Sights

GEOLOGICAL LANDMARKS

★ **The Narrows**

NATURE SITE | This sinuous 16-mile crack in the earth where the Virgin River flows over gravel and boulders is one of the world's most stunning gorges. If you hike through it, you'll find yourself surrounded—sometimes nearly boxed in—by smooth walls stretching high into the heavens. Plan to get wet, and beware that flash floods can occur here, especially in spring and summer. Check on the weather before you enter. ✉ *Zion National Park* ✛ *Begins at Riverside Walk.*

MUSEUMS

Zion Human History Museum

MUSEUM | This informative museum tells the park's story from the perspective of its human inhabitants, among them Ancestral Puebloans and early Mormon settlers. Permanent exhibits illustrate how humans have dealt with wildlife, plants, and natural forces. Temporary exhibits have touched on everything from vintage park employee photography to the history of Union Pacific Railroad hotels. Don't miss the incredible view of Towers of the Virgin from the back patio. ✉ *Zion Canyon Scenic Dr., ½ mile north of south entrance* ☎ *435/772–3256* ⊠ *Free.*

PICNIC AREAS

The Grotto

RESTAURANT—SIGHT | **FAMILY** | Get your food to go at the Zion Lodge, take a short walk to this scenic retreat, and dine beneath a shady oak. Amenities include drinking water, picnic tables, and restrooms, but there are no fire grates. A trail from here leads to the Emerald Pools. ✉ *Off Zion Canyon Scenic Dr., at Grotto.*

Zion Nature Center
RESTAURANT—SIGHT | FAMILY | On your way to or from the Junior Ranger Program you can feed your kids at the center's picnic area. When the center is closed, use the restrooms in South Campground. ✉ *Zion National Park* ✛ *Near entrance to South Campground, ½ mile north of south entrance.*

SCENIC DRIVES
★ Zion Canyon Scenic Drive
SCENIC DRIVE | Vividly colored cliffs tower 2,000 feet above the road that meanders north from Springdale along the floor of Zion Canyon. As you roll through the narrow, steep canyon you'll pass the Court of the Patriarchs, the Sentinel, and the Great White Throne, among other imposing rock formations. From February through November, unless you're staying at the lodge, Zion Canyon Scenic Drive is accessed only by park shuttle. You can drive it yourself at other times. ✉ *Off Hwy. 9.*

Zion–Mount Carmel Highway and Tunnels
SCENIC DRIVE | Two narrow tunnels as old as the park itself lie between the east entrance and Zion Canyon on this breathtaking 12-mile stretch of Highway 9. One was once the longest man-made tunnel in the world. As you travel the (1.1-mile) passage through solid rock, five arched portals along one side provide fleeting glimpses of cliffs and canyons. When you emerge you'll find that the landscape has changed dramatically. Large vehicles require traffic control and a $15 permit, available at the park entrance, and have restricted hours of travel. This includes nearly all RVs, trailers, dual-wheel trucks, and campers. The Canyon Overlook Trail starts from a parking area between the tunnels. ✉ *Hwy. 9, 5 miles east of Canyon Junction* ⊕ *www.nps.gov/zion/ planyourvisit/the-zion-mount-carmel-tunnel.htm.*

SCENIC STOPS
Checkerboard Mesa
NATURE SITE | It's well worth stopping at the pull-out 1 mile west of Zion's east entrance to observe the distinctive waffle patterns on this huge white mound of sandstone. The stunning crosshatch effect visible today is the result of eons of freeze-and-thaw cycles that caused vertical fractures, combined with erosion that produced horizontal bedding planes. ✉ *Zion–Mount Carmel Hwy.*

Court of the Patriarchs
NATURE SITE | This trio of peaks bears the names of, from left to right, Abraham, Isaac, and Jacob. Mount Moroni is the reddish peak on the far right that partially blocks the view of Jacob. Hike the trail that leaves from the Court of the Patriarchs Viewpoint, 1½ miles north of Canyon Junction, to get a much better view of the sandstone prophets. ✉ *Zion Canyon Scenic Dr.*

Great White Throne
NATURE SITE | Dominating the Grotto picnic area near Zion Lodge, this massive Navajo sandstone peak juts 2,000 feet above the valley floor. The popular formation lies about 3 miles north of Canyon Junction. ✉ *Zion Canyon Scenic Dr.*

Weeping Rock
NATURE SITE | Surface water from the rim of Echo Canyon spends several thousand years seeping down through the porous sandstone before exiting at this picturesque alcove 4½ miles north of Canyon Junction. A paved walkway climbs ¼ mile to this flowing rock face where wildflowers and delicate ferns grow. In fall, the maples and cottonwoods burst with color, and lizards point the way down the path, which is too steep for wheelchairs or strollers. A major rockslide closed the Weeping Rock Trail in summer 2019; check with visitor center to see if it has reopened. ✉ *Zion Canyon Scenic Dr.*

TRAILS

★ Angels Landing Trail

TRAIL | As much a trial as a trail, this path beneath the Great White Throne, which you access from the Lower West Rim Trail, is one of the park's most challenging hikes. Early on you work your way through Walter's Wiggles, a series of 21 switchbacks built out of sandstone blocks. From there you traverse sheer cliffs that have chains bolted into the rock face to serve as handrails in some (but not all) places. In spite of its hair-raising nature, this trail is popular. Allow 2½ hours round trip if you stop at Scout's Lookout (2 miles), and four hours if you keep going to where the angels (and birds of prey) play. The trail is 5 miles round trip and is not appropriate for children or those who are uneasy about heights. *Difficult.* ⊠ *Zion National Park* ⚐ *Trailhead: off Zion Canyon Scenic Dr. at the Grotto.*

★ Canyon Overlook Trail

TRAIL | FAMILY | The parking area just east of Zion–Mount Carmel tunnel leads to this popular trail, which is about 1 mile round trip and takes about an hour to finish. From the breathtaking overlook at the trail's end you can see the West and East temples, the Towers of the Virgin, the Streaked Wall, and other Zion Canyon cliffs and peaks. The elevation change is 160 feet. There's no shuttle to this trail and the parking area often fills up—try to come very early or late in the day to avoid crowds. *Moderate.* ⊠ *Zion National Park* ⚐ *Trailhead: off Hwy. 9 just east of Zion–Mount Carmel tunnel.*

Emerald Pools Trail

TRAIL | FAMILY | Multiple waterfalls cascade (or drip, in dry weather) into algae-filled pools along this trail, about 3 miles north of Canyon Junction. The path leading to the lower pool is paved and appropriate for strollers and wheelchairs. If you've got any energy left, keep going past the lower pool. The ¼ mile from there to the middle pool becomes rocky and somewhat steep but offers increasingly scenic views. A less crowded and exceptionally enjoyable return route follows the Kayenta Trail, connecting to the Grotto Trail. Allow 50 minutes for the 1¼-mile round-trip hike to the lower pool, and an hour more each round trip to the middle (2 miles) and upper pools (3 miles). *Lower, easy. Upper, moderate.* ⊠ *Zion National Park* ⚐ *Trailhead: off Zion Canyon Scenic Dr., at Zion Lodge or the Grotto.*

Grotto Trail

TRAIL | FAMILY | This flat trail takes you from Zion Lodge, about 3 miles north of Canyon Junction, to the Grotto picnic area, traveling for the most part along the park road. Allow 20 minutes or less for the walk along the ½-mile trail. If you are up for a longer hike and have two or three hours, connect with the Kayenta Trail after you cross the footbridge, and head for the Emerald Pools. You will begin gaining elevation, and it's a steady, steep climb to the pools, which you will begin to see after about 1 mile. *Easy.* ⊠ *Zion National Park* ⚐ *Trailhead: off Zion Canyon Scenic Dr. at the Grotto.*

Hidden Canyon Trail

TRAIL | This steep, 2-mile round-trip hike takes you up 850 feet in elevation. Not too crowded, the trail is paved all the way to Hidden Canyon. Allow about three hours for the round-trip hike. A massive rockfall in summer 2019 resulted in the closure of this trail—check with the visitor center for updates. *Moderate–Difficult.* ⊠ *Zion National Park* ⚐ *Trailhead: off Zion Canyon Scenic Dr. at Weeping Rock.*

★ Narrows Trail

TRAIL | After leaving the paved ease of the Gateway to the Narrows trail behind, walk on the riverbed itself. You'll find a pebbly shingle or dry sandbar path, but when the walls of the canyon close in, you'll be forced into the chilly waters of the Virgin River. A walking stick and good shoes are a must. Be prepared to swim, as chest-deep holes may occur even when water levels are low. Check with park rangers about the likelihood of flash floods. A day trip up the lower section of the Narrows is 6 miles one-way to the turnaround point. Allow at least five hours round trip. *Difficult.* ⊠ *Zion National Park* ✛ *Trailhead: off Zion Canyon Scenic Dr., at end of Riverside Walk.*

Pa'rus Trail

TRAIL | FAMILY | An approximately 1¾-mile, relatively flat paved walking and biking path, Pa'rus parallels and occasionally crosses the Virgin River. Starting at South Campground, ½ mile north of the South Entrance, the walk proceeds north along the river to the beginning of Zion Canyon Scenic Drive. Along the way you'll take in great views of the Watchman, the Sentinel, the East and West temples, and Towers of the Virgin. Leashed dogs are allowed on this trail. Wheelchair users may need assistance. *Easy.* ⊠ *Zion National Park* ✛ *Trailhead: at Canyon Junction.*

Riverside Walk

TRAIL | FAMILY | This 2.2-mile round-trip hike shadows the Virgin River. In spring, wildflowers bloom on the opposite canyon wall in lovely hanging gardens. The trail, which begins 6½ miles north of Canyon Junction at the end of Zion Canyon Scenic Drive, is the park's most visited trail, so be prepared for crowds in high season. Riverside Walk is paved and suitable for strollers and wheelchairs, though some wheelchair users may need assistance. Round trip it takes about 90 minutes. At the end, the much more challenging Narrows Trail begins. *Easy.* ⊠ *Zion National Park* ✛ *Trailhead: off Zion Canyon Scenic Dr. at Temple of Sinawava.*

Watchman Trail

TRAIL | For a dramatic view of Springdale and a look at lower Zion Creek Canyon and the Towers of the Virgin, this strenuous hike begins on a service road east of Watchman Campground. Some springs seep out of the sandstone, nourishing the hanging gardens and attracting wildlife. There are a few sheer cliff edges, so supervise children carefully. Plan on two hours for this 3.3-mile round-trip hike that has a 368-foot elevation change. *Moderate.* ⊠ *Zion National Park* ✛ *Trailhead: at Zion Canyon Visitor Center.*

🍴 Restaurants

Castle Dome Café & Snack Bar

$ | CAFÉ | Next to the shuttle stop at Zion Lodge, this small fast-food restaurant is both convenient and enjoys a lovely shaded outdoor patio. You can grab a banana, burger, smoothie, or salad to go, order local brews from the Beer Garden cart, or enjoy a dish of ice cream while soaking up the views of the surrounding geological formations. **Known for:** quick bites; gorgeous views; nice beer selection. $ *Average main: $6* ⊠ *Zion Lodge, Zion Canyon Scenic Dr.* ☎ *435/772–7700* ⊕ *www.zionlodge.com/dining* ☉ *Closed Dec.–Feb.*

Red Rock Grill

$$ | AMERICAN | The fare at this restaurant at Zion Lodge includes steaks, seafood, and Western specialties such as pecan-encrusted trout and jalapeño-topped bison cheeseburgers headlining the dinner menu. Photos of the surrounding landscape adorn the walls of the spacious dining room, which has enormous windows taking in the scenery, and the large patio has gorgeous views of the real thing. **Known for:** dinner reservations necessary in summer; astounding views inside and out; only full-service restaurant in the park. $ *Average main: $19* ⊠ *Zion Lodge, Zion Canyon Scenic Dr.* ☎ *435/772–7760* ⊕ *www.zionlodge.com/dining.*

Hotels

★ Zion Lodge

$$$$ | HOTEL | For a dramatic location inside the park, you'd be hard-pressed to improve on a stay at the historic Zion Lodge: the canyon's jaw-dropping beauty

Take a shuttle or scenic horseback ride within the walls of Zion Canyon.

surrounds you, access to trailheads is easy, and guests can drive their cars on the lower half of Zion Park Scenic Drive year-round. **Pros:** handsome hotel in the tradition of historic park properties; incredible views; bike rentals on-site. **Cons:** pathways are dimly lit (bring a flashlight); spotty Wi-Fi, poor cell service; books up months ahead. $ *Rooms from: $229* ✉ *Zion Canyon Scenic Dr.* ☎ *888/297–2757 reservations only, 435/772–7700* ⊕ *www.zionlodge.com* ⇨ *122 rooms* ⊙ *No meals.*

Kolob Canyons

Sights

SCENIC DRIVES
Kolob Canyons Road
SCENIC DRIVE | The beauty starts modestly at the junction with Interstate 15, but as you move along this 5-mile road the red walls of the Kolob finger canyons rise suddenly and spectacularly out of the earth. With the crowds left behind at Zion Canyon, this drive offers the chance to take in incredible vistas at your leisure. Trails include the short but rugged Middle Fork of Taylor Creek Trail, which passes two 1930s homestead cabins, culminating 2¾ miles later in the Double Arch Alcove. During heavy snowfall Kolob Canyons Road may be closed. ✉ *I–15, Exit 40.*

Kolob Terrace Road
SCENIC DRIVE | This 21-mile road begins 14 miles west of Springdale at Virgin and winds north to Kolob Reservoir. The drive meanders in and out of the park boundaries, crossing several important trailheads, all the while overlooking the cliffs of North Creek. A popular day-use trail (permit required) leads past fossilized dinosaur tracks to the Subway, a stretch of the stream where the walls of the slot canyon close in so tightly as to form a near tunnel. Farther along the road you reach the Wildcat Canyon trailhead, which connects to the path overlooking the North Guardian Angel. The road terminates at the reservoir, beneath

8,933-foot Kolob Peak. Although paved, this narrow, twisting road is not recommended for RVs. Because of limited winter plowing, the road is closed from November or December through April or May. ⊠ *Zion National Park ⊹ Begins in Virgin at Hwy. 9.*

SCENIC STOPS
Lava Point
VIEWPOINT | Infrequently visited, this area has a primitive campground and two nearby reservoirs that offer the only significant fishing opportunities. Lava Point Overlook, one of the highest viewpoints in the park, provides a panoramic view of Zion Canyon from the north. The higher elevation here makes it much cooler than the Zion Canyon area. Park visitors looking for a respite from crowds and heat find the campground a nice change of pace, though the six sites fill up quickly and are only open May through September. ⊠ *Zion National Park ⊹ Kolob Terrace Rd to Lava Point Rd then turn right.*

Kolob Canyons Viewpoint
RESTAURANT—SIGHT | Enjoy a shaded meal with a view at this picnic site 100 yards down the Timber Creek Trail, 5 miles from Kolob Canyons Visitor Center. ⊠ *Zion National Park ⊹ On Timber Creek Trail at end of Kolob Canyons Rd.*

TRAILS
Taylor Creek Trail
TRAIL | This trail in the Kolob Canyons area descends parallel to Taylor Creek, sometimes crossing it, sometimes shortcutting benches beside it. The historic Larsen Cabin precedes the entrance to the canyon of the Middle Fork, where the trail becomes rougher. After the old Fife Cabin, the canyon bends to the right into Double Arch Alcove, a large, colorful grotto with a high blind arch (or arch "embryo") towering above. To Double Arch it's 2½ miles one way—about four hours round trip. The elevation change is 450 feet. *Moderate.* ⊠ *Zion National Park ⊹ Trailhead: at Kolob Canyons Rd., about 1½ miles east of Kolob Canyons Visitor Center.*

Activities

BIKING
Zion Cycles
BICYCLING | This shop just outside the park rents bikes by the hour or longer, sells parts, and has a full-time mechanic on duty. You can pick up trail tips and other advice from the staff here. They also offer guided road-biking treks in the park and mountain-biking excursions elsewhere in Southern Utah. ⊠ *868 Zion Park Blvd., Springdale* ☎ *435/772–0400* ⊕ *www.zioncycles.com* ⊠ *Guided tours from $175; bike rentals from $40/day.*

CAMPING
South Campground. All the sites here are under big cottonwood trees that provide some relief from the summer sun. The campground operates on a reservation system. ⊠ *Hwy. 9, ½ mile north of south entrance* ☎ *435/772–3256, 877/444–6777* ⊕ *www.recreation.gov.*

Watchman Campground. This large campground on the Virgin River operates on a reservation system between March and November, but you do not get to choose your site. ⊠ *Access road off Zion Canyon Visitor Center parking lot* ☎ *435/772–3256, 877/444–6777* ⊕ *www.recreation.gov.*

HORSEBACK RIDING
Canyon Trail Rides
HORSEBACK RIDING | **FAMILY** | Grab your hat and boots and see Zion Canyon the way the pioneers did—on a horse or mule. Easygoing, one-hour and half-day guided rides are available (minimum age 7 and 10 years, respectively). Maximum weight is 220 pounds. These friendly folks have been around for years, and are the only outfitter for trail rides inside the park. Reservations are recommended and can be made online. ⊠ *Across from Zion Lodge* ☎ *435/679–8665* ⊕ *www.canyonrides.com* ⊠ *From $45.*

BRYCE CANYON NATIONAL PARK

Updated by
Shelley Arenas

⊙ Sights	🍴 Restaurants	🛏 Hotels	💼 Shopping	🍸 Nightlife
★★★★★	★★★☆☆	★★★★★	★★★★☆	★★☆☆☆

WELCOME TO
BRYCE CANYON NATIONAL PARK

TOP REASONS TO GO

★ **Hoodoo heaven:** The boldly colored, gravity-defying limestone tentacles reaching skyward—called hoodoos—are Bryce Canyon's most recognizable attraction.

★ **Famous fresh air:** With some of the clearest skies in the nation, the park offers views that, on a clear day, can extend more than 100 miles and into three states.

★ **Spectacular sunrises and sunsets:** The deep orange and crimson hues of the park's hoodoos are intensified by the light of the sun at either end of the day.

★ **Dramatically different zones:** From the highest point of the rim to the canyon base, the park spans 2,000 feet, so you can explore three unique climatic zones: spruce-fir forest, ponderosa-pine forest, and pinyon pine-juniper forest.

★ **Snowy fun:** Bryce gets an average of 87 inches of snowfall a year, and is a popular destination for skiers and snowshoe enthusiasts.

Bryce Canyon National Park isn't a single canyon, but rather a series of natural amphitheaters on the eastern edge of the Paunsaugunt Plateau. The park's scenic drive runs along a formation known as the Pink Cliffs and offers more than a dozen amazing overlooks. One strategy is to drive without stops to the end of the 18-mile road and turn around, stopping at the scenic overlooks—which will then all be conveniently on the right side of the road, on the return drive. From the main park road you can also access the most popular hiking trails down into the canyons. A handful of roads veer east of the scenic drive to access other points of interest. For relief from the frequent heavy traffic and scarce parking during the spring–fall high season, leave your car outside the park and ride the free (once you've paid the park entrance fee) shuttle buses.

1 Bryce Amphitheater. It's the heart of the park. From here you can access the historic Bryce Canyon Lodge as well as Sunrise, Sunset, and Inspiration points. Walk to Bryce Point at sunrise to view the mesmerizing collection of massive hoodoos known as Silent City.

2 Under the Rim. The 23-mile Under-the-Rim Trail is the best way to reach Bryce Canyon backcountry. It can be a challenging three-day adventure or half day of fun via one of the four access points from the main road. Several primitive campgrounds line the route.

3 Rainbow and Yovimpa Points. The end of the scenic road, but not of the scenery, here you can hike a trail to see some ancient bristlecone pines and look south into Grand Staircase-Escalante National Monument.

4 Bryce Canyon City. Just a few miles from the visitor center and right on the shuttle route, this "company town" was incorporated in 2007 by the owners of the Ruby's Inn nearly a century after it first began welcoming guests. Though there are less than 200 year-round residents, thousands of tourists stay here each year to explore the adjacent park and partake in events like the town's winter festival.

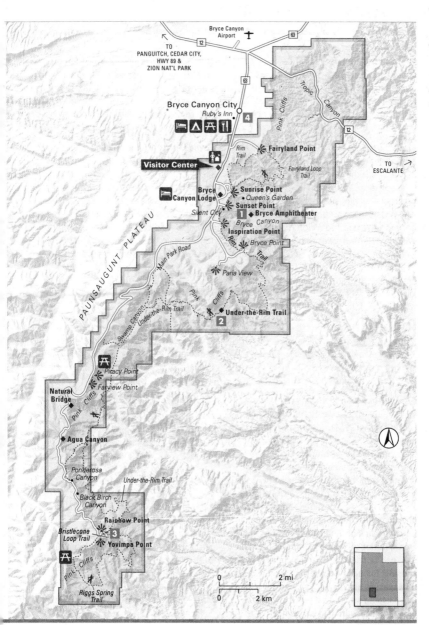

Bryce Canyon Airport

12

63

TO PANGUITCH, CEDAR CITY, HWY 89 & ZION NAT'L PARK

63

Pink Cliffs

Tropic Canyon

Bryce Canyon City
Ruby's Inn

4

12

TO ESCALANTE

Rim Trail

Fairland Point

Fairland Loop Trail

Visitor Center

Sunrise Point

Bryce Canyon Lodge

Queen's Garden

Sunset Point

Silent City

Bryce Amphitheater

1

Bryce Canyon

PAUNSAUGUNT PLATEAU

Inspiration Point

Bryce Point

Rim Trail

Main Park Road

Paria View

Pink Cliffs

Under-the-Rim Trail

Under-the-Rim Trail

2

Swamp Canyon

Piracy Point

Fairview Point

Natural Bridge

Pink Cliffs

Agua Canyon

Ponderosa Canyon

Under-the-Rim Trail

Black Birch Canyon

Rainbow Point

Bristlecone Loop Trail

3

Yovimpa Point

Pink Cliffs

Riggs Spring Trail

0   2 mi

0   2 km

A land that captures the imagination and the heart, Bryce is a favorite among the Southwest's national parks.

Although its splendor has been well-known for decades, Bryce Canyon wasn't designated a national park until 1928. Bryce Canyon is known for its fanciful hoodoos, best viewed at sunrise or sunset, when the light plays off the red rock.

In geological terms, Bryce is actually an amphitheater, not a canyon. The hoodoos in the amphitheater took on their unusual shapes because the top layer of rock—cap rock—is harder than the layers below it. If erosion undercuts the soft rock beneath the cap too much, the hoodoo will tumble. Bryce continues to evolve today, but the hoodoos are a permanent feature; old ones may die, but new ones are constantly forming as the amphitheater rim recedes.

Planning

When to Go

Around Bryce Canyon National Park and the nearby Cedar Breaks National Monument area, elevations approach and surpass 9,000 feet, making for temperamental weather, intermittent and seasonal road closures due to snow, and downright cold nights well into June. The air is cooler on the rim of the canyon than it is at lower altitudes. ■ TIP→ **If you choose to see Bryce Canyon April through October, you'll be visiting with the rest of the world. During this period, traffic on the main road can be heavy and parking limited, so consider taking one of the park shuttle buses. RV access is also limited to a handful of lots and camping areas, most of them near the park entrance, during these months.**

If it's solitude you're looking for, come to Bryce any time between November and February. The park is open all year long, so if you come during the cooler months you might just have a trail all to yourself.

FESTIVALS AND EVENTS

Bryce Canyon Winter Festival. This event at the Best Western Ruby's Inn features cross-country ski races, snow-sculpting contests, ski archery, ice-skating, and kids' snow boot races. Clinics to hone skills such as snowshoeing and photography also take place, and there's plenty of entertainment, too. ☎ *435/834–5341, 866/866–6616* ⊕ *www.rubysinn.com.*

Quilt Walk Festival. During the bitter winter of 1864, Panguitch residents set out over the mountains to fetch provisions from the town of Parowan, 40 miles away. Legend says the men, frustrated and ready to turn back, laid a quilt on the snow and knelt to pray. Soon they realized the quilt had kept them from sinking into the snow. Spreading quilts before them as they walked, leapfrog style, the men traveled to Parowan and back. This four-day event in June commemorates the event with quilting classes, a tour of pioneer homes, tractor pull, dinner-theater, and other events. ☎ *435/690–9228* ⊕ *www.quiltwalk.org.*

Getting Here and Around

AIR

The nearest commercial airport to Bryce Canyon, Cedar City Regional Airport is 80 miles west and has daily direct flights from Salt Lake City. The airports in Salt Lake City and Las Vegas

AVERAGE HIGH/LOW TEMPERATURES					
JAN.	FEB.	MAR.	APR.	MAY	JUNE
37/15	38/17	45/23	54/29	64/37	75/45
JULY	AUG.	SEPT.	OCT.	NOV.	DEC.
80/53	77/50	70/42	58/32	45/23	36/15

are the closest major ones to the park—each is about a four-hour drive.

BUS

A shuttle bus system operates in Bryce Canyon from mid-April through mid-October. Buses start at 8 am and run every 10 to 15 minutes until 8 pm in summer and 6 pm in early spring and October; they're free once you pay park admission. The route begins at the Shuttle Station north of the park, where parking is available (visitors can also park at Ruby's Inn or Ruby's Campground outside the park entrance and catch the shuttle there). It stops at the visitor center, lodge, campgrounds, and all the main overlooks and trailheads.

CAR

The closest major cities to Bryce Canyon are Salt Lake City and Las Vegas, each about 270 miles away. You reach the park via Highway 63, just off of Highway 12, which connects U.S. 89 just south of Panguitch with Torrey, near Capitol Reef National Park. You can see the park's highlights by driving along the well-maintained road running the length of the main scenic area. Bryce has no restrictions on automobiles on the main road, but from spring through fall you may encounter heavy traffic and full parking lots—it's advisable to take the shuttle bus at this time.

Park Essentials

ACCESSIBILITY

Most park facilities were constructed between 1930 and 1960. Some have been upgraded for wheelchair accessibility, while others can be used with some

assistance. The Sunset campground offers two sites with wheelchair access. Few of the trails, however, can be managed in a standard wheelchair due to the sandy, rocky, or uneven terrain. The section of the Rim Trail between Sunrise and Inspiration points is wheelchair accessible. The 1-mile Bristlecone Loop Trail at Rainbow Point has a hard surface and could be used with assistance, but several grades do not meet accessibility standards. Accessible parking is marked at all overlooks and public facilities.

PARK FEES

The entrance fee is $35 per vehicle for a seven-day pass and $20 for pedestrians or bicyclists, and includes unlimited use of the park shuttle. An annual Bryce Canyon park pass, good for one year from the date of purchase, costs $40. If you leave your private vehicle outside the park at the shuttle staging area or Ruby's Inn or Campground, the one-time entrance fee is $35 per party and includes transportation on the shuttle.

A $5 backcountry permit, available from the visitor center, is required for camping in the park's interior, allowed only on Under-the-Rim Trail and Rigg's Spring Loop, both south of Bryce Point. Campfires are not permitted.

PARK HOURS

The park is open 24/7, year-round. It's in the Mountain time zone.

CELL PHONE RECEPTION

Cell phone reception is hit-or-miss in the park, with some of the higher points along the main road your best bet. The lodge and visitor center have limited (it can be slow during busy periods) Wi-Fi,

Bryce Canyon in One Day

Begin your day at the **visitor center** to get an overview of the park and to purchase books and maps. Watch the 20-minute film and peruse the excellent exhibits about the natural and cultural history of Bryce Canyon. Then, proceed to the historic **Bryce Canyon Lodge**. From here, stroll along the relaxing **Rim Trail**. If you have the time and stamina to walk into the amphitheater, the portion of the Rim Trail near the lodge gets you to the starting point for either of the park's two essential hikes, the **Navajo Loop Trail** from **Sunset Point** or the **Queen's Garden Trail** that connects Sunset to **Sunrise Point.**

Afterward (or if you skip the hike), drive the 18-mile **main park road**, stopping at the overlooks along the way. Allowing for traffic, and if you stop at all 13 overlooks, this drive will take you between two and three hours.

If you have the time for more walking, a short, rolling hike along the **Bristle-cone Loop Trail** at **Rainbow Point** rewards you with spectacular views and a cool walk through a forest of bristlecone pines.

End your day watching the sunset at **Inspiration Point** or dinner at Bryce Canyon Lodge.

and there are pay phones at a few key spots in the park, but these are gradually being removed.

Hotels

Lodgings in and around Bryce Canyon include both rustic and modern options, but all fill up fast in summer. Bryce Canyon Lodge is the only hotel inside the park, but there are a number of options in Bryce Canyon City, just north of the park's entrance. Nearby Panguitch and Tropic, and Escalante a bit farther away, are small towns with a number of additional budget and mid-range hotels, and these places tend to have more last-minute availability. *Hotel reviews have been shortened. For full information, visit Fodors.com.*

What It Costs

$	$$	$$$	$$$$
RESTAURANTS			
under $16	$16–$22	$23–$30	over $30
HOTELS			
under $125	$125–$175	$176–$225	over $225

Restaurants

Dining options in the park proper are limited to a few options in or near Bryce Canyon Lodge; you'll also find a handful of restaurants serving mostly standard American fare within a few miles of the park entrance, in Bryce Canyon City. Venture farther afield—to Tropic and Escalante to the east, and Panguitch and Hatch to the west—and the diversity of culinary offerings increases a bit.

Visitor Information

PARK CONTACT INFORMATION Bryce Canyon National Park. ☎ *435/834–5322* ⊕ *www.nps.gov/brca.*

Bryce Ampitheater

Here at the central part of the park, you'll find the visitor center, lodge, campgrounds, and many of the most popular trails and viewpoints. A convenient free shuttle runs a loop through this area, stopping at eight main spots where you can get out and explore. It also runs through the nearby town of Bryce Canyon City, so you don't need to bring your vehicle if you're staying at one of the hotels just outside the park.

Sights

HISTORICAL SIGHTS
Bryce Canyon Lodge
BUILDING | The lodge's architect, Gilbert Stanley Underwood, was a national park specialist, having designed lodges at Zion and Grand Canyon before turning his T-square to Bryce in 1924. The results are worth a visit as this National Historic Landmark has been faithfully restored, right down to the lobby's huge limestone fireplace, and log and wrought-iron chandelier. Inside the historic building, the only remaining hotel built by the Grand Circle Utah Park Company, are a restaurant and gift shop, as well as information on park activities. The lodge operation includes several historic log cabins and two motels nearby on the wooded grounds, just a short walk from the rim trail. Everything but the Sunset Motel (which is open early March–late December) shuts down from early November through late March. ⊠ *Off Hwy. 63* ☎ *435/834–8700* ⊕ *www.bryce-canyonforever.com.*

SCENIC DRIVES
★ Main Park Road
SCENIC DRIVE | Following miles of canyon rim, this thoroughfare gives access to more than a dozen scenic overlooks between the park entrance and Rainbow Point. Major overlooks are rarely more than a few minutes' walk from the parking areas, and many let you see more than 100 miles on clear days. Remember that all overlooks lie east of the road. To keep things simple, proceed to the southern end of the park and stop at the overlooks on your northbound return; they will all be on the right side of the road. Allow two to three hours to travel the entire 36-mile round trip. The road is open year-round, but may close temporarily after heavy snowfalls. Keep your eyes open for wildlife as you drive. Trailers are not allowed at Bryce Point and Paria View, but you can park them at the parking lot across the road from the visitor center. RVs can drive throughout the park (with limited parking options spring through fall), and vehicles longer than 25 feet are not allowed at Paria View. ⊠ *Bryce Canyon National Park.*

SCENIC STOPS
Agua Canyon
VIEWPOINT | This overlook in the southern section of the park, 12 miles south of the park entrance, has a nice view of several standout hoodoos. Look for the top-heavy formation called the Hunter, which actually has a few small hardy trees growing on its cap. As the rock erodes, the park evolves; snap a picture because the Hunter may look different the next time you visit. ⊠ *Bryce Canyon National Park* ⊕ *www.nps.gov/brca/planyourvisit/aguacanyon.htm.*

Bryce Point
VIEWPOINT | After absorbing views of the Black Mountains and Navajo Mountain, you can follow the Under-the-Rim Trail and go exploring beyond Bryce Amphitheater to the cluster of top-heavy hoodoos known collectively as the Hat Shop.

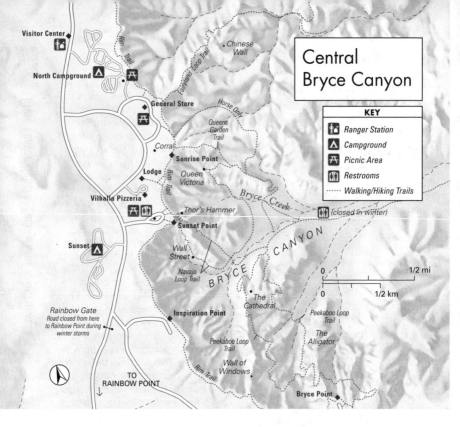

Or, take a left off the Under-the-Rim Trail and hike the challenging Peekaboo Loop Trail with its geological highlight, the **Wall of Windows.** Openings carved into a wall of rock illustrate the drama of erosion that formed Bryce Canyon. ⊠ *Inspiration Point Rd., 5½ miles south of park entrance.*

Fairyland Point

VIEWPOINT | Best visited as you exit the park, this scenic overlook adjacent to Boat Mesa, ½ mile north of the visitor center and a mile off the main park road, has splendid views of Fairyland Amphitheater and its delicate, fanciful forms. The Sinking Ship and other formations stand before the grand backdrop of the Aquarius Plateau and distant Navajo Mountain. Nearby is the Fairyland Loop trailhead—it's a stunning five-hour hike in summer and a favorite of snowshoers in winter. ⊠ *Off Hwy. 63.*

★ Inspiration Point

VIEWPOINT | Not far (1½ miles) east along the Rim Trail from Bryce Point is Inspiration Point, site of a wonderful vista on the main amphitheater and one of the best places in the park to see the sunset. (You will have plenty of company and hear a variety of languages as the sun goes down.) ⊠ *Inspiration Point Rd.* ⊕ *www.nps.gov/brca/planyourvisit/inspiration.htm.*

Natural Bridge

VIEWPOINT | Formed over millions of years by wind, water, and chemical erosion, this 85-foot rusty-orange arch formation—one of several rock arches in the park—is an essential photo op. Beyond the parking lot lies a rare stand of aspen trees, their leaves twinkling in the wind. Watch out for distracted drivers at this stunning viewpoint.

✉ *Main park road, 11 miles south of park entrance* ⊕ *www.nps.gov/brca/ planyourvisit/naturalbridge.htm.*

North Campground

VIEWPOINT | FAMILY | Across the road and slightly east of the Bryce Canyon Visitor Center, this popular campground has a couple of scenic picnic areas plus a general store and easy trail access. ✉ *Main park road ⊹ ½ mile south of visitor center.*

★ Sunrise Point

VIEWPOINT | Named for its stunning views at dawn, this overlook a short walk from Bryce Canyon Lodge is one of the park's most popular stops. It's also the trailhead for the Queen's Garden Trail and the Fairyland Loop Trail. You have to descend the Queen's Garden Trail to get a glimpse of the regal **Queen Victoria,** a hoodoo that appears to sport a crown and glorious full skirt. The trail is popular and marked clearly, but a bit challenging with 350 feet of elevation change. ✉ *Off Hwy. 63.*

Sunset Point

VIEWPOINT | Watch the late-day sun paint the hoodoos here. You can see **Thor's Hammer,** a delicate formation similar to a balanced rock, from the rim, but when you hike 550 feet down into the amphitheater on the Navajo Loop Trail you can walk through the famous and very popular Wall Street—a deep, shady "slot" canyon. The point is near Bryce Canyon Lodge. ✉ *Bryce Canyon National Park.*

TRAILS
Fairyland Loop Trail

TRAIL | Hike into whimsical Fairyland Canyon on this trail that gets more strenuous and less crowded as you progress along its 8 miles. It winds around hoodoos, across trickles of water, and finally to a natural window in the rock at Tower Bridge, 1½ miles from Sunrise Point and 4 miles from Fairyland Point. The pink-and-white badlands and hoodoos surround you the whole way. Don't feel like you have to go the whole distance

to make it worthwhile. But if you do, allow at least five hours round-trip with 1,700 feet of elevation change. *Difficult.* ✉ *Bryce Canyon National Park ⊹ Trailheads: at Fairyland Point and Sunrise Point.*

VISITOR CENTERS
★ Bryce Canyon Visitor Center

INFO CENTER | FAMILY | Even if you're anxious to hit the hoodoos, the visitor center—just to your right after the park entrance station—is the best place to start if you want to know what you're looking at and how it got there. Rangers staff a counter where you can ask questions or let them map out an itinerary of "must-sees" based on your time and physical abilities. There are also multimedia exhibits, Wi-Fi, books, maps, backcountry camping permits for sale, and the Bryce Canyon Natural History Association gift shop, whose proceeds help to support park programs and conversation. ✉ *Hwy. 63* ☏ *435/834–5322* ⊕ *www.nps.gov/brca.*

Restaurants

★ Bryce Canyon Lodge Restaurant

$$$ | AMERICAN | With a high-beam ceiling, tall windows, and a massive stone fireplace, the dining room at this historic lodge set among towering pines abounds with rustic western charm. The kitchen serves three meals a day (reservations aren't accepted, so be prepared for a wait), and the dishes—highlights of which include buffalo sirloin steak, burgundy-braised bison stew, and almond-and-panko-crusted trout—feature organic or sustainable ingredients whenever possible. **Known for:** good selection of local craft beers; delicious desserts, including fudge brownie sundae and six-layer carrot cake; hearty breakfasts. Ⓢ *Average main: $28* ✉ *Off Hwy. 63* ☏ *435/834–8700* ⊕ *www.brycecanyonforever.com/dining* ⊘ *Closed early Nov.–late Mar.*

Word of Mouth

"It was early morning when I took this photo looking out across Bryce Canyon. With a chill still in the air we hiked to the edge of the canyon, and were rewarded with this breathtaking view."
—photo by Pete Foley, Fodors.com member

Valhalla Pizzeria & Coffee Shop

$ | PIZZA | FAMILY | A quick and casual 40-seat eatery across the parking lot from Bryce Canyon Lodge, this pizzeria and coffee shop is a good bet for an inexpensive meal, especially when the lodge dining room is too crowded. Coffee shop choices include an espresso bar, house-made pastries, and fresh fruit, or kick back on the tranquil patio in the evening and enjoy fresh pizza or salad. **Known for:** convenient and casual; decent beer and wine selection; filling pizzas. $ *Average main: $13* ✉ *Off Hwy. 63* ☎ *435/834– 8709* ⊕ *www.brycecanyonforever.com/ pizza* ⊗ *Closed mid-Sept.–mid-May.*

Hotels

★ Bryce Canyon Lodge

$$$ | HOTEL | This historic, rugged stone-and-wood lodge close to the amphitheater's rim offers western-style rooms with semi-private balconies or porches in two motel buildings, suites in the historic inn, and cozy, beautifully designed lodgepole pine–and–stone cabins, some with cathedral ceilings and gas fireplaces. **Pros:** close proximity to canyon rim and trails; lodge is steeped in history and has loads of personality; cabins have fireplaces and exude rustic charm. **Cons:** closed in winter; books up fast; no TVs or air-conditioning. $ *Rooms from: $223* ✉ *Off Hwy. 63* ☎ *435/834–8700, 877/386–4383* ⊕ *www. brycecanyonforever.com* ⊗ *Closed Jan.– early Mar.* ⇌ *113 rooms* ⦿ *No meals.*

Shopping

Bryce Canyon Lodge Gift Shop

CONVENIENCE/GENERAL STORES | Here you can buy Native American and South-western crafts such as pottery and jewelry, T-shirts, jackets, dolls, and books. ✉ *Bryce Canyon Lodge, Hwy. 63, 2 miles south of park entrance* ☎ *435/834–8700* ⊗ *Closed mid-Nov.–late Mar.*

Bryce Canyon Pines General Store

CONVENIENCE/GENERAL STORES | Buy groceries, T-shirts, hats, books, post-cards, and camping items that you might have left behind, as well as snacks, drinks, juices, and quick meals at this multipurpose facility at Sunrise Point. Picnic tables under pine trees offer a shady break. ✉ *Bryce Canyon National Park* ✛ *About ½ mile off the main park road, 2 miles south of the park entrance* ☎ *435/834–5441.*

Under the Rim

Bryce Canyon's longest trail leads back-packers under the rim of the park's plateau that edges the natural amphitheater. Hiking the full 23-mile Under the Rim Trail will require an overnight stay, though there are some shorter trails to access parts of this area on day hikes. On clear nights, the stargazing can be amazing.

Sights

TRAILS
Hat Shop Trail

TRAIL | The sedimentary haberdashery sits 2 miles from the trailhead. Hard gray caps balance precariously atop narrow pedestals of softer, rust-color rock. Allow three to four hours to travel this some-what strenuous but rewarding 4-mile round-trip trail, the first part of the longer Under-the-Rim Trail. *Moderate.* ✉ *Bryce Canyon National Park* ✛ *Trailhead: at Bryce Point, 5½ miles south of park entrance.*

Navajo Loop Trail

TRAIL | FAMILY | One of Bryce's most popular and dramatic attractions is this steep descent via a series of switchbacks leading to Wall Street, a slightly claustro-phobic hallway of rock only 20 feet wide in places with walls 100 feet high. After a walk through the Silent City, the northern end of the trail brings Thor's Hammer into view. A well-marked intersection offers a shorter way back via Two Bridges Trail or continuing on the Queen's Garden Trail to Sunrise Point. For the short version allow at least an hour on this 1½-mile trail with 550 feet of elevation change. *Moderate.* ⊠ *Bryce Canyon National Park* ✛ *Trailhead: at Sunset Point, near Bryce Canyon Lodge.*

★ Navajo/Queen's Garden Combination Loop

TRAIL | FAMILY | By walking this extended 3-mile loop, you can see some of the best of Bryce; it takes a little more than two hours. The route passes fantastic formations and an open forest of pine and juniper on the amphitheater floor. Descend into the amphitheater from Sunrise Point on the Queen's Garden Trail and ascend via the Navajo Loop Trail; return to your starting point via the Rim Trail. *Moderate.* ⊠ *Bryce Canyon National Park* ✛ *Trailheads: at Sunset and Sunrise points, 2 miles south of park entrance.*

★ Peekaboo Loop

TRAIL | The reward of this steep trail is the Wall of Windows and the Three Wise Men. Horses use this trail in spring, summer, and fall and have the right-of-way. Start at Bryce, Sunrise, or Sunset Point and allow four to five hours to hike the 5-mile trail or 7-mile double-loop. *Difficult.* ⊠ *Bryce Canyon National Park* ✛ *Trailheads: at Bryce Point, 5½ miles south of park entrance; Sunrise and Sunset points, near Bryce Canyon Lodge.*

Queen's Garden Trail

TRAIL | FAMILY | This hike is the easiest way down into the amphitheater, with 350 feet of elevation change leading to a short tunnel, quirky hoodoos, and lots of like-minded hikers. It's the essential Bryce "sampler." Allow two hours total to hike the 1½-mile trail plus the ½-mile rimside path and back. *Easy.* ⊠ *Bryce Canyon National Park* ✛ *Trailhead: at Sunrise Point, 2 miles south of park entrance.*

Under-the-Rim Trail

TRAIL | Starting at Bryce Point, the trail travels 23 miles to Rainbow Point, passing through the Pink Cliffs, traversing Agua Canyon and Ponderosa Canyon, and taking you by several springs. Most of the hike is on the amphitheater floor, characterized by up-and-down terrain among stands of ponderosa pine; the elevation change totals about 1,500 feet. It's the park's longest trail, but four trailheads along the main park road allow you to connect to the Under-the-Rim Trail and cover its length as a series of day hikes. Allow at least two days to hike the route in its entirety, and although it's not a hoodoo-heavy hike there's plenty to see to make it a more leisurely three-day affair. *Difficult.* ⊠ *Bryce Canyon National Park* ✛ *Trailheads: at Bryce Point, Swamp Canyon, Ponderosa Canyon, and Rainbow Point.*

Rainbow and Yovimpa points

Heading south from park entrance, this is as far as you can drive on the 18-mile park road. The area includes a short, easy trail through the forest as well as a longer difficult trail. The viewpoints at Rainbow and Yovimpa look to the north and south, so you'll want to visit both. Many visitors like to drive to this part of the park first then drive back north.

Sights

SCENIC DRIVES AND OVERLOOKS

★ Rainbow and Yovimpa points

VIEWPOINT | Separated by less than half a mile, Rainbow and Yovimpa points offer two fine panoramas facing opposite directions. Rainbow Point's best view is to the north overlooking the southern rim of the amphitheater and giving a glimpse of Grand Staircase–Escalante National Monument; Yovimpa Point's vista spreads out to the south. On an especially clear day you can see all the way to Arizona's highest point, Humphrey's Peak 150 miles away. Yovimpa Point also has a shady and quiet

Yovimpa Point looks to the south of Bryce Canyon, offering a spectacular view.

picnic area with tables and restrooms. You can hike between them on the easy Bristlecone Loop Trail or tackle the more strenuous 9-mile Riggs Spring Loop Trail, which passes the tallest point in the park. This is the outermost auto stop on the main road, so visitors often drive here first and make it their starting point, then work their way back to the park entrance. ⊠ *End of main park road, 18 miles south of park entrance.*

TRAILS
Bristlecone Loop Trail
TRAIL | This 1-mile trail with a modest 200 feet of elevation gain lets you see the park from its highest points of more than 9,000 feet, alternating between spruce and fir forest and wide-open vistas out over Grand Staircase–Escalante National Monument and beyond. You might see yellow-bellied marmots and dusky grouse, critters not found at lower elevations in the park. Plan on 45 minutes to an hour. *Easy.* ⊠ *Bryce Canyon National Park* ✢ *Trailhead: at Rainbow Point parking lot, 18 miles south of park entrance.*

Riggs Spring Loop Trail
TRAIL | One of the park's two true backpacker's trails, this rigorous 9-mile path has an overnight option at the Yovimpa Pass, Riggs Spring, or Corral Hollow campsites. You'll journey past groves of twinkling aspen trees and the eponymous spring close to the campsite. Start at either Yovimpa or Rainbow point and be prepared for 1,500 feet of elevation change. Campers need to check in at the visitor center ahead of time for backcountry permits. *Difficult.* ⊠ *Bryce Canyon National Park* ✢ *Trailheads: at Yovimpa and Rainbow points, 18 miles south of park entrance.*

Bryce Canyon City

Right outside the park, this village has several lodging and dining options, shops, gas, tourist attractions, and other helpful amenities for park visitors. The park shuttle bus makes several stops in the town.

Sights

MUSEUMS

Bryce Wildlife Adventure

MUSEUM | FAMILY | Imagine a zoo frozen in time: this 14,000-square-foot private museum contains more than 1,600 butterflies and 1,000 taxidermy animals in tableaux mimicking actual terrain and animal behavior. The animals and birds come from all parts of the world. An African room has baboons, bush pigs, Cape buffalo, and a lion. There's also a collection of living deer that kids delight in feeding, and ATV and bike rentals for touring scenic Highway 12 and the Paunsaugunt Plateau. ✉ *1945 W. Hwy. 12, Bryce Canyon City* ☎ *435/834–5555* 🌐 *www.brycewildlifeadventure.com* 🎟 *$8* ⏲ *Closed mid-Nov.–Mar.*

SCENIC DRIVES

U.S. 89/Utah's Heritage Highway

LOCAL INTEREST | Winding north from the Arizona border all the way to Spanish Fork Canyon, an hour south of Salt Lake City, U.S. 89 is known as the Heritage Highway for its role in shaping Utah history. At its southern end, Kanab (see the Zion National Park chapter) is known as "Little Hollywood," having provided the backdrop for many famous Western movies and TV commercials. The town has since grown considerably into a major recreation hub and a base for visiting Zion, Bryce, and the North Rim of the Grand Canyon. Other towns north along this famous road may not have the same notoriety in these parts, but they do offer eye-popping scenery as well as some lodging and dining options relatively close to Bryce Canyon.

Restaurants

Bryce Canyon Pines Restaurant

$$ | AMERICAN | Inside the Bryce Canyon Pines Motel, about 6 miles northwest of Bryce Canyon National Park, this down-home, family-friendly roadhouse decorated with Old West photos and memorabilia serves reliably good stick-to-your-ribs breakfasts, hefty elk burgers, rib-eye steaks, and Utah rainbow trout. But the top draw here is homemade pie, which comes in a vast assortment of flavors, from banana-blueberry cream to boysenberry. **Known for:** delectable pies; friendly staff; plenty of kids' options. [$] *Average main: $16* ✉ *Hwy. 12, mile marker 10, Bryce Canyon City* ☎ *435/834–5441* 🌐 *www.brycecanyonrestaurant.com.*

Hotels

Best Western Bryce Canyon Grand Hotel

$$$ | HOTEL | If you appreciate creature comforts but can do without much in the way of local personality, this four-story hotel just outside the park fits the bill—rooms are relatively posh, with comfortable mattresses, pillows, and bedding, spacious bathrooms, and modern appliances, and there's an outdoor pool and pleasant patio. **Pros:** clean, spacious rooms; lots of amenities and activities; short drive or free shuttle ride from Bryce Canyon. **Cons:** no pets allowed; pricey during busy times; standard chain ambience. [$] *Rooms from: $220* ✉ *30 N. 100 E, Bryce Canyon City* ☎ *866/866–6634, 435/834–5700* 🌐 *www.brycecanyongrand.com* 🛏 *164 rooms* 🍴 *Free breakfast.*

Best Western Plus Ruby's Inn

$$$ | HOTEL | FAMILY | This bustling Southwestern-themed hotel has expanded over the years to include various wings with rooms that vary widely in terms of size and character. **Pros:** lots of services and amenities; short drive or free shuttle ride into the park; nice indoor pool. **Cons:** can get very busy, especially when the big tour buses roll in; too big for charm or a quiet getaway; uneven quality of restaurants. [$] *Rooms from: $190* ✉ *26 S. Main St., Bryce Canyon City* ☎ *435/834–5341, 866/866–6616* 🌐 *www.rubysinn.com* 🛏 *368 rooms* 🍴 *Free breakfast.*

Bryce Canyon Pines

$$ | **HOTEL** | Most rooms in this motel complex tucked into the woods 6 miles southwest of the park entrance have excellent mountain views. **Pros:** guided horseback rides; outdoor pool and hot tub; lively restaurant famed for homemade pies. **Cons:** thin walls; room quality varies widely; furnishings are a bit dated. [$] *Rooms from: $150* ✉ *Hwy. 12, mile marker 10, Bryce Canyon City* ☎ *800/892–7923* 🌐 *www.brycecanyon-motel.com* 🛏 *46 rooms* 🍴 *No meals.*

Shopping

Ruby's General Store

CONVENIENCE/GENERAL STORES | It may not be one of the area's geological wonders, but this giant mercantile center almost has to be seen to be believed. On a busy evening it is bustling with tourists plucking through souvenirs that range from sweatshirts to wind chimes. There is also Western wear, children's toys, a holiday-gift gallery, and groceries. Even the camping equipment is in ample supply. Need a folding stove, sleeping bag, or fishing gear? You will find it at Ruby's. You can also cross Main Street to where this ever-expanding complex has added a line of shops trimmed like an Old West town, complete with candy store and rock shop. ✉ *26 S. Main St.* ☎ *435/834–5484.*

Activities

Most visitors explore Bryce Canyon by car, but the hiking trails are far more rewarding. At these elevations, you'll have to stop to catch your breath more often if you're used to being closer to sea level. It gets warm in summer but rarely uncomfortably hot, so hiking farther into the depths of the park is not difficult, so long as you don't pick a hike that is beyond your abilities.

AIR TOURS

Bryce Canyon Airlines & Helicopters

TOUR—SPORTS | For a bird's-eye view of Bryce Canyon National Park, take a dramatic helicopter ride or airplane tour over the fantastic sandstone formations. Longer full-canyon tours and added excursions to sites such as the Grand Canyon, Monument Valley, and Zion are also offered. Flights last from 35 minutes to four hours. ☎ *435/834–8060* 🌐 *www.rubysinn.com/scenic-flights* 🎟 *From $110.*

CAMPING

The two campgrounds in Bryce Canyon National Park fill up fast, especially in summer, and are family-friendly. All are drive-in, except for the handful of back-country sites that only backpackers and gung-ho day hikers ever see.

North Campground. A cool, shady retreat in a forest of ponderosa pines, this is a great home base for campers visiting Bryce Canyon. You're near the general store, The Lodge, trailheads, and the visitor center. Reservations are accepted for some RV sites; for the rest it's first-come, first-served, and the campground usually fills by early afternoon in July, August, and September. Just be aware that some sites feel crowded and un-private. ✉ *Main park road, ½ mile south of visitor center* ☎ *435/834–5322.*

Sunset Campground. This serene alpine campground is within walking distance of Bryce Canyon Lodge and many trail-heads. Most of the 100 or so sites are filled on a first-come, first-served basis, but 20 tent sites can be reserved up to six months in advance. The campground fills by early afternoon in July though September, so secure your campsite before you sightsee. Reservations are required for the group site. As one of the most accessible hiking areas of the park, it can be crowded. ✉ *Main park road, 2 miles south of visitor center* ☎ *435/834–5322.*

HIKING

To get up close and personal with the park's hoodoos, set aside a half day to hike into the amphitheater. Remember, after you descend below the rim you'll have to get back up. The air gets warmer the lower you go, and the altitude will have you huffing and puffing unless you're very fit. The uneven terrain calls for lace-up shoes on even the well-trodden, high-traffic trails and sturdy hiking boots for the more challenging ones. No below-rim trails are paved. For trail maps, information, and ranger recommendations, stop at the visitor center. Bathrooms are at most trailheads but not down in the amphitheater. ⇨ *For more information on hiking trails, see the Sights sections, above.*

RANGER-LED HIKES
★ Full Moon Hike

HIKING/WALKING | Rangers lead guided hikes on the nights around each full moon (two per month). You must wear heavy-traction shoes, and reserve a spot on the day of the hike. In peak season the tickets are distributed through a lottery system. Schedules are posted at the visitor center and on the park's website. No flashlights are allowed and children must be at least 8 years old. ✉ *Bryce Canyon National Park* ⊕ *www.nps.gov/brca/planyourvisit/fullmoonhikes.htm.*

Rim Walk

HIKING/WALKING | Join a park ranger for a ½-mile, 75-minute-long stroll along the gorgeous rim of Bryce Canyon starting at the Sunset Point overlook. Reservations are not required for the walk, which is offered twice daily from Memorial Day through Labor Day weekends, then usually daily the rest of the year. Check with the visitor center or the park website for details. ✉ *Bryce Canyon National Park* ⊕ *www.nps.gov/brca/planyourvisit/ranger-programs.htm.*

HORSEBACK RIDING
Canyon Trail Rides

HORSEBACK RIDING | Descend to the floor of the Bryce Canyon amphitheater via horse or mule—most visitors have no riding experience so don't hesitate to join in. A two-hour ride ambles along the amphitheater floor through the Queen's Garden before returning to Sunrise Point. The half-day expedition follows Peekaboo Loop Trail, winds past the Fairy Castle, and passes the Wall of Windows before returning to Sunrise Point. Two rides a day of each type leave in the morning and early afternoon. There are no rides in winter. ✉ *Bryce Canyon Lodge, Off Hwy. 63* ☎ *435/679–8665, 435/834–5500 Bryce Canyon reservations* ⊕ *www.canyonrides.com* 🐎 *From $65.*

Ruby's Horseback Adventures

HORSEBACK RIDING | **FAMILY** | Ride to the rim of Bryce Canyon, venture through narrow slot canyons in Grand Staircase–Escalante National Monument, or even retrace the trails taken by outlaw Butch Cassidy more than 100 years ago. Rides last from 90 minutes to all day. Kids must be seven or older to ride, in some cases 10. Wagon rides to the rim of Bryce Canyon are available for all ages, as are sleigh rides in winter. ✉ *Bryce Canyon National Park* ☎ *866/782–0002* ⊕ *www.horserides.net* 🐎 *From $68.*

WINTER ACTIVITIES
Ruby's Winter Activities Center

SKIING/SNOWBOARDING | **FAMILY** | This facility grooms miles of private, no-cost trails that connect to the ungroomed trails inside the park. Rental snowshoes, ice skates, and cross-country ski equipment are available. ✉ *Hwy. 63, 1 mile north of park entrance, Bryce Canyon City* ☎ *435/834–5341, 866/866–6616* ⊕ *www.rubysinn.com/winter-activities.*

Chapter 10

SOUTHWESTERN UTAH

Updated by
Andrew Collins

👁 Sights	🍴 Restaurants	🛏 Hotels	🛍 Shopping	🍸 Nightlife
★★★★★	★★★☆☆	★★★★★	★★★★☆	★★☆☆☆

WELCOME TO SOUTHWESTERN UTAH

TOP REASONS TO GO

★ **Access amazing national parks:** This part of the state contains the scenic dining and lodging hubs for visits to Zion, Bryce Canyon, and Capitol Reef national parks.

★ **Travel through history:** Imagine life during the pioneer days as you explore the historic sites and museums of St. George and ghost towns outside Springdale and Kanab.

★ **Drive the Scenic Byway:** With its hair-raising twists and turns, spectacular Highway 12 begins just outside Panguitch and passes through Red Canyon and Grand Staircase–Escalante National Monument on its way to Capitol Reef National Park.

★ **Shakespeare and more:** Watch productions of the Bard's work in three handsome theaters in Cedar City during the Utah Shakespeare Festival.

★ **Bliss out:** Treat yourself at a luxuriant spa, shoot a round of golf, and partake of sophisticated resort dining with views of red rock canyons and lava-capped mountains in and around St. George.

1 Cedar City. Home to Southern Utah University, this bustling community has some of the region's top cultural draws, including the Utah Shakespeare Festival.

2 Brian Head. This alpine hamlet is most famous as the state's southernmost ski town, but in summer it's also the nearest base for exploring Cedar Breaks National Monument.

3 St. George. This desert metropolis boasts a slew of diversions, from tony golf and spa resorts to a historic downtown filled with excellent museums and lively eateries.

4 Springdale. Adjoining the southern boundary of Zion National Park, this gorgeously situated village on the Virgin River is an ideal base for exploring the park.

5 Tropic. Tiny Tropic is handy for visiting Bryce Canyon National Park.

6 Escalante. Since the designation of surrounding Grand Staircase–Escalante National Monument, this picturesque village on Highway 12 has become one of the region's top recreation hubs.

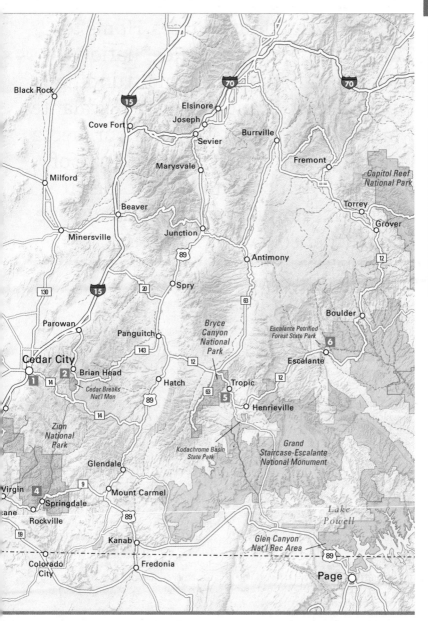

Just two hours by desert highway north of the glittering lights of Las Vegas lies one of the most beautiful and distinctive regions of the United States. Home to Zion, Bryce, and Capitol Reef national parks as well as the vast and stunning wilderness of Grand Staircase–Escalante National Monument, this outdoor mecca is anchored by the fast-growing city of St. George, which is itself surrounded by shimmering white and red sandstone and blackened lava formations.

Elsewhere in the region you'll find small recreational base communities—such as Cedar City, Kanab, Escalante, and Torrey—all of which offer plenty of charms, from hip coffeehouses and fine art galleries to breathtaking scenic drives and rugged hikes.

Southwestern Utah is a landscape of both adrenaline thrills and peaceful relaxation—head for one of the swanky spas in St. George for the ultimate rejuvenating getaway. Seasonal fare, like the renowned Utah Shakespeare Festival, and a growing number of noteworthy dining options and one-of-a-kind lodgings make this a region worth slowing down and spending time to discover. You'll find southern Utah's best alpine skiing in Brian Head and opportunities for mountain biking, horseback trail rides, jeep tours, and wildlife viewing throughout the region, and in St. George you'll also find a clutch of renowned golf courses. As you venture to some of the more remote sections of the area, visiting canyons and mesas rich with Native American history and where Butch Cassidy and the Sundance Kid once roamed, it's easy to feel as though you've traveled back in time. And at night, when the dark alpine sky pulses with stars, you can almost imagine you're on another planet.

MAJOR REGIONS

South-Central Washington County. Many of southwestern Utah's Mormon settlers arrived from the American South and brought the name "Dixie" with them, a nickname for the area which is falling out of favor. Sunny and hot St. George, the region's main population center, offers an impressive mix of hip eateries, swanky resort hotels, and both cultural and recreational attractions. Locals from the north migrate here during cold months. To the north, Cedar City and Brian's Head are smaller but don't lack for engaging diversions.

Along U.S. 89. From the Arizona border, U.S. 89, which is known as the Heritage Highway for its role in shaping Utah history, winds west through Paria Canyon and then turns north in Kanab and winds through the Sevier River Valley past Panguitch on its way into the center of the state. The small towns along this route are excellent bases for visiting nearby Zion and Bryce Canyon national parks.

Along Highway 12. Branching off from U.S. 89, this designed Scenic Byway passes near Bryce Canyon National Park before twisting and turning through 1.9 million-acre Grand Staircase–Escalante National Monument and then turning north toward Capitol Reef National Park. Here as well you'll find several towns to stay in and explore.

Planning

When to Go

Year-round, far southwestern Utah is the warmest region in the state. St. George is usually the first city in Utah to break 100°F every summer, and even the winters remain mild at these lower desert elevations. Despite the summer's heat, most people visit the area from June to September—prime season for national park touring—making the off-season winter months preferable if you wish to avoid crowds and sweltering (but arid) heat. If you do decide to brave the heat, wear sunscreen and drink lots of water, regardless of your activity level, but also pack some warmer clothes if you're venturing into the national parks, Brian Head and Dixie National Forest, or the U.S. 89 and Highway 12 corridors, as even in July and August, nights cool down significantly in these high-elevation climates.

Getting Here and Around

Most visitors to the region drive or take the bus here from Las Vegas (two hours away) or Salt Lake City (a little over four hours), but the airport in St. George is served by most major airlines and is a good option if you're spending most of your trip in this part of the state. However you get here, you absolutely need a car to get around. Most major car rental agencies have offices in downtown St. George as well as out at the airport. Enterprise and Budget also have offices in Cedar City.

AIR

Small, modern, and convenient St. George Regional Airport (SGU) has daily flights to Salt Lake City (Delta), Denver (United), and Phoenix (American). Las Vegas's McCarran International Airport (LAS) is 120 miles south of St. George, and Salt Lake International Airport is 300 miles north. Salt Lake/St. George Express buses make numerous trips per day between McCarran Airport and St. George, and a handful of trips north from St. George to Salt Lake City, with a stop in Cedar City.

AIRPORT CONTACTS McCarran International Airport. ✉ 5757 Wayne Newton Blvd., Las Vegas ☎ 702/261–5211 ⊕ www.mccarran.com. **St. George Regional Airport.** ✉ 4550 S. Airport Way, St. George ☎ 435/627–4080 ⊕ www.flysgu.com.

AIRPORT SHUTTLE Salt Lake/St. George Express. ✉ 805 S. Bluff St., St. George ☎ 208/656–8824 ⊕ www.saltlakeexpress.com.

CAR

Interstate 15, the main corridor through southwestern Utah, connects St. George and Cedar City with Las Vegas and Salt Lake City and also intersects with Interstate 70 about 75 miles north of Cedar City. It's actually quite pretty for an interstate, but the scenery becomes even more dramatic as you venture onto the region's main two-lane highways, such as Highway 9 through Springdale and Zion National Park, Highways 14 and 143 through Brian Head and Dixie National Forest, U.S. 89 through Paria Canyon, Kanab, and Panguitch, and Highway 12 through Bryce City, Tropic, Escalante, and Torrey. ■TIP→ **If you travel between I–15 and U.S. 89 via Highway 9, you must pay the $35 admission fee to Zion National Park even if you do not plan to stop and visit. If you're planning to visit Zion and at least two other parks, however, you should think about buying an Interagency Annual Pass for $80.**

In winter, Highway 143—the primary access road to Brian Head and Cedar Breaks National Monument—occasionally closes when there's heavy snowfall, and Highway 148 shuts down all winter, typically from mid-November through February. Utah Department of Transportation provides free, up-to-the-minute interactive road conditions. You can also download the app or check conditions online (⊕ udottraffic.utah.gov).

Keep in mind that services are few and far between on back roads in this part of the state, especially as you head east from the Interstate 15 corridor. Cell service can be spotty in these areas, too. It's best to download maps and top off your gas tank before you set out to explore these areas.

Restaurants

Cedar City and Springdale offer a number of distinctive options, and perhaps most surprisingly, tiny Kanab now boasting a handful of truly sophisticated destination eateries. In Escalante and Torrey, too, it's become easier to find fair-trade coffee, vegetarian options, and creative dining.

Utah has unique wine and liquor laws, but these days, most of the nicer restaurants in bigger communities serve beer, wine, or cocktails. Still, especially in smaller towns, it's a good idea to call ahead and confirm if alcohol is served and also how late dinner is available, as many establishments close by 8 or 9 in the region's more remote communities. *Restaurant reviews have been shortened. For full information, visit Fodors.com.*

Hotels

Budget, midrange, and a handful of upscale chain properties make up the lion's share of lodging options in St. George and the larger towns in the region. *Hotel reviews have been shortened. For full information, visit Fodors.com.*

What it Costs			
$	$$	$$$	$$$$
RESTAURANTS			
under $16	$16–$22	$23–$30	over $30
HOTELS			
under $125	$125–$175	$176–$225	over $225

Cedar City

250 miles southwest of Salt Lake City.

Rich iron-ore deposits captured the attention of Mormon leader Brigham Young. He ordered a Church of Jesus Christ of Latter-day Saints mission be established here in what is now southwestern Utah's second largest community, with a population of about 33,000 (up from just 13,000 in 1990). The first ironworks and foundry opened in 1851 and operated for only eight years; problems with the furnace, flooding, and hostility between settlers and regional Native Americans eventually put out the flame. Residents then turned to ranching and agriculture for their livelihood, and Cedar City has thrived ever since as an agricultural and, since the founding of Southern Utah University in 1897, educational point of the state.

The Southern Utah University campus hosts the city's most popular event, the Utah Shakespeare Festival, with a two-month season that continues to get longer as its reputation grows. This attractive, youthful city is well situated for exploring the Brian Head area and Cedar Breaks National Monument.

GETTING HERE AND AROUND
Interstate 15 cuts right through Cedar City. Though downtown is walkable, you'll want a car to explore further afield.

FESTIVALS
★ Utah Shakespeare Festival
FESTIVALS | Since 1962, Cedar City has gone Bard-crazy, staging productions of Shakespeare's plays the end of June through late October in three theaters on the Southern Utah University campus, the largest of which is open-air. The Tony award–winning festival also features literary seminars, backstage tours, cabarets featuring festival actors, and an outdoor pre-show with Elizabethan performers. Try to book well in advance, as many performances sell out. ☎ *435/586–7878, 800/752–9849* ⊕ *www.bard.org.*

ESSENTIALS
VISITOR INFORMATION Visit Cedar City and Brian Head. ✉ *581 N. Main St.* ☎ *435/586–5124* ⊕ *www.visitcedarcity. com.*

 Sights

Dixie National Forest
FOREST | The forest's expansive natural area is divided into four noncontiguous swaths covering a total of nearly 2 million acres. Adjacent to three national parks, two national monuments, and several state parks, the forest has 26 campgrounds in a variety of backdrops

lakeside, mountainside, and in the depths of pine and spruce forests. Recreational opportunities abound, including hiking, picnicking, horseback riding, and fishing. ✉ *Dixie National Forest Headquarters, 1789 N. Wedgewood La.* ☎ *435/865–3700* ⊕ *www.fs.usda.gov/dixie.*

Frontier Homestead State Park Museum
MUSEUM | This interactive living history museum devoted to the county's early iron industry is home to a number of interesting attractions, including a bullet-scarred stagecoach that ran in the days of Butch Cassidy, and the oldest standing home in all of southern Utah, built in 1851. Local artisans demonstrate pioneer crafts, and numerous mining artifacts and tools are on display. ✉ *585 N. Main St.* ☎ *435/586–9290* ⊕ *www. frontierhomestead.org* 🎟 *$4* 🕑 *Closed Sun. in Sept.–May.*

IG Winery
WINERY/DISTILLERY | In a state with few wineries, this popular operation in downtown Cedar City sources grapes from respected vineyards in California's Napa and Sonoma valleys, Washington's Columbia Valley, and Oregon's Rogue Valley. The Bordeaux-style reds are well-crafted, though spendy, while more moderately priced Tempranillo and Sangiovese also have plenty of fans. With exposed brick walls and hardwood floors, the handsome tasting room is hung with local art and warmed by a fireplace in winter. There's also a sunny patio, and live bands perform regularly. ✉ *59 W. Center St.* ☎ *435/867–9463* ⊕ *www. igwinery.com* 🕑 *Closed Sun. and Mon.*

Southern Utah Museum of Art
MUSEUM | Set in a striking modern building designed in 2016 to resemble the region's canyons and rock formations, this excellent regional art museum with a peaceful sculpture garden is part of Southern Utah University's cultural compound, along with the Utah Shakespeare Festival theaters. The galleries feature selections from the museum's

permanent collection of some 2,000 works—including pieces by Renoir, Dalí, and Thomas Hart Benton—along with rotating shows that shine a light on emerging regional artists as well as students and faculty. ✉ *13 S. 300 W* ☎ *435/586–5432* ⊕ *www.suu.edu/pva/suma* ⊙ *Closed Sun.*

Restaurants

★ Centro Woodfired Pizzeria

$ | **PIZZA** | You can watch your handmade artisanal pizza being pulled from the fires of the brick oven, then sit back and enjoy a seasonal pie layered with ingredients such as house-made fennel sausage and wood-roasted cremini mushrooms. The creamy vanilla gelato layered with a balsamic reduction and sea salt is highly addictive. **Known for:** house-made sausage; good wine and beer list; creative desserts. $ *Average main: $14* ✉ *50 W. Center St.* ☎ *435/867–8123* ⊕ *www.centropizzeria.com.*

Chef Alfredo's Ristorante Italiano

$$ | **ITALIAN** | With linen tablecloths, a decent wine list, and soft music playing in the background, this charmingly old-school restaurant tucked away in a strip mall serves authentic Sicilian-style Italian food. Highlights include traditional antipasto appetizers and specials like butternut ravioli or eggplant Parmesan, plus linguine and clam sauce, chicken parmigiana, fettuccine primavera, and the like. **Known for:** romantic atmosphere; flatbread pizzas; tender steaks. $ *Average main: $22* ✉ *2313 W. 400 N* ☎ *435/586–2693* ⊕ *www.chefalfredos.com* ⊙ *No lunch weekends.*

Erawan Thai

$$ | **THAI** | In a nondescript but conveniently located shopping center just off the interstate, this excellent Thai restaurant has a cheerful, inviting rustic-wood interior with paintings, crafts, and cannisters of imported tea. The kitchen turns out deftly prepared renditions of classic—chicken satay, massaman shrimp curry, tom kha soup—and more creative fare, like mango-curry-fried rice. **Known for:** attractive, art-filled space; crispy duck with several preparations; extensive selection of teas. $ *Average main: $17* ✉ *1190 Sage Dr.* ☎ *435/267–0391* ⊕ *www.erawanthai-ut.com* ⊙ *Closed Sun.*

★ The French Spot

$$ | **FRENCH** | This tiny takeout patisserie in the center of downtown is a favorite stop for lattes and cold brew, crepes, salads, heartier dinner specials (salmon, filet mignon), and ethereal pastries and sweets, including a rotating selection of chocolate, berry, lemon, and seasonal tarts. Although primarily a to-go option that's perfect for stocking up before a hiking or biking adventure, in warm weather you can also dine on the cute patio out front. **Known for:** picnic supplies to enjoy before a show at the nearby Utah Shakespeare Festival; scrambled-egg breakfast croissants with ham, bacon, Gruyère, or smoke salmon; colorful macarons. $ *Average main: $17* ✉ *5 N. Main St.* ☎ *347/886–8587* ⊕ *www.thefrenchspot-cafe.com* ⊙ *Closed Mon.*

Milt's Stage Stop

$$$ | **STEAKHOUSE** | Cabin decor, friendly service, and canyon views are the hallmarks of this dinner spot 10-minutes southeast of downtown Cedar City by car. Expect traditional, hearty steak house cuisine: rib-eye steaks, prime rib, and seafood dishes, accompanied by loaded baked potatoes, deep-fried zucchini, and similar sides. **Known for:** scenic alpine setting; hefty steaks and seafood; chocolate lava cake. $ *Average main: $27* ✉ *3560 E. Hwy. 14* ☎ *435/586–9344* ⊕ *www.miltsstagestop.com* ⊙ *No lunch.*

PorkBelly's Eatery

$ | **AMERICAN** | As the name suggests, this airy contemporary restaurant is a meat-lover's paradise. Starting with tri-tip eggs Benedict and chicken and waffles at breakfast, pulled-pork sandwiches, carne asada nachos, and bacon-mushroom-cheddar burgers follow. **Known for:** mammoth portions of meat-centric fare; smoked baby back ribs on weekends; the chicken bomb (a jalapeño stuffed with cream cheese and sausage and wrapped in chicken and bacon). [$] *Average main: $14* ✉ *565 S. Main St.* ☎ *435/586–5285* 🌐 *www.porkbellyseatery.com* 🕒 *Closed Mon. No dinner Sun.*

Rusty's Ranch House

$$ | **STEAKHOUSE** | Locals have long considered the meals at this fun, if a bit touristy, Old West–style roadhouse some of the best in the region. They serve steaks, barbecue brisket and baby-back ribs, towering burgers, sweet coconut shrimp, and other classics. **Known for:** extensive cocktail selection; quirky Western vibe; Granny's hot-caramel apple cobbler. [$] *Average main: $21* ✉ *2275 E. Hwy. 14* ☎ *435/586–3839* 🌐 *www.rustysranchhouse.com* 🕒 *Closed Sun. No lunch.*

Coffee and Quick Bites

Bulloch's Drug Store

$ | **CAFÉ** | **FAMILY** | Built in 1917 and remodeled to retain its historic character, this landmark building in downtown Cedar City contains an old-fashioned drug store, complete with a soda fountain from the 1950s. Enjoy ice cream, shakes, sundaes, and malts, or try one of the uniquely flavored sodas. **Known for:** decadent ice cream sundaes; big selection of penny candies; cool old building. [$] *Average main: $6* ✉ *91 N. Main St.* ☎ *435/586–9651* 🌐 *www.bullochdrug.com* 🕒 *Closed Sun. No dinner.*

Hotels

Abbey Inn Cedar City

$ | **HOTEL** | Just off the interstate and near Southern Utah State University, this two-story economical motel has spacious rooms with exterior entrances, fridges, microwaves, and—in the case of suites—kitchens and hot tubs. **Pros:** 10-minute walk to downtown and festival venues; lots of dining options nearby; nice indoor pool and fitness center. **Cons:** road noise for some rooms; bland setting amid fast-food restaurants and chains; cookie-cutter room decor. [$] *Rooms from: $116* ✉ *940 W. 200 N* ☎ *435/586–9966, 800/325–5411* 🌐 *www.abbeyinncedar.com* 🛏 *83 rooms* 🍴 *Free breakfast.*

★ **Amid Summer's Inn Bed & Breakfast**

$ | **B&B/INN** | This enchanting 1930s cottage-style inn, set along a quiet tree-lined street close to Southern Utah University campus, has individually decorated rooms with literary themes, lavish antiques, and fine artwork. **Pros:** friendly, knowledgeable staff; exceptional breakfasts and decadent baked goods; two blocks from Shakespeare Festival and downtown. **Cons:** some rooms are accessible only by a narrow stairway; may be too intimate for some; books up well in advance in summer. [$] *Rooms from: $119* ✉ *140 S. 100 W* ☎ *435/586–2600* 🌐 *www.amidsummersinn.com* 🛏 *10 rooms* 🍴 *Free breakfast.*

★ **Iron Gate Inn**

$$ | **B&B/INN** | Set in a grand downtown second empire Victorian home that underwent an ambitious renovation before becoming a B&B, this gracious lodging has seven large, period-furnished rooms with well-designed modern bathrooms; some have private sitting areas or direct access to verandas and the inn's fragrant gardens. **Pros:** steps from Shakespeare Festival and downtown; impressive gourmet breakfast included; Jacuzzi and firepit in lush back garden. **Cons:** frilly Victorian decor may not suit every taste; friendly cats and dogs live on premises but could be an issue for some; fills up on summer weekends. [$] *Rooms from: $129* ✉ *100 N. 200 W* ☎ *435/383–5133* 🌐 *www.theirongateinn.com* 🛏 *7 rooms* 🍴 *Free breakfast.*

SpringHill Suites by Marriott Cedar City
$$ | **HOTEL** | Just off Interstate 15 on the quiet south side of Cedar City, this modern and well-equipped all-suites property is convenient to downtown and the Shakespeare Festival and has some nice features for families or guests staying a few days, including in-room kitchenettes, sitting areas, a 24/7 guest food and beverage pantry, and a well-equipped gym and indoor pool. **Pros:** easy freeway access and 5-minute drive to downtown; mountain views from many rooms; bright, contemporary rooms and common spaces. **Cons:** not within walking distance of downtown; indoor pool can feel stuffy in summer; a little pricier than most properties in town. [$] *Rooms from: $149* ✉ *1477 S. Old Hwy. 91* ☎ *435/586–1685* 🌐 *www.marriott.com* 🛏 *72 suites* 🍴 *Free breakfast.*

Activities

RECREATIONAL AREAS

Coal Creek Trail
PARK—SPORTS-OUTDOORS | It's easy, even if you're pushing a stroller, to get out into nature in this sunny, mile-high community. Perfect for strolling, jogging, biking, or running, this 3.4-mile paved multipurpose trail starts in Bicentennial Park and cuts in a southeasterly direction right through the center of town, paralleling the scenic creek for which it's named and eventually joining with the similarly paved Cedar Canyon Trail. Other non-paved hiking trails also spur off from the Cedar Creek Trail and into the surrounding foothills. ✉ *Bicentennial Park, 660 W. 1045 N* 🌐 *www.cedarcity.org.*

Brian Head

29 miles east of Cedar City.

This tiny town's Brian Head Resort is Utah's southernmost and highest ski area at well over 9,000 feet, but the area's summer recreation, especially mountain biking, has also developed energetically in recent years. There are now more than 200 miles of trails for bikers, many of which are served by chairlift or shuttle services. The bright red-orange rock formations of Cedar Breaks Monument are several miles south of town.

GETTING HERE AND AROUND

Most of the year, from Cedar City, you take Highway 14 east to highways 143 and 148 north. But in winter, when Highway 148 is closed, you'll need to take Interstate 15 north to Parowan and then Highway 143 south. Whichever way you arrive, the drive takes about the same amount of time (45 minutes to an hour) and is wonderfully scenic.

Sights

★ **Brian Head Peak Observation**
SCENIC DRIVE | This 11,312-foot stone lookout hut was built by the Civilian Conservation Corps (CCC) in 1935 atop the highest summit in Iron County. You can see for miles in every direction, as far as Nevada and Arizona, enjoying especially dramatic views of nearby Cedar Breaks National Monument. The windy and dramatic nearly 3-mile drive along unpaved Forest Road 047 from Hwy. 143 is part of the fun; note that it's a short 0.2-mile hike from the parking area to the summit, and that when there's snow, the last section of road is closed to vehicles, but you can still hike or snowshoe up to the top. You can also hike to the summit from the junction of Rocky Road and Hwy. 143—the rugged and picturesque trek is about 3½ miles each way. ✉ *end of Forest Rd. 047* 🌐 *www.fs.usda.gov/dixie.*

★ **Cedar Breaks National Monument**
NATURE SITE | From the rim of Cedar Breaks, a 3-mile-long natural amphitheater plunges a half-mile into the Markagunt Plateau. Short alpine hiking trails along the rim and few crowds make this a wonderful summer stop. Most visitors are content to photograph the monument

from one of the handful of overlooks alongside the road—which means the intrepid hiker, skier, or snowshoer can easily find solitude along the trails. In fact, winter is one of the best times to visit, when snow drapes the red-orange formations. Call ahead for road conditions (the road is sometimes closed due to heavy snowfall), and keep in mind that all visitor facilities are closed from October through late May. ✉ *Hwy. 148 ✣ 3½ miles north of Hwy. 14* ☎ *435/586–9451* 🌐 *www.nps.gov/cebr* 🎟 *$7* 🕒 *Visitor center closed mid-Oct.–late May.*

Hotels

Best Western Premier Brian Head Hotel & Spa

$$ | RESORT | With its stunning scenery and prime location, this modern mission-style lodge is a great base for outdoor adventures and offers a number of amenities, including a bar and grill, outdoor deck, indoor pool, hot tubs, and a spa where you can enjoy a range of body and beauty treatments. **Pros:** comfortable base for outdoor recreation; full-service spa and pool; rooms have mountain views. **Cons:** can get pricey on winter weekends; breakfast costs extra; on-site restaurant gets mixed reviews. [$] *Rooms from: $145* ✉ *314 Hunter Ridge Rd.* ☎ *435/677–9000* 🌐 *www.bwpbrianheadhotel.com* 🛏 *100 rooms* 🍴 *No meals.*

Cedar Breaks Lodge & Spa

$$ | RESORT | At an altitude of 9,600 feet, this lodge-style resort near Brian Head's popular ski slopes offers scenic views, and although some rooms may show their age, all are decorated in a warm and rustic style that suits the setting. **Pros:** many recreational amenties; easy access to skiing, hiking, and mountain biking; scenic mountain views. **Cons:** early (10 am) check-out; no a/c; quality of on-site restaurant is hit-or-miss. [$] *Rooms from: $150* ✉ *223 Hunter Ridge Rd.* ☎ *435/677–3000, 800/438–2929* 🌐 *www.cedarbreakslodge.com* 🛏 *118 rooms* 🍴 *No meals.*

Activities

BICYCLING

SKIING AND SNOWBOARDING

Brian Head Ski Resort

SKIING/SNOWBOARDING | Eight lifts (including two high-speed quads) transport skiers to this popular resort's 71 runs (evenly divided among expert, intermediate, and beginner terrain), which cover more than 650 acres and encompass a vertical drop of about 1,400 feet, with peak elevation nearing 11,000 feet. A half-pipe, trails, and a terrain park attract snowboarders. From the top of the resort's peak, you can see the red-rock cliffs of Cedar Breaks National Monument to the southwest. During summer and fall, the resort is a favorite with mountain bikers and hikers. ✉ *329 S. Hwy. 143* ☎ *866/930–1010* 🌐 *www.brianhead.com* 🎟 *Lift tickets $45–$62.*

Georg's Ski Shop and Bikes

BICYCLING | Just down the road from Brian Head Resort, this popular ski shop has new and rental skis, snowboards, and bikes. The friendly staff is experienced at helping both beginning and advanced skiers find the perfect gear. ✉ *612 S. Hwy. 143* ☎ *435/677–2013* 🌐 *www.georgsskishop.com.*

St. George

50 miles southwest of Cedar City.

Believing the mild year-round climate ideal for growing cotton, Brigham Young dispatched 309 LDS families in 1861 to found St. George. They were to raise cotton and silkworms and to establish a textile industry, to make up for textile shortages resulting from the Civil War.

The fourth fastest-growing metropolitan area in the country, St. George has become the cultural and recreational hub of southern Utah, a favorite place to relocate among both retirees who appreciate the warm winters and younger families and entrepreneurs lured by the high quality of life, stunning scenery, and growing number of restaurants, shops, and other services.

GETTING HERE AND AROUND

This burgeoning and increasingly sprawling city is bisected by Interstate 15, and although the very heart of downtown is pedestrian-friendly, you need a car to visit outlying attractions.

FESTIVALS

Dixie Roundup

FESTIVALS | Dozens of professional rodeo cowboys from across the West take part in this three-day mid-September event held since the 1930s. Team roping, saddle-bronc riding, and bull riding are among the main attractions, along with the always entertaining mutton-busting competition for the kids and the rodeo parade. ⊠ *St. George* ⊕ *www.stgeorge-lions.com.*

St. George Arts Festival

ARTS FESTIVALS | Artisan booths, food, children's activities, and entertainment (including cowboy poets) are all part of this Town Square festival held Friday and Saturday before Easter. ⊠ *St. George* ⊕ *www.sgartfestival.com.*

ESSENTIALS

Greater Zion Convention & Visitors Bureau ⊠ *20 N. Main St.* ☎ *435/634–5747* ⊕ *www.greaterzion.com.*

 Sights

Brigham Young Winter Home

HOUSE | Mormon leader Brigham Young spent the last seven winters of his life in the warm, sunny climate of St. George. Built of adobe on a sandstone-and-basalt foundation and now a museum, this two-story home with pretty green and red trim and well-tended gardens contains a portrait of Young over one fireplace, and furnishings from the late 19th century. Visits are by guided tour. ⊠ *67*

W. 200 N ☎ *435/673–2517* ⊕ *history. churchofjesuschrist.org* ⊠ *Free.*

Kayenta Art Village

ARTS VENUE | In the heart of an upscale, contemporary planned community in Ivins, not far from Tuacahn Center for the Arts and Red Mountain Resort, this scenic little arts district contains several of southern Utah's top galleries, including Gallery 873; known for jewelry and ceramics; Kayenta Desert Arboretum & Desert Rose Labyrinth, which visitors can freely stroll through; Zia Pottery Studio, a co-op operated by talented local potters; and several others. Set against a red rock landscape, it's an enchanting neighborhood to stroll through, especially during the Art in Kayenta outdoor festival in mid-October. Also check to see what's on at the Center for the Arts at Kayenta—which presents lectures, movies, theater, and concerts—or grab a bite at the excellent Xetava Gardens Café. ⊠ *875 Coyote Gulch Ct., Ivins* ☎ *435/688–8535* ⊕ *www. kayentautah.com.*

★ Red Cliffs Desert Reserve

INFO CENTER | Encompassing the convergence of the Mojave, Great Basin, and Colorado Plateau desert zones, this pristine 62,000 tract of red-rock wilderness begins several miles north of St. George and was established in 2009 to protect the habitat of the desert tortoise. However, countless other flora and fauna—including gila monsters and chuckwallas—thrive in this unique transition zone that can be accessed through miles of designated hiking, mountain biking, and horseback trails. The best place to start your adventure is by visiting the reserve's contemporary visitor center in downtown St. George, where you'll find live animals, interactive exhibits, and staff who can advise you on hikes and other ways to visit. You can pick up trail maps here or download detailed PDF maps from the reserve website. The trail sections closest to St. George include City Creek and Paradise Canyon. Although it adjoins the reserve and is part of the same ecosystem, popular Snow Canyon State Park is administered separately. ⊠ *Visitor Center, 10 N. 100 E* ☎ *435/634–5759* ⊕ *www. redcliffsdesertreserve.com.*

★ Red Hills Desert Garden

GARDEN | Opened in 2015 as the state's first botanic garden devoted to desert conservation, Red Hills is a beautiful spot for a peaceful stroll as well as a great place to learn about water-efficient plants. More than 5,000 of them—including fragrant mesquite trees, prickly pear cactus, blue agave, Joshua trees, weeping yucca, and desert willows—thrive here, along with a meandering stream that's stocked with desert suckers, Virgin River chub, and other native species. Paths also lead past a number of boulders that preserve the tracks of dinosaurs that roamed here some 200 million years ago. The garden adjoins rugged Pioneer Park, a 52-acre expanse of rock-climbing and hiking terrain with barbecue pits, picnic pavilions and tables, and both short and long trails. ⊠ *375 E. Red Hills Pkwy.* ☎ *435/673–3617* ⊕ *www.redhillsdesertgarden.com.*

★ Snow Canyon State Park

NATIONAL/STATE PARK | Named not for winter weather but after a pair of pioneering Utahans named Snow, this gem of a state park—about 10 miles north of St. George—is filled with natural wonders. Hiking trails lead to lava cones, sand dunes, cactus gardens, and high-contrast vistas. From the campground you can scramble up huge sandstone mounds and overlook the entire valley. Park staff lead occasional guided hikes. ⊠ *1002 Snow Canyon Dr., Ivins* ☎ *435/628–2255* ⊕ *stateparks.utah.gov* ⊠ *$10 per vehicle.*

St. George Art Museum

MUSEUM | FAMILY | The downtown centerpiece of St. George's growing art scene occupies an attractively reimagined former sugar-beet warehouse. The permanent collection celebrates the works of mostly regionally based potters, photographers, and painters, many of them depicting the region's spectacular landscapes. Rotating exhibits highlight local history and lore and showcase emerging contemporary talents. There's also a Family Discover Center, with materials for kids to create their own works. ⊠ *47 E. 200 N* ☎ *435/627–4525* ⊕ *www. sgcity.org/artmuseum* ⊠ *$3* ⊗ *Closed Sun.*

St. George Children's Museum

MUSEUM | FAMILY | Located next to Town Square Park and the downtown library and set inside a former school building with a striking red-stone exterior, this impressive museum contains two floors of touch-friendly exhibits that will stimulate kids' imaginations, including an earthquake-simulation table, a science discovery lab, a transportation center with planes and an auto shop, and a miniature version of St. George's famed Tuacahn theater. ⊠ *86 S. Main St.* ☎ *435/986–4000* ⊕ *www.sgchildrensmuseum.org* ⊠ *$5* ⊗ *Closed Sun. and also Mon. in Aug.–Feb.*

St. George Dinosaur Discovery Site at Johnson Farm

ARCHAEOLOGICAL SITE | FAMILY | Unearthed in 2000 by property developers, this site preserves and exhibits ancient footprints left by dinosaurs from the Jurassic Period millions of years ago. Fossils unearthed here are also on display in the modern museum, where accurate replicas portray the creatures that left these tantalizing remains, and themed displays cover many details of the Jurassic era. There's an interactive area for children and a Dino Park outside the museum with shaded picnic tables and a Walk Through Time exhibit. ⊠ *2180 E. Riverside Dr.* ☎ *435/574–3466* ⊕ *www.dinosite.org* ⊠ *$8.*

St. George Tabernacle

RELIGIOUS SITE | This is one of the best-preserved pioneer buildings in the entire state, and it is still used for public meetings and programs for the community. Mormon settlers began work on the tabernacle just a few months after the city of St. George was established in June 1863. Upon completion of the sandstone building's 140-foot clock tower 13 years later, Brigham Young formally dedicated the site. You can visit the building by guided tour. ✉ *18 S. Main St.* ☎ *435/628–4072* 🌐 *history.churchofjesuschrist.org.*

St. George Temple

RELIGIOUS SITE | The red-sandstone temple, plastered over with white stucco, was completed in 1877 and was the first Mormon temple in Southwest Utah. It has served as a meeting place for both Mormons and other congregations over the decades. Today, only members of the Church of Jesus Christ of Latter-day Saints can enter the temple, but a visitor center next door offers guided tours of the visitor center and grounds. ✉ *250 E. 400 S* ☎ *435/673–5181* 🌐 *www.churchofjesuschrist.org.*

Restaurants

Aragosta

$$$$ | **MODERN AMERICAN** | With a palatial dining room with chandeliers and white napery, this elegant restaurant east of downtown (and formerly in Ivins) specializes in haute American and European fare and is a favorite destination for special occasions. Think rich creamy lobster bisque with Spanish sherry, risotto with black truffles and grilled prawns, fall-off-the-bone lamb osso buco, and chateaubriand for two. **Known for:** steaks with decadent sauces and sides; refined service; impressive wine list. $ *Average main: $33* ✉ *1386 E. 100 S* ☎ *435/313–0611* 🌐 *www.aragostautah.com.*

Benja Thai and Sushi

$ | **THAI** | In a stone-walled dining room in downtown's charming Ancestor Square, you can dine on authentic hot-and-sour soups, papaya and larb salads, ginger chicken, whole crispy red snapper with spicy basil sauce, and other Thai dishes, as well as offerings from an extensive sushi menu. The room's tapestries, intricate wood carvings, and lilting music give it warmth and tranquility, and large windows provide views of the landscaped courtyard dotted with quaint historic buildings. **Known for:** huge selection of sushi rolls and nigiri; charming setting; mango cheesecake. $ *Average main: $14* ✉ *2 W. St. George Blvd.* ☎ *435/628–9538* 🌐 *benjathai.com* ⏲ *Closed Sun.*

Cliffside Restaurant

$$ | **MODERN AMERICAN** | This strikingly situated restaurant beside the Inn on the Cliff Hotel offers dazzling St. George Valley views from both the dining room and patio, making it an especially popular spot for sunset dinners. The kitchen turns out well-prepared modern American fare, with an emphasis on steaks and seafood—consider the seared flat-iron steak with chimichurri sauce, or almond-crusted Idaho trout with farro pesto, broccolini, and a beurre blanc sauce. **Known for:** eye-popping views; buttermilk chicken-fried chicken; decadent, seasonally changing desserts. $ *Average main: $22* ✉ *511 S. Tech Ridge Dr.* ☎ *435/319–6005* 🌐 *www.cliffsiderestaurant.com* ⏲ *Closed Sun.*

Irmita's Casita

$ | **MEXICAN** | **FAMILY** | A standby for tasty Mexican-American fare in various locations around town since 1993, this humble spot serves affordable, no-nonsense food that can be quite spicy if requested. Specialties include spicy pork tortas, massive burritos smothered in red or green sauce, and shrimp enchiladas. **Known for:** steak chilaquiles at breakfast; chicken mole poblano; Mexican soft drinks and juices. $ *Average main: $10* ✉ *95 W. 700 S* ☎ *435/703–9162* 🌐 *www.irmitascasita.net* 💳 *No credit cards* ⏲ *Closed Sun.*

Morty's Cafe

$ | **MODERN AMERICAN** | **FAMILY** | At this funky updated take on a burger joint on the east side of downtown, the brick walls are hung with local art for sale. Creatively topped beef and veggie burgers are offered, plus breakfast burritos, several varieties of quinoa salad, and thick milkshakes. **Known for:** breakfast sandwiches and burritos served all day; three-bean veggie burgers with chipotle mayo; salted peanut butter milkshakes. [$] *Average main: $8* ✉ *702 E. St. George Blvd.* ☎ *435/359–4439* 🌐 *www.mortyscafe.com* 🕒 *Closed Sun.*

★ Painted Pony

$$$$ | **MODERN AMERICAN** | Shaded patio dining overlooking Ancestor Square and contemporary Southwestern art on the walls provide a romantic setting. Enjoy contemporary American fare with an emphasis on seasonal ingredients, many from the owners' private organic garden. **Known for:** knowledgeable servers; one of the best wine lists in town; seasonally changing bread pudding. [$] *Average main: $32* ✉ *2 W. St. George Blvd.* ☎ *435/634–1700* 🌐 *www.painted-pony.com* 🕒 *No lunch Sun.*

700 Degree Artisan Pizza

$ | **PIZZA** | After a hike in nearby Pioneer Park or Red Hills Desert Garden, fuel up on delicious blistered-crust pizzas at this hip eatery and taproom that's also known for its impressive selection of craft beers and sodas as well as wines on tap. Favorite pies include the Arugula Bianca with roasted garlic, prosciutto, pecorino Romano, and truffle oil, and the spice-lover's Purgatory, which has a spicy tomato base along with calabrese salami, pepperoncini, jalapeños, and sweet-and-hot Italian sausage. **Known for:** pizzas with interesting toppings; wood-fired meatballs, garlic bread, and other sides; dessert pizzas topped with Nutella and ricotta cheese. [$] *Average main: $14* ✉ *974 W. Sunset Blvd.* ☎ *435/703–6700* 🌐 *www.700degree.pizza* 🕒 *Closed Mon.*

★ Wood Ash Rye

$$$ | **MODERN AMERICAN** | With a white-tile open kitchen, marble tables, and a wood-beam ceiling, this scene-y farm-to-table restaurant and bar in the swanky Advenire Hotel has quickly become St. George's destination for people-watching and deftly crafted seasonal cuisine. The sharing-friendly menu changes regularly but always features a selection of cheeses and charcuterie, and typical offerings include grilled octopus with preserved lemon and smoked olive oil, and grilled duck with artichoke, tomatillo aioli, and crispy skin. **Known for:** innovative cocktails and mocktails; oysters served raw, charbroiled, or fried; rotating selection of house-made ice creams and sorbets. [$] *Average main: $25* ✉ *25 W. St. George Blvd.* ☎ *435/522–5020* 🌐 *www.theadvenirehotel.com.*

★ Xetava Gardens Cafe

$$ | **MODERN AMERICAN** | This beautifully designed adobe oasis in the Kayenta Art Village in Ivins, about 10 miles northwest of St. George, offers gracious indoor and outdoor seating, the latter overlooking fragrant high-desert gardens. Pronounced Zah-Tah-Vah, the space began as a coffee bar and is still a source of lattes and mochas, but you'll also find an eclectic selection of globally inspired all-day fare, including avocado breakfast ciabattas, wild-caught mahimahi green curry, peach-glazed organic chicken, and wild mushroom burgers. **Known for:** location near several art galleries; well-curated beer, wine, and cocktail list; coconut-lime cake. [$] *Average main: $17* ✉ *815 Coyote Gulch Ct., Ivins* ☎ *435/656–0165* 🌐 *www.xetava.com* 🕒 *No dinner Mon.–Wed.*

☕ Coffee and Quick Bites

FeelLove Coffee

$ | **CAFÉ** | Head to this light-filled, high-ceilinged café just off the east side's Virgin River bike and jogging trail for well-crafted coffees, teas, and lemonades as well as an assortment of tasty, generally healthy, dishes. Start the day with an egg-avocado toast or a turmeric-tofu scramble, and for lunch or dinner, try the vegan Greek salad, turkey–Munster cheese baguette, or "nachos" topped with sliced apples, date caramel, almond butter, and pistachios. **Known for:** live music some evenings; Thai, matcha, and other sweet tea lattes; fresh-baked desserts, including many vegan options. [$] *Average main: $10* ✉ *558 E. Riverside Dr.* ☎ *435/922–1717* 🌐 *www.feellovecoffee.com.*

Hotels

★ The Advenire

$$$ | **HOTEL** | A strikingly contemporary, upscale hotel that's directly across the street from the buzzy shopping and dining of Ancestor Square, this stylish member of Marriott Bonvoy's indie-spirited Autograph Collection exudes hipness with its hardwood floors, bold-print pillows and chairs, high-tech entertainment center, and cushy bedding. **Pros:** stylish, cosmopolitan decor; superb on-site restaurant; steps from downtown dining and retail. **Cons:** neighborhood can be busy and crowded at times; steep cleaning fee if you bring a pet; a bit pricey. [$] *Rooms from: $189* ✉ *25 W. St. George Blvd.* ☎ *435/522–5022* 🌐 *www.theadvenirehotel.com* 🛏 *60 rooms* 🍴 *No meals.*

Best Western Coral Hills

$ | **HOTEL** | **FAMILY** | This reasonably priced two-story motel set against a back drop of red hills is a handy choice for being a short walk from many restaurants, shops, and downtown attractions, and heated indoor and outdoor pools promise relaxation after a busy day. **Pros:** suites have deep jetted tubs; pool and hot tub set within a red rock grotto; lots of dining options nearby. **Cons:** some issues with street noise; breakfast is basic; kids often congregate around the pools. [$] *Rooms from: $105* ✉ *125 E. St. George Blvd.* ☎ *435/673–4844* 🌐 *www.coralhills.com* 🛏 *98 rooms* 🍴 *Free breakfast.*

The Inn at Entrada

$$$ | **HOTEL** | Hikers, spa goers, and—above all—golfers flock to this plush boutique resort set amid the red-rock canyons northwest of downtown, surrounded by a world-class Johnny Miller–designed golf course, and offering a top-notch spa, pool, and fitness facility. **Pros:** adjoins one of the top golf courses in the state; attractive Southwest-inspired contemporary decor; terrific spa. **Cons:** 10- to 15-minute drive from downtown dining; nongolfers may feel a little out of place; can get very expensive depending on time of year. [$] *Rooms from: $192* ✉ *2588 W. Singua Trail* ☎ *435/634–7100* 🌐 *www.innatentrada.com* 🛏 *54 units* 🍴 *No meals.*

★ Inn on the Cliff

$$ | **HOTEL** | It's all about the panoramic views at this exceptionally well-maintained mid-century modern boutique hotel set high on a ridge overlooking downtown St. George and the red rocks beyond. **Pros:** reasonable rates for such a nice property; stunning views; continental breakfast delivered to your room. **Cons:** breakfast is a bit meager; too far to walk from downtown; restaurant closed on Sunday. [$] *Rooms from: $170* ✉ *511 S. Tech Ridge Dr.* ☎ *435/216–5864* 🌐 *www.innonthecliff.com* 🛏 *27 rooms* 🍴 *Free breakfast.*

★ Red Mountain Resort

$$$$ | **RESORT** | This luxurious red-rock hideaway, with its stunning surroundings near the mouth of Snow Canyon, offers a range of outdoor adventures and fitness and wellness options, from fitness classes, hikes, and yoga sessions to red clay–lavender body wraps and warm Himalayan salt stone massages. **Pros:** world-class spa and fitness facilities; handsome contemporary design fits in with natural surroundings; a range of meal, spa, and activity packages available. **Cons:** caters more to activity-seekers than those looking to relax; 15-minute

drive northwest of St. George; all those potential treatment, activity, and meal add-ons can get pricey. $ *Rooms from: $235* ☒ *1275 E. Red Mountain Circle, Ivins* ☎ *435/673–4905, 877/246–4453* ⊕ *www.redmountainresort.com* ⤵ *106 units* ⦿ *No meals.*

Seven Wives Inn Bed & Breakfast

$$ | B&B/INN | Named for an ancestor of the owner who indeed had seven wives, this quaint bed-and-breakfast occupies two Victorian homes on a pretty tree-lined street and is full of historic charm. **Pros:** nice outdoor pool and sundeck; short walk from Ancestor Square and downtown attractions; distinctive historic ambience. **Cons:** often books up well-ahead on summer weekends; a bit too old-fashioned for some tastes; not ideal for kids. $ *Rooms from: $135* ☒ *217 N. 100 W* ☎ *435/628–3737* ⊕ *www. sevenwivesinn.com* ⤵ *13 rooms* ⦿ *Free breakfast.*

Nightlife

★ George's Corner

BARS/PUBS | A lively hub of bustling Ancestor Square, this welcoming tavern is open all day for casual dining but is also one of the city's relatively few late-night options for drinks and live music. The spacious bar decorated with historic black-and-white photos of the area offers a nice selection of cocktails and regional craft brews. ☒ *2 W. St. George Blvd.* ☎ *435/216–7311* ⊕ *www.georgescorner-restaurant.com.*

Zion Brewery Station II

BREWPUBS/BEER GARDENS | Southwestern Utah's best craft brewery is based in Springdale but also operates this hip taproom with pool tables and a patio near Ancestor Square. ☒ *142 N. Main St.* ☎ *435/673–7644* ⊕ *www.zionbrewery.com.*

Performing Arts

Tuacahn

CONCERTS | At this magnificent outdoor amphitheater nestled in a natural red-sandstone cove, you can watch touring Broadway musicals and concerts by noted pop artists. ☒ *1100 Tuacahn Dr., Ivins* ☎ *800/746–9882, 435/652–3300* ⊕ *www.tuacahn.org.*

🛍 Shopping

★ Rowley's Red Barn

FOOD/CANDY | FAMILY | Set in a red barn just a 10-minute drive northeast of St. George, this outpost of the legendary family farm and fruitstand in central Utah is a favorite stop for delicious apples, cherries, peaches, pears, and watermelons, along with several items grown out of state, including oranges and pineapples. Be sure to sample the fresh-pressed apple juice and cider, and the ice cream parlor doles out tasty treats, including shakes and apple cider slushes. ☒ *25 N. 300 W, Washington* ☎ *435/652–6611* ⊕ *www.rowleysredbarn.com.*

Urban Renewal

HOUSEHOLD ITEMS/FURNITURE | In the heart of Ancestor Square's retail district, this big housewares emporia carries all sorts of fun curiosities and gifts for the home, from larger tables and chairs to antique farm implements, vintage toys and collectibles, old books, interesting kitchen goods, and more. ☒ *5 E. 100 N* ☎ *435/236–3838* ⊕ *www.facebook.com/byjennylarsen.*

Activities

BICYCLING

Bicycles Unlimited

BICYCLING | A trusted southern Utah biking resource, this shop rents bikes and sells parts and accessories, and offers maps and advice about great rides in the area. ☒ *90 S. 100 E* ☎ *435/673–4492, 888/673–4492* ⊕ *www.bicyclesunlimited.com.*

GOLF

★ Entrada at Snow Canyon Country Club

GOLF | Opened in 1996 and surrounded by a spectacular desert landscape, this challenging course designed by Johnny Miller was featured in the Disney movie *High School Musical 2*. Ranked among the top courses in the Southwest for its perfectly manicured greens and stylish clubhouse, this is a private course, but it is accessible to guests staying at the Inn at Entrada, which offers stay-and-play packages. ✉ *2511 W. Entrada Trail* ☎ *435/986–2207* ⊕ *www.golfentrada.com* 💲 *$110–$150* 🏌 *18 holes, 7062 yards, par 72.*

The Ledges Golf Course

GOLF | Seven miles north of St. George, this state-of-the-art course designed by Matt Dye features meticulously maintained greens and an impressive backdrop of red rock combined with panoramic views of Snow Canyon State Park. The difficult back nine may be a bit intimidating for less experienced golfers. ✉ *1585 Ledges Pkwy.* ☎ *435/634–4640* ⊕ *www.ledges.com/golf-course* 💲 *$65–$110* 🏌 *18 holes, 7200 yards, par 72.*

Springdale

40 miles east of St. George.

Although small, this gorgeously situated town of about 600 has more than doubled in population since 1990, thanks in large part to its being directly adjacent to Zion National Park. Hotels, restaurants, and shops continue to pop up, yet the town still manages to maintain its small-town charm.

GETTING HERE AND AROUND

You'll need a car to get to Springdale, via Highway 9, but getting around once you're here is easy. The complimentary canyon-road shuttle bus—from April through October—makes getting from one end of Springdale to the other stress-free, with bus stops throughout town, and connecting service to the free shuttle into Zion National Park. It's also a pleasant town to stroll through, with shops, galleries, and restaurants all in a central district. In winter, when there are fewer crowds, a car is handy for getting around town or visiting the park.

Sights

Grafton

GHOST TOWN | FAMILY | A stone school, dusty cemetery, and a few wooden structures are all that remain of the nearby town of Grafton, which is between Springdale and Hurricane, a few miles west of the turnoff onto Bridge Road in Rockville. This ghost town has been featured in films such as *Butch Cassidy and the Sundance Kid*. ✉ *Hwy. 250 S.*

 Restaurants

Bit & Spur

$$ | SOUTHWESTERN | This laid-back Springdale institution has been delighting locals and tourists since the late 1980s, offering a well-rounded menu that includes fresh fish and pasta dishes, but the emphasis is on creative Southwestern fare such as roasted-sweet-potato tamales and chili-rubbed rib-eye steak. Craft beers and the popular house-made sangria complement the zesty cuisine. **Known for:** creative margaritas; live music; outdoor dining by a fountain beneath shade trees. 💲 *Average main: $20* ✉ *1212 Zion Park Blvd.* ☎ *435/772–3498* ⊕ *www.bitand-spur.com* ⊘ *No lunch.*

★ King's Landing Bistro

$$$ | MODERN AMERICAN | Request to be seated on the patio—with dramatic views of the area's red rock monoliths—when dining at this casually stylish bistro at the downtown Springdale's popular Driftwood Lodge hotel. The artfully presented cuisine here tends toward creative American—king salmon with saffron couscous, roast chicken with artichoke tapenade—but you'll find some international, mostly Mediterranean, influences in the form of charred Spanish octopus and some one or two outstanding pastas. **Known for:** interesting artisan cocktail list; emphasis on local and seasonal produce and vegetables; rich desserts, including a classic tiramisu. $ *Average main: $24* ✉ *1515 Zion Park Blvd.* ☎ *435/772–7422* ⊕ *www.klbzion.com* ⊘ *Closed Sun. No lunch.*

Oscar's Cafe

$ | **SOUTHWESTERN** | **FAMILY** | Prepare for an active day with a filling breakfast, or reward yourself after a long hike with lunch or dinner at this welcoming Southwestern café with a big, inviting patio offering stunning mountain views. The pork verde breakfast burrito and huevos rancheros are hearty and delicious, and excellent lunch and dinner options include flame-broiled garlic burgers topped with provolone cheese, and shrimp tacos with a creamy lime sauce. **Known for:** blue-corn nachos with cheese and gaucamole; extensive selection of creative burgers; a large heated patio. $ *Average main: $15* ✉ *948 Zion Park Blvd.* ☎ *435/772–3232* ⊕ *www.oscarscafe.com.*

Park House Cafe

$ | **AMERICAN** | Notable for its big patio with fantastic views into the park and for one of the better selections of vegan and vegetarian dishes in town, this funky little café decorated with colorful artwork serves plenty of tasty meat and egg dishes, too. The grilled ham Benedict has plenty of fans, as do buffalo burgers with havarti cheese and apple-pear-berry salads with organic greens, feta, and walnuts. **Known for:** breakfast served all day; full slate of espresso drinks and smoothies; ice cream sundaes and banana splits. $ *Average main: $12* ✉ *1880 Zion Park Blvd.* ☎ *435/772–0100* ⊘ *Closed Tues. No dinner.*

Spotted Dog Café

$$ | **MODERN AMERICAN** | At this upscale light-filled restaurant with an eclectic menu that typically includes pastas and meat dishes, the staff makes you feel right at home even if you saunter in wearing hiking shoes. The exposed wood beams and large windows that frame the surrounding trees and rock cliffs set a Western mood, with tablecloths and original artworks supplying a dash of refinement. **Known for:** impressive but accessible wine list; extensive breakfast buffet; much of the produce is grown on-site. $ *Average main: $22* ✉ *Flanigan's Inn, 428 Zion Park Blvd.* ☎ *435/772–0700* ⊕ *www.flanigans.com/dining* ⊘ *Limited hrs Nov.–Mar. No lunch.*

Zion Pizza & Noodle Co.

$$ | **PIZZA** | **FAMILY** | Creative pizzas and a kickback atmosphere make this a great place to replenish after a trek through the canyon. Meat lovers can dive into the Cholesterol Hiker pizza, topped with pepperoni, Canadian bacon, and Italian sausage, but the Thai chicken and rosemary-garlic pies are also delicious. **Known for:** stone-slate pizzas with creative toppings; lovely garden seating; good craft beer list. $ *Average main: $16* ✉ *868 Zion Park Blvd.* ☎ *435/772–3815* ⊕ *www.zionpizzanoodle.com* ⊘ *No lunch. Closed Dec.–Feb.*

☕ Coffee and Quick Bites

★ Deep Creek Coffee Company

$ | **CAFÉ** | Stop by this cheerful coffeehouse with hanging air-plants and several tables on a spacious side patio to fuel up before your big park adventure, or for some healthy sustenance to take with you. Hearty açaí and miso-quinoa bowls, avocado toast with poached eggs, bagels with house-made schmears, and Belgian waffles with banana and Nutella are among the tasty offerings. **Known for:** opens at 6 am daily; refreshing house-made cold brew; delicious smoothies. $ *Average main: $9* ✉ *932 Zion Park Blvd.* ☎ *435/669–8849* ⊕ *www.deepcreekcoffee.com* ⊘ *No dinner.*

Hotels

★ Cable Mountain Lodge

$$$ | **HOTEL** | This contemporary lodge with a large swimming pool is the closest hotel in Springdale to Zion—it's a scenic five-minute walk over a foot bridge across the Virgin River. **Pros:** steps from Zion National Park's south entrance; many suites have full kitchens; beautiful picnic area along river with gas grills and tables. **Cons:** no breakfast (but a coffeehouse and market steps away); not all rooms have park views; no pets. [$] *Rooms from: $199* ✉ *147 Zion Park Blvd.* ☎ *435/772–3366, 877/590–3366* 🌐 *www.cablemountainlodge.com* 🛏 *52 rooms* 🍴 *No meals.*

Cliffrose Springdale, Curio Collection by Hilton

$$$$ | **HOTEL** | The canyon views, acres of lush lawns and flowers, and pool and two-tier waterfall hot tubs at this stylish riverside hotel make it more than a place to rest your head, and you could throw a rock across the river and hit Zion National Park. **Pros:** close to Zion's south entrance; enchanting grounds and views; good restaurant serving breakfast and dinner. **Cons:** steep rates; lots of foot and car traffic nearby; no elevator. [$] *Rooms from: $289* ✉ *281 Zion Park Blvd.* ☎ *435/772–3234* 🌐 *www.cliffroselodge.com* 🛏 *52 rooms* 🍴 *No meals.*

★ Desert Pearl Inn

$$$$ | **HOTEL** | Offering spacious rooms with vaulted ceilings, oversize windows, sitting areas, small kitchens with wet bars and dishwashers, and a pleasing contemporary decor, this riverside lodge is special. **Pros:** spacious, smartly designed rooms; excellent restaurant adjacent to hotel; rooms facing river have balconies or terraces. **Cons:** often books up well in advance spring through fall; breakfast costs extra; pets not permitted. [$] *Rooms from: $249* ✉ *707 Zion Park Blvd.* ☎ *435/772–8888, 888/828–0898* 🌐 *www.desertpearl.com* 🛏 *73 rooms* 🍴 *No meals.*

Driftwood Lodge

$$ | **HOTEL** | The rooms at this friendly roadside lodge are among the most reasonably priced in town, even for the premium units, which have balconies or patio along with great views of the Virgin River and surrounding canyons. **Pros:** excellent value; superb restaurant; attractive pool and picnic area. **Cons:** least expensive rooms have no view or balcony; breakfast costs extra; no pets. [$] *Rooms from: $139* ✉ *1515 Zion Park Blvd., Springville* ☎ *435/772–3262* 🌐 *www.driftwoodlodge.net* 🛏 *63 rooms* 🍴 *No meals.*

Flanigan's Inn

$$ | **HOTEL** | A tranquil, nicely landscaped inn with canyon views and a small pool, Flanigan's has big, comfortable accommodations, including two private villas, and suites that sleep six; some units have a patio or a deck. **Pros:** easy shuttle ride or pleasant walk to Zion Canyon Visitor Center; a meditation maze on the hilltop; great seasonal on-site restaurant. **Cons:** not all rooms have views; smaller property that tends to book up quickly; breakfast, though discounted, isn't complimentary (and is unavailable in winter). [$] *Rooms from: $159* ✉ *428 Zion Park Blvd.* ☎ *435/772–3244* 🌐 *www.flanigans.com* 🛏 *34 rooms* 🍴 *No meals.*

Shopping

Bumbleberry Gifts

CLOTHING | Next to the Bumbleberry Inn, this colorful souvenir shop is best known for its fresh-baked bumbleberry pies and bumbleberry jams. There's also fudge in a riot of flavors, along with both cheesy (fridge magnets, shot glasses) and more practical (mugs, caps, t-shirts, hoodies) gifts and keepsakes. ✉ *897 Zion Park Blvd.* ☎ *435/772–3224* 🌐 *www.bumbleberrygifts.com.*

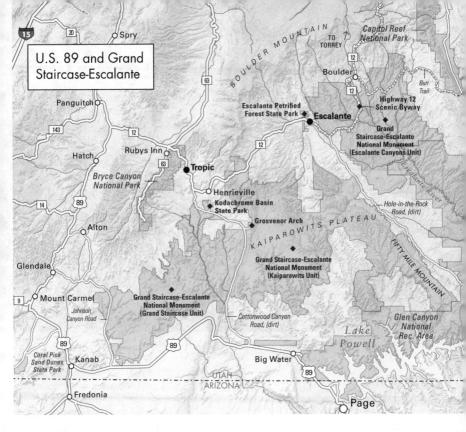

U.S. 89 and Grand Staircase-Escalante

David J. West Gallery

ART GALLERIES | The radiant photography of artist David West captures Zion's natural setting in its full grandeur, along with Bryce, Cedar Breaks, Arches, and other stunning spots throughout Utah and the Southwest. The gallery also stocks contemporary landscape paintings by Michelle Condrat and geologically inspired pottery by Bill Campbell. ⊠ *801 Zion Park Blvd.* ☎ *435/772–3510* ⊕ *www. davidjwest.com.*

Sol Foods Supermarket

FOOD/CANDY | Stop by this market specializing in healthy, organic foods for sandwiches, salads, and vegetarian snacks or box lunches for your adventures into the park. Also be sure to poke around the affiliated and well-stocked hardware and camping store next door. A few blocks closer to the park entrance, the owners also operate Hoodoos General Store, which dispenses espresso drinks, ice cream, pizza, and more gourmet goodies. ⊠ *995 Zion Park Blvd.* ☎ *435/772–3100* ⊕ *www.solfoods.com.*

★ **Worthington Gallery**

ART GALLERIES | The emphasis at this superb gallery set inside an 1880s pioneer home is on regional art, including pottery, works in glass, jewelry, beguiling copper wind sculptures by Lyman Whitaker, and paintings that capture the dramatic beauty of Southern Utah. ⊠ *789 Zion Park Blvd.* ☎ *435/772–3446* ⊕ *www. worthingtongallery.com.*

Grand Staircase–Escalante National Monument is the area's main draw.

Tropic

28 miles east of Panguitch.

Essentially an extension of nearby Bryce Canyon City and thus a similar base for exploring the majestic rock formations of Bryce Canyon National Park—many of which you can see from town—Tropic has around 500 residents and a handful of eateries and lodgings, some of them excellent. Keep in mind that many businesses shut down or greatly slow down in winter.

GETTING HERE AND AROUND

Just down the hill from Bryce Canyon, tiny Tropic is along Highway 12.

🍴 Restaurants

★ Stone Hearth Grille

$$$$ | **MODERN AMERICAN** | With sweeping panoramas toward Bryce Canyon from the back deck, an art-filled dining room with a stone fireplace, and some of the most accomplished modern American fare within an hour's drive of the park, this refined yet unpretentious restaurant on the outskirts of tiny Tropic is well worth a splurge. Favorites here include grilled artichoke with hollandaise sauce, radicchio Caesar salad, bone-in grilled pork chops with cheddar-potato fondue, and several preparations of local grass-fed steaks. **Known for:** breathtaking views; well-curated wine list; great children's menu. [$] *Average main: $31* ✉ *1380 W. Stone Canyon La., Tropic* ☎ *435/679–8923* 🌐 *www.stonehearthgrille.com* 🕓 *Closed Nov.–mid-Mar.*

🛏 Hotels

★ Stone Canyon Inn

$$$ | **B&B/INN** | Although not actually in the park, this stunningly situated luxury inn lies just east of Bryce Canyon, and rooms and the excellent on-site restaurant, Stone Hearth Grille, have astounding views of the park's hoodoos—there's even a trailhead nearby that accesses some of Bryce's best trails. **Pros:** the most stylish rooms in the area; fantastic

restaurant on-site; soaking tubs and fireplaces in some rooms. **Cons:** on the pricey side; not within walking distance of downtown shops and restaurants; no breakfast. $ *Rooms from: $195* ✉ *1380 W. Stone Canyon La., Tropic* ☎ *435/679–8611, 866/489–4680* ⊕ *www.stonecanyoninn.com* ⤴ *15 rooms* ❢◎❢ *No meals.*

Escalante

38 miles east of Tropic.

Though the Dominguez and Escalante expedition of 1776 came nowhere near this area, the town's name does honor the Spanish explorer. It was bestowed nearly a century later by a member of a survey party led by John Wesley Powell, charged with mapping this remote area. Today, this friendly little town is home to a steadily growing crop of lodgings, eateries, and tour operators. Escalante is the northern gateway to Grand Staircase–Escalante National Monument, an amazing 1.9-million acre wilderness that earned monument status in September 1996.

Unlike parks and monuments operated by the national park service, Grand Staircase–Escalante is administered by the Bureau of Land Management (BLM), and visiting its key attractions requires a bit more research and effort than, for example, Bryce or Capitol Reef, which are relatively more compact and accessible. A good way to plan your visit is to stop by one of the several visitor centers in the area, such as the Escalante Interagency office right in town or the BLM Visitor Center in Cannonville. If you're entering the monument from the south, you might also want to check out the BLM visitor centers in Kanab and Big Water. Given that many of this enormous national monument's top attractions are in remote areas with limited signage and accessed via unpaved roads, it may be

worth hiring one of the many experienced outfitters and guides in the area, especially if it's your first time in the area. You'll find more details about some of the monument's top attractions—including Calf Creek Falls and the several sites on or just off of Hole-in-the-Rock Road—in this section.

GETTING HERE AND AROUND

Escalante is accessible by Highway 12, one of the prettiest drives in the state, especially the stretch that runs north to Boulder. You can explore the vast Grand Staircase–Escalante National Monument via unpaved roads and sometimes pretty rough roads, ideally with a four-wheel-drive vehicle, although in dry weather, a passenger car can handle some areas. Most access points are off of Highway 12. It costs nothing to enter the park, but fees apply for camping and backcountry permits.

ESSENTIALS

VISITOR INFORMATION Cannonville BLM Visitor Center. ✉ *10 Center St., Cannonville* ☎ *435/826–5640* ⊕ *www.blm.gov.* **Escalante Interagency Visitor Center.** ✉ *755 W. Main St.* ☎ *435/826–5499* ⊕ *www.blm.gov/visit/escalante-interacgency-visitor-center.*

TOURS

In addition to the local guides listed below, also check the Kanab, Boulder, and Torrey tour sections, as most outfitters in those areas also offer Grand Staircase–Escalante adventures.

Escape Goats

SPECIAL-INTEREST | This noted family-owned operation offers a variety of day and evening hikes, multiday backpacking trips, and photo and artist tours, which can be customized to any ability or age. The company provides shuttle services, too. ✉ *Escalante* ☎ *435/826–4652* ⊕ *www.escalantecanyonguides.com* ⤴ *From $150.*

Excursions of Escalante

EXCURSIONS | Hiking, backpacking, photography, and canyoneering tours in the Escalante region are custom-fit to your needs and abilities by experienced guides. Canyoneers will be taken into the slot canyons to move through slot chutes or rappel down walls and other obstacles. All gear and provisions are provided whether it's a day hike or multiday adventure. ⊠ *125 E. Main St.* ☏ *800/839–7567, 435/826–4714* ⊕ *www.excursionsofescalante.com* 🖃 *From $155.*

★ Utah Canyon Outdoors

SPECIAL-INTEREST | Run by a young husband and wife team with extensive experience in Utah as naturalists and guides, this stellar outfitter also occupies an outdoor gear shop and coffeehouse in a charming little converted house in downtown Escalante. In addition to full-day hikes through slot canyons and the area's other dramatic features, the company also offers Escalante yoga experiences. ⊠ *325 W. Main St.* ☏ *435/826–4967* ⊕ *www.utahcanyonoutdoors.com* 🖃 *From $140.*

Sights

★ Calf Creek Falls Recreation Area

BODY OF WATER | **FAMILY** | One of the more easily accessible and rewarding adventures in the area, this picturesque canyon rife with oak trees and cacti and sandstone pictographs is reached via a 6-mile round-trip hike that starts at Calf Creek Campground, which is just 15 miles east of Escalante and 12 miles south of Boulder along scenic Highway 12. The big payoff, and it's especially pleasing on warm days, is a 126-foot spring-fed waterfall. The pool at the base is a beautiful spot for a swim or picnic. ⊠ *Hwy. 12* ☏ *435/826–5499* ⊕ *www.blm.gov/visit/lower-calf-creek-falls-trail* 🖃 *$5 per vehicle.*

Escalante Petrified Forest State Park

BODY OF WATER | **FAMILY** | This park just 2 miles outside Escalante protects a huge repository of petrified wood, easily spotted along two short but moderately taxing hiking trails (the shorter and steeper of the two, the Sleeping Rainbows Trail requires some scrambling over boulders). Of equal interest is the park's Wide Hollow Reservoir, which has a swimming beach and is popular for kayaking, standup paddling, trout fishing, and birding. ⊠ *710 N. Reservoir Rd.* ☏ *435/826–4466* ⊕ *stateparks.utah.gov* 🖃 *$8 per vehicle.*

Hell's Backbone Road

SCENIC DRIVE | For a scenic, topsy-turvy backcountry drive or a challenging mountain-bike ride, follow 35-mile Hell's Backbone Road (aka Forest Road 153) from Escalante, where it begins as Posey Lake Road, to Boulder. Built by the Civilian Conservation Corps in the early 1930s, it's a gravel-surface alternate route that's arguably even more spectacular than scenic Highway 12. You can make the drive with an ordinary passenger car in summer (it's impassable in winter), assuming dry conditions, but a four-wheel-drive vehicle is more comfortable. Allow about two hours to drive it. ⊠ *Hell's Backbone Rd.* ⊕ *www.fs.usda.gov/dixie.*

★ Highway 12 Scenic Byway

SCENIC DRIVE | Keep your camera handy and steering wheel steady along this entrancing 123-mile route between Escalante and Torrey, just west of Capitol Reef National Park. Though the highway starts at the intersection of U.S. 89, west of Bryce Canyon National Park, the stretch that begins in Escalante is one of the most spectacular. Be sure to stop at the scenic overlooks; almost every one will give you an eye-popping view, and information panels let you know what you're looking at. Pay attention while driving, though; the paved road is twisting and steep, and at times climbs over a hogback with sheer drop-offs on both sides. ⊠ *Hwy. 12.*

Hole-in-the-Rock Road

NATIONAL/STATE PARK | On the way to southeastern Utah in 1879, Mormon pioneers chipped and blasted a narrow passageway in solid rock, through which they lowered their wagons. The Hole-in-the-Rock Trail, now a very rugged 60-mile unpaved washboard road (aka BLM 200), leads south from Highway 12, 5 miles east of Escalante, to the actual hole-in-the-rock site in Glen Canyon Recreation Area. The original passageway ends where the canyon has been flooded by the waters of Lake Powell—you can hike the half-mile from the end of the road to a dramatic viewpoint overlooking the lake. Just keep in mind that it can take up to three hours to drive to the end of the road, and high-clearance vehicles are best (and a requirement when muddy—check with the Escalante BLM visitor center before setting out). However, there are some amazing hiking spots located off the road, including Zebra Slot Canyon (at mile 8.5), Devil's Garden (at mile 12), Peekaboo Gulch (off Dry Fork Road, at mile 26), and Dance Hall Rock (at mile 36). ✉ *Hole in the Rock Road* ☎ *435/826–5499* 🌐 *www.nps.gov/glca.*

★ **Kodachrome Basin State Park**

NATIONAL/STATE PARK | **FAMILY** | Yes, it is named after the old-fashioned color photo film, and once you see it you'll understand why the National Geographic Society gave it the name. The stone spires known as "sand pipes" cannot be found anywhere else in the world. Hike any of the trails to spot some of the 67 pipes in and around the park. The short Angels Palace Trail takes you quickly into the park's interior, up, over, and around some of the badlands. Note that the oft-photographed Shakespeare Arch collapsed in April 2019, although the trail leading to it is still open. ✉ *off Cottonwood Canyon Rd., Cannonville* ☎ *435/679–8562* 🌐 *stateparks.utah.gov* 🎟 *$10 per vehicle.*

🍴 Restaurants

★ **Escalante Outfitters**

$ | **MODERN AMERICAN** | This warm and inviting log cabin–style restaurant—part of a popular tour operator, camp store, and cabin and camping compound—is a great place to sit back and relax after a day of hiking, fly-fishing, or road-tripping. Try one of the creatively topped pizzas, a veggie sandwich, or an apple-pecan-arugula salad, or drop in for one of the best cups of (fair trade) coffee in the region, and a light breakfast to kick off the day. **Known for:** one of the better craft beer selections in the region; lively and fun dining room; fine coffees, quiches, and pastries in the morning. [$] *Average main: $12* ✉ *310 W. Main St.* ☎ *435/826–4266* 🌐 *www.escalanteoutfitters.com.*

☕ Coffee and Quick Bites

★ **Kiva Koffeehouse**

$ | **CAFÉ** | This fun stop along scenic Highway 12 at mile marker 73.86, 13 miles east of Escalante, was constructed by the late artist and inventor Bradshaw Bowman, who began building it when he was in his eighties and spent two years finding and transporting the 13 Douglas-fir logs surrounding the structure. The distinctive eatery with amazing views serves homemade soups, bagel sandwiches, salads, and desserts, and an array of espresso drinks. **Known for:** breathtaking canyon views; breakfast sandwiches and bagels; housemade pies and cupcakes. [$] *Average main: $10* ✉ *7386 Hwy. 12* ☎ *435/826–4550* 🌐 *www.kivakoffeehouse.com* 💳 *No credit cards* 🕒 *Closed Nov.–Mar. and Tues. No dinner.*

🛏 Hotels

Canyon Country Lodge

$$ | **HOTEL** | A boutique hotel on the outskirts of town, just off Highway 12, Canyon Country Lodge contains 28 spacious rooms—many of them with northerly views toward Escalante Canyon—comfortably outfitted with smart TVs, microwaves, refrigerators, and modern tile bathrooms. **Pros:** stylishly decorated; nice indoor pool and hot tub; close to but just outside downtown. **Cons:** 15-minute walk to most dining options; on-site restaurant gets mixed reviews; no elevator. $ *Rooms from: $159* ⊠ *760 E. Hwy. 12* ☎ *435/826–4545, 844/367–3080* ⊕ *www.canyoncountry-lodge.com* ⇆ *28 rooms* ⓘ *Free breakfast.*

Circle D Motel

$ | **HOTEL** | Although there's nothing fancy about this low-slung adobe motel on the edge of downtown Escalante, the simple rooms have all the basics you need for a comfortable night or two, including microwaves, fridges, coffeemakers, HDTVs, and individual climate control, and one larger suite can sleep six and has a kitchenette. **Pros:** short walk from downtown businesses; casual restaurant with a pleasant patio; among the lowest rates in the area. **Cons:** standard rooms are small; no pool or gym; no breakfast. $ *Rooms from: $85* ⊠ *475 W. Main St.* ☎ *435/826–4297* ⊕ *www.escalantecircledmotel.com* ⇆ *22 rooms* ⓘ *No meals.*

★ Entrada Escalante Lodge

$$ | **HOTEL** | Each of the eight rooms in this smart, contemporary lodge in Escalante has a patio with grand views of the surrounding mountains, plus plenty of cushy perks like French presses and fresh-ground coffee, plush bedding, and 50-inch smart TVs. **Pros:** great restaurant; stunning views of Grand Staircase–Escalante National Monument; pets, including horses, are welcome. **Cons:** books up well ahead many weekends; in a very secluded, small town; no gym or pool. $ *Rooms from: $149* ⊠ *480 W. Main St.* ☎ *435/826–4000* ⊕ *www.entradaescalante.com* ⇆ *8 rooms* ⓘ *No meals.*

Escalante Outfitters

$ | **B&B/INN** | A one-stop shop for planning and buying gear for your outdoor adventure, or if you're traveling on a budget and don't care about amenities, the seven log

bunkhouse cabins here share a single bathhouse, and tent sites are also available (there's also one larger family cabin that sleeps four and has its own bath). **Pros:** firepit, grills, and picnic tables; pet-friendly; lots of tours available. **Cons:** cabins are tiny; you may have to wait in line for a shower; some cabins have only bunk beds. $ *Rooms from: $55* ⊠ *310 W. Main St.* ☎ *435/826–4266* ⊕ *www.escalanteoutfitters.com* ⇆ *8 cabins* ⓘ *No meals.*

★ Slot Canyons Inn B&B

$$ | **B&B/INN** | In a dramatic, New Mexico adobe–style building 5 miles west of town, this upscale inn with spacious rooms and lots of big windows is set at the mouth of a canyon on the edge of the national monument—in fact, there's hiking right outside your door, and the hosts can provide guidance on other great treks in the region. **Pros:** utterly peaceful and enchanting setting; within a short hike of petroglyphs and dramatic cliffs; many rooms have jetted soaking tubs. **Cons:** very remote setting; the one economically priced room is a little small; not within walking distance of town. $ *Rooms from: $135* ⊠ *3680 Hwy. 12* ☎ *435/826–4901, 866/889–8375* ⊕ *www.slotcanyonsinn.com* ⇆ *11 rooms* ⓘ *Free breakfast.*

 Nightlife

★ 4th West Pub

BARS/PUBS | In a part of the world where nightlife typically consists of listening to coyotes howl beneath a starlit sky, it's nice to have one good late-night (late meaning 10 or 11 pm, depending on the season) option. 4th West Pub is a great place to socialize, shoot pool, and sip craft beer and cocktails. In this stylishly converted 1940s former service station, there's live music, art classes, trivia matches, and other fun events some evenings, and the kitchen turns out an array of tasty bar snacks, from nachos to panini. ⊠ *425 W. Main St.* ☎ *435/826–4525* ⊕ *www.4wpub.com.*

Chapter 11

ARCHES
NATIONAL PARK

11

Updated by
Stina Sieg

👁 **Sights**
★★★★★

🍴 **Restaurants**
★★★☆☆

🛏 **Hotels**
★★★★★

🛍 **Shopping**
★★★★☆

🍸 **Nightlife**
★★☆☆☆

WELCOME TO
ARCHES NATIONAL PARK

TOP REASONS TO GO

★ **Arch appeal:** Nowhere in the world has as large an array or quantity of natural arches.

★ **Legendary landscape:** A photographer's dream—no wonder it's been the chosen backdrop for many Hollywood films.

★ **Treasures hanging in the balance:** Landscape Arch and Balanced Rock look like they might topple any day. And they could—the features in this park erode and evolve constantly.

★ **Fins and needles:** Fins are thin, parallel walls of eroding rock that slowly disintegrate into tower-like "needles." The spaces around and between them will carve their way into your memories like the wind and water that formed them.

Southeastern Utah's Arches National Park boasts some of the most unimaginable rock formations in the world. Off U.S. 191, Arches (along with Canyonlands National Park) is in Moab, 230 miles southeast of Salt Lake City and 27 miles south of Interstate 70.

1 Devils Garden. 18 miles from the visitor center, this is the end of the paved road in Arches. It has the park's only campground, a picnic area, and access to drinking water. Trails in Devils Garden lead to Landscape Arch and several other noteworthy formations.

2 Fiery Furnace. About 14 miles from the visitor center this area is so labeled because its orange spires of rock look much like tongues of flame. Reservations are required, and can be made up to six months in advance, to join the twice-daily ranger-guided treks, or you can obtain a permit to visit Fiery Furnace on your own, but only experienced, well-prepared hikers should attempt this option.

3 Delicate Arch/Wolfe Ranch. A spur road about 11.7 miles from the visitor center leads to the moderately strenuous 3-mile round-trip trail and viewpoints for the park's most famous feature—Delicate Arch. To see it from below, follow the road to the viewpoint, then walk to either easily accessible viewing area.

4 The Windows. Reached on a spur 9.2 miles from the visitor center, here you can see many of the park's natural arches from your car or on an easy rolling trail.

5 Balanced Rock. This giant rock teeters atop a pedestal, creating a 128-foot formation of red rock grandeur right along the roadside, about 9 miles from the visitor center.

6 Petrified Dunes. Just a tiny pull-out about 5 miles from the visitor center, stop here for pictures of acres and acres of petrified sand dunes.

7 Courthouse Towers. The Three Gossips, Sheep Rock, and Tower of Babel are all here. Enter this section of the park 3 miles past the visitor center. The Park Avenue Trail winds through the area.

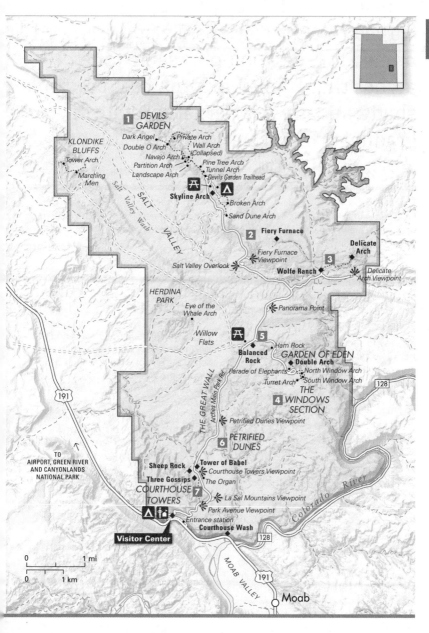

1 DEVILS GARDEN

KLONDIKE BLUFFS
Tower Arch
Marching Men

Dark Angel
Double O Arch
Navajo Arch
Partition Arch
Landscape Arch
Private Arch
Wall Arch (Collapsed)
Pine Tree Arch
Tunnel Arch
Devils Garden Trailhead
Skyline Arch
Broken Arch
Sand Dune Arch

SALT VALLEY
Salt Valley Wash

2 Fiery Furnace
Fiery Furnace Viewpoint
Salt Valley Overlook

3 Delicate Arch
Wolfe Ranch
Delicate Arch Viewpoint

HERDINA PARK
Eye of the Whale Arch
Willow Flats
Panorama Point

5 Ham Rock
Balanced Rock
GARDEN OF EDEN
Double Arch
North Window Arch
South Window Arch
Parade of Elephants
Turret Arch
4 THE WINDOWS SECTION

THE GREAT WALL
Arches Main Park Rd
Petrified Dunes Viewpoint

6 PETRIFIED DUNES

Sheep Rock
Tower of Babel
Courthouse Towers Viewpoint
Three Gossips
The Organ
7 COURTHOUSE TOWERS
La Sal Mountains Viewpoint
Park Avenue Viewpoint
Entrance station
Courthouse Wash

Visitor Center

TO AIRPORT, GREEN RIVER AND CANYONLANDS NATIONAL PARK

191
128
Colorado River

0   1 mi
0   1 km

MOAB VALLEY
191
Moab

More than 1.5 million visitors come to Arches annually, drawn by the red rock landscape and its wind- and water-carved rock formations. The park is named for the 2,000-plus sandstone arches that frame horizons, cast precious shade, and are in a perpetual state of gradual transformation, the result of constant erosion.

Fancifully named attractions like Three Penguins, Queen Nefertiti, and Tower of Babel stir curiosity, beckoning visitors to stop and marvel. Immerse yourself in this spectacular landscape, but don't lose yourself entirely—summer temperatures frequently exceed 100°F, and water is hard to come by inside the park boundaries.

It's easy to spot some of the arches from your car, but take the time to step outside and walk beneath the spans and giant walls of orange rock. This gives you a much better idea of their proportion. You may feel as writer Edward Abbey did when he awoke on his first day as a park ranger in Arches: that you're walking in the most beautiful place on Earth.

It's especially worthwhile to visit as the sun goes down. At sunset, the rock formations glow, and you'll often find photographers behind their tripods waiting for magnificent rays to descend on Delicate Arch or other popular sites. The Fiery Furnace earns its name as its narrow fins glow red just before the sun dips below the horizon. Full-moon nights are particularly dramatic in Arches as the creamy white Navajo sandstone reflects light, and eerie silhouettes are created by towering fins and formations.

Planning

When to Go

The busiest times of year are spring and fall. In the spring blooming wildflowers herald the end of winter, and temperatures in the 70s and 80s bring the year's largest crowds. The crowds remain steady in summer as the thermostat often exceeds 100°F and above in July and August. Sudden dramatic cloudbursts create rainfalls over red rock walls in late-summer "monsoon" season.

Fall means clear, warm days and crisp, cool nights. The park is much quieter in winter, and from December through February you can hike many of the trails in relative solitude. Snow occasionally falls in the valley beneath La Sal Mountains, and when it does, Arches is a photographer's paradise, with a serene white dusting over slickrock mounds and natural rock windows.

Arches in One Day

There's no food service in the park, so pack snacks, lunch, and plenty of water and electrolytes before you head into Arches. Also plan ahead to get tickets to the daily ranger-led Fiery Furnace walks, held spring through fall. It's a highlight for those who are adventurous and in good shape (see *Ranger Programs* for details). The one-day itinerary below is based on what to do on a day that you can't visit Fiery Furnace. If you do take a Fiery Furnace walk, you should also have time to drive the park road and perhaps walk on the Park Avenue Trail. If you have a third day, take a rafting trip on the nearby Colorado River.

Start as early as sunrise for cool temperatures and some of the best natural light, and head out on the 3-mile round-trip hike on the **Delicate**

Arch Trail. The route is strenuous but extremely rewarding. Next head to **Devils Garden**, another great spot for morning photography, where you'll also find the easy, primarily flat trail to **Landscape Arch**, the second of the park's two must-see arches. If you're a fairly experienced hiker, continue on to **Double O**, but note that this portion of the trail is moderately difficult. Along the way, picnic in the shade of a juniper or in a rock alcove. By the time you return you'll be ready to see the rest of the park by car, with some short strolls on easy paths.

In the mid- to late afternoon, drive to **Balanced Rock** for photos, then on to **Windows.** Depending on what time the sun is due to set, go into town for dinner before or after you drive out to Delicate Arch or along the park road to watch the sun set the rocks aglow.

11

Arches National Park PLANNING

AVERAGE HIGH/LOW TEMPERATURES					
JAN.	**FEB.**	**MAR.**	**APR.**	**MAY**	**JUNE**
44/22	52/28	64/35	71/42	82/51	93/60
JULY	**AUG.**	**SEPT.**	**OCT.**	**NOV.**	**DEC.**
100/67	97/66	88/55	74/42	56/30	45/23

Getting Here and Around

AIR
Moab is served by tiny Canyonlands Field Airport, which has daily service to Denver on United Airlines and a couple of car rental agencies. The nearest midsize airport is Grand Junction Regional Airport in Grand Junction, Colorado, which is approximately 110 miles from Moab and is served by several major airlines.

CAR
The park entrance is just off U.S. 191 on the north side of downtown Moab, 28 miles south of Interstate 70 and 130 miles north of the Arizona border. Arches is also about 30 miles from the Island in the Sky section and 80 miles from the Needles District of Canyonlands National Park. If you're driving to Arches from points east on Interstate 70, consider taking Exit 214 in Utah (about 50 miles west of Grand Junction, CO), and continuing south on picturesque Highway 128, the Colorado River Scenic Byway, about 50 miles to

Moab. Bear in mind that services can be sparse on even major roads in these parts.

Branching off the main, 18-mile park road—officially known as Arches Scenic Road—are two spurs, one 2½ miles to the Windows section and one 1.6 miles to Delicate Arch trailhead and viewpoint. There are several four-wheel-drive roads in the park; always check at the visitor center for conditions before attempting to traverse them. The entrance road into the park can back up midmorning to early afternoon during busy periods. You'll encounter less traffic early in the morning or at sunset.

Park Essentials

ACCESSIBILITY

Not all park facilities meet federally mandated accessibility standards, but as visitation to Arches increases, the park continues efforts to increase accessibility. Visitors with mobility impairments can access the visitor center, all park restrooms, and two campsites in the Devils Garden Campground (4H is first-come, first served, while site 7 can be reserved up to six months in advance Mar.–Oct.). The Park Avenue Viewpoint is a paved path with a slight decline near the end, and both Delicate Arch and Balanced Rock viewpoints are partially hard-surfaced. For those with visual disabilities, visitor center exhibits include audio recordings and some tactile elements. You can also request an audio version of the park brochure (or listen to it on the park website ⊕ www.nps.gov/arch). Large-print and braille versions of park information are also available at the visitor center.

PARK FEES AND PERMITS

Admission to the park is $30 per vehicle, $25 per motorcycle, and $15 per person entering on foot or bicycle, valid for seven days. To encourage visitation to the park during less busy times, a $50 local park pass grants you admission to both Arches and Canyonlands parks as well as

Natural Bridges and Hovenweep national monuments for one year.

PARK HOURS

Arches National Park is open year-round, seven days a week, around the clock. It's in the Mountain time zone.

CELL PHONE RECEPTION

Cell phone reception is spotty in the park and in general is strongest whenever the La Sal mountains are visible. There are pay phones outside the visitor center.

Hotels

Though there are no hotels or cabins in the park itself, in the surrounding area every type of lodging is available, from economy chain motels to B&Bs and high-end, high-adventure resorts. It's important to know when popular events are held, however, as accommodations can, and do, fill up weeks ahead of time.

Restaurants

In the park itself, there are no dining facilities and no snack bars. Supermarkets, bakeries, and delis in downtown Moab will be happy to make you food to go. If you bring a packed lunch, there are several picnic areas from which to choose.

Visitor Information

PARK CONTACT INFORMATION Arches National Park. ⊠ N. U.S. 191 ☎ 435/719–2299 ⊕ www.nps.gov/arch.

VISITOR CENTER

Arches Visitor Center
With well-designed hands-on exhibits about the park's geology, wildlife, and history; helpful rangers; a water station; and a bookstore; the center is a great way to start your park visit. It also has picnic tables and something that's rare in the park: cell service for many carriers. ⊠ N. U.S. 191 ☎ 435/719–2299 ⊕ nps.gov/arch.

Devils Garden

18 miles north of the visitor center.

At the end of the paved road in Arches, Devils Garden is the most developed area of the park, with the park's only campground and drinking water. It's also the site of the busiest trailheads.

 ## Sights

GEOLOGICAL FORMATIONS
Skyline Arch
NATURE SITE | FAMILY | A quick walk from the parking lot at Skyline Arch, 16½ miles from the park entrance, gives you closer views and better photos. The short trail is less than a half mile round-trip and only takes a few minutes to travel. ⊠ *Devils Garden Rd.*

SCENIC DRIVES
★ Arches Main Park Road
SCENIC DRIVE | The main park road and its two short spurs are extremely scenic and allow you to enjoy many park sights from your car. The main road leads through Courthouse Towers, where you can see Sheep Rock and the Three Gossips, then alongside the Great Wall, the Petrified Dunes, and Balanced Rock. A drive to the Windows section takes you to attractions like Double Arch, and you can see Skyline Arch along the roadside as you approach the Devils Garden campground. The road to Delicate Arch allows hiking access to one of the park's main features. Allow about two hours to drive the 45-mile round trip, more if you explore the spurs and their features and stop at viewpoints along the way. ⊠ *Arches National Park.*

PICNIC AREAS
★ Devils Garden
NATIONAL/STATE PARK | FAMILY | There are grills, water, picnic tables, and restrooms here and, depending on the time of day, some shade from junipers and rock walls. It's a good place for lunch before

or after a hike. ⊠ *End of main road, 18 miles from park entrance.*

TRAILS
Broken Arch Trail
TRAIL | An easy walk across open grassland, this loop trail passes Broken Arch, which is also visible from the road. The arch gets its name because it appears to be cracked in the middle, but it's not really broken. The trail is 1¼ miles round trip, but you can extend your adventure to about 2 miles round trip by continuing north past Tapestry Arch and through Devils Garden Campground. *Easy.* ⊠ *Arches National Park ⊹ Trailhead: off Devils Garden Rd., 16½ miles from park entrance.*

★ Devils Garden Trail
TRAIL | Landscape Arch is a highlight of this trail but is just one of several arches within reach, depending on your ambitions. It's an easy ¾-mile one-way (mostly gravel, relatively flat) trip to Landscape Arch, one of the longest stone spans in the world. Beyond Landscape Arch the scenery changes dramatically and the hike becomes more strenuous, as you must climb and straddle slickrock fins and negotiate some short, steep inclines. Finally, around a sharp bend, the stacked spans that compose Double O Arch come suddenly into view. Allow up to three hours for this round-trip hike of just over 4 miles. For a still longer (about a 7-mile round-trip) and more rigorous trek, venture on to see a formation called Dark Angel and then return to the trailhead on the primitive loop, making the short side hike to Private Arch. The hike to Dark Angel is a difficult route through fins. Other possible (and worthwhile) detours lead to Navajo Arch, Partition Arch, Tunnel Arch, and Pine Tree Arch. Allow about five hours for this adventure, take plenty of water, and watch your route carefully. Pick up the park's useful guide to Devils Garden, or download it from the website before you go. *Moderate–Difficult.* ⊠ *Arches National Park ⊹ Trailhead: on Devils Garden Rd., end of main road, 18 miles from park entrance.*

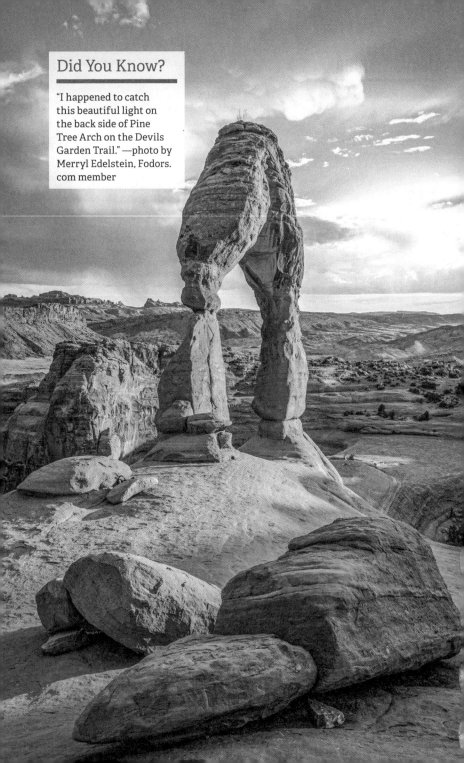

Did You Know?

"I happened to catch this beautiful light on the back side of Pine Tree Arch on the Devils Garden Trail." —photo by Merryl Edelstein, Fodors. com member

Landscape Arch

TRAIL | This natural rock opening, which measures 306 feet from base to base and looks like a delicate ribbon of rock bending over the horizon, is the longest geologic span in North America. In 1991, a slab of rock about 60 feet long, 11 feet wide, and 4 feet thick fell from the underside, leaving it even thinner. You reach it via a rolling, gravel, 1.6-mile-long trail. *Easy–Moderate.* ⊠ *Arches National Park* ✛ *Trailhead: at Devils Garden Rd., at end of main road, 18 miles north of park entrance.*

Tower Arch Trail

TRAIL | Check with park rangers before attempting the dirt road through Salt Valley to Klondike Bluffs parking area. If rains haven't washed out the road, a trip to this seldom-visited area provides a solitude-filled hike culminating in a giant rock opening. Allow from two to three hours for this 3½-mile round-trip hike, not including the drive. *Moderate.* ⊠ *Arches National Park* ✛ *Trailhead: at Klondike Bluffs parking area, 24½ miles from park entrance, 7¾ miles off main road.*

Fiery Furnace

14 miles north of hte park entrance.

Fewer than 10% of the park's visitors ever descend into the chasms and washes of Fiery Furnace (a permit or a ranger-led hike is the only way to go), but you can gain an appreciation for this twisted, unyielding landscape from the Overlook. At sunset, the rocks glow a vibrant flamelike red, which gives the formation its daunting moniker.

 Sights

TOURS

★ Fiery Furnace Walk

TOUR—SIGHT | Join a park ranger on a 2½-hour scramble through a labyrinth of rock fins and narrow sandstone canyons.

You'll see arches and other eye-popping formations that can't be viewed from the road. You should be very fit and not afraid of heights or confined spaces for this moderately strenuous experience. Wear sturdy hiking shoes, sunscreen, and a hat, and bring at least a liter of water. Guided walks into the Fiery Furnace are offered mid-April through September, usually a few times a day (hours vary), and leave from Fiery Furnace Viewpoint, about 15 miles from the park visitor center. Tickets for the morning walks must be reserved (at ⊕ *www.recreation. gov*) and are available beginning six months in advance and up to four days before the day of the tour. Tickets for afternoon Fiery Furnace walks must be purchased in person at the park visitor center, ideally as soon as you arrive in Moab and as far ahead as seven days before your hike. Children ages 5–12 are charged half-price; kids under 5 are not allowed. Book early as the program usually fills months prior to each walk. ⊠ *Arches National Park* ✛ *Trailhead: on Arches Scenic Dr.* ▦ *$16* ☾ *Guided hikes not offered Oct.–mid-April.*

TRAILS

Fiery Furnace

TRAIL | This area of the park has taken on a near-mythical lure for park visitors, who are drawn to challenging yet breathtaking terrain. Rangers strongly discourage inexperienced hikers from entering here—in fact, you can't enter without watching a video about how to help protect this very special section of the park and obtaining a permit ($6). Reservations can be made up to six months in advance to get a spot on the 2-mile round-trip ranger-led hikes ($16), offered mid-April–September, through this unique formation. A hike through these rugged rocks and sandy washes is challenging but fascinating. Hikers will need to use their hands at times to scramble up and through narrow cracks and along vertigo-inducing ledges above drop-offs, and there are no trail markings. If you're not familiar with the

Furnace you can easily get lost or cause damage, so watch your step and use great caution. For information about reservations, see Ranger Programs Overview above. The less intrepid can view Fiery Furnace from the Overlook off the main road. *Difficult.* ☒ *Arches National Park* ⊹ *Trailhead: off main road, about 14 miles from park entrance.*

Sand Dune Arch Trail

TRAIL | FAMILY | You may return to the car with shoes full of bright red sand from this giant sandbox in the desert—it's fun exploring in and around the rock. Set aside five minutes for this shady, 530-yard walk and plenty of time if you have kids, who will love playing amid this dramatic landscape. Never climb on this or any other arch in the park, no matter how tempting—it's illegal, and it could result in damage to the fragile geology or personal injury. The trail intersects with the Broken Arch Trail—you can visit both arches with an easy 1½-mile round-trip walk. *Easy.* ☒ *Arches National Park* ⊹ *Trailhead: off Arches Scenic Dr., about 16½ miles from park entrance.*

Delicate Arch/ Wolfe Ranch

13 miles north of the park entrance.

The iconic symbol of the park and the state (it appears on many of Utah's license plates), Delicate Arch is tall and prominent compared to many of the spans in the park—it's big enough that it could shelter a four-story building. The arch is a remnant of an Entrada Sandstone fin; the rest of the rock has eroded and it now frames La Sal Mountains in the background. Drive 2.2 miles off the main road to the viewpoint to see the arch from a distance, or hike right up to it from the trailhead that starts near Wolfe Ranch. The trail, 1.2 miles off the main road, is a moderately strenuous 3-mile

round-trip hike with no shade or access to water. It's especially picturesque shortly after sunrise or before sunset.

Sights

HISTORIC SIGHTS

Wolfe Ranch

HISTORIC SITE | Civil War veteran John Wesley Wolfe and his son started a small ranch here in 1888. He added a cabin in 1906 when his daughter Esther and her family came west to live. Built out of Fremont cottonwoods, the rustic one-room cabin still stands on the site. Look for remains of a root cellar and a corral as well. Even older than these structures is the nearby Ute rock-art panel by the Delicate Arch trailhead. About 150 feet past the footbridge and before the trail starts to climb, you can see images of bighorn sheep and figures on horseback, as well as some smaller images believed to be dogs. ☒ *Off Delicate Arch Rd.*

TRAILS

★ Delicate Arch Trail

TRAIL | To see the park's most famous freestanding arch up close takes effort and won't offer you much solitude—but it's worth every step. The 3-mile round-trip trail ascends via steep slickrock, sandy paths, and along one narrow ledge (at the very end) that might give pause to anyone afraid of heights. Plus, there's almost no shade. First-timers should start early to avoid the midday heat in summer. Still, at sunrise, sunset, and every hour in between, it's the park's busiest trail. Bring plenty of water, especially in the warmer months, as heatstroke and dehydration are very real possibilities. Allow two to three hours, depending on your fitness level and how long you care to linger at the arch. If you go at sunset or sunrise, bring a headlamp or flashlight. Don't miss Wolfe Ranch and some ancient rock art near the trailhead. *Moderate–Difficult.* ☒ *Arches National Park* ⊹ *Trailhead: on Delicate Arch Rd., 13 miles from park entrance.*

A hike the "The Windows" is 1-mile round-trip.

The Windows

11¾ miles north of the park entrance.

As you head north from the park entrance, turn right at Balanced Rock to find this concentration of natural windows, caves, and needles. Stretch your legs on the easy paths that wind between the arches and soak in a variety of geological formations.

Sights

GEOLOGICAL FORMATIONS
Double Arch

NATURE SITE | In the Windows section of the park, 11¾ miles from the park entrance, Double Arch has appeared in several Hollywood movies, including *Indiana Jones and the Last Crusade.* From the parking lot you can also take the short and easy Window Trail to view North Window, South Window, and Turret Arch. ⊠ *The Windows Rd.*

TRAILS
Double Arch Trail

TRAIL | FAMILY | If it's not too hot, it's a simple walk to here from Windows Trail. This relatively flat trek leads to two massive arches that make for great photo opportunities. The ½-mile round trip gives you a good taste of desert flora and fauna. *Easy.* ⊠ *Arches National Park* ⊹ *Trailhead: 2½ miles from main road, on Windows Section spur road.*

The Windows

TRAIL | FAMILY | An early stop for many visitors to the park, a trek through the Windows gives you an opportunity to get out and enjoy the desert air. Here you'll see three giant openings in the rock and walk on a trail that leads right through the holes. Allow about an hour on this gently inclined, 1-mile round-trip hike. As most visitors don't follow the "primitive" trail around the backside of the two windows, take advantage if you want some desert solitude. The primitive trail adds an extra half hour to the hike. *Easy.* ⊠ *Arches National Park*

274

⚓ Trailhead: on the Windows Rd., 12 miles from park entrance.

Balanced Rock

9¼ miles north of the park entrance.

One of the park's favorite sights, this rock is visible for several minutes as you approach—and just gets more impressive and mysterious as you get closer. The formation's total height is 128 feet, with the huge balanced rock rising 55 feet above the pedestal. Be sure to hop out of the car and walk the short (⅓-mile) loop around the base.

 Sights

PICNIC AREAS
Balanced Rock Picnic Area
VIEWPOINT | The view is the best part of this picnic spot opposite Balanced Rock parking area. There's no water, but there are tables. If you sit just right you might find some shade under a small juniper; otherwise, this is an exposed site. Pit toilets are nearby. ⊠ *9¼ miles from park entrance on main road.*

TRAILS
Balanced Rock Trail
TRAIL | FAMILY | You'll want to stop at Balanced Rock for photo ops, so you may as well walk the easy, partially paved trail around the famous landmark. This is one of the most accessible trails in the park and is suitable even for small children. The 15-minute stroll is only about ⅓ mile round trip. *Easy.* ⊠ *Arches National Park ⚓ Trailhead: approximately 9¼ miles from park entrance.*

Park Avenue Trail
TRAIL | The first named trail that park visitors encounter, this is a relatively easy, 2-mile round-trip walk (with only one small hill but a somewhat steep descent into the canyon) amid walls and towers that vaguely resemble a New York City skyline. You'll walk under the gaze of

Queen Nefertiti, a giant rock formation that some observers think has Egyptian-looking features. If you are traveling with companions, make it a one-way, 1-mile downhill trek by having them pick you up at the Courthouse Towers Viewpoint. Allow about 45 minutes for the one-way journey. *Easy–Moderate.* ⊠ *Arches National Park ⚓ Trailhead: 2 miles from park entrance on main park road.*

Petrified Dunes

5 miles north of the visitor center.

 Sights

Petrified Dunes
NATURE SITE | FAMILY | Just a tiny pull-out, this memorable stop features acres upon acres of reddish-gold, petrified sand dunes. There's no trail here, so roam as you like while keeping track of where you are. If you do lose your way, heading west will take you back to the main road. ⊠ *Arches National Park ⚓ 6 miles from park entrance.*

Courthouse Towers

3 miles north of the visitor center.

This collection of towering rock formations looks unreal from a distance and even more breathtaking up close. The Three Gossips does indeed resemble a gaggle of wildly tall people sharing some kind of secret. Sheep Rock is right below, with the massive Tower of Babel just a bit north. Enter this section of the park 3 miles past the visitor center. The extremely popular Park Avenue Trail winds through the area.

◉ Sights

SCENIC STOPS
Courthouse Wash
NATURE SITE | Although this rock-art panel fell victim to an unusual case of vandalism in 1980, when someone scoured the petroglyphs and pictographs that had been left by four cultures, you can still see ancient images if you take a short walk from the parking area on the left-hand side of the road, heading south. ⊠ *U.S. 191, about 2 miles south of Arches entrance.*

Activities

Arches lies in the middle of one of the adventure capitals of the United States. Deep canyons and towering walls are everywhere you look. Thousand-foot sandstone walls draw rock climbers from across the globe. Hikers can choose from shady canyons or red rock ridges that put you in the company of the West's big sky. The Colorado River forms the southeast boundary of the park and can give you every grade of white-water adventure. Moab-based outfitters can set you up for just about any sport you may have a desire to try: mountain biking, ATVs, dirt bikes, four-wheel-drive vehicles, kayaking, climbing, stand-up paddleboarding, and even skydiving. Within the park, it's best to stick with basics such as hiking, sightseeing, and photography. Climbers and other adventure seekers should always inquire at the visitor center about restrictions, which can also be seen on the park's website.

BIRD WATCHING
Within the park you'll definitely see plenty of the big, black, beautiful ravens. Look for them perched on top of a picturesque juniper branch or balancing on the bald knob of a rock. Noisy black-billed magpies populate the park, as do the more melodic canyon and rock wrens. Lucky visitors may spot a red-tailed hawk and hear its distinctive call. Serious birders will have more fun visiting the Nature Conservancy's Scott M. Matheson Wetlands Preserve, 5 miles south of the park. The wetlands is home to more than 200 species of birds including the wood duck, western screech owl, indigo bunting, and plumbeous vireo.

CANYONEERING
Desert Highlights
CLIMBING/MOUNTAINEERING | This guide company takes adventurous types on descents and ascents through canyons (with the help of ropes), including those found in the Fiery Furnace at Arches National Park. Full-day and multiday canyoneering treks are available to destinations both in and near the national parks. ⊠ *16 S. 100 E, Moab* ☎ *435/259–4433* ⊕ *www.deserthighlights.com* ✉ *From $105.*

CAMPING
Campgrounds in and around Arches range from sprawling RV parks with myriad amenities to quaint, shady retreats near a babbling brook. The Devils Garden Campground in the park is a wonderful spot to call home for a few days, though it is often full and lacks an RV dump station. More than 350 campsites are operated in the vicinity by the Bureau of Land Management—their sites on the Colorado River and near the Slickrock Trail are some of the nicest (and most affordable, at just $20/night) in the area. The most centrally located campgrounds in Moab generally accommodate RVs.

IN THE PARK
Devils Garden Campground. This campground is one of the most unusual—and gorgeous—in the West, and in the national park system, for that matter. ⊠ *End of main road, 18 miles from park entrance* ☎ *435/719–2299, 877/444–6777 for reservations* ⊕ *www.recreation.gov.*

OUTSIDE THE PARK
Bureau of Land Management Campgrounds.
Most of the 350 sites at 26 different
BLM campgrounds are in the Moab area,
including some stunning sites along
the Colorado River (Highway 128 and
Highway 279), Sand Flats Recreation
Area (near the Slickrock Trail), and Canyon
Flats Recreation Area (outside Needles
District of Canyonlands). ☎ *435/259–2100*
⊕ *www.blm.gov/utah/moab.*

Canyonlands RV Resort and Campground.
Although this camping park is in downtown Moab, the campground is astride
Pack Creek and has many shade trees.
✉ *555 S. Main St., Moab* ☎ *435/259–
6848 or 877/415–3991* ⊕ *www.
sunrvresorts.com/resorts/west/utah/
canyonlands-rv-resort-campground/.*

Moab Valley RV Resort and Campground.
Near the Colorado River, this campground with an expansive view feels
more like a mall than a campground
with its abundant space, activities, and
services. ✉ *1773 N. U.S. 191, Moab*
☎ *435/259–4469 or 877/418–8535*
⊕ *www.sunrvresorts.com/resorts/west/
utah/moab-valley/.*

Slickrock Campground.
At one of Moab's
older campgrounds you'll find lots of
mature shade trees and all the basic
amenities, plus a swimming pool.
✉ *1415 N. Main St., Moab* ☎ *435/259–
7660 or 888/991–5329* ⊕ *www.
sunrvresorts.com/resorts/west/utah/
slickrock-campground/.*

Up the Creek Campground.
Perhaps the
quietest of the in-town campgrounds, Up
the Creek lies under big cottonwoods on
the banks of Mill Creek. ✉ *210 E. 300 S,
Moab* ☎ *435/260–1888* ⊕ *www.moab-
campground.com.*

FOUR-WHEELING
With thousands of acres of nearby
Bureau of Land Management lands to
enjoy, it's hardly necessary to use the
park's limited trails for four-wheel adventures. You can, however, go backcountry

riding in Arches on the Willow Flats Road.
Parallel to the Salt Valley Road is also a
dirt track simply called the 4 Wheel Drive
Road, which is very sandy and requires
experienced drivers. Don't set out for
an expedition without first stopping at
the visitor center to learn of current
conditions.

HIKING
Getting out on any one of the park trails
will surely cause you to fall in love with
this Mars-like landscape. But remember,
you are hiking in a desert environment
and approximately 1 mile above sea level.
Many people succumb to heat and dehydration because they do not drink enough
water. Park rangers recommend a gallon of
water per day per person, plus electrolytes.

ROCK CLIMBING AND CANYONEERING
Rock climbers travel from across the
country to scale the sheer red rock walls
of Arches National Park and surrounding
areas. Most climbing routes in the park
require advanced techniques. Permits are
not required, but climbers are encouraged
to register for a free permit, either online
or at a kiosk outside the visitor center.
Climbers are responsible for knowing park
regulations, temporary route closures,
and restricted routes. Two popular routes
ascend Owl Rock in the Garden of Eden
(about 10 miles from the visitor center);
the well-worn route has a difficulty of
5.8, while a more challenging option is
5.11 on a scale that goes up to 5.13-plus.
Many climbing routes are available in the
Park Avenue area, about 2.2 miles from
the visitor center. These routes are also
extremely difficult climbs. No commercial
outfitters are allowed to lead rock-climbing
excursions in the park, but guided canyoneering (which involves ropes, rappelling,
and some basic climbing) is allowed, and
permits are required for canyoneering.
Before climbing, it's imperative that you
stop at the visitor center and check with a
ranger about climbing regulations.

Chapter 12

CANYONLANDS NATIONAL PARK

Updated by
Stina Sieg

⊙ Sights   🍴 Restaurants   🛏 Hotels   🛍 Shopping   🍸 Nightlife

★★★★★   ★★★☆☆   ★★★★★   ★★★★☆   ★★☆☆☆

WELCOME TO
CANYONLANDS NATIONAL PARK

TOP REASONS TO GO

★ **Endless vistas:** The view from Island in the Sky stretches for miles as you look out over millennia of sculpting by wind and rain.

★ **Seeking solitude:** Needles, an astoundingly beautiful part of the park to explore on foot, sees very few visitors—it can sometimes feel like you have it all to yourself.

★ **Radical rides:** The Cataract Canyon rapids and the White Rim Trail are world-class adventures by boat or bike.

★ **Native American artifacts:** View rock art and Ancestral Puebloan dwellings in the park.

★ **Wonderful wilderness:** Some of the country's most untouched landscapes are within the park's boundaries, and they're worth the extra effort needed to get there.

★ **The night skies:** Far away from city lights, Canyonlands is ideal for stargazing.

Canyonlands National Park, in southeastern Utah, is divided into three distinct land districts, as well as the separate Horseshoe Canyon, so it can be a little daunting to visit. It's exhausting, but not impossible, to explore the Island in the Sky and Needles in the same day. For many, rafting through the waterways is the best way to see the park. The Green and Colorado, while very different today as a result of man-made dams than when John Wesley Powell explored them in the mid-1800s, are spectacular.

1 **Island in the Sky.** From any of the overlooks here you can see for miles and look down thousands of feet to canyon floors. Chocolate-brown canyons are capped by white rock, and deep-red monuments rise nearby.

2 **Needles.** Pink, orange, and red rock is layered with white rock and stands in spires and pinnacles around grassy meadows. Extravagantly red mesas and buttes interrupt the horizon as in a picture postcard of the Old West.

3 **The Maze.** Only the most intrepid adventurers explore this incredibly remote mosaic of rock formations. There's a reason Butch Cassidy hid out here.

4 **Horseshoe Canyon.** Plan on several hours of dirt-road driving to get here, but the famous rock-art panel "Great Gallery" is a grand reward at the end of a long hike.

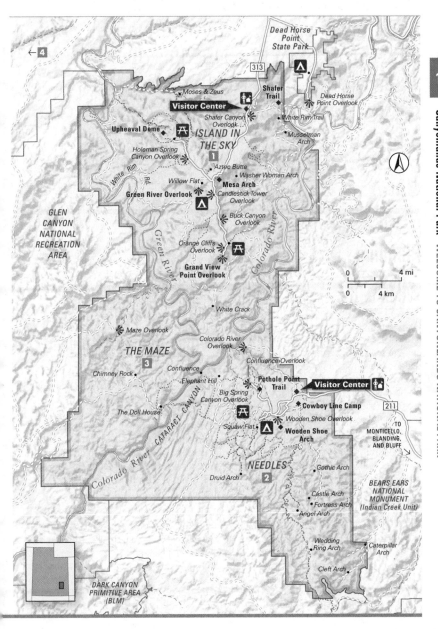

Canyonlands is truly four parks in one, but the majority of visitors drive through the panoramic vistas of Island in the Sky and barely venture anywhere else. Plan a day to explore the Needles district and see the park from the bottom up. Float down the Green and Colorado rivers on a family-friendly rafting trip, or take on the white water in the legendary Cataract Canyon.

Planning

When to Go

Gorgeous weather means that spring and fall are most popular. Canyonlands is seldom crowded, but in spring backpackers and four-wheelers populate the trails and roads. During Easter week, some of the four-wheel-drive trails in the park are used for Jeep Safari, an annual event drawing thousands of visitors to Moab.

The crowds thin out by July as the thermostat reaches 100°F and higher for about four weeks. It's a great time to get out on the Colorado or Green River winding through the park. October can be a little rainy, but the region receives only 8 inches of rain annually.

The well-kept secret is that winter, except during occasional snow storms, can be a great time to tour the park. Crowds are gone, snowcapped mountains stand in the background, and key roads in Island in the Sky and Needles

are well-maintained (although it's wise to check the park website for conditions). Winter here is one of nature's most memorable shows, with red rock dusted white and low-floating clouds partially obscuring canyons and towers.

Getting Here and Around

AIR
Moab is served by tiny Canyonlands Field Airport, which has daily service to Denver on SkyWest/United Airlines and a couple of car rental agencies. The nearest mid-sized airport is Grand Junction Regional Airport in Grand Junction, Colorado, which is approximately 110 miles from Moab and is served by most major airlines.

CAR
Off U.S. 191, Canyonlands' Island in the Sky Visitor Center is 29 miles from Arches National Park and 32 miles from Moab on Highway 313 west of U.S. 191; the Needles District is 80 miles from Moab and reached via Highway 211, 34 miles west of U.S. 191.

Canyonlands in One Day

Your day begins with a choice: Island in the Sky or Needles. If you want expansive vistas looking across southeast Utah's canyons, head for the island, where you stand atop a giant mesa. If you want to walk among Canyonlands' spires and buttes, Needles is your destination. If you have a second or third day in the area, consider contacting an outfitter to take you on a rafting or 4X4 trip.

■ TIP→ **Before venturing into the park, top off your gas tank, pack a picnic lunch, and stock up on plenty of water and electrolytes.**

Island in the Sky

Make your first stop along the main park road at the visitor center to learn about ranger talks or special programs. Next visit **Shafer Canyon Viewpoint,** where a short walk takes you out on a finger of land with views of the canyon over both sides. From here you can see Shafer Trail's treacherous descent as it hugs the canyon walls below.

Then drive to **Mesa Arch.** Grab your camera and water bottle for the short hike out to the arch perched on the cliff's edge. After your excursion, take the spur road to Upheaval Dome, with its picnic spot in the parking lot.

A short walk takes you to the first viewpoint of this crater. If you still have energy, 30 more minutes and a little sense of adventure, continue to the second overlook.

Retrace your drive to the main park road and continue to **Grand View Point.** Stroll along the edge of the rim, and see how many landmarks you can spot in the distance. White Rim Overlook is the best of the scenic spots, particularly if you're not afraid of heights and venture all the way out to the end of the rocky cliffs (no guardrail here). On the way back to dinner in Moab, spend an hour in Dead Horse Point State Park.

Needles

If you can stay overnight as well, then begin the day by setting up camp at Needles Campground or one of the other wonderful group camping areas in Needles. Then hit the **Joint Trail,** or any of the trails that begin from the campground, and spend the day hiking in the backcountry. Save an hour for the brief but terrific little hike to **Cave Springs,** and be sure to drive to the end of the park road to check out Big Spring Canyon Overlook. Sleep under countless stars.

12

Canyonlands National Park PLANNING

AVERAGE HIGH/LOW TEMPERATURES					
JAN.	FEB.	MAR.	APR.	MAY	JUNE
44/22	52/28	64/35	71/42	82/51	93/60
JULY	AUG.	SEPT.	OCT.	NOV.	DEC.
100/67	97/66	88/55	74/42	56/30	45/23

Before starting a journey to any of Canyonlands' three districts, make sure your gas tank is topped off, as there are no services inside the large park. The

Maze is especially remote, 135 miles from Moab, and actually a bit closer (100 miles) to Capitol Reef National Park. In the Island in the Sky District, it's about 12 miles from the entrance station to Grand View Point, with a 5-mile spur to Upheaval Dome. The Needles scenic drive is 10 miles from the entrance station, with two spurs, about 3 miles each. Roads in the Maze—suitable only for high-clearance, four-wheel-drive vehicles—wind for hundreds of miles through the rugged canyons. Within the parks, it's critical that you park only in designated pull-outs or parking areas.

Park Essentials

ACCESSIBILITY
There are currently no trails in Canyonlands accessible to people in wheelchairs, but Grand View Point, Buck Canyon Overlook, and Green River Overlook at Island in the Sky are wheelchair accessible. In Needles, the visitor center, restrooms, Squaw Flat Campground, and Wooden Shoe Overlook are wheelchair accessible. The visitor centers at the Island in the Sky and Needles districts are also accessible, and the park's pit toilets are accessible with some assistance.

PARK FEES AND PERMITS
Admission is $30 per vehicle, $15 per person on foot or bicycle, and $25 per motorcycle, good for seven days. Your Canyonlands pass is good for all the park's districts. There's no entrance fee to the Maze District of Canyonlands. A $55 local park pass grants you admission to both Arches and Canyonlands as well as Natural Bridges and Hovenweep national monuments for one year.

You need a permit for overnight backpacking, four-wheel-drive camping, river trips, and mountain-bike camping. Online reservations can be made four months in advance on the park website (⊕ www. nps.gov/cany). Four-wheel-drive day use in Salt, Horse, and Lavender canyons and all motorized vehicles and bicycles on the Elephant Hill and White Rim trails also require a permit, which you can obtain

online up to 24 hours before your trip or in person at visitor centers.

PARK HOURS
Canyonlands National Park is open 24 hours a day, seven days a week, year-round. It is in the Mountain time zone.

CELL PHONE RECEPTION
Cell phone reception may be available in some parts of the park, but not reliably so. Public telephones are at the park's visitor centers.

Restaurants

There are no dining facilities in the park, although Needles Outpost campground, a mile from Needles Visitor Center, has a small solar-powered store with snacks and drinks. Moab has a multitude of dining options, and there are a few very casual restaurants in Blanding (in Blanding, restaurants don't serve alcohol and are typically closed Sunday), plus a couple of excellent eateries a bit farther south in Bluff.

Hotels

There is no lodging in the park. Most visitors—especially those focused on Island in the Sky—stay in Moab or perhaps Green River, but the small towns of Blanding and Bluff—which have a smattering of motels and inns—are also convenient for exploring the Needles District.

Visitor Information

Stop by the **Island in the Sky Visitor Center** or **Needles District Visitor Center** for restrooms and water (water is seasonal at Island in the Sky, but there's no food service or general store in either section). In addition, the remote **Hans Glat Ranger Station** in the Maze has a pit toilet but no water or food.

PARK CONTACT INFORMATION Canyonlands National Park. ☎ 435/719–2313
⊕ www.nps.gov/cany.

Island in the Sky

Sights

SCENIC DRIVES

Island in the Sky Park Road

SCENIC DRIVE | This 12-mile-long main road
inside the park is bisected by a 5-mile
side road to the Upheaval Dome area.
To enjoy dramatic views, including the
Green and Colorado river basins, stop at
the overlooks and take the short walks.
Once you get to the park, allow at least
two hours—and ideally four—to explore.
⊠ *Island in the Sky.*

SCENIC STOPS

Green River Overlook

VIEWPOINT | From the road it's just 100
yards to this stunning view of the Green
River to the south and west. It's not
far from Island in the Sky (Willow Flat)
campground. ⊠ *About 1 mile off Upheaval Dome Rd., Island in the Sky ⊹ 7 miles
from visitor center.*

White Rim Overlook Trail

VIEWPOINT | The cliffs fall away on three
sides at the end of this one-mile level
hike until you get a dramatic view of the
White Rim and Monument Basin. There
are restrooms at the trailhead. ⊠ *Grand
View Point, Island in the Sky.*

TRAILS

Aztec Butte Trail

TRAIL | The highlight of the 2-mile round-
trip hike is the chance to see Ancestral
Puebloan granaries. The view into Taylor
Canyon is also nice. *Moderate.* ⊠ *Island
in the Sky ⊹ Trailhead: Upheaval Dome
Rd., about 7 miles from visitor center.*

★ Grand View Point Trail

TRAIL | This 360-degree view is the main
event for many visitors to Island in the
Sky. Look down on the deep canyons

of the Colorado and Green rivers, which
have been carved by water and erosion
over the millennia. Many people just stop
at the paved overlook and drive on, but
you'll gain breathtaking perspective by
strolling along this 2-mile round-trip, flat
cliffside trail. On a clear day you can see
up to 100 miles to the Maze and Needles
districts of the park and each of Utah's
major laccolithic mountain ranges: the
Henrys, Abajos, and La Sals. *Easy.* ⊠ *End
of main park road, Island in the Sky ⊹ 12
miles from visitor center.*

★ Mesa Arch Trail

TRAIL | If you don't have time for the
2,000 arches in nearby Arches National
Park, you should take the easy, half-mile
round-trip walk to Mesa Arch. After the
overlooks this is the most popular trail
in the park. The arch is above a cliff that
drops 800 feet to the canyon bottom.
Through the arch, views of Washerwom-
an Arch and surrounding buttes, spires,
and canyons make this a favorite photo
opportunity. ⊠ *Off main park road, Island
in the Sky ⊹ 6 miles from visitor center.*

Shafer Trail

TRAIL | This rough trek that leads to the
100-mile White Rim Road was probably first established by ancient Native
Americans, but in the early 1900s
ranchers used it to drive cattle into the
canyon. Originally narrow and rugged, it
was upgraded during the uranium boom,
when miners hauled ore by truck from
the canyon floor. Check out the road's
winding route down canyon walls from
Shafer Canyon Overlook before you drive
it to see why it's mostly used by daring
four-wheelers and energetic mountain
bikers. Off the main road, less than 1
mile from the park entrance, it descends
1,400 feet to the White Rim. Check with
the visitor center about road conditions
before driving the Shafer Trail. It's often
impassable after rain or snow. ⊠ *Island
in the Sky.*

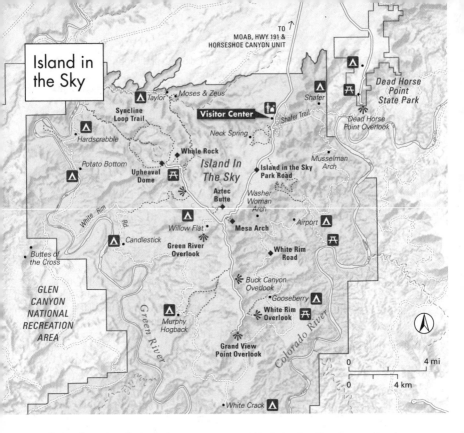

Island in the Sky

TO
MOAB, HWY 191 &
HORSESHOE CANYON UNIT

Taylor • Moses & Zeus
Syncline Loop Trail
Visitor Center
Shafer Trail
Dead Horse Point State Park
Dead Horse Point Overlook
Hardscrabble
Neck Spring
Whale Rock
Potato Bottom
Upheaval Dome
Island In The Sky
Island in the Sky Park Road
Musselman Arch
White Rim Rd
Aztec Butte
Washer Woman Arch
Buttes of the Cross
Candlestick
Willow Flat
Green River Overlook
Mesa Arch
Airport
White Rim Road
GLEN CANYON NATIONAL RECREATION AREA
Green River
Buck Canyon Overlook
Gooseberry
White Rim Overlook
Murphy Hogback
Grand View Point Overlook
Colorado River

0   4 mi
0   4 km

• White Crack

★ Upheaval Dome Trail

TRAIL | This mysterious crater is one of the wonders of Island in the Sky. Some geologists believe it's an eroded salt dome, but others think it was made by a meteorite. Either way, it's worth the steep hike to see it and decide for yourself. The moderate hike to the first overlook is about a half-mile; energetic visitors can continue another half-mile to the second overlook for an even better perspective. The trail is steeper and rougher after the first overlook. Round trip to the second overlook is 2 miles. The trailhead has restrooms and a picnic area. *Moderate.* ⊠ *End of Upheaval Dome Rd., Island in the Sky* ✛ *11 miles from visitor center.*

Whale Rock Trail

TRAIL | If you've been hankering to walk across some of that pavement-smooth stuff they call slickrock, the hike to

Whale Rock will make your feet happy. This 1-mile round-trip adventure, which culminates with a tough final 100-foot climb and features some potentially dangerous dropoffs, takes you to the very top of the whale's back. Once you get there, you are rewarded with great views of Upheaval Dome and Trail Canyon. *Moderate.* ⊠ *Island in the Sky* ✛ *Trailhead: Upheaval Dome Rd., 10 miles from visitor center.*

VISITOR CENTER

★ Island in the Sky Visitor Center

INFO CENTER | The gateway to the world-famous White Rim Trail, this visitor center 21 miles from U.S. 191 draws a mix of mountain bikers, hikers, and tourists. Enjoy the orientation film, then browse the bookstore for information about the region. Exhibits help explain animal adaptations as well as some of the history of the park. Check the website or at the center for a daily schedule of ranger-led programs. ⊠ *Off Hwy. 313, Island in the Sky* ☎ *435/259–4712* ⊙ *Closed late Dec.– early Mar.*

Needles

⊙ Sights

HISTORIC SIGHTS
Cowboy Camp

HISTORIC SITE | FAMILY | This fascinating stop on the 0.6-mile round-trip **Cave Spring Trail** is an authentic example of cowboy life more than a century ago. You do not need to complete the entire trail (which includes two short ladders and some rocky hiking) to see the 19th-century artifacts at Cowboy Camp. ⊠ *End of Cave Springs Rd., Needles* ⊹ *2.3 miles from visitor center.*

SCENIC DRIVES
Needles District Park Road

SCENIC DRIVE | You'll feel like you've driven into a Hollywood Western as you roll along the park road in the Needles District. Red mesas and buttes rise against the horizon, blue mountain ranges interrupt the rangelands, and the colorful red-and-white needles stand like soldiers on the far side of grassy meadows. Definitely hop out of the car at a few of the marked roadside stops, including both overlooks at Pothole Point. Allow at least two hours in this less-traveled section of the park. ⊠ *Needles.*

SCENIC STOPS
Needles District Picnic Area

VIEWPOINT | The most convenient picnic spot in the Needles District is a sunny location on the way to Big Spring Canyon Overlook. There are picnic tables, but no other amenities. ⊠ *Needles* ⊹ *Main park road, 5 miles west of visitor center.*

Wooden Shoe Arch Overlook

VIEWPOINT | FAMILY | Kids enjoy looking for the tiny window in the rock that looks like a wooden shoe with a turned-up toe. If you can't find it on your own, there's a marker to help you. ⊠ *Off main park road, Needles* ⊹ *2 miles from visitor center.*

TRAILS
★ Cave Spring Trail

TRAIL | One of the best, most interesting trails in the park takes you past a historic cowboy camp, precontact rock art, and great views. Two wooden ladders and one short, steep stretch may make this a little daunting for the extremely young or old, but it's also a short hike (0.6 mile round trip), features some shade, and has many notable features. *Moderate.* ⊠ *Needles* ⊹ *Trailhead: end of Cave Springs Rd., 2.3 miles from visitor center.*

★ Joint Trail

TRAIL | Part of the Chesler Park Loop, this trail follows a series of deep, narrow fractures in the rock. A shady spot in summer, it will give you good views of the Needles formations for which the district is named. The loop travels briefly along a four-wheel-drive road and is 11 miles round trip; allow at least five hours to complete it. *Difficult.* ⊠ *Needles* ⊹ *Trailhead: Elephant Hill parking lot, 6 miles from visitor center.*

Pothole Point Trail

TRAIL | Microscopic creatures lie dormant in pools that fill only after rare rainstorms. When the rains do come, some eggs hatch within hours and life becomes visible. If you're lucky, you'll hit Pothole Point after a storm. The dramatic views of the Needles and Six Shooter Peak make this easy, 0.6-mile round trip worthwhile. Plan for about 45 minutes. There's no shade, so wear a hat and take plenty of water. ⊠ *Off main road, Needles* ⊹ *5 miles from visitor center.*

12

Canyonlands National Park NEEDLES

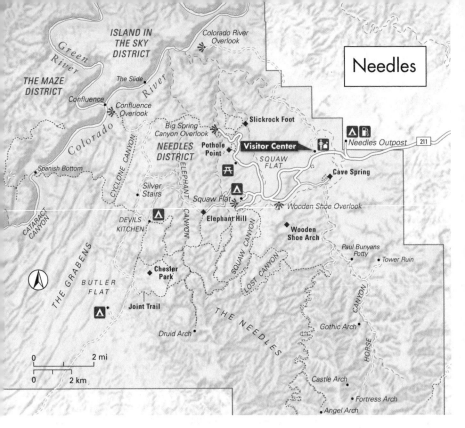

ISLAND IN
THE SKY
DISTRICT

Colorado River
Overlook

THE MAZE
DISTRICT

Green River

The Slide

Confluence

Confluence
Overlook

Colorado River

Slickrock Foot

Big Spring
Canyon Overlook

NEEDLES
DISTRICT

Pothole
Point

Visitor Center

Needles Outpost

211

Spanish Bottom

CYCLONE CANYON

Silver
Stairs

ELEPHANT CANYON

Squaw Flat

SQUAW
FLAT

Cave Spring

Wooden Shoe Overlook

CATARACT CANYON

THE GRABENS

DEVILS
KITCHEN

Elephant Hill

SQUAW CANYON

LOST CANYON

Wooden
Shoe Arch

Paul Bunyans
Potty

Tower Ruin

BUTLER
FLAT

Chesler
Park

Joint Trail

THE NEEDLES

CANYON

Gothic Arch

Druid Arch

HORSE CANYON

Castle Arch

0   2 mi

0   2 km

Fortress Arch

Angel Arch

Needles

Slickrock Trail

TRAIL | Wear a hat and carry plenty of water
if you're on this trail—you won't find any
shade along the 2.4-mile round-trip trek.
This is the rare frontcountry site where you
might spot one of the few remaining native
herds of bighorn sheep in the national
park system. Nice panoramic views. *Easy.*
⊠ *Needles* ✛ *Trailhead: main park road, 6
miles from visitor center.*

VISITOR CENTER
Needles District Visitor Center

INFO CENTER | This gorgeous building is
34 miles from U.S. 191 via Highway
211, near the park entrance. Needles is
remote, so it's worth stopping to inquire
about road, weather, and park conditions.
You can also watch the interesting orientation film, refill water bottles, and get
books, trail maps, and other information.
⊠ *off Hwy. 211, Needles* ☎ *435/259–4711*
🕐 *Closed late Nov.–early Mar.*

The Maze

Sights

VISITOR CENTER
Hans Flat Ranger Station

INFO CENTER | Only experienced and
intrepid visitors will likely ever visit this
remote outpost—on a dirt road 46 miles
east of Highway 24 in Hanksville. The
office is a trove of books, maps, and
other documents about the unforgiving
Maze District of Canyonlands, but rangers will strongly dissuade any inexperi-
enced off-road drivers and backpackers
to proceed into this truly rugged wilderness. Just to get here you must drive 46
miles on a dirt road that is sometimes
impassable even to 4X4 vehicles. There's
a pit toilet, but no water, food, or services
of any kind. If you're headed for the backcountry, permits cost $30 per group for

up to 14 days. Rangers offer guided hikes in Horseshoe Canyon on most weekends in spring and fall. ■TIP→ **Call the ranger station for road conditions leading to Horseshoe Canyon/Hans Flat, as rain can make travel difficult.** ⊠ *Jct. of Recreation Rds. 777 and 633, Maze* ☎ *435/259–2652.*

Horseshoe Canyon

◉ Sights

Horseshoe Canyon Trail

TRAIL | This remote region of the park is accessible by dirt road, and only in good weather. Park at the lip of the canyon and hike 7 miles round trip to the Great Gallery, considered by some to be the most significant rock-art panel in North America. Ghostly life-size figures in the Barrier Canyon style populate the amazing panel. The hike is moderately strenuous, with a 700-foot descent. Allow at least six hours for the trip and take a gallon of water per person. There's no camping allowed in the canyon, although you can camp on top near the parking lot. *Difficult.*
■TIP→ **Call Hans Flat Ranger Station before heading out, because rain can make the access road a muddy mess.** ⊠ *Horseshoe Canyon* ✛ *Trailhead: 32 miles east of Hwy. 24.*

Activities

AERIAL TOURS

Redtail Air Adventures

TOUR—SPORTS | This company's daily, regional tours give you an eagle's-eye view of the park, and you'll walk away with new respect and understanding of the word "wilderness." The Canyonlands Tour, one of several flightseeing options, lasts for one hour. A two-person minimum applies. ⊠ *Canyonlands Field Airport, 94 W. Aviation Way, Moab* ✛ *Off U.S. 191* ☎ *435/259–7421* ⊕ *flyredtail. com* ✉ *From $184 per person.*

BICYCLING

In addition to the company listed below, **Rim Tours** and **Western Spirit Cycling Adventures** offer tours in both Arches and Canyonlands.

Magpie Cycling

BICYCLING | Professional guides and mountain biking instructors lead groups (or lone riders) on daylong and multiday bike trips exploring the Moab region's most memorable terrain, including the White Rim, Needles, and the Maze. If you need to rent a bike, Magpie can meet you at its preferred shop, Poison Spider Bicycles (☎ *800/635–1792* ⊕ *poisonspiderbicycles.com*). ⊠ *Moab* ☎ *435/259–4464* ⊕ *www.magpiecycling. com* ✉ *Day tours from $150, multiday from $875.*

RECOMMENDED TRAILS

Mountain bikers from all over the world like to brag that they've conquered the 100 miles of **White Rim Road.** The trail's fame is well-deserved: it traverses steep roads, broken rock, and dramatic ledges, as well as long stretches that wind through the canyons and look down onto others. If you're biking White Rim without an outfitter, you'll need careful planning, vehicle support, and much sought-after backcountry reservations. Permits are available no more than four months, and no less than two days, prior to permit start date. There is a 15-person, three-vehicle limit for groups. Day-use permits are also required and can be obtained at the Island in the Sky visitor center or reserved 24 hours in advance through the park's website. Follow the turn-off about 1 mile from the entrance, then 11 miles further along Shafer Trail in Island in the Sky.

BOATING AND RAFTING

In Labyrinth Canyon, north of the park boundary, and in Stillwater Canyon, in the Island in the Sky District, the river is quiet and calm and there's plenty of shoreside camping. The Island in the Sky leg of the Colorado River, from Moab to its confluence with the Green River

Serious mountain bikers traverse all 100 miles of White Rim Road.

and downstream a few more miles to Spanish Bottom, is ideal for both canoeing and for rides with an outfitter in a large, stable jet boat. If you want to take a self-guided flat-water float trip in the park you must obtain a $30 permit, which you have to request by mail or fax. Make your upstream travel arrangements with a shuttle company before you request a permit. For permits, contact the reservation office at park headquarters (☎ 435/259–4351).

Below Spanish Bottom, about 64 miles downstream from Moab, 49 miles from the Potash Road ramp, and 4 miles south of the confluence, the Colorado churns into the first rapids of legendary Cataract Canyon. Home of some of the best white water in the United States, this piece of river between the Maze and the Needles districts rivals the Grand Canyon stretch of the Colorado River for adventure. During spring melt-off these rapids can rise to staggering heights and deliver heart-stopping excitement. The canyon cuts through the very heart of Canyonlands, where you can see this amazing wilderness area in its most pristine form. The water calms down a bit in summer. Outfitters will take you for the ride of your life in this wild canyon, where the river drops more steeply than anywhere else on the Colorado River (in ¾ mile, the river drops 39 feet). You can join an expedition lasting anywhere from one to six days, or you can purchase a $20 permit for a self-guided trip from park headquarters.

Oars

WHITE-WATER RAFTING | FAMILY | This well-regarded outfitter can take you for several days of rafting the Colorado, Green, and San Juan rivers. Hiking/interpretive trips are available in Canyonlands and Arches. ✉ *Moab* ☎ *435/259–5865, 800/346–6277* ⊕ *www.oars.com/utah* 🖃 *From $109.*

Sheri Griffith Expeditions

BOATING | FAMILY | In addition to trips through the white water of Cataract, Westwater, and Desolation canyons, on the Colorado and Green rivers, this company also offers specialty expeditions for women, writers, photographers, and families. One of their more luxurious expeditions features dinners cooked by a professional chef and served on linen-covered tables. Cots and other sleeping amenities also make roughing it a little more comfortable. ✉ *2231 S. U.S. 191, Moab* ☎ *435/259–8229, 800/332–2439* ⊕ *www.griffithexp.com* ✈ *From $185.*

CAMPING

Canyonlands campgrounds are some of the most beautiful in the national park system. At the Needles District, campers will enjoy fairly private campsites tucked against red rock walls and dotted with pinyon and juniper trees. At Island in the Sky, starry nights and spectacular vistas make the small campground an intimate treasure. Hookups are not available in either of the park's campgrounds; however, some sites are long enough to accommodate units up to 28 feet long.

IN THE PARK
Needles Campground. The defining features of the camp sites at Squaw Flat are house-size red rock formations, which provide some shade, offer privacy from adjacent campers, and make this one of the more unique campgrounds in the national park system. ✉ *Off main road, about 3 miles from park entrance, Needles* ☎ *435/259–4711.*

Willow Flat Campground. From this little campground on a mesa top, you can walk to spectacular views of the Green River. Most sites have a bit of shade from juniper trees. ✉ *Off main park road, about 7 miles from park entrance, Island in the Sky* ☎ *435/259–4712.*

OUTSIDE THE PARK
Dead Horse Point State Park Campground. But for the name, this gem of a site has every attribute of a great national park campground: a stunning location and view atop a mesa, well-maintained pads, room for RVs, and a canopy of infinite

stars nightly. It fills up at about the same pace as the national park campgrounds. ✉ *Dead Horse Point State Park, Hwy. 313* ☎ *435/259–2614* ⊕ *www.stateparks. utah.gov.*

FOUR-WHEELING
RECOMMENDED TRAILS
Winding around and below the Island in the Sky mesa top, the dramatic, 100-mile **White Rim Road** is not just for bikers. It offers a once-in-a-lifetime driving experience for four-wheeling as well. As you tackle Murphy's Hogback, Hardscrabble Hill, and more formidable obstacles, you will get some fantastic views of the park. Attempting to travel the loop in one day is not recommended—plan instead to camp overnight with advance reservations, which can be made up to four months in advance (book ASAP for busy spring and fall weekends). Day-use permits, which are available at the park visitor center or 24 hours in advance through the park website, are required for motorized and bicycle trips on White Rim Road. Bring plenty of water, a spare tire, and a jack, as no services are available on the road. White Rim Road starts at the end of Shafer Trail.

This remote, rugged **Flint Trail** is the most popular in the Maze District, but it's not an easy ride. It has 2 miles of switchbacks that drop down the side of a cliff face. You reach Flint Trail from the Hans Flat Ranger Station, 46 miles from the closest paved road. From Hans Flat to the end of the road at the Doll House it's a 41-mile drive that takes at least six hours one-way. The Maze is not recommended as a day trip, so you'll have to purchase an overnight backcountry permit for $30. Despite its remoteness, the Maze District can fill to capacity during spring and fall, so plan ahead.

The first 3 miles of the **Elephant Hill Trail** in the Needles District are passable by all vehicles, but don't venture out without asking about road conditions. For the rest of the trail, only 4X4 vehicles are allowed.

The route is so difficult that many people get out and walk—it's faster than you can drive it in some cases. The trek from Elephant Hill Trailhead to Devil's Kitchen is 3½ miles; from the trailhead to the Confluence Overlook, it's a 14½-mile round trip and requires at least eight hours. Don't attempt this without a well-maintained 4X4 vehicle and spare gas, tires, and off-road knowledge. A day-use permit, which is available at the park visitor center or 24 hours in advance through the park website, is required for motorized and bicycle trips on the Elephant Hill Trail.

HIKING

At Canyonlands National Park you can immerse yourself in the intoxicating colors, smells, and textures of the desert. ⚠ **Make sure to bring water and electrolytes, as dehydration is the number-one cause of search-and-rescue calls here.**

ISLAND IN THE SKY

Island in the Sky has several easy and moderate hikes that are popular with day-trippers, including the **Aztec Butte Trail, Grand View Point Trail, Upheaval Dome Trail,** and **Whale Rock Trail.** ⇨ *For more information on these popular trails, see Sights.*

If you're up for a strenuous day of hiking, try the 8-mile **Syncline Loop Trail,** which follows the canyons around Upheaval Dome. You get limited views of the dome itself as you actually make a complete loop around the outside of the crater. This challenging trek—best avoided during the hot summer months—requires some route-finding and scrambling through boulder fields, plus tackling some steep switchbacks—the total elevation gain is 1,300 feet. Carry a map, a flashlight, and extra water and food. You'll get some sheltering afternoon shade if you hike the trail clockwise. The trailhead is on Upheaval Dome Road, 12 miles from the park entrance.

NEEDLES

Both the **Cave Spring Trail** and **Slickrock Trail** are popular with day-trippers to the Needles section of Canyonlands, suitable for most hikers young or old, though the former requires one to climb two wooden ladders. Others are considerably more difficult and require experience.

Chesler Park is a grassy meadow dotted with spires and enclosed by a circular wall of colorful "needles." One of Canyonlands' more popular trails, the **Chesler Viewpoint Trail,** leads through the area to the famous **Joint Trail,** one of the park's star attractions, though a moderately difficult hike.

Chapter 13

MOAB AND SOUTHEASTERN UTAH

Updated by
Stina Sieg

◉ Sights
★★★★★

🍴 Restaurants
★★★☆☆

🛏 Hotels
★★★☆☆

🛍 Shopping
★★☆☆☆

🍸 Nightlife
★☆☆☆☆

WELCOME TO
MOAB AND SOUTHEASTERN UTAH

TOP REASONS TO GO

★ **Beauty from another world:** The terra-cotta expanse of open desert here is unparalleled.

★ **Get out and play:** Mountain and road biking, rafting, rock climbing, hiking, four-wheeling, and cross-country skiing are all wildly popular.

★ **Creature comforts:** Though remote, southeastern Utah—and Moab, in particular—has an array of lodging and dining options, including elegant bistros, fancy hotels, and quaint bed-and-breakfasts.

★ **Catch a festival:** Especially in the spring and summer months, this area is chock-full of gatherings focused on art, music, and recreation.

★ **Another state of being:** There's something about being in such intense beauty so far from everything that creates a friendly, informal culture in which time and money aren't the main focus. Once that red dirt gets in your blood, you might never leave.

1 Moab. This increasingly busy heart of the area is full of shops, restaurants, and hotels.

2 Green River. This small town right off the interstate is a place to stock up on supplies and gas before heading off on farther-flung adventures.

3 Blanding. This tiny place isn't a huge draw on its own but is close to several natural wonders and two Native American reservations.

4 Bluff. A small, arty town with a big personality, Bluff has a few great places to stay and eat and many historic buildings that are fun to stroll past.

5 Natural Bridges National Monument. The remote park features three of its namesake spans of red rock, including the Sipapu Bridge, one of the largest natural bridges in the world.

6 Lake Powell. One of the biggest recreation draws in the Southwest, millions of visitors come to this giant reservoir every year to boat, swim, and fish.

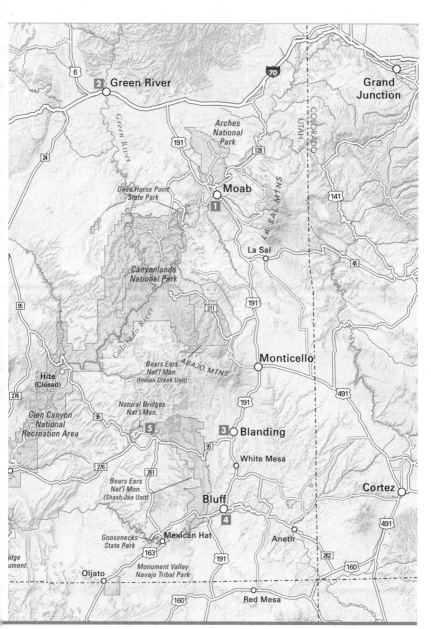

6

2 **Green River**

70

Grand Junction

Green River

Arches National Park

191

128

COLORADO UTAH

24

Dead Horse Point State Park

Moab

1

LA SAL MTNS

141

La Sal

45

Canyonlands National Park

95

Colorado River

211

191

Bears Ears Nat'l Mon. (Indian Creek Unit)

ABAJO MTNS

Monticello

Hite (Closed)

Natural Bridges Nat'l Mon.

191

491

276

Glen Canyon National Recreation Area

95

5

3 **Blanding**

95

White Mesa

276

261

Bears Ears Nat'l Mon. (Shash Jáa Unit)

Bluff

4

Cortez

491

idge ument

Goosenecks State Park

Mexican Hat

163

Monument Valley Navajo Tribal Park

191

Aneth

262

160

Oljato

160

Red Mesa

Southeastern Utah, especially Moab, is full of converts, and not so much in a religious sense. These are people formerly from suburbs or cities who came here long ago for vacation and never truly left. They may have spent just a few days surrounded by the vast desert and the clean, welcoming rivers, but in that short time, the land became a part of them. Moab has a certain kind of magic to it, as anyone who has ever visited will tell you, and many stay for the empty beauty of the region.

Although the towns tend to be visually simple in this part of the state, the beauty that surrounds them is awe-inspiring. You can hear about the canyons, arches, and natural bridges, but no words come close to their enormous presence.

Ostensibly, visitors arrive to run the gorgeous stretch of the Colorado River near Moab or to explore the unique landscape of the area's national parks and monuments. Or perhaps they are history buffs, excited to explore the ancient ruins and rock art left behind by various Native American tribes. For the most part, tourists come out of curiosity to find out if this landscape is just as special and disarming as they have heard it is. After just a little while in this unique canvas, you'll understand how it can be so hard to leave.

MAJOR REGIONS

Moab. Small but unbelievably busy in spring, summer, and fall, Moab is on the Colorado River, south of I–70 on U.S. 191. More than 100 miles from any large town, it's close to nothing, and its residents are just fine with that.

Southeastern Utah. From Green River to Mexican Hat, this large swath of desert has a very small population. The most easily reached destinations are the small towns right on U.S. 191 or I–70, but some of the most beautiful stops require substantial but worthwhile detours off these main roads. Lake Powell, about three hours southwest of Moab, remains a favorite among visitors and locals alike.

Utah scenery is dramatic, from the wide span of water at Lake Powell to the huge, sandstone formations (called "mittens") in Monument Valley. Around Green River you'll encounter a world of agriculture and boating, with melon stands popping up in the late summer and fall. Farther south you'll see the influence of Native American culture including ancient rock art and dwellings. Along the way to Mexican Hat, you'll enjoy Navajo tacos and handmade jewelry.

Planning

When to Go

The most enjoyable times to be in this part of Utah are the beginning and end of high season, March and October, respectively. April and May have the best weather—and the biggest crowds. May to September is the best time to hit the river, but is also when the towns and national parks are filled with people, and the temperatures can be downright fiery. From the beginning of November through the end of February some restaurants and stores shut down, and things can get eerily quiet. To compensate, almost all hotels offer steep discounts (sometimes as much as 40% off high-season prices), which can make visiting in the off-season a steal.

Planning Your Time

With its variety of restaurants and lodgings, Moab is a great place to base your southeastern Utah adventures. From here, it's an easy drive to both **Arches** and **Canyonlands** national parks, each of which require at least a day to take in. At Arches, hike to the famous **Delicate Arch.** At **Canyonlands,** the **Island in the Sky District** is a stunning area to visit, with its crow's-nest views of deep canyons, thin spires, and the Colorado River. After a few days surrounded by rock and dust, you can spend one or several more days on the **Green, San Juan,** or **Colorado** river. Outfitters also offer half-day, one-day,

or multiday trips on mountain bikes and jeeps, if either of those are more your speed. Many side trips from Moab can be taken in a day, some worthwhile treks being to the **La Sal Mountains, Goblin Valley State Park,** and the little town of **Bluff.** More southern locales, like **Natural Bridges National Monument, Lake Powell,** and **Monument Valley,** are much more enjoyable with an overnight stay.

Getting Here and Around

AIR

The nearest large airport to southeastern Utah is Walker Field Airport in Grand Junction, Colorado, 110 miles from Moab, but you can catch a regional flight directly to Moab. Rental cars are now available at the Moab Airport; advanced reservations are highly recommended.

AIR CONTACTS Grand Junction Regional Airport. ⊠ 2828 Walker Field Dr., Grand Junction ☏ 970/244–9100 ⊕ www.gjairport.com.

CAR

To reach southeastern Utah from Salt Lake City, take I–15 to U.S. 6 and then U.S. 191 south. From Colorado or more eastern locations, use I–70 or U.S. 491. Take U.S. 191 from either Wyoming or Arizona. Most roads are well-maintained two-lane highways, though snow can be a factor during winter travel. Be sure your car is in good working order and keep the gas tank topped off, as there are long stretches of empty road between towns.

INFORMATION Utah State Road Conditions. ☏ 511 toll-free within Utah, 866/511–8824 toll-free outside Utah ⊕ www.udot.utah.gov.

Restaurants

Including a few surprising twists, Moab-area restaurants have anything you might crave. The other smaller towns in southeastern Utah don't have quite the culinary kaleidoscope, and focus on all-American cuisine. Though not the best destination for vegetarians or those with a restricted diet, the comfort food will satisfy after a day of activity. *Restaurant reviews have been shortened. For full information, visit Fodors.com.*

Hotels

Every type of lodging is available in southeastern Utah, from economy chain motels, to B&Bs and high-end, high-adventure resorts. Some of the best values in Moab are condominiums available for rent. Start with the Moab Travel Council for listings and suggestions of accommodations to suit your group size and budget. There are 26 BLM (Bureau of Land Management) campgrounds in the area, all for $20, all first-come, first-served. *Hotel reviews have been shortened. For full information, visit Fodors.com.*

CONTACTS Moab Property Management. ✉ 11850 Highway 191, Suite A6 ☎ 435/259–5955, 800/505–5343, 435/514–7281 ⊕ www.moabutahlodging.com.

What It Costs			
$	$$	$$$	$$$$
RESTAURANTS			
under $16	$16–$22	$23–$30	over $30
HOTELS			
under $125	$125–$175	$176–$225	over $225

Moab

When you first drive down crowded Main Street (Moab's commercial, downtown strip), you might not get the town's appeal right away. The wide thoroughfare is lined with T-shirt shops and touristy restaurants. But don't let Moab's impersonal exterior fool you; take a few walks, visit some of the town's locally owned stores and eateries, and talk to some of the residents, and you'll realize this is a town centered on community. Local theater, local radio, and local art rule. At its core, this is a frontier outpost, where people have had to create their own livelihoods for more than 100 years. In the late 1880s, it was settled as a farming and ranching community. By the 1950s it became a center for uranium mining after Charlie Steen found a huge deposit of the stuff outside town. After about a decade of unbelievable monetary success, there was a massive downturn in the mining industry, and Moab plunged into an economic free fall. Then came tourism. Moab was able to rebuild itself with the dollars of sightseers, four-wheelers, bikers, and boaters. Today the town is dealing with environmental and development issues while becoming more and more popular with tourists and second-homeowners from around the world. No matter how it changes, though, one thing never will: this town has a different flavor from any other found in the state.

GETTING HERE AND AROUND
Although Moab is friendly to bikes and pedestrians, the only practical way to reach it is by car. If you're coming from the south, U.S. 191 runs straight into Moab. If you're arriving from Salt Lake City, travel 50 miles via I-15, then go 150 miles southeast via U.S. 6, and finally 30 miles south via U.S. 191. Signs for Moab will be obvious past Green River. ■ TIP→ **If you are approaching from the east on I–70, take Exit 214 into the ghost town of Cisco, and then drive down Colorado River Scenic Byway—Route 128 into Moab. The views of the river, rocks, and mesas are second to none.**

FESTIVALS
As much as Moab is a place for the outdoors, it's also a spot to experience extremely popular festivals and events in

a small-town setting. For the most part, these are time-honored institutions that draw quite a crowd of both locals and visitors. The free paper *Moab Happenings* is a great resource for all that's going on around town.

Canyonlands PRCA Rodeo

FESTIVALS | FAMILY | Cowboys come to the Old Spanish Trail Arena (just south of Moab) for three days in late May or early June to try their luck at thrashing bulls and broncs at this annual Western tradition. ✉ *3641 S. U.S. 191* ⊕ *www.moabcanyonlandsrodeo.com.*

Easter Jeep Safari

FESTIVALS | For more than a week each year, Easter Jeep Safari draws thousands of 4x4 vehicles to Moab to tackle some of the toughest backcountry roads in America. For all other visitors (and some locals), this is a good time of year to avoid town. ✉ *Moab* ☎ *435/259–7625* ⊕ *www.rr4w.com.*

★ Moab Arts Festival

ARTS FESTIVALS | FAMILY | Every Memorial Day weekend, artists from across the West gather at Moab's Swanny City Park to show their wares, including pottery, photography, and paintings. This fun, free festival is small enough to be manageable and sells a variety of affordable artworks and crafts. Expect lots of food, plus activities for the kids. Most days have live music and local theater on two stages. ✉ *400 N. 100 W* ☎ *435/259–2742* ⊕ *www.moabartsfestival.org.*

★ Moab Folk Festival

MUSIC FESTIVALS | Some of America's top folk artists converge in Moab each November to perform on indoor and outdoor stages. Past artists have included Richard Thompson, Shawn Colvin, Bruce Cockburn, Loudon Wainwright III, and Ferron. ✉ *Moab* ☎ *435/259–3198* ⊕ *www.moabfolkfestival.com.*

Moab Music Festival

MUSIC FESTIVALS | Moab's red rocks resonate with world-class music—classical, jazz, and traditional—during this annual festival held at indoor and outdoor venues including the city park, local auditoriums, private homes, and a natural stone grotto along the Colorado River. Musicians from all over the globe perform, and it's one of the West's top music showcases. The festival starts the Thursday before Labor Day and runs about two weeks. ✉ *Moab* ☎ *435/259–7003* ⊕ *www.moabmusicfest.org.*

Pumpkin Chuckin' Festival

FESTIVALS | FAMILY | This unique event brings together the diverse Moab community on the last Saturday of October. This festival may not be like any other you've attended; here, people from all over the Southwest build contraptions—catapults, trebuchets, and slingshots—that send pumpkins across the sky. Live music, about 25 vendor booths, and typically beautiful weather make this a popular event. Proceeds go toward the Youth Garden Project. ✉ *Grand County High School, 400 E. and Red Devil Dr.* ☎ *435/259–2326* 🎟 *$10.*

TOURS

Canyonlands by Night & Day

BOAT TOURS | Since 1963 this outfitter has been known for its Sound and Light Show Jet Boat Tour, a two-hour, after-dark boat ride on the Colorado River (March–October). While illuminating the canyon walls with 40,000 watts, the trip includes music and narration highlighting Moab's history, Native American legends, and geologic formations along the river. A dutch oven dinner is included, though you can exclude it and save $10. Daytime jet boat tours are offered, too, as well as tours by Hummer, airplane, and helicopter (land and air tours are offered year-round). ✉ *1861 U.S. 191* ☎ *435/259–2628, 800/394–9978* ⊕ *www.canyonlandsbynight.com* 🎟 *Boat tour with dinner from $79.*

ESSENTIALS

The Moab Information Center is right in the heart of town and it's the best place to find information on Arches and Canyonlands national parks. Hours vary, but in the peak tourist season it's open until at least 7 pm, and for a few hours each morning and afternoon in winter.

VISITOR INFORMATION Discover Moab Information Center. ⊠ *25 E. Center St.* ☎ *435/259–8825* ⊕ *www.discovermoab. com.*

 Sights

★ Colorado River Scenic Byway—Highway 128

SCENIC DRIVE | One of the most scenic drives in the Four Corners region, Highway 128 intersects U.S. 191, 3 miles south of Arches. The 44-mile highway runs along the Colorado River with 2,000-foot red rock cliffs rising on both sides. This gorgeous river corridor is home to a winery, orchards, and a couple of luxury lodging options. It also offers a spectacular view of world-class climbing destination Fisher Towers before winding north to Interstate 70. Give yourself an hour to 90 minutes to drive it. ⊠ *Hwy. 128.*

Colorado River Scenic Byway—Highway 279

SCENIC DRIVE | If you're interested in Native American rock art, Highway 279 northwest of Moab is a perfect place to spend a couple of hours immersed in the past.

To get there, go north on U.S. 191 for about 3½ miles and turn left onto Highway 279. If you start late in the afternoon, the cliffs will be glowing orange as the sun sets. Along the first part of the route you'll see signs reading "Indian Writings." Park only in designated areas to view the petroglyphs on the cliff side of the road. At the 18-mile marker you'll see Jug Handle Arch. A few miles beyond this point the road turns to four-wheel-drive only, and takes you into the Island in the Sky District of Canyonlands. Do not continue onto the Island in the Sky unless you are in a high-clearance four-wheel-drive vehicle with a full gas tank and plenty of water. Allow about two hours round-trip for the Scenic Byway drive. ■ **TIP→ If you happen to be in Moab during a heavy rainstorm, Highway 279 is also a good option for viewing the amazing waterfalls caused by rain pouring off the cliffs on both sides of the Colorado River.** ⊠ *Hwy. 279.*

★ Dead Horse Point State Park

NATIONAL/STATE PARK | FAMILY | One of the gems of Utah's state park system, right at the edge of the Island in the Sky section of Canyonlands, this park overlooks a sweeping oxbow of the Colorado River some 2,000 feet below. Dead Horse Point itself is a small peninsula connected to the main mesa by a narrow neck of land. As the story goes, cowboys used to drive wild mustangs onto the point and pen them there with a brush fence. There's a modern visitor center with a coffee shop and museum. The park's Intrepid trail system is popular with mountain bikers and hikers alike. Be sure to walk the 4-mile rim trail loop and drive to the park's eponymous point if it's a nice day. ⊠ *Hwy. 313, Canyonlands National Park* ☎ *435/259–2614, 800/322–3770 camping reservations* ⊕ *stateparks. utah.gov* ⊠ *$20 per vehicle.*

Moab Museum

MUSEUM | FAMILY | Exhibits on the history, geology, and paleontology of the Moab area include settler-era antiques, and ancient and historic Native Americans are remembered in displays of baskets, pottery, sandals, and other artifacts. Displays also chronicle early Spanish expeditions into the area, regional dinosaur finds, and the history of uranium discovery. ⊠ *118 E. Center St.* ☎ *435/259–7985* ⊕ *www. moabmuseum.org* ⊠ *$5* ⊙ *Closed Sun.*

Scott and Norma Matheson Wetlands Preserve

NATURE PRESERVE | FAMILY | Owned and operated by the Nature Conservancy, this is the best place in the Moab area for bird-watching. The 894-acre oasis is home to more than 200 species, including such treasures as the pied-billed grebe, the cinnamon teal, and the northern flicker. It's also a great place to spot beavers and muskrats playing in the water. Hear a big "Slap!" on the water? That's a beaver warning you that you're too close. Always remember to respect the wildlife preserved in these areas, and enjoy the nature you find here. An information kiosk greets visitors just inside the preserve and a boardwalk winds through the property to a viewing shelter. To reach the preserve, turn northwest off U.S. 191 at Kane Creek Boulevard and continue northwest approximately 2 miles. ✉ *934 W. Kane Creek Blvd.* ☎ *435/259–4629* 🌐 *www.nature.org* 🎟 *Free.*

🍴 Restaurants

From juicy steaks and fresh sushi to rich Mexican and savory Thai, there are enough menu options in Moab to keep you satiated.

Antica Forma

$ | ITALIAN | Moab's best pizza joint, which has a wildly popular original location in the northeastern Utah town of Vernal, offers an extensive list of thin-crust wood-fired pizzas with a variety of toppings, plus plenty of classic antipasto (mussels in white wine, homemade burrata, arancini) and pasta options. Have a seat at one of the granite-top tables under high ceilings in the dining room, peruse the carefully chosen wine and beer list, and tuck into one of the specialty pies, perhaps the white pie with pistachio pesto, Italian sausage, homemade mozzarella, pecorino romano, basil, and olive oil. **Known for:** delicious thin crusts (both traditional and gluten-free); extensive craft beer selection; creative pizza toppings. [$] *Average main: $15* ✉ *267 N. Main St.* ☎ *435/355–0167* 🌐 *www.anticaforma.com.*

★ Desert Bistro

$$$$ | MODERN AMERICAN | Moab's finest dining experience is found in a small adobe house just off Main Street. Whether you eat inside or on either of the peaceful patios, anticipate thoughtful flavor combinations in artful salads, locally sourced beef, and delicious vegetables. **Known for:** excellent service; large wine selection; bison entrées. [$] *Average main: $38* ✉ *36 S. 100 W* ☎ *435/259–0756* 🌐 *www.desertbistro.com* 🕒 *Closed Dec.–Feb., Mon. in Sept. and Oct., and Mon. and Tues. in Nov. No lunch.*

La Sal House

$$ | MODERN AMERICAN | Named for the soaring mountain range southeast of town, this stylish dinner house with exposed timber, tile floors, and leather banquettes has elevated Moab's culinary and cocktail scene to new heights. Both classic and new cocktails prime diners for the extraordinary seasonally inspired dishes, which might include a beet salad with whipped blue cheese, pecans, and locally produced fig vinaigrette, followed by Colorado lamb with cauliflower, chickpeas, rainbow chard, house-made naan, and lemon aioli. **Known for:** stellar craft cocktails; innovative food with global influences; reasonable prices for such gourmet fare. [$] *Average main: $20* ✉ *11 E. 100 N* ☎ *435/259–5725* 🌐 *lasalhouse.com* 🕒 *Closed Sun. and Mon. No lunch.*

Miguel's Baja Grill

$ | MEXICAN | This isn't the cheapest Mexican menu around, but it's definitely the best. Not your standard south-of-the-border fare, the food here comes from the culinary spirit of Baja, California, which means some excellent seafood dishes like ceviche, a tangy blend of raw fish, onions, tomatoes, and spices. **Known for:** house-made margaritas; big portions; fresh seafood (despite desert locale). [$] *Average*

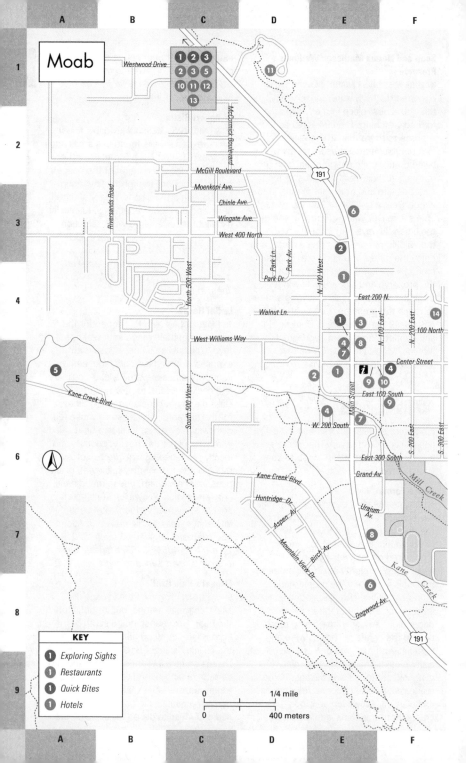

Moab

Westwood Drive

McCormick Boulevard

McGill Boulevard

Moenkopi Ave.

Chinle Ave.

Wingate Ave.

West 400 North

Park Ln.

Park Av.

Park Dr.

N. 100 West

East 200 N.

N. 100 East

N. 200 East

100 North

Walnut Ln.

West Williams Way

Center Street

Main Street

East 100 South

Riversands Road

North 500 West

South 500 West

Kane Creek Blvd.

W. 200 South

East 300 South

S. 200 East

S. 300 East

Grand Av.

Mill Creek

Kane Creek Blvd.

Huntridge Dr.

Uranium Av.

Aspen Av.

Mountain View Dr.

Birch Av.

Dogwood Av.

Kane Creek

191

191

KEY

- Exploring Sights
- Restaurants
- Quick Bites
- Hotels

0   1/4 mile

0   400 meters

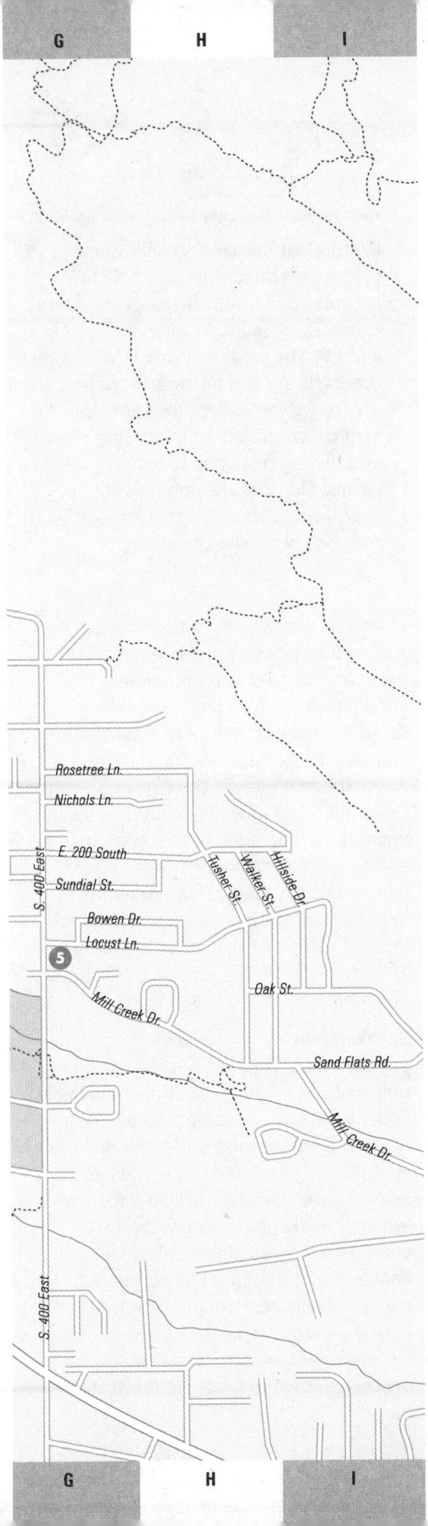

Sights ▼

1 Colorado River
  Scenic Byway -
  Highway 128.............**C1**
2 Colorado River
  Scenic Byway—
  Highway 279.............**C1**
3 Dead Horse Point
  State Park **C1**
4 Moab Museum...........**F5**
5 Scott and Norma
  Matheson
  Wetlands Preserve.....**A5**

Restaurants ▼

1 Antica Forma.............**E4**
2 Desert Bistro **E5**
3 La Sal House **E4**
4 Miguel's Baja Grill **E5**
5 Milt's Stop and Eat......**G6**
6 Moab Brewery............**E8**
7 Moab Diner...............**E6**
8 Moab Garage Co.........**E5**
9 Sabaku Sushi.............**E5**
10 Singha Thai Cuisine **E5**
11 Sunset Grill **D1**

Quick Bites ▼

1 Quesadilla Mobilla.......**E4**
2 Sweet Cravings
  Bakery + Bistro **E3**

Hotels ▼

1 Best Western Plus
  Canyonlands Inn.........**E5**
2 Big Bend
  Campground **C1**
3 Dead Horse Point
  State Park
  Campgrounds **C1**
4 Gonzo Inn.................**E5**
5 Goose Island
  Campground **C1**
6 Hampton Inn..............**E3**
7 Moab Nightly Rentals ...**E5**
8 Moab Red Stone Inn **E7**
9 Moab Rustic Inn **F5**
10 Moab Springs Ranch....**C1**
11 Red Cliffs Lodge..........**C1**
12 Sorrel River Ranch
  Resort & Spa **C1**
13 SpringHill Suites by
  Marriott Moab **C1**
14 Sunflower Hill
  Luxury Inn **F4**

Rosetree Ln.
Nichols Ln.
E. 200 South
S. 400 East
Sundial St.
Tusher St.
Walker St.
Hillside Dr.
Bowen Dr.
Locust Ln.
⑤
Mill Creek Dr.
Oak St.
Sand Flats Rd.
Mill Creek Dr.
S. 400 East

G   H   I

main: $15 ✉ *51 N. Main St.* ☎ *435/259–6546* 🕒 *Closed Dec.–Feb. No lunch.*

Milt's Stop and Eat

$ | **FAST FOOD** | **FAMILY** | Since 1954, Milt's has offered delicious burgers and shakes from an unassuming, off-Main Street drive-up stand. About all that's changed is that the Buffalo Burger is now nearly as popular as the beef version. **Known for:** tasty burgers and shakes; local institution; friendly, vintage feel. [$] *Average main: $6* ✉ *356 Millcreek Dr.* ☎ *435/259–7424* 🌐 *www.miltsstopandeat.com.*

Moab Brewery

$ | **AMERICAN** | Moab's first microbrewery is known for its Scorpion Pale Ale, Squeaky Bike Nut Brown Ale, and an assortment of other brews from light to dark. The on-site restaurant is spacious and comfortable and decorated with kayaks, bikes, and other adventure paraphernalia. **Known for:** lively crowd; house-made gelato; very good craft beer. [$] *Average main: $14* ✉ *686 S. Main St.* ☎ *435/259–6333* 🌐 *www.themoabbrewery.com.*

Moab Diner

$ | **AMERICAN** | **FAMILY** | For breakfast (served all day), plus lunch and dinner, this neon-lighted retro diner and ice cream shop is a favorite place of old-time Moabites who appreciate the reasonable prices and good-size portions of reliably tasty American fare, from caramelized-pecan pancakes to green-chili cheeseburgers. Friendly servers whisk quickly amid the bustling dining room, and kids love the banana splits, milkshakes, and other sweet treats for dessert. **Known for:** opens at 6 am; malted milkshakes; green chili served on or as a side with many dishes. [$] *Average main: $9* ✉ *189 S. Main St.* ☎ *435/259–4006* 🌐 *www.moabdiner.com* 🕒 *Closed Sun.*

★ **Moab Garage Co.**

$ | **ECLECTIC** | Set in a vintage redbrick storefront on downtown Moab's busiest block, this urbane café and ice-cream shop also offers enough hearty savory dishes throughout the day—plus a well-curated selection of beer and wine—to serve as a legit breakfast, lunch, or dinner option. Consider the Liege-style waffles with fresh berries or avocado toast early in the day, or a veggie "meatball" or fancy grilled cheese sandwich (the preparation of the latter changes daily), Cobb salad, or street tacos later in the day. **Known for:** nitro-infused ice cream; superb coffee; cool, centrally located hangout. [$] *Average main: $9* ✉ *78 N. Main St.* ☎ *435/554–8467* 🌐 *moabgarageco.com* 🕒 *Closed Tues.*

Sabaku Sushi

$$ | **JAPANESE** | Sushi in the remote desert may seem surprising, but the chefs here know what they're doing. The fish is flown in fresh several times a week, the veggies are crisp, and the sauces are spicy—locals particularly love the spicy tuna roll with cucumber and avocado served with sriracha and eel sauce. **Known for:** fresh and artfully prepared sushi; friendly service; good sake selection. [$] *Average main: $17* ✉ *90 E. Center St.* ☎ *435/259–4455* 🌐 *www.sabakusushi.com* 🕒 *Closed Mon. No lunch.*

Desert Soundtrack

KZMU, Moab Community Radio Since 1992, locals have tuned in to KZMU for solar-powered, off-the-grid community radio. At 106.7 and 90.1 FM, the programming is an eccentric quilt of music and community news shows provided entirely by local volunteers, showcasing everything from pop to country twang. Don't be shy about calling in a request. ✉ *Moab* ☎ *435/259–5968 request line* 🌐 *www.kzmu.org.*

Singha Thai Cuisine

$ | **THAI** | Authentic Thai food may not be what you expect to find in the middle of the desert, and that's exactly why this cozy, central place so highly recommended by locals. Some of the tastiest dishes here are the noodle options, such as the tangy pad Thai or the spicy, pan-fried drunken noodles. **Known for:** affordable, especially the lunch specials; friendly service; tasty traditional favorites, including noodles and curry. $ *Average main: $15 ⊠ 92 E. Center St. ☎ 435/259–0039* ⊙ *Closed Sun.*

Sunset Grill

$$$ | **AMERICAN** | This cliffside home of former uranium kingpin Charlie Steen offers the best views of any restaurant in town, especially at sunset—the dining room's big windows take in the Colorado River and surrounding red rocks. The traditional American fare—including filet mignon, prime rib, sautéed Idaho trout, and shrimp scampi—is generally well-prepared if not especially inventive. **Known for:** historical setting; stunning view; slow-roasted prime rib. $ *Average main: $25 ⊠ 900 N. Main St. ☎ 435/259–7146* ⊕ *www.moabsunsetgrill.com* ⊙ *Closed Sun. No lunch.*

☕ Coffee and Quick Bites

Quesadilla Mobilla

$ | **MEXICAN FUSION** | Opened by a young, outdoorsy couple with a passion for southeastern Utah, this food truck permanently moored on a prominent downtown corner serves adventurous, delicious—if not necessarily authentic—quesadillas. Order at the window and dine at one of the outdoor tables in the pretty landscaped courtyard, or take your meal with you on an outdoor adventure. **Known for:** huge portions; great food for picnics or hikes; very affordable. $ *Average main: $9 ⊠ 95 N. Main St. ☎ 435/260–0289* ⊕ *www.quesadillamobilla.com* ⊙ *No dinner.*

★ Sweet Cravings Bakery + Bistro

$ | **BAKERY** | **FAMILY** | In addition to doling out some of the largest and most delicious cookies and cinnamon rolls you've ever tried, this cheerful and informal bakery café presents a terrific roster of breakfast and lunch panini, wraps, and sandwiches, and daily comfort foods like potpies and soups. Baked goods are all from scratch, gluten-free options abound, produce is local, meats are preservative-free, and coffee is 100% Rainforest Alliance and organic. **Known for:** hefty cinnamon rolls; many gluten-free options; local produce and ingredients. $ *Average main: $10 ⊠ 397 N. Main St. ☎ 435/259–8983* ⊕ *www.cravemoab.com* ⊙ *No dinner.*

Hotels

★ Best Western Plus Canyonlands Inn

$$$ | **HOTEL** | **FAMILY** | The confluence of Main and Center streets is the epicenter of Moab, and this comfortable, contemporary, impeccably clean hotel anchors the intersection, providing a perfect base for families. **Pros:** steps from many restaurants; sparkling, contemporary rooms; complimentary breakfast alfresco on outdoor patio. **Cons:** central location can feel a bit crowded at busy times; books up far in advance; pool is closed in winter (but hot tub is open year-round). $ *Rooms from: $199 ⊠ 16 S. Main St. ☎ 435/259–2300* ⊕ *www.bestwestern.com* ↵ *80 rooms* ⫩ *Free breakfast.*

Gonzo Inn

$$$ | **HOTEL** | This eclectic inn stands out for its fun design, brightly colored walls, desert-inspired art, and varnished adobe construction. **Pros:** unique, spotless, and hip; steps to Main Street; pool and hot tub. **Cons:** interior hallways can be dark; no elevator; not all rooms have a good view. $ *Rooms from: $209 ⊠ 100 W. 200 S ☎ 435/259–2515* ⊕ *www.gonzoinn.com* ↵ *43 rooms* ⫩ *Free breakfast.*

Hampton Inn
$$$$ | **HOTEL** | **FAMILY** | This property features a huge lobby with plenty of room to spread out and newly renovated rooms a modern, simple aesthetic. **Pros:** reliably clean and chic; walking distance from downtown; hot breakfast included. **Cons:** no pets; noise insulation could be improved; like most spots in Moab, gets pricey in the busy season. [$] *Rooms from: $229* ✉ *488 N. Main St.* ☎ *435/259–3030* 🌐 *hamptoninn.hilton.com* 🛏 *79 rooms* 🍴 *Free breakfast.*

Moab Nightly Rentals
$$$ | **RENTAL** | **FAMILY** | Guests can choose from two downtown properties: **Cali Conchitta,** a 19th-century Victorian with a main house, outbuildings, and a pleasant garden; or **Desert Gardens,** a small collection of updated rooms with a vintage exterior and a large, shaded backyard. **Pros:** good value considering the amenities offered; easy walk to the hub of town; both locations offer serene backyards. **Cons:** the least expensive rooms are a bit small; no pool; not all rooms allow pets. [$] *Rooms from: $179* ✉ *33 N. Main St.* ☎ *435/259–4961* 🌐 *www.moabnightly.rentals* 🛏 *8 rooms* 🍴 *No meals.*

Moab Red Stone Inn
$$ | **HOTEL** | One of the best bargains in town, this timber-frame motel offers small, clean rooms at the south end of the Moab strip near restaurants and shops. **Pros:** walking distance to many restaurants and shops; the price is right; all rooms have small kitchenettes. **Cons:** pool is at sister property across busy Main Street; no frills; rooms close to the road are noisy. [$] *Rooms from: $139* ✉ *535 S. Main St.* ☎ *435/259–3500, 800/772–1972* 🌐 *www.moabredstone.com* 🛏 *52 rooms* 🍴 *No meals.*

Moab Rustic Inn
$ | **HOTEL** | One of the best values amid Moab's increasingly pricey lodging landscape, this homey downtown sister property to Red Cliffs Lodge is, as the name suggests, rustic, but the 35 rooms are all clean and comfortable, and provide ample room for families or friends traveling together. **Pros:** most rooms sleep at least four guests; terrific value; nice pool and barbecue area. **Cons:** simple (but comfortable) furnishings; downtown location is busy at times; can book up months in advance, especially the apartments. [$] *Rooms from: $100* ✉ *120 E. 100 S* ☎ *435/259–6177* 🌐 *www.moabrusticinn.com* 🛏 *35 rooms* 🍴 *Free breakfast.*

Moab Springs Ranch
$$$$ | **RENTAL** | **FAMILY** | First developed by William Grandstaff in the late 19th century, this 18-acre property about 3 miles from Arches and 1 mile from downtown Moab features spacious, studio-style bungalows (completed in 2019) and town houses, set by a meandering spring and decades-old sycamores, mulberries, and cottonwoods. **Pros:** scenic setting is a respite; boutique accomodations; features hiking trails and sits on a bike path into town. **Cons:** about a 30-minute walk from downtown; some U.S. 191 traffic noise; most units have two-night minimum stays. [$] *Rooms from: $235* ✉ *1266 N. Highway 191* ☎ *435/259–7891* 🌐 *www.moabspringsranch.com* 🛏 *35 units* 🍴 *No meals.*

Red Cliffs Lodge
$$$$ | **RESORT** | Discovered in the late 1940s by director John Ford, this former ranch was the setting for several 1950s Westerns, and you can feel transported into one as you gaze onto the Colorado River and high canyon walls from your simple but elegant room. **Pros:** beautiful spot, with peaceful canyon and river views; many luxury amenities and great restaurant; private cabins are woodsy but modern. **Cons:** drive to town can be long during busy season; spotty cell service; not all rooms have river or creek views. [$] *Rooms from: $289* ✉ *Hwy. 128, mile marker 14* ☎ *435/259–2002,*

866/812–2002 🌐 *www.redcliffslodge.com* 🛏 *110 rooms* 🍴 *No meals.*

Sorrel River Ranch Resort & Spa

$$$$ | RESORT | One of the premier luxury resorts in the Southwest, this lodge on the banks of the Colorado River, 17 miles north of Moab, is the ultimate destination for a relaxing and plush getaway, especially if you enjoy spa treatments. **Pros:** swanky spa and restaurant; luxurious rooms; red rock setting along the Colorado River. **Cons:** drive to town is long during the busy season; steep rates; breakfast not included. [$] *Rooms from: $599* ✉ *Hwy. 128* ✣ *Mile marker 17.5* ☎ *435/259–4642* 🌐 *www.sorrelriver.com* 🛏 *59 rooms* 🍴 *No meals.*

SpringHill Suites by Marriott Moab

$$$ | HOTEL | FAMILY | Views of the Colorado River are sure to wow guests at this all-suites hotel that shares a large pool area and hot tub with the neighboring sister property, the similarly excellent (and usually a bit more affordable) Fairfield by Marriott. **Pros:** attractive pool area; views of river and red rocks; spacious rooms with nice amenities. **Cons:** not within walking distance of downtown; pricey during popular periods; on a busy road. [$] *Rooms from: $209* ✉ *1865 N. U.S. 191* ☎ *435/259–5350* 🌐 *www.marriott.com* 🛏 *99 suites* 🍴 *Free breakfast.*

★ Sunflower Hill Luxury Inn

$$$ | B&B/INN | Near the heart of old downtown Moab, this thriving turn-of-the-20th-century inn is all about comfort and the guest experience, with elegant interiors and lush surroundings. **Pros:** just blocks from town; beautifully appointed rooms; friendly hosts. **Cons:** children younger than 10 not allowed; some rooms are a bit dark; not ideal if you prefer a larger property. [$] *Rooms from: $219* ✉ *185 N. 300 E* ☎ *435/259–2974, 800/662–2786* 🌐 *www.sunflowerhill.com* 🛏 *12 rooms* 🍴 *Free breakfast.*

CAMPGROUNDS

Big Bend

$ | RENTAL | FAMILY | Both RVs and tents can camp at this spot on the Colorado River directly across from the eastern cliffs of Arches National Park. **Pros:** riverside location with great red rock views; sandy beach; shade. **Cons:** no drinking water; no hookups for RVs; the Colorado may look tranquil, but its currents can be deadly, be careful if you have children with you. [$] *Rooms from: $20* ✉ *7.5 miles from U.S. 191 on Rte. 128, Arches National Park* ☎ *435/259–2100* 🌐 *www.blm.gov* 🛏 *23 sites* 🍴 *No meals.*

Dead Horse Point State Park Campgrounds

$ | RENTAL | FAMILY | This park's recent improvements, including a new visitor center, miles of new mountain-bike trails, and freshly installed electrical hookups available at every RV site, have made it the darling of park rangers and all who visit. **Pros:** beautiful setting; amenities for large RVs; mountain-bike trails. **Cons:** fills up very quickly; though there is water available, there are no water hookups at campsites; higher prices than nearby BLM camping spots. [$] *Rooms from: $35* ✉ *Dead Horse Point State Park, Rte. 313* ✣ *18 miles off U.S. 191, near the entrance to Canyonlands* ☎ *435/259–2614, 800/322–3770 reservations* 🌐 *stateparks.utah.gov* 🛏 *52 sites* 🍴 *No meals.*

Goose Island Campground

$ | RENTAL | FAMILY | The first campground north of Moab on stunningly beautiful Hwy. 128, this campground is suitable for RVs and tents. **Pros:** close to Arches and Moab, but far enough away for solitude; incredible red rock views and riverside location; affordable. **Cons:** not much shade, so most sites are fairly exposed; no drinking water; the fast-moving Colorado may be a concern if you have small children with you. [$] *Rooms from: $20* ✉ *1.4 miles from U.S. 191 on Rte. 128, Arches National Park* 🌐 *www.blm.gov* 🛏 *18 sites* 🍴 *No meals.*

Nightlife

Moab's nightlife can be pretty quiet, especially in winter. In high season, live bands perform every weekend.

World Famous Woody's Tavern

BARS/PUBS | An old-school style tavern that's a favorite hangout for locals, this Main Street standby offers beer, bands, and a little bit of ruckus. The front porch still looks like a perfect place to ride up and secure a horse, and there is a great patio. ⊠ *221 S. Main St.* ☎ *435/259–3550.*

Shopping

Shopping opportunities are plentiful in Moab, with art galleries, jewelry stores, and shops carrying T-shirts and souvenirs throughout Main Street.

ART GALLERIES

Lema's Kokopelli Gallery

ART GALLERIES | The Lema family has built a reputation for fair prices on a large selection of Native American and Southwest-themed jewelry, art, pottery, rugs, and more. Everything sold here is authentic. ⊠ *70 N. Main St.* ☎ *435/259–5055* ⊕ *www.kokopellioutlet.com.*

Moab Art Walk

Moab galleries and shops celebrate the perfect weather of spring and fall with a series of exhibits. Art Walks are held the second Saturday of the month from April through June and September through November. Stroll the streets (5–8 pm) to see and purchase original works by Moab and regional artists. ⊠ *Moab* ☎ *435/259–6272* ⊕ *www.moabartwalk.com.*

Tom Till Gallery

ART GALLERIES | Moab photographer Tom Till is internationally known for his stunning original photographs of the Arches and Canyonlands areas, as well as other regions of the world. The gallery features mostly images of southeastern Utah, but also other gorgeous remote places to fuel your wanderlust. ⊠ *61 N. Main St.* ☎ *435/259–9808* ⊕ *tomtill.com.*

BOOKS

Back of Beyond Books

BOOKS/STATIONERY | FAMILY | A Main Street treasure, this comprehensive shop features books on the American West, environmental studies, Native American cultures, water issues, and Western history, as well as rare antiquarian books on the Southwest. There's also a nice nook for kids. ⊠ *83 N. Main St.* ☎ *435/259–5154, 800/700–2859* ⊕ *www. backofbeyondbooks.com.*

SUPPLIES

Dave's Corner Market

CONVENIENCE/GENERAL STORES | You can get most anything you may need here for your travels, including some of the best cappuccino and Colombian coffee in town. The store is also the heartbeat of the local community, where everyone gossips, discusses local politics, and swaps info on the best hiking and adventure spots. ⊠ *401 Mill Creek Dr.* ☎ *435/259–6999.*

Desert Thread

TEXTILES/SEWING | This friendly yarn shop owned by two sisters is a big deal when you consider it's the only one for more than a hundred miles. Look for locally produced yarn and roving, plus classes, and a night of "social stitching" every Wednesday. ⊠ *29 E. Center St.* ☎ *435/259–8404* ⊕ *www.desertthread.com.*

GearHeads

SPECIALTY STORES | If you forget anything for your camping, climbing, hiking, or other outdoor adventure, you can get a replacement here. GearHeads is packed with essentials, and fun extras like booties and packs for your dog, water filtration straws, and cool souvenirs. The store's owners invented a high-end LED flashlight that has become very popular with the U.S. military, available at the store. ⊠ *1040 S. Main St.* ☎ *435/259–4327* ⊕ *www.moabgear.com.*

Walker Drug Co.
CONVENIENCE/GENERAL STORES | A Moab landmark since the 1950s, this is as close as you'll get to a department store for more than 100 miles. Besides pharmacy and drugstore items, you can buy all the essentials, including camping supplies, swimsuits, hats, sunglasses, and souvenirs. The pharmacy section is closed on weekends. ⊠ *290 S. Main St.* ☎ *435/259–5959.*

⚓ Activities

Moab's towering cliffs and deep canyons can be intimidating, and some are unreachable without the help of a guide. Fortunately, guide services are abundant in Moab. Whether you are interested in a 4x4 expedition into the rugged backcountry, a river-rafting trip, a jet-boat tour on calm water, bicycle tours, rock-art tours, or a scenic flight, you can find the pro to help you on your way. It's always best to make reservations. Book the Fiery Furnace tour in Arches National Park at least one month in advance; you can book as early as six months in advance.

SHUTTLES
If you need a ride to or from your trailhead or river trip put-in point, a couple of Moab companies provide the service (and also provide airport shuttle service by reservation), with vehicles large enough to handle most groups. Coyote's website is worth checking out for trail and river conditions and other information. Inquiries for Roadrunner are handled by Dual Sport, under the same ownership.

Coyote Shuttle
BICYCLING | ⊠ *55 W. 300 S* ☎ *435/260–2097* ⊕ *www.coyoteshuttle.com.*

Roadrunner Shuttle
BOATING | ⊠ *Deal Sport Utah, 197 W. Center St.* ☎ *435/259–9402* ⊕ *www. roadrunnershuttle.com.*

FOUR-WHEELING
There are thousands of miles of four-wheel-drive roads in and around Moab suitable for all levels of drivers. Seasoned 4x4 drivers might tackle the daunting Moab Rim, Elephant Hill, or Poison Spider Mesa. Novices will be happier touring Long Canyon, Hurrah Pass. If you're not afraid of precipitous cliff edges, the famous Shafer Trail may be a good option for you. Expect to pay around $75 for a half-day tour and $120 for a full day; multiday safaris usually start at around $600. Almost all of Moab's river-running companies also offer four-wheeling excursions.

Coyote Land Tours
FOUR-WHEELING | FAMILY | Imposing Mercedes Benz Unimog trucks (which dwarf Hummers) take you to parts of the backcountry where you could never wander on your own. Technical tours challenge drivers with imposing rock formations, washes, and assorted obstacles, and there are tamer sunset excursions and camp-style ride-and-dine trips. They stand by their money-back "great time" guarantee. ⊠ *Moab* ☎ *435/260–6056* ⊕ *www. coyotelandtours.com* ⊠ *From $59.*

Dual Sport Utah
FOUR-WHEELING | If you're into dirt biking, this is the only outfitter in Moab specializing in street-legal, off-road dirt-bike tours and rentals. New in 2020, you can also rent pedal-assist, electric bikes. Follow the Klondike Bluffs trail to Arches, or negotiate the White Rim Trail in Canyonlands in a fraction of the time you would spend on a mountain bike. ⊠ *197 W. Center. St.* ☎ *435/260–2724* ⊕ *www. dualsportutah.com* ⊠ *$300 for rentals.*

High Point Hummer & ATV
FOUR-WHEELING | FAMILY | You can rent vehicles, including ATVs, UTVs, and Jeeps, or get a guided tour of the backcountry in open-air Hummer vehicles or ATVs, or dune buggy–like "side-by-sides" that seat up to six people. The enthusiastic owners love families and small,

intimate groups, and offer hiking and canyoneering as well. ✉ *301 S. Main St.* ☏ *435/259–2972, 877/486–6833* ⊕ *www. highpointhummer.com* ⊐ *From $69.*

HIKING

For a great view of the Moab Valley and surrounding red-rock country, hike up the steep **Moab Rim Trail.** For something a little less taxing, hike the shady, cool path of **Grandstaff Canyon,** which is off Route Highway 129. At the end of the trail you'll find giant Morning Glory Arch towering over a serene pool created by a natural spring. If you want to take a stroll through the heart of Moab, hop on the **Mill Creek Parkway,** which winds along the creek from one side of town to the other. It's paved and perfect for bicycles, strollers, or joggers. For a taste of slick-rock hiking that feels like the backcountry but is easy to access, try the **Corona Arch Trail** off Highway 279. You'll be rewarded with two large arches hidden from view of the highway. The Moab Information Center carries a free hiking trail guide.

MOUNTAIN BIKING

Mountain biking originated in Moab, and the region has earned the well-deserved reputation as the mountain-biking capital of the world. Riders of all ages and skill levels are drawn to the many rugged roads and trails found here. One of the most popular routes is the **Slickrock Trail,** a stunning area of steep Navajo Sandstone dunes a few miles east of Moab. ■**TIP**➔ **Beginners should master the 2⅓-mile practice loop before attempting the longer, and very challenging, 10-mile loop.** More moderate rides can be found on the **Gemini Bridges** or **Monitor and Merrimac** trails, both found off U.S. 191 north of Moab. **Klondike Bluffs,** north of Moab, is an excellent novice ride, as are sections of the newer trails in the Klonzo trail system. The Moab Information Center carries a free biking trail guide. Mountain-bike rentals range from $40 for a good bike to $75 for a top-of-the-line workhorse. If you want to go on a

guided ride, expect to pay between $120 and $135 per person for a half-day, and $155 to $190 for a full day, including the cost of the bike rental. You can save money by joining a larger group to keep the per-person rates down; even a party of two will save drastically over a single rider. Several companies offer shuttles to and from the trailheads.

Chile Pepper Bike Shop

BICYCLING | For mountain bike rentals, sales, service, and gear, plus espresso, stop here before you set out. ✉ *702 S. Main St.* ☏ *435/259–4688* ⊕ *www. chilebikes.com.*

★ Poison Spider Bicycles

BICYCLING | In a town of great bike shops, this fully loaded shop is one of the best. Poison Spider serves the thriving road-cycling community as well as mountain bikers. Rent, buy, or service your bike here. You can also arrange for shuttle and guide services and purchase merchandise. Want to ship your bike to Moab for your adventure? Poison Spider will store it until you arrive and the staff will reassemble it for you and make sure everything is in perfect working order. ✉ *497 N. Main St.* ☏ *435/259–7882, 800/635–1792* ⊕ *www.poisonspiderbicy-cles.com.*

Rim Tours

BICYCLING | Reliable, friendly, and professional, Rim Tours has been taking guests on guided one-day or multiday mountain-bike tours, including Klondike Bluffs (which enters Arches) and the White Rim Trail (inside Canyonlands) since 1985. Road-bike tours as well as bike rentals are also available. Bike skills a little rusty? Rim Tours also offers mountain-bike instructional tours. For all tours, the larger the group, the cheaper the price per person. ✉ *1233 S. U.S. 191* ☏ *435/259–5223* ⊕ *www.rimtours.com* ⊐ *Tours start at $155 for a solo rider.*

Western Spirit Cycling Adventures

BICYCLING | Head here for fully supported, go-at-your-own-pace, multiday mountain-bike and road-bike tours throughout the western states, including trips to Canyonlands, Bears Ears, and the 140-mile Kokopelli Trail, which runs from Grand Junction, Colorado, to Moab. Guides versed in the geologic wonders of the area cook up meals worthy of the scenery each night. Ask about family rides, and road bike trips, too. Electric bicycles are available. ⊠ *478 S. Mill Creek Dr.* ☎ *435/259–8732, 800/845–2453* ⊕ *www.westernspirit.com* ☏ *From $995.*

MULTISPORT

Outdoor lovers wear many hats in Moab: boaters, bikers, and even Jeep-drivers. Here are a few companies that cater to a range of adventure seekers.

Adrift Adventures

BOATING | FAMILY | This outfitter takes pride in well-trained guides who can take you via foot, raft, kayak, 4x4, jet boat, stand-up paddleboard, and more, all over the Moab area, including the Colorado and Green rivers and Arches Jeep and hiking adventures. They also offer history, movie, and rock-art tours. They've been in business since 1977 and have a great reputation around town. ⊠ *378 N. Main St.* ☎ *435/259–8594, 800/874–4483* ⊕ *www.adrift.net* ☏ *From $49.*

Moab Adventure Center

BOATING | FAMILY | At the prominent storefront on Main Street you can schedule most any type of local adventure experience you want, including rafting, 4x4 tours, scenic flights, hikes, balloon rides, and a couple of excellent bus overview tours of Arches highlights. You can also purchase clothing and outdoor gear for your visit. ⊠ *225 S. Main St.* ☎ *435/259–7019, 866/904–1163* ⊕ *www.moabadventurecenter. com* ☏ *From $89.*

NAVTEC

BOATING | FAMILY | Doc Williams was the first doctor in Moab in 1896, and some of his descendants never left, sharing his love for the area through this rafting, canyoneering, and 4x4 company. Whether you want to explore the region by boat, boots, or wheels, you'll find a multitude of one-day and multiday options here. ⊠ *321 N. Main St.* ☎ *435/259–7983, 800/833–1278* ⊕ *www.navtec.com* ☏ *From $69.*

Oars

WHITE-WATER RAFTING | FAMILY | This well-regarded outfitter can take you for several days of rafting the Colorado, Green, and San Juan rivers. Hiking/interpretive trips are available in Canyonlands and Arches. ⊠ *Moab* ☎ *435/259–5865, 800/346–6277* ⊕ *www.oars.com/utah* ☏ *From $109.*

RIVER EXPEDITIONS

On the Colorado River northeast of Arches and very near Moab, you can take one of America's most scenic—but not intimidating—river-raft rides. The river rolls by the red Fisher Towers as they rise into the sky in front of the La Sal Mountains. A day trip on this stretch of the river will take you about 15 miles. Outfitters offer full, half, or multiday adventures here. Upriver, in narrow, winding Westwater Canyon near the Utah–Colorado border, the Colorado River cuts through the oldest exposed geologic layer on Earth. Most outfitters offer this trip as a one-day getaway, but you may also take as long as three days to complete the journey. A permit is required from the Bureau of Land Management (BLM) in Moab to run Westwater Canyon.

★ Canyon Voyages Adventure Co.

BOATING | FAMILY | This is an excellent choice for rafting or kayaking adventures on the Colorado River—including the Fisher Towers section—or Green River. Don and Denise Oblak run a friendly, professional company with a retail store and rental shop that's open year-round.

Most customers take one-day trips, but they also offer multiday itineraries, guided tours, and rentals. They also operate a great kayak school. Ask about stand-up paddleboarding, biking, and horseback riding, too. ⊠ *211 N. Main St.* ☎ *435/241–3846,* ⊕ *www.canyonvoyages.com* ✉ *From $65.*

Holiday River Expeditions
BOATING | FAMILY | Since 1966, this outfitter has offered one-day and multiday trips on the San Juan, Green, and Colorado rivers, including inside Canyonlands National Park. They also offer multisport trips, women's retreats, and bike adventures, including the White Rim Trail. ⊠ *2075 E. Main St., Green River* ☎ *435/564–3273, 800/624–6323* ⊕ *www.bikeraft.com* ✉ *From $210.*

ROCK CLIMBING
Rock climbing is an integral part of Moab culture. The area's rock walls and towers bring climbers from around the world, and a surprising number end up sticking around. Moab offers some of the best climbing challenges in the country, and any enthusiast will find bliss here.

Desert Highlights
CLIMBING/MOUNTAINEERING | This guide company takes adventurous types on descents and ascents through canyons (with the help of ropes), including those found in the Fiery Furnace at Arches National Park. Full-day and multiday canyoneering treks are available to destinations both in and near the national parks. ⊠ *16 S. 100 E* ☎ *435/259–4433* ⊕ *www.deserthighlights.com* ✉ *From $105.*

★ Moab Cliffs & Canyons
CLIMBING/MOUNTAINEERING | In a town where everyone seems to offer rafting and 4x4 expeditions, Moab Cliffs & Canyons focuses on canyoneering, climbing, and rappelling—for novice and veteran adventurers. Prices vary according to how many people sign up. This is the outfitter that provided technical assistance to the crew on the movie *127 Hours.*

⊠ *253 N. Main St.* ☎ *435/259–3317, 877/641–5271* ⊕ *www.cliffsandcanyons.com* ✉ *From $175.*

Pagan Mountaineering
CLIMBING/MOUNTAINEERING | Climbers in need of gear and advice on local terrain should speak with the knowledgeable staff here, who can help plot your adventure. ⊠ *59 S. Main St., No. 2* ☎ *435/259–1117* ⊕ *paganclimber.com.*

SKYDIVING
Because the area gets only a few days of rain, the skydiving season is long, lasting from March 1 to November 15.

Skydive Moab
FLYING/SKYDIVING/SOARING | Find the best view of Moab and the surrounding landscape with something you can check off your bucket list. You're in good hands at Skydive Moab. All flights take off from Moab's Canyonlands Field, 16 miles north of town. They also host the annual Mother of All Boogies Skydiving Festival each year in September. ⊠ *Canyonlands Field/Moab Airport, Hwy. 191 N* ☎ *435/259–5867* ⊕ *www.skydivemoab.com* ✉ *From $169 for a tandem skydive.*

Green River

70 miles west of the Colorado state line and about 50 miles northwest of Moab.

The town of **Green River** and the namesake river that runs through it are historically important. Early Native Americans used the river for centuries; the Old Spanish Trail crossed it, and the Denver and Rio Grande Railroad bridged it in 1883. Some say the "green" refers to the color of the water; others claim it's named for the plants along the riverbank. And yet another story gives the credit to a mysterious trapper named Green. Whatever the etymology, Green River remains a sleepy little town, and a nice break from some of the more "hip" tourist communities in southern Utah.

Green River has some less expensive—·but also less noteworthy—dining and lodging options, and the excellent John Wesley Powell River History Museum. Each September the fragrance of fresh cantaloupe, watermelon, and honeydew fills the air, especially during Melon Days, a family-fun harvest celebration held annually on the third weekend of the month. As Moab hotels have become more expensive and crowded spring through fall, many park visitors have taken to staying farther south in the small southeastern Utah towns of **Blanding** and **Bluff,** and even 110 miles away up in **Grand Junction, Colorado,** a city of about 63,000 that's come into its own in recent years with a quaint, historic downtown and close proximity to gorgeous Colorado National Monument.

GETTING HERE AND AROUND

Reaching Green River is as easy as finding I–70. The town is 180 miles southeast of Salt Lake City, 100 miles west of Grand Junction, Colorado, and 50 miles northwest of Moab.

ESSENTIALS
FESTIVALS
Melon Days

FESTIVALS | In southeast Utah there's nothing quite like the taste of the fresh cantaloupe, watermelon, and honeydew grown along the Green River. For more than a century, locals have celebrated the harvest with Melon Days the third weekend of September. This small-town event features a parade (watch for the 25-foot watermelon slice to roll down the street), a fair, a melon queen contest, plenty of music, square dancing, a canoe race, and thousands of pounds of Green River's famous melons. The parade winds down Main Street to OK Anderson City Park, where the festival is held. If you're lucky enough to be in the area for Melon Days, don't miss it. ⊠ *Main St. and Green River Blvd.* ☎ *888/564–3600* ⊕ *melon-days. com.*

 Sights

Crystal Geyser

NATURE SITE | If you're very lucky, you might get to catch this geyser in action. It erupts every 14 to 16 hours for sometimes as long as 30 minutes. The water can shoot up as high as 80 to 100 feet, but hasn't for many years. Researchers studying the cold-water geyser believe it's been partially plugged by people throwing rocks into the hole to force the geyser to erupt.

On the banks of the Green River, 10 miles south of town, you'll get a good taste of the backcountry on a bumpy, dirt road. Mineral deposits have created a dramatic orange terrace surrounding the eruption site. The staff at the Green River Information Center, which is in the John Wesley Powell River History Museum, can provide detailed directions and updated road conditions. ⊠ *Green River.*

★ Goblin Valley State Park

NATURE SITE | FAMILY | Strange-looking "hoodoos" rise up from the desert landscape 12 miles north of Hanksville, making Goblin Valley home to hundreds of strange goblin-like rock formations with a dramatic orange hue. Short, easy trails wind through the goblins making it a fun walk for kids and adults. ⊠ *Hwy. 24* ☎ *435/275–4584* ⊕ *stateparks.utah.gov* ⊠ *$15 per vehicle.*

Green River State Park

NATIONAL/STATE PARK | A shady respite on the banks of the Green River, this park is best known for its golf course. It's also the starting point for boaters drifting along the river through Labyrinth and Stillwater canyons. Fishing and bird-watching are favorite pastimes here. ⊠ *450 S. Green River Rd.* ☎ *435/564–3633, 800/322–3770 for campground reservations* ⊕ *stateparks.utah.gov* ⊠ *$5 per vehicle.*

★ John Wesley Powell River History Museum

MUSEUM | FAMILY | Learn what it was like to travel down the Green and Colorado rivers in the 1800s in wooden boats. A series of displays tracks the Powell Party's arduous, dangerous 1869 journey, and visitors can watch the award-winning film *Journey Into the Unknown* for a cinematic taste of the white-water adventure. The center also houses the River Runner's Hall of Fame, a tribute to those who have followed in Powell's wake. River-themed art occupies a gallery and there's a dinosaur exhibit on the lower level. ✉ *1765 E. Main St.* ☎ *435/564–3427* ⊕ *www.johnwesleypowell.com* ▧ *$6* ⊘ *Closed Mon. in winter.*

Sego Canyon Rock Art Interpretive Site

ARCHAEOLOGICAL SITE | Sego is one of the most dramatic and mystifying rock-art sites in the entire state. Large, ghostlike rock-art figures painted and etched by Native Americans approximately 4,000 years ago cover these canyon walls. There's also art left by the Ute from the 19th century. Distinctive for their large anthropomorphic figures, and for horses, buffalo, and shields painted with red-and-white pigment, these rare drawings are a must-see. ✉ *I–70, Exit 187, Thompson Springs* ✛ *25 miles east of Green River on I–70, at Exit 187 go north onto Hwy. 94 through Thompson Springs* ☎ *435/259–2100 Bureau of Land Management Office in Moab* ⊕ *www.blm.gov.*

Restaurants

Ray's Tavern

$ | AMERICAN | In little downtown Green River, Ray's is something of a Western legend and a favorite hangout for river runners. The bar that runs the length of this 1940s restaurant reminds you this is still a tavern and a serious watering hole—but all the photos and rafting memorabilia make it comfortable for families as well. **Known for:** legendary burgers; great people-watching; homemade apple pie. $ *Average main: $12* ✉ *25 S. Broadway* ☎ *435/564–3511* ⊕ *www.raystavern.com.*

Tamarisk Restaurant

$ | AMERICAN | Views of the Green River make this no-frills restaurant a nice stop after a long drive. Though the interior has gotten hipper in recent years, the breakfast, lunch, and dinner menus are filled with the same classic diner favorites the spot has been serving up for decades. **Known for:** great river view; Navajo tacos; salad bar. $ *Average main: $12* ✉ *1710 E. Main St.* ⊕ *www.tamariskrestaurant.com.*

🛏 Hotels

River Terrace Hotel

$$ | HOTEL | The peaceful setting, on the bank of the Green River, is conducive to a good night's rest, and this nicely maintained hotel is conveniently less than 2 miles off Interstate 70, although nearly an hour's drive from Arches. **Pros:** shady riverside location (be sure to request a river-view room); reasonable rates; on-site restaurant. **Cons:** in a sleepy town with few attractions; not within distance of downtown Green River; about 50 miles north of Moab. $ *Rooms from: $141* ✉ *1740 E. Main St.* ☎ *435/564–3401, 877/564–3401* ⊕ *www.river-terrace.com* ⇄ *50 rooms* ❑ *Free breakfast.*

Activities

RIVER FLOAT TRIPS

Bearing little resemblance to its name, Desolation Canyon acquaints those who venture down the Green River with some of the last true American wilderness: a lush, verdant canyon, where the rapids promise more laughter than fear. It's a favorite destination of canoe paddlers, kayakers, and novice rafters. May through September, raft trips can be arranged by outfitters in Green River or Moab. South of town the river drifts at a lazier pace through Labyrinth and Stillwater canyons, and the stretch south to Mineral Bottom in Canyonlands is best suited to canoes and motor boats.

For river-trip outfitters, see the Moab Activities section.

Blanding

126 miles south of Green River.

For nearly the first 20 years of its history, this small town near the base of the Abajo and Henry mountains was known as Grayson. This changed when wealthy Thomas Bicknell offered a huge library of books to any town willing to take his name. In the end, another town got the name, and Blanding was honored with Bicknell's wife's maiden name, as well as a share of the book bounty.

There is famously little to do around here, yet many residents love it for its peaceful quality. As the biggest town in San Juan County and the gateway to several national monuments, state parks, and two Native American reservations, it remains vital in its own way.

GETTING HERE AND AROUND
The town is about 90 minutes from Moab traveling south on U.S. 191.

ESSENTIALS
VISITOR INFORMATION Blanding Visitor Center. ✉ *12 N. Grayson Pkwy.* ☎ *435/678–3662* ⊕ *www.blanding-ut.gov.*

 Sights

Dinosaur Museum
MUSEUM | FAMILY | Skeletons, fossils, footprints, and reconstructed dinosaur skins are all on display at this small museum. Hallways hold a collection of movie posters featuring Godzilla and other monsters dating back to the 1930s. ✉ *754 S. 200 W* ☎ *435/678–3454* ⊕ *www.dinosaur-museum.org* 🎟 *$4.50* 🕙 *Closed mid-Oct.–mid-Apr.*

★ Edge of the Cedars State Park Museum
MUSEUM | FAMILY | Behind what is one of the nation's foremost museums dedicated to the Ancestral Puebloan culture, an interpretive trail leads to an ancient village that they once inhabited. Portions have been partially excavated, and visitors can climb down a ladder into a 1,000-year-old ceremonial room called a kiva. The museum displays a variety of pots, baskets, spear points, and rare artifacts—even a pair of sandals said to date back 1,500 years. ✉ *660 W. 400 N* ☎ *435/678–2238* ⊕ *stateparks.utah.gov* 🎟 *$5* 🕙 *Closed Sun.*

Hovenweep National Monument
NATIONAL/STATE PARK | The best place in southeast Utah to see ancient tower ruins dotting the scenic cliffs, if you're headed south from Canyonlands and have an interest in Ancestral Puebloan culture, a visit to this monument is a must. Park rangers strongly advise following printed maps and signs from U.S. 191 near Blanding, Utah, or County Road G from Cortez, Colorado. GPS is not reliable here. Once you get there, you'll find unusual tower structures (which may have been used for astronomical observation) and ancient dwellings. ✉ *Hovenweep Rd.* ☎ *970/562–4282* ⊕ *www.nps.gov/hove.*

Newspaper Rock State Historic Monument
NATIVE SITE | FAMILY | One of the West's most famous rock-art sites, about 15 miles west of U.S. 191, this site contains Native American designs engraved on the rock over the course of 2,000 years. Early pioneers and explorers to the region named the site Newspaper Rock because they believed the rock, crowded with drawings, constituted a written language with which early people communicated. Archaeologists now agree that the petroglyphs do not represent language. ✉ *Hwy. 211.*

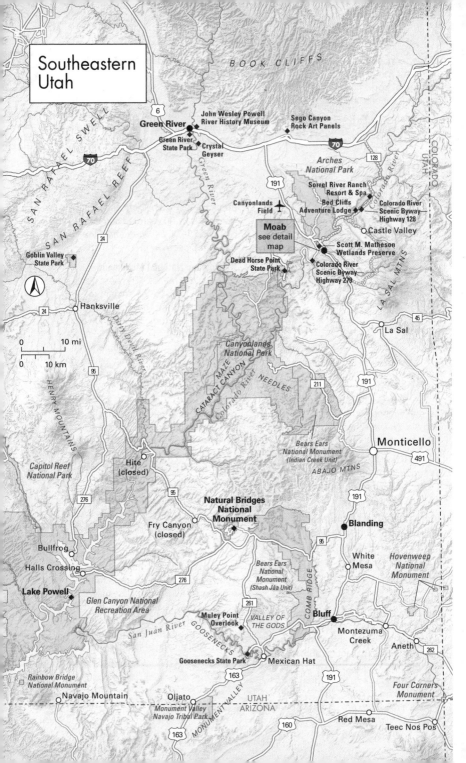

Southeastern Utah

BOOK CLIFFS

SAN RAFAEL SWELL

SAN RAFAEL REEF

Green River

John Wesley Powell
River History Museum

Sego Canyon
Rock Art Panels

Green River
State Park

Crystal
Geyser

Green River

Arches
National Park

Canyonlands
Field

Sorrel River Ranch
Resort & Spa
Red Cliffs
Adventure Lodge

Colorado River
Scenic Byway
Highway 128

Moab
see detail
map

Castle Valley

Scott M. Matheson
Wetlands Preserve

Goblin Valley
State Park

Dead Horse Point
State Park

Colorado River
Scenic Byway
Highway 279

LA SAL MTNS

Hanksville

La Sal

DIRTY DEVIL RIVER

Canyonlands
National Park

MAZE

CATARACT CANYON

Colorado River

NEEDLES

HENRY MOUNTAINS

Capitol Reef
National Park

Hite
(closed)

Bears Ears
National Monument
(Indian Creek Unit)

Monticello

ABAJO MTNS

Fry Canyon
(closed)

**Natural Bridges
National
Monument**

Blanding

White
Mesa

Hovenweep
National
Monument

Bullfrog

Halls Crossing

Lake Powell

Glen Canyon National
Recreation Area

Bears Ears
National
Monument
(Shash Jáa Unit)

COMB RIDGE

Bluff

Montezuma
Creek

Aneth

Muley Point
Overlook

VALLEY OF
THE GODS

San Juan River

GOOSENECKS

Goosenecks State Park

Mexican Hat

Four Corners
Monument

Rainbow Bridge
National Monument

Navajo Mountain

Oljato

Monument Valley
Navajo Tribal Park

MONUMENT VALLEY

UTAH
ARIZONA

Red Mesa

Teec Nos Pos

0   10 mi

0   10 km

Restaurants

Homestead Steak House

$ | AMERICAN | The folks here specialize in authentic Navajo fry bread and Navajo tacos. At lunch the popular—and massive—sheepherder's sandwich is made with fry bread, and comes with your choice of beef, turkey, or ham, and all the trimmings. **Known for:** homemade soups; Friday night seafood; banana pudding. $ *Average main: $14* ✉ *121 E. Center St.* ☎ *435/678–3456* ⊕ *www.homesteadsteakhouseut.com* ⊘ *Closed Sun.*

🛏 Hotels

Inn at the Canyons

$ | HOTEL | One of the largest properties in Monticello, which is just under an hour from Needles District Visitor Center, this is also one of the comfiest, with a heated indoor pool and a hot tub that's just what the doctor ordered for soaking adventure-weary bodies. **Pros:** close to Needles district of Canyonlands; year-round indoor pool and hot tub; pets allowed on request. **Cons:** sits near the main road through town, so might be noisy; in a sleepy town; rooms are clean not memorable. $ *Rooms from: $115* ✉ *533 N. Main St., Monticello* ☎ *435/587–2458* ⊕ *www.monticellocanyonlandsinn.com* ⇱ *43 rooms* ⦿ *Free breakfast.*

Stone Lizard Lodge

$$ | HOTEL | This rustic yet classy spot stands out from the local hotel chains and motor lodges with its individually decorated rooms, all with local art on the walls and Navajo-style rugs on the hardwood floors. **Pros:** one of the most comfortable lodgings around; hearty continental breakfast, with several hot items and homemade baked goods; calming garden area. **Cons:** smallish rooms (due to being built in the 1940s); more expensive than most other lodgings in the area; a limited number of pet-friendly rooms (and only dogs are allowed). $ *Rooms from:* *$134* ✉ *88 W. Center St.* ☎ *435/678–3323* ⊕ *www.stonelizardlodge.com* ⇱ *17 rooms* ⦿ *Free breakfast.*

Bluff

25 miles south of Blanding via U.S. 191.

Bluff is a tiny but unexpectedly cool town that's built a reputation for fun events. Like Moab, it doesn't have a palpable Mormon feel, and it remains a mini–melting pot of Navajos, river rats, hippies, and old-time Utahns. Surrounded by red-rock mesas, its cell phone service is spotty at best.

Settled in 1880, Bluff is one of southeastern Utah's oldest towns. Mormon pioneers from the original Hole in the Rock journey built a ranching empire that made the town, at one time, the richest per capita in the state. Although this early period of affluence passed, several historic Victorian-style homes remain. Pick up the free brochure "Historic Bluff by Bicycle and on Foot" at any business in town. Most of the original homes from the 1880 town-site of Bluff City are part of the Bluff Historic District. In a dozen or so blocks, there are 42 historic structures, most built between about 1890 and 1905.

GETTING HERE AND AROUND

Bluff is just under two hours from Moab south on U.S. 191.

FESTIVALS

Bear Dance

CULTURAL FESTIVALS | Every September you can see traditional Ute ceremonial dances at the Bear Dance. This amazing event is sponsored by the Ute Mountain Ute Tribe in a four-day celebration held Labor Day weekend on the Ute Reservation. The powwow and dance represent the end of summer and the impending hibernation of the bear. ✉ *Beaver La., White Mesa* ☎ *435/678–3621.*

Bluff Arts Festival

ARTS FESTIVALS | A growing local artist community shows off its talent during this annual festival in mid-October. Each year features a different theme, and touts four days of artist receptions, lectures, and workshops, along with the Bluff Film Festival. ✉ *Bluff* ☎ *435/672–2253.*

Bluff International Balloon Festival

FESTIVALS | Colorful hot-air balloons—some from as far away as England—take to the skies over Valley of the Gods and the town of Bluff during this mid-January festival. It's always a friendly crowd, and the balloon pilots often will trade a free ride if you help as part of their chase crew. Attend the "glow in" if weather allows, and see balloons illuminated against the night sky by the flame from the propane heaters that fill them with hot air. Bring warm clothing and expect crisp, clear weather. ✉ *Bluff* ☎ *435/672–2341.*

👁 Sights

Four Corners Monument

LOCAL INTEREST | The Navajo Nation manages this interesting landmark about 65 miles southeast of Bluff and 6 miles north of Teec Nos Pos, Arizona. Primarily a photo-op spot, you'll also find Navajo and Ute artisans selling authentic jewelry and crafts, as well as traditional foods. It's the only place in the United States where four states meet at one single point. Surveyors now believe the monument—a stone and metal marker sitting at the intersection of Colorado, Arizona, Utah, and New Mexico—is at least 1,800 feet east of the correct spot. The small entry fee of $5 per person is cash-only, so be sure to get money prior to heading out. ✉ *Four Corners Monument Rd., off U.S. 160.*

Sand Island Recreation Site

NATIVE SITE | Three miles southwest of Bluff you'll find a large panel of Ancestral Puebloan rock art. The panel includes several large images of Kokopelli, the mischief-maker from Puebloan lore. ✉ *U.S. 191* ☎ *435/587–1500 Monticello BLM office.*

★ Valley of the Gods

SCENIC DRIVE | A red fairyland of slender spires and buttes, the Valley of the Gods is a smaller version of Monument Valley. Approximately 15 miles west of Bluff, you can take a pretty drive through this relatively unvisited area on the 17-mile-long Valley of the Gods Road, which begins on U.S. 163 and ends on Highway 261. **■ TIP→ The road is unpaved but should be drivable as long as it's dry.** ✉ *Mexican Hat* ☎ *435/587–1500* 🌐 *www.bluffutah.org/valley-of-the-gods.*

🍴 Restaurants

Comb Ridge Eat and Drink

$ | **AMERICAN** | Get a feel for the local color at one of the best restaurants in the area, with big wooden posts breaking up the barn-like space, and works by local artists on the walls. The menu is filled with burgers, pizzas, and salads, all with creative flairs. **Known for:** large portions; vegetarian options; excellent coffee and desserts. [$] *Average main: $15* ✉ *680 S. U.S. 191* ☎ *435/485–5555* 🌐 *www.combridgeeatanddrink.com* 🕒 *Closed Sun.*

Cottonwood Steakhouse

$$$ | **STEAKHOUSE** | The ribs served here will blow your mind, and the charming Old West theme begins when you drive up to the rustic, false-front exterior. Inside, animal pelts, guns, and other memorabilia of the era adorn the walls. **Known for:** outstanding barbecue ribs; decadent homemade desserts; old-timey look, in and out. [$] *Average main: $23* ✉ *409 W. Main St.* ☎ *435/672–2282* 🌐 *www.cottonwoodsteakhouse.com* 🕒 *Closed Nov.–Mar. No lunch.*

Twin Rocks Cafe

$ | **SOUTHWESTERN** | Part of the appeal of eating at this colorful diner-style spot in tiny Bluff is that the restaurant sits beneath a striking pair of 150-foot-tall rock spires. There's also an outstanding Navajo trading post inside, and the kitchen turns out tasty and hearty Native American and Southwestern fare, from Navajo fry-bread French toast with local peaches in the morning to burgers, beef stew, and chili at lunch and dinner. **Known for:** Navajo fry bread; locally crafted jewelry and weavings in the trading post; delicious and filling breakfasts. $ *Average main: $13* ⊠ *913 E. Navajo Twins Dr.* ☎ *435/672–2341* ⊕ *www.twinrockscafe. com* ☾ *No dinner Sun.–Thurs. during winter.*

Hotels

★ Desert Rose Inn and Cabins
$$ | HOTEL | Bluff's largest and most upscale hotel, which also contains two of the region's best restaurants, is an attractive, wood-sided lodge with a huge two-story front porch. **Pros:** rustic-elegant room furnishings; fitness center in adjacent building; pool and hot tub. **Cons:** nearly two-hour drive to Needles District; remote town without many amenities; a bit spendy for the area. $ *Rooms from: $169* ⊠ *701 W. Main St.* ☎ *435/672–2303* ⊕ *www.desertroseinn.com* ⤴ *53 rooms* ⊖| *No meals.*

Recapture Lodge
$ | HOTEL | Rooms at this family-operated inn are basic and clean, mostly with wood paneling; there's also a playground and pool. **Pros:** set on shady grounds with riverside chairs and walking trails; pool and hot tub; pets and horses welcome. **Cons:** nearly two-hour drive to Needles District; older property with small rooms and basic amenities; pool not close to rooms. $ *Rooms from: $98* ⊠ *250 E. Main St.* ☎ *435/672–2281* ⊕ *https://www. recapturelodge.com* ⤴ *26 rooms* ⊖| *Free breakfast.*

Shopping

★ Valley of the Gods
SCENIC DRIVE | A red fairyland of slender spires and buttes, the Valley of the Gods is a smaller version of Monument Valley. Approximately 15 miles west of Bluff, you can take a pretty drive through this relatively unvisited area on the 17-mile-long Valley of the Gods Road, which begins on U.S. 163 and ends on Highway 261.

■ **TIP→ The road is unpaved but should be drivable as long as it's dry.** ⊠ *Mexican Hat* ☎ *435/587–1500* ⊕ *www.bluffutah.org/ valley-of-the-gods.*

Activities

RIVER EXPEDITIONS
While somewhat calmer than the Colorado, the San Juan River offers some truly exceptional scenery and abundant opportunities to visit archaeological sites. It can be run in two sections: from Bluff to Mexican Hat, or from Mexican Hat to Lake Powell. Near Bluff (3 miles southwest on U.S. 191), the Sand Island Recreation Site is the launch site for most river trips. You'll find a primitive campground there as well. Permits from the Bureau of Land Management are required for floating on the San Juan River.

Bureau of Land Management, Monticello Field Office
BOATING | For permits, contact the Bureau of Land Management, Monticello Field Office. ⊠ *365 N. Main St., Monticello* ☎ *435/587–1544* ⊕ *www.blm.gov/ut.*

Wild River Expeditions
BOATING | FAMILY | The San Juan River is one of the prettiest floats in the region, and this reliable outfitter can take you on one- to seven-day trips. They are known for educational adventures that emphasize the geology, natural history, and archaeological wonders of the area. ⊠ *2625 S. U.S. 191* ☎ *435/672–2244* ⊕ *www. riversandruins.com* ⊠ *From $199.*

Stunning Lake Powell is worth the journey.

Natural Bridges National Monument

The scenery and rock formations found in this national monument must be seen to be believed.

Sights

Natural Bridges National Monument
NATIONAL/STATE PARK | FAMILY | Stunning natural bridges, ancient Native American ruins, and magnificent scenery throughout make Natural Bridges National Monument a must-see if you have time to make the trip. Sipapu is one of the largest natural bridges in the world, spanning 268 feet and standing 220 feet tall. You can take in the Sipapu, Owachomo, and Kachina bridges via an 8.6-mile round-trip hike that meanders around and under them. A 13-site primitive campground is an optimal spot for stargazing. The national monument is 40 miles from Blanding. ⊠ *Hwy. 275, off Hwy. 95*

☎ *435/692–1234* ⊕ *www.nps.gov/nabr* 💳 *$20 per vehicle.*

Lake Powell

The placid waters of Lake Powell allow you to depart the landed lifestyle and float away on your own houseboat. With 96 major side canyons spread across 186 miles, you can spend months exploring more than 2,000 miles of shoreline. Every water sport imaginable awaits, from waterskiing to fishing. Small communities around marinas in Page (Arizona), Bullfrog, Wahweap, Hite, and Hall's Crossing have hotels, restaurants, and shops where you can restock vital supplies.

GETTING HERE AND AROUND
AIR
Getting here can be your biggest challenge, so it's best to plan ahead whenever possible. Contour Airlines serves Page, Arizona, from Phoenix and Las Vegas. To get to Bullfrog, Utah, it's a

two-and-a-half-hour drive from Canyonlands Airport in Moab (served by United) and three-and-a-half hours from Walker Field Airport in Grand Junction, Colorado.

CAR

Many people visit Lake Powell as part of grand drives across the southwestern United States. Bullfrog, Utah, is about 300 miles from Salt Lake City via I–15 to I–70 to U.S. 95 south. Take I–70 from Colorado and the east. Take U.S. 191 from either Wyoming or Arizona. Most roads are well-maintained two-lane highways, though snow can be a factor in winter. Be sure your car is in good working order, as there are long stretches of empty road, and top off the gas tank whenever possible.

INFORMATION Utah State Road Conditions.

☎ 511 toll-free within Utah, 866/511–8824 toll-free outside Utah ⊕ www.udot.utah.gov.

FERRY

Hall's Crossing Marina is the eastern terminus of the ferry. You and your vehicle can float across a 3-mile stretch of the lake to the Bullfrog Basin Marina in 25 minutes; from there it is an hour's drive north to rejoin Highway 95. Ferries run several times each day (less frequently during the off-season). Call ahead for departures information.

Lake Powell Ferry

✉ Hall's Crossing Marina, Hwy. 276 ☎ 435/684–3088 ⊕ www.lakepowell.com 💲 $25 per car.

Sights

Lake Powell

NATIONAL/STATE PARK | With a shoreline longer than America's Pacific coast, Lake Powell is the heart of the huge 1.25-millon-acre **Glen Canyon National Recreation Area.** Created by the Glen Canyon Dam—a 710-foot wall of concrete in the Colorado River—Lake Powell took 17 years to fill. The second-largest

man-made lake in the nation, it extends through terrain so rugged that it was the last major area of the country to be mapped. Red cliffs ring the lake and twist off into 96 major canyons and countless inlets with huge, red-sandstone buttes randomly jutting from the sapphire waters.

The most popular thing to do at Lake Powell is to rent a houseboat and chug leisurely across the lake, exploring coves and inlets. You'll have plenty of company, though, since more than 2 million people visit the lake each year. Fast motorboats, Jet Skis, and sailboats all share the lake. Unless you love crowds and parties, it's best to avoid visiting during Memorial Day or Labor Day weekends. It's also important to check with the National Park Service for current water levels, closures, and other weather-related conditions.

Guided day-tours are available for those who don't want to rent a boat of their own. A popular full-day or half-day excursion sets out from the Bullfrog and Hall's Crossing marinas to **Rainbow Bridge National Monument.** This is the largest natural bridge in the world, and its 290-foot-high, 275-foot-wide span is a breathtaking sight. The main National Park Service visitor center is at Bullfrog Marina; a gas station, campground, general store, and boat docks are there for supplies, snacks, and chit-chat with locals. ✉ Bullfrog visitor center, Hwy. 276 ☎ 435/684–7420 ⊕ www.nps.gov/glca.

🛏 Hotels

★ Amangiri

$$$$ | **RESORT** | One of just two U.S. properties operated by the famously luxurious Aman resort company, this ultraplush and ultraexpensive 34-suite compound lies just a few miles north of Lake Powell on a 600-acre plot of rugged high desert, soaring red-rock cliffs, and jagged mesas. **Pros:** stunning accommodations inside and out; exceedingly gracious and

professional staff; world-class restaurant and spa. **Cons:** many times more expensive than most accommodations in the area; extremely remote; airy, super-sleek rooms are gorgeous but not everyone's idea of cozy. [$] *Rooms from: $3500* ✉ *1 Kayenta Rd., Canyon Point* ✢ *15 miles northwest of Page, off U.S. 89* ☎ *435/675–3999, 877/695–3999* 🌐 *www.amanresorts.com* 🛏 *34 suites* 🍴 *All meals.*

Defiance House Lodge
$$ | **HOTEL** | At the Bullfrog Marina, this cliff-top lodge has comfortable and clean rooms anyone can appreciate, but the real draw is the view of the lake. **Pros:** beautiful lakefront setting; adjacent restaurant; pets allowed for nightly fee. **Cons:** very remote; no general store for miles; aging rooms. [$] *Rooms from: $150* ☎ *435/684–2233, 888/896–3829* 🌐 *www.lakepowell.com* 🛏 *48 rooms* 🍴 *No meals.*

Dreamkatchers Lake Powell Bed and Breakfast
$$ | **B&B/INN** | This sleek, contemporary Southwestern-style home sits on a bluff just a few miles northwest of Lake Powell and 15 miles from Page. **Pros:** peaceful and secluded location perfect for stargazing; delicious breakfasts; laid-back, friendly hosts. **Cons:** often booked months in advance; few services in the remote surrounding area; late check-in not available. [$] *Rooms from: $175* ✉ *1055 S. American Way, Big Water* ☎ *435/675–5828* 🌐 *www.dreamkatchers-lakepowell.com* ⏲ *Closed mid-Nov.–mid-Mar.* 🛏 *3 rooms* 🍴 *Free breakfast.*

Activities

Lake Powell Resorts & Marinas
TOUR—SPORTS | Boating and fishing are the major sports at Lake Powell. Conveniently, all powerboat rentals and tours are conducted by this company. Daylong tours (departing from Wahweap Marina near Page, Arizona) go to Rainbow Bridge or Antelope Canyon. There's also a tour that goes into some of the more interesting canyons and a dinner cruise. The company rents houseboats for anyone looking to make their stay here last. ✉ *Bullfrog Marina, Rte. 276* ☎ *800/528–6154* 🌐 *www.lakepowell.com* 🎟 *Tours start at $48.*

Index

Photo Credits

Front Cover: David Noton Photography / Alamy [Description: The night sky over Delicate Arch, Arches National Park, Utah, USA]. **Back cover, from left to right:** Byelikova/Dreamstime, vjohnnya123/iStockphoto, FashionStock.com/Shutterstock. **Spine:** Franfoto/Dreamstimes. **Interior, from left to right:** David Pettit/Visit Utah (1). Larry C. Price/Visit Utah (2). **Chapter 1: Experience Utah:** Sandra Salvas/Visit Utah (6-7). Courtesy of Deer Valley Resort (8). Maridav / Shutterstock (9). Utah Office of Tourism (9). Johnnya123/Dreamstime (10). Courtesy of Natural History Museum of Utah (10). Utah Office of Tourism/Steve Greenwood (10). Nyokki/Shutterstock (11). Michael Runkel Utah / Alamy (12). Sharron Schiefelbein - www.agefotostock.com (12). Ian Dagnall / Alamy (12). Greg Gard / Alamy (13). Douglas Pulsipher/Visit Salt Lake City (13). imageBROKER / Alamy (14). Jakub Zajic/Shutterstock (14). Dndavis/Dreamstime (15). Bettie Grace Miner (18). Mike Tittel (18). Courtesy of Alta's Rustler Lodge (18). St. Regis, Deer Valley (19). Eric Schramm Photography/Solitude Mountain Resort (19). Matt Morgan/Visit Utah (20). Larry C. Price/Visit Utah (20). Tristanbnz/Dreamstime.com (20). Galyna Andrushko/Shutterstock (21). Atmosphere1/Shutterstock (21). TREVORHOOPERPHOTO.COM 2018/Courtesy Of HighWest Distillery (22). Bill Coker Photography/ Courtesy of Red Iguana (23). **Chapter 3: Salt Lake City:** f11photo/Shutterstock (51). Sopotnicki/Shutterstock (58). Nagel Photography/Shutterstock (64). Chris Curtis/Shutterstock (84). Kristi Blokhin/Shutterstock (97). **Chapter 4: Park City and the Southern Wasatch:** johnnya123/iStockphoto (101). Sean Pavone/iStockphoto (111). johnnya123/iStockphoto (126). Johnny Adolphson/Shutterstock (132). Robert Crum/Shutterstock (142). **Chapter 5: Northern Utah:** Guy In Utah/Shutterstock (145). Ritu Manoj Jethani/Shutterstock (155). Guy In Utah/Shutterstock (159). Layne V. Naylor/Shutterstock (163). **Chapter 6: Dinosaurland and Eastern Utah:** jnerad/Shutterstock (173). Claudia Johnson/Shutterstock (182). Zack Frank/Shutterstock (191). Galyna Andrushko/Shutterstock (194). **Chapter 7: Capitol Reef National Park:** JeniFoto/Shutterstock (197). Edmund Lowe Photography/Shutterstock (204). **Chapter 8: Zion National Park:** Checubus/Shutterstock (209). bjul/Shutterstock (219). **Chapter 9: Bryce Canyon National Park:** Lorcel/Shutterstock (221). Michele Kemper/Dreamstime (230). Humorousking207/Dreamstime (233). **Chapter 10: Southwestern Utah:** Harry Beugelink/Shutterstock (237). Will Sylwester/Shutterstock (258). **Chapter 11: Arches National Park:** Colin D. Young/Shutterstock (263). kylepostphotography/shutterstock (270). Checubus/Shutterstock (273). **Chapter 12: Canyonlands National Park:** Edwin Verin/shutterstock (277). Alex Grichenko/Dreamstime (288). **Chapter 13: Moab and Southeastern Utah:** Dmitry Pichugin/Shutterstock (291). Johnny Adolphson/Shutterstock (318). **About Our Writers:** All photos are courtesy of the writers.

Every effort has been made to trace the copyright holders, and we apologize in advance for any accidental errors. We would be happy to apply the corrections in the following edition of this publication.

Notes

Notes

Notes

Notes

Notes

Notes

Notes

Fodor's UTAH

Publisher: Stephen Horowitz, *General Manager*

Editorial: Douglas Stallings, *Editorial Director*; Jill Fergus, Jacinta O'Halloran, Amanda Sadlowski, *Senior Editors*; Kayla Becker, Alexis Kelly, Rachael Roth, *Editors*

Design: Tina Malaney, *Director of Design and Production*; Jessica Gonzalez, *Graphic Designer*; Mariana Tabares, *Design and Production Intern*

Production: Jennifer DePrima, *Editorial Production Manager*; Elyse Rozelle, *Senior Production Editor*; Monica White, *Production Editor*

Maps: Rebecca Baer, *Senior Map Editor*; Mark Stroud (Moon Street Cartography), David Lindroth, *Cartographers*

Photography: Viviane Teles, *Senior Photo Editor*; Namrata Aggarwal, Ashok Kumar, Carl Yu, *Photo Editors*; Rebecca Rimmer, *Photo Intern*

Business and Operations: Chuck Hoover, *Chief Marketing Officer*; Robert Ames, *Group General Manager*; Devin Duckworth, *Director of Print Publishing*; Victor Bernal, *Business Analyst*

Public Relations and Marketing: Joe Ewaskiw, *Senior Director Communications & Public Relations*

Fodors.com: Jeremy Tarr, *Editorial Director*; Rachael Levitt, *Managing Editor*

Technology: Jon Atkinson, *Director of Technology*; Rudresh Teotia, *Lead Developer*; Jacob Ashpis, *Content Operations Manager*

Writers: Shelly Arenas, Andrew Collins, Stina Sieg, Jenie Skoy

Editors: Rachael Roth, Douglas Stallings and Amanda Sadlowski

Production Editor: Elyse Rozelle

7th Edition

ISBN 978-1-64097-344-2

ISSN 1547–870X

All details in this book are based on information supplied to us at press time. Always confirm information when it matters, especially if you're making a detour to visit a specific place. Fodor's expressly disclaims any liability, loss, or risk, personal or otherwise, that is incurred as a consequence of the use of any of the contents of this book.

SPECIAL SALES

This book is available at special discounts for bulk purchases for sales promotions or premiums. For more information, e-mail SpecialMarkets@fodors.com.

PRINTED IN CANADA

10 9 8 7 6 5 4 3 2 1

About Our Writers

 Shelley Arenas grew up in eastern Washington and has lived in the Seattle area since college. She's been a regular contributor to *Fodor's Pacific Northwest* and other guidebooks for more than a decade; she's also co-authored a book about Seattle for families and writes for several regional publishers. She updated Travel Smart, Capitol Reef National Park, Zion National Park, and Bryce Canyon National Park this edition.

 Former Fodor's staff editor **Andrew Collins** is based in Mexico City but spends much of his time traveling throughout the United States. A long-time contributor to more than 200 Fodor's guidebooks, including Pacific Northwest, Santa Fe, New England, Inside Mexico City, and National Parks of the West, he's also written for dozens of mainstream and LGBTQ publications — Travel + Leisure, New Mexico Magazine, AAA Living, The Advocate, and Canadian Traveller among them. Additionally, Collins teaches travel writing and food writing for New York City's Gotham Writers Workshop. You can find more of his work at AndrewsTraveling.com.

 Stina Sieg has been in love with the desert ever since she moved to New Mexico a vintage trailer at the age 22. She's worked for newspapers and radio stations across the Southwest — including in Moab, Utah — and now cools her heels just over the Colorado border in Grand Junction, where she's the Western Slope reporter for Colorado Public Radio. For this edition, she updated the Dinosaurland and Eastern Utah, Arches National Park, and Moab and Southeastern Utah chapters.

Jenie Skoy is a freelance writer and photographer living in lush Southern Oregon where she is between mountains and the sea. Utah is her second home. When she's not road-tripping, you can find her making homemade gnocchi and a mean bolognese sauce or playing the guitar and singing to her tomato plants. For this edition, Jenie update the Park City and the Southern Wasatch chapter.